A MESSAGE FROM OUTER SPACE?

On Saturday, November 16, 1974, a message was beamed from the giant radio antenna at Arecibo, Puerto Rico, toward a distant cluster of stars at the edge of the Milky Way, known as Messier 13. The message is traveling at the speed of light and will take 24,000 years to arrive. It can be converted into a television picture which will explain to the watchers that a planet called Earth is dominated by a species whose genetic construction is mediated by the chemical molecule known as deoxyribonucleic acid—DNA.

When I examined the "message," I had an eerie feeling I had seen it before. And I had ... I had see it at Toro Muerto in the Andean mountains, scratched on a rock 14,000 years ago.

If we sent a cryptic message to space encompassing our essence in a few signs and mathematical symbols, was it possible that some arriving explorer left his own very clear imprint on the Toro Muerto plain?

Bantam Books by Alan and Sally Landsburg

IN SEARCH OF ANCIENT MYSTERIES
THE OUTER SPACE CONNECTION

THE OUTER
SPACE
CONNECTION

by Alan and Sally Landsburg

PHOTOGRAPHS BY ANDREW REICHLINE

This book is dedicated to
the memory of Harry Landsburg.
His death has left an unfillable gap
in our lives.
His immortality is ensured.

RLI: $\dfrac{\text{VLM 9 (VLR 8–10)}}{\text{IL 9–adult}}$

THE OUTER SPACE CONNECTION
A Bantam Book / July 1975

Published simultaneously in the United States and Canada

Bantam Books are published by Bantam Books, Inc. Its trade-
mark, consisting of the words "Bantam Books" and the por-
trayal of a bantam, is registered in the United States Patent
Office and in other countries. Marca Registrada. Bantam
Books, Inc., 666 Fifth Avenue, New York, New York 10019.

PRINTED IN THE UNITED STATES OF AMERICA

Contents

ACKNOWLEDGMENTS:

We gratefully acknowledge the valuable contribution of the literary and editorial work of our colleague, Fred Warshofsky.

With the exception of the credited photographs, the picture section of *The Outer Space Connection* was photographed in locations around the world by Andrew Reichline. We are grateful for his creative talent and his technical skill under difficult conditions.

We would also like to thank Deborah Blum, who involved herself in an incredible job of research and was always there to assist us with her knowledge, ideas, and creativity.

Foreword
by
Rod Serling

One of the qualities I admire in others is the ability to tell a story. I have spent the greater part of my professional life enslaved to ideas that demand the proper setting. When the opening gambit has an irresistible sparkle, I'm easily lured into the web of the tale.

When Alan and Sally Landsburg approached me with "that glint" in their eyes, I became wary I was facing storytellers with the consummate ability to snare me. More than two years ago, they spun out a piece of verbal legerdemain that carried me into their search for ancient mysteries. All my antennae were out, therefore, when they offered to show me something that they said was "unusual." I knew the bait was being dropped.

Down from the book shelf came an innocent looking box. Under the glass panel set in its top, however, was one of the most ominous realities I had ever encountered: it was a mummy's hand. Before I had a chance to censor the thought, the words had come out of my mouth, "What are you doing with that thing?" Alan's smile told me I was in for a good story.

"There are some people, Rod," Alan said, "who do not believe that it is possible to recreate the human being when all we have left is a mummified hand." I told them that I didn't, either, and settled back. What I heard in the next half hour set my hair on end.

I was given a demonstration of how ancient Egyptians had gone about mummifying the remains of their kings. I learned in fascinating detail how mummies were preserved so that a replication might be made from an individual cell that had been kept intact. Very gradually layers of archaeological data were peeled back to reveal the probability of advanced biochemical knowledge existing on Earth thousands of years ago. The events of the past were cross-referenced with today's scientific research that confirmed the essential idea Alan and Sally were presenting. They ventured into the science of cloning, the process of "creating life," touched on live embryo transport and examined life preservative nutrients drawn from the pharmacopoeia of folk medicine. We were very much like time travelers viewing strange occurrences in ancient times and then seeing their reflections in modern biological experimentation. I was engrossed in a world more clearly the province of the fiction writer than the journalist.

I know the Landsburgs too well, however, to think that any part of the tale was fictional. Alan had spent most of his working life documenting on film the crucial events of our time and the important stories of progress in science and technology. Sally is a lecturer at a Los Angeles college.

The central theme of their story was as important to me as I believe it will be to you. The research that went in to creating this book and the motion picture "The Outer Space Connection" deals primarily with one of man's oldest and fondest dreams. The subject is immortality, the probability that you and I can live forever. If immortality is as real as it is portrayed in the work of scientists around the world, then the Landsburgs' contention that we are on the threshold of "the outer space connection" might be borne out. I believe it. See if you do.

1

The Question We Couldn't Get Out of Our Minds

I was surprised when Dr. Ray Cameron handed me a parka. The office air-conditioner was humming away and the temperature outside was in the low nineties, a not untypical fall day in La Jolla, California. I had gone to the Scripps Institute of Oceanography to film an amazing discovery made by Dr. Cameron, a microbiologist who had been one of an international team of scientists examining the depths below the ice of the Antarctic, seeking information about its geological history.

Dr. Cameron noticed my puzzled expression as I glanced at the heavy jacket he'd given me, and explained that the cores we were about to see—plugs of Antarctic soil and rock extracted from deep beneath the frozen surface—were kept in a refrigerated building. Coring has been going on for some time now, at various depths in the world's oceans and at the Poles. Much of Earth's past, changes in climate, the processes of mountain building, island making, and continental shifting, can be deduced from these cores of rock and earth. They are a geological record of millions of years, clearly readable by examining each layer.

Dr. Cameron, whose homebase is the Darwin Research Institute at Dana Point, was using Scripps Institute's cold-storage facilities for his cores. They represented something very special in the history of Earth, for locked within their frozen grasp was something never before seen by man. We left Dr. Cameron's office, blinking in the warm sun, and headed for the ice lockers. At the door we struggled into our parkas, then entered.

Our breath hung in the air like smoke. The cold, actually a few degrees above freezing, was such a marked contrast to the warmth outside that I felt as if I had suddenly plunged into an icy sea. Despite the parka, I shivered as I looked around the huge room. Row upon row of shelves rose from floor to ceiling. Each shelf was crammed with steel tubes three feet long and four inches in diameter, capped with red plastic seals. Collectively the cores inside those tubes represented billions of years of Earth's history. Each was a sample drilled at one of hundreds of sites all over the globe. Dr. Cameron consulted a chart and began reading the numbers inked on the red caps. At last he pulled out one tube, cradled it in his arms, and headed for the door.

In the lab section he uncapped a tube and with small tweezers pulled out a pinch of substance. It was a core sample possibly one million years old. He placed it on a glass slide, mixed in a drop or two of an oily liquid, and covered it with a glass slip. He passed the slide slowly over the flame of a Bunsen burner for two or three seconds, then slipped it onto a microscope stage. His eyes pressed against the twin oculars and his hands played delicately with the neural knobs at the side of the instrument. Then he stepped back and told me to take a look.

I peered into the eyepiece. In the light-bathed circular field a number of small, round objects were moving with the leisurely ease of fish in a pool.

"They're alive!" I exclaimed.

"Yes," Dr. Cameron said softly, "they are indeed alive."

He didn't have to say any more because I was staring in astonishment at a rather small cluster of bacteria moving about on a slide. But these bacteria were unlike any that had ever before been seen by man. Uncovered quite by accident in the frozen earth and rock of the Antarctic, the bacteria were the oldest known living things. The strata from which the cores had come, geologists estimated, was possibly one million years old, which meant that these microscopic bits of life may well have been just as old. It was hard to hold down my excitement at seeing living matter that might date back to a time when Earth was a far different place.

I looked up and saw Ray Cameron's bemused expression.

"I know how you feel," he said. "It was like a thunderbolt to us when we saw it. They're a biologist's dream come true."

"Or a nightmare," I said. "What if they were like . . . like . . ."

"The Andromeda Strain?" Cameron anticipated my flood of science fiction questions. "Dangerous to man, a contagion that could wipe out Earth? No," he went on, "there's a better chance that our environment is mortally dangerous to them."

I went back to the microscope and stared again at the squirming figures. Life had returned to them after millennia, after the equivalent of a hundred thousand human life spans. I knew little of bacteria classification so the forms I was seeing meant little to me, but I was beginning to sense the implications of their very existence. The tiny fragments of matter had, in a way, achieved man's oldest wish—immortality. Life, they seemed to tell me, could be continued for an incomprehensibly long period of time. Time. Time enough to make long journeys to the nearest stars and even to the end of the galaxy. Time enough to encounter those whose existence might have been joined to ours in the initial burst of creation that first seeded life on Earth. One-million-year-old bacteria frozen in a state of suspended animation, restored to life by the accidental bite of a drill and the warmth of a lab, represented both a claim to immortality and a connection to the origin of man. As I watched the bacteria I realized that immortality was in fact the outer space connection.

I had worked for three years seeking answers to an increasing number of questions about mysteries of our distant past. Working with my wife, Sally, I had written a book called *In Search of Ancient Mysteries,* an examination of the evidence which led me to suspect that man's origin was attributable to an infusion of life from outer space. Along with Fred Warshofsky, a brilliant documentary filmmaker, I had fashioned a television special based on *In Search of Ancient Mysteries.* At Ray Cameron's lab the quest had begun again. I had started to probe deeper still into the specific questions of how and when an alien presence from somewhere in outer space had contributed the vital spark of our existence. One possible answer lay before me. Immortality was the key. If in fact immortality, in one form or another, was possible, then many of the insoluble problems we'd encountered in the early days of research might be solved.

I now had a basis on which to continue and expand my efforts to pinpoint the outer space connection. Three of us, Sally, Fred Warshofsky, and I, decided to fan out across the world seeking new information to illuminate our theory. A new film, called *The Outer Space Connection,* was born at that moment. I will narrate the results of our research and travels, but this book and the film are, in fact, the products of dedicated effort of the two people working along with me.

We were searching for immortality or at least evidence that it could exist. If immortality was not possible then neither were deep space voyages. I had accumulated enough indications of extraterrestrial influence to convince me that there had been visits to Earth in the past. I was sure that whoever or whatever had visited did not come from our own solar system. We have already explored enough of it to know that Mars has no little green men and there is no man on the moon. The visitor must have come from a system elsewhere in the galaxy. Logic dictates that it be a system not too different from our own, a sun circled by planets. At least one of those planets should be similar to Earth in size and in distance from its sun, and have a combination of warmth, water, and atmosphere that would permit life to begin. To that equation, add time. Not the mere four and a half billion years of existence Earth has known, but perhaps half again as much.

The nearest sun fitting that description is the star Kruger 60. *It is sixty trillion miles away from Earth.* Such numbers are almost impossible for us to comprehend. If, for example, you were to count one number every second for eight hours a day, you would need every day of your life to reach the number one billion. One trillion is a billion followed by five zeros. Sixty trillion is so huge a number that astronomers don't even use it. Rather, they measure the distance between stars in terms of light-years, the time it takes light, which travels at 186,000 miles per second, to reach us on Earth. Herein lies one of the major problems of extended space travel. The speed of light may in fact be the speed limit of the universe; it may be an unattainable speed.

We used to think that a mile a minute was fast. A mile a minute is sixty miles an hour. A mile a second is sixty times faster, or thirty-six hundred miles an hour. Escape velocity achieved by our spacecraft—that is, the speed needed to escape Earth's gravitational attraction and enter space—is seventeen thousand miles an hour, or almost five miles a second. Once in space, vehicles accelerate because of the diminishing gravitational attraction of the body they have just left and the increasing gravitational pull exerted by the body lying along the path on which the vehicle is traveling.

By using the enormous gravitational pull of Jupiter as a sort of slingshot, *Pioneer 10,* one of our unmanned explorers, has become the fastest-traveling object we have ever launched into space. Assuming it is headed in the right direction, it will take *Pioneer 10* a hundred thousand years to reach Kruger 60.

The journey from Kruger 60 to Earth, regardless of the technological advancement of the beings making the trip, would have consumed such vast quantities of time as to demand immortality on the part of the voyagers. Immortality—that was the idea I couldn't get out of my mind, the concept that seemed to be lurking behind all of the ancient mysteries I had been exploring. I knew where I had to go next. To Uxmal and the ancient, mysterious Mayan Temple of Death.

2

The Mayan Mystery

I waited at the foot of a steep, narrow path as a busload of Scandinavian tourists clambered down the trail from the principal Mayan Temple of Uxmal. I felt uneasy. I was belabored by the sense that I was seeking new information from a played-out source. Uxmal is one of the main stops on any tour of Mexico's steaming Yucatan Peninsula. Thousands of amateur cameramen had photographed the ruins of one of the last Mayan strongholds from every conceivable angle. Archaeologists had examined each structure in the settlement and rendered their own view of Mayan life based on available artifacts. But I wanted to see it again.

As I climbed toward the temple the heat of jungle summer plastered my shirt to my back. What a dreadful place, I kept thinking. Why would anyone, especially the Mayas, a highly civilized people who left evidence of great technological accomplishments, choose to live here? The word *choose* stuck in my mind. Perhaps their decision had nothing to do with choice. It seemed highly unlikely that anyone would willingly undertake crop farming in such an environment. There had to be another answer, and it was my guess that they had come to the Yucatan, to Uxmal and neighboring Chichen Itza, to hide. Who or what had chased them to this remote outpost?

I was standing before a stone altar made of massive boulders carefully sculpted to interlock. Beyond the altar was the Temple of the Priests, gleaming white in the noonday sun. I had forgotten its immensity—almost four hundred feet long and half again as wide. Some of the intricate sculpture was still visible along its facade, but most of the carvings had been stripped away by scavengers, beginning with the armies of Cortez in the sixteenth century and continuing through to the thoughtless souvenir hunters of today.

A civilization with the engineering skill to create lasting structures, a people who invented the figure zero to facilitate mathematical calculation, a culture that created a yearly calendar accurate to within seventeen seconds in 365 days, why would the Mayas take flight from the onslaught of less advanced societies? They never fought invaders. Instead, they retreated deeper and deeper into undesirable places, seemingly in fear of contact with any other people. Why, damnit, why?

I entered the temple and found it dark, damp, and stripped of every artifact. I wanted to locate an area described by John Stephens, a nineteenth century explorer who was responsible for the rediscovery of lost Mayan cities. In *Incidents of Travel in Central America,* he had reported finding an artifact he described as a smooth, black, glasslike surface which Mayan priests consulted when making crucial decisions. Stephens made no other mention of the object. I felt that his perspective in examining it was limited by the perception of nineteenth century man. In light of today's knowledge, a black, glasslike surface, used for communication, might well have been a television receiver.

I wandered from one barren room to another, empty of all but the chirping bats awakened by my flashlight. No, I wouldn't find Stephens' magical black screen, but I fancied I could see a convocation of priests requesting guidance and help from a television receiver tuned to a vehicle traveling somewhere in space. I gave up then and returned to the reality of the hot sun and the other structures at Uxmal.

There was the ubiquitous Mayan pyramid to which modern mythology had given the name Pyramid of the Magicians. It is possible that the Mayas invented this mystic building form whose purpose we are just beginning to divine. I photographed the structure for later reference and made a note to ask Dr. Patrick Flanagan, an expert in pyramid energy, his view of why the Mayas had constructed so many of them.

I started to fight my way along an overgrown path leading away from the settlement. I was headed for the remains of a structure that is usually bypassed. I had missed it on my first visit, content with the guide's opinion that there wasn't much to see. On the map of Uxmal the ruin is called the House of Death. In fact, there was almost nothing left of the building. A fragment of one wall still stood but I had to strip away a mass of vines to examine it. At that moment I understood why the name House of Death had been applied to the small temple: a skull and two crossed bones had been carved at the base of the wall. Then I stopped short. Sure, a skull and crossed bones had become our modern symbol for poison, but Mayan symbols and language glyphs originated in the distant past. The mistake that had been made, I felt, was applying modern logic to the interpretation of an ancient sign.

I looked at the carving again. It did not have the traditional character of the figures engraved on other Mayan temples. What little is known of the Mayan language was drawn from interpretation of symbols used repeatedly in all the surviving artifacts. Each pictograph is highly stylized, and the exact same figures appear in calendars and mathematical computations, making it easy to sort out a possible meaning for each sign. Nowhere had I seen a graphic representation equal to the skull and crossed bones of Uxmal's House of Death.

What if the symbol meant *life,* not death? What if the Mayas possessed a method of preserving life through some form of surgical transplant? What if the House of Death was the storehouse of parts or . . . ? I realized that I was letting my imagination run away with me, but I had hit a new track and I wanted to follow it. Too, I had the beginning of an explanation for the self-imposed isolation of the Mayas. I saw the possibility that the Mayas might have thought physical contact with the other people was a source of fatal contamination and so fled to regions where they could survive and adapt themselves to the stressful elements in Earth's environment. All the while they might have kept their colony alive with a knowledge of immortality. I had an absorbing thought to occupy my time on the flight back to the United States; I knew I would have to define the limits of immortality.

I had been treating the word *immortality* rather cavalierly, it seemed. With the vision of the structures at Uxmal clearly in my mind I kept coming up against the definition of *immortality*. *Webster's Dictionary* says it is "exemption from death and annihilation, unending existence." But is that what I really mean? "Unending" is a long, long time. The notion of immortality began to squirm away from me and it seemed that now was the time to clearly outline the concept.

Existence is life, and that has to be the key word. But what exactly are the criteria of life? Walking, talking, awareness, breathing, eating. These are not quite enough, for we already have a number of machines that perform these functions. Robot explorers have been on the moon, have flown past several of the planets in our solar system and reported what they had seen back to other machines on Earth. The star of one modern television commercial is an anthropomorphic dummy with a beating heart and lungs that breathe. He is used to teach fledgling MDs to recognize the sounds of heartbeat and respiration in the healthy and ailing body. A few years ago a group of engineers and physicists at Johns Hopkins University got together and built a robot whose sole task was to feed himself. His food was electricity, and he roamed the halls of the Advanced Physics Building seeking electrical outlets, poking his prongs into them, and gluttonously "eating." No, these criteria do not spell life, nor do the traditional vital signs of heartbeat and respiration mean that an organism is alive.

For some years medical circles have debated the question of how to determine when a person is dead. At one time there was no problem, for the doctor could presume that death had come when the patient's heart had stopped beating and his breathing ceased. Of course, an MD could, if he wanted to, wait until rigor mortis set in before actually declaring his patient dead, but not much was going to change things, owing to the shortage of real miracles in recent years. But today we seem to be rediscovering techniques that may have been used thousands of years ago, techniques that call into question our traditional concepts of death.

Even minor advances such as electric defibrillators that shock the heart to a rhythmic beat, mechanical respirators that breathe for the patient, and a host of sophisticated chemical agents have been so successful that they have blurred the one sharp line that for the doctor separated life from death. Moreover, with the increasing success of transplants the demand for human organs has become extreme. Doctors are forced into the ghoulish position of waiting for a patient to die so that a vital organ may be extracted and dropped into the body of another in an attempt to restore him to good health.

"The essential organ system we have to think about for death," says Dr. Robert White of Cleveland Western Reserve Medical School, "is the brain, and what we have to have defined for us is a period or area where we can be absolutely sure that the individual will not recover even though his heart and lungs are working. If we know by some chemical test, by some electrical test, or perhaps by some examination that these individuals are never going to recover, then the question would be upon us whether or not we should define these people as in a category of no recovery and as a consequence be justified in removing one or more of their organs."

To help clarify the idea I had stumbled onto at Uxmal I wanted to examine Dr. White's work more closely. His interest in testing life can be best appreciated in the context of his work. He transplants brains. Dr. White's effort was admittedly experimental as he was in fact transplanting the brain not as an end per se but simply as a means of keeping it alive outside its natural container, the cranium. The idea was to study a living brain in an isolated, controlled environment without having to peer at a shadowy picture of it through layers of bone. From these studies may come the answer to the question of bodily life and death, but Dr. White's problems, once he had decided upon this course of experimentation, were just beginning. First there was the selection of the experimental animal. Human beings were, for obvious reasons, ruled out. The ideal experimental animal was then determined to be the rhesus monkey, which has a brain the size of a human baby's. Next was the question of surgical technique: Did one simply punch a hole in the skull and hope that the brain would sort of leak out? Obviously not. The bony skull around the brain had to be removed and then the brain had to be separated from the spinal cord. With the brain isolated, all sorts of monitoring devices were put into use, providing a great deal of information about the neurochemistry, neurophysiology, and other systems that operate in the brain but had never before been seen alive from this particular vantage point. This was still not a transplant, which technically is the removal of an organ from one body and its reimplantation into a second body. Inevitably this was the direction in which Dr. White was headed. To keep his naked, living brain alive he needed a miniature heart-lung machine, but this kept the brain alive for only a few hours. There was no way to remove the toxic product of brain metabolism, so it died. To solve the problem Dr. White began to devise a miniature artificial kidney, but at this point the engineering requirements overwhelmed the experiment and so Dr. White did what he probably should have done in the first place: he transplanted his isolated brain into the body of another monkey and plugged it into the femoral artery of the leg, where it gained the continuous supply of oxygenated blood and the use of two perfectly healthy, functioning kidneys.

There was something tantalizing about all this, and I pursued the subject in an interview with Dr. Fernando Cabiezas, a Peruvian neurosurgeon at the University of San Marco. "Cabie," as he is known by just about everyone in Peruvian intellectual circles, is also an accomplished amateur archaeologist specializing in Incan neurosurgery. We were sitting in the courtyard of the Cuzco Archaeological Museum, surrounded by some of

the most ancient and beautiful things ever found in the
Andes. At Cabie's feet were an assortment of skulls,
each with one or more holes in it.

"These skulls," he said with an expansive wave
meant to include virtually all of the Andean plateau,
"are just a small sample of the tremendous amount
of skulls that were found in the graves of the ancient
Peruvians. I think that, all in all, we have studied more
than ten thousand skulls that have been unearthed in
this area." Cabie picked up one of the skulls and his
fingers traced a ring in each of the four holes that made
the top of the cranium look like a lace doily. "This one
is a rather interesting specimen. We find that this man
suffered four operations, and he survived every one of
them! Either he was a very sick man or he had a very
persistent surgeon. But he was an excellent technician. These two openings," he said, pointing at silver-
dollar-sized holes, "are right over very dangerous
sites. Even right now, with all the techniques that we
use, we would be very much afraid of operating in
these sites. And this man survived each of the four
operations."

"How can you tell?" I asked. "Neurosurgeons have
been known to bury their mistakes."

"See the way the bone around the hole is smooth
and tapers off to a very thin layer of bone?" Cabie said.
"This shows a healing process. Bone cells have grown
again around the edges, and if this man had lived long
enough, say forty or fifty years after the surgery, it
would have been a very small hole or perhaps no hole
at all, but a newly cut bone has sharp vertical sides
with none of the tapering growth produced by healing.
There must have been a lot of successful neurosurgery
around here because at one site, the Talca, in Chile, I
would say that eighty-five percent of the skulls showed
healed trepanations, new cell growth. An eighty-five
percent survival rate is an excellent result."

That last statement finished our film interview and
the crew began to strike lights and coil up cables. We
were now simply underfoot, no longer the focus of attention but merely two clumsy, nonworking people who
were in the way. As we left the courtyard I noticed that

in the glass cases lining the walls a number of mummies—skeletons, really, their flesh long since rotted away—were displayed like bundles of old clothes. Many were in the fetal position, knees drawn up to chest, arms wrapped about the knees. In many, the mummified sinews that once held bones in place had broken away and jaws had opened in silent appeal, hands dropped down in piteous pleadings that would never be seen by anyone save an occasional tourist visiting the museum. For a moment I felt unaccountably sad, and then just as quickly the mood lifted. Quite obviously these long-dead people had benefited from medical and surgical skills that might easily have equaled or surpassed our own.

"How many of the skulls which you have studied might have contained transplanted brains?" I asked Cabie, thinking of Dr. White's experimental work. For a moment he looked at me and then burst out laughing. "I'm quite serious," I said.

"Well then, you deserve a serious answer. You see, there are two basic ways of transplanting a brain. One is to lift off the top of the cranium, much the way you remove the top of a shell from a soft-boiled egg, lift the brain out after severing its connection with the spinal cord, and then drop it into a similarly prepared skull. The difficulty, of course, is in making the neuro-connections that will enable the brain to be supported by and control its new body. I have seen no evidence of cranial lifts of the sort required for a brain transplant."

"But there are other ways," I suggested. "The Guthrie-Demikhov techniques." Charles Guthrie and Vladimir Demikhov were transplant pioneers separated by fifty years but united by interest in brain transplants. Their technique, first used by Guthrie at the Rockefeller Institute in New York in 1908 and subsequently by Demikhov in Moscow in 1959, grafted the entire head onto the body of another animal. In both procedures the experimental animals were dogs and the recipient kept his own head as well as gaining the new one. Demikhov's two-headed dog lived for twenty-two days and even though its nourishment, respiration, and blood supply were furnished by the host, the grafted head salivated and blinked one eye, an indication that a number of neural connections may have been made between host and graft head.

"We've never looked for any evidence that heads were transplanted," said Cabie, "but I still don't feel that there is any reason to. There is more than enough evidence of Incan neurological skills, and that's the area in which my studies are concentrated." His tone indicated that he did not want to pursue this any further.

Despite Dr. Cabiezas' reluctance, there was some evidence that the ancient Peruvians transplanted many of the body's organs. Medical historian R. L. Moody specifically cited "bone transplants and other less obvious organ transplants." (*Mystery of the Ancients,* by Eric and Craig Umland) We found remainders of the skills of these ancient Andeans in remote mountain villages where a caste of medical priests, called Collahu Aya, still minister to the sick. "They do not talk," noted anthropologist Jacques Bergier. "They travel throughout South America, treating illness, and carry with them in boxes medicines that we have not been able to identify." (*Mystery of the Ancients*)

Certainly the herbalists of the ancient world were skilled pharmacists, and their knowledge is in use today in many of the formulations we consider to be the most advanced products of modern pharmacology. There is ample evidence that the skills of the ancient healers were not limited to a sort of mumbo-jumbo folk medicine. Their surgical skills, already amply demonstrated for us in Cuzco, are equal to the most sophisticated transplants being done today. The Samhita, an eighth century B.C. surgical text, contained specific transplant techniques. A Chinese document dated 300 B.C. reported the following account of a remarkable event:

One day Chen Au Chao called on the surgeon's friends Chen and Ch'aio. He gave them a toxic drink, and they were unconscious for three days. Then Chao operated and opened their stomachs and explored the heart. After removing and interchanging their organs, he gave them a wonderful drug and the two men went home recovered.

There may, of course, be more than a little poetic license in the story. It nonetheless seems to indicate more than a passing familiarity with the technique of transplanting the body's organs.

Still another account, this one from Africa, told of the heart of a ten-year-old girl being placed in the chest of a fifty-eight-year-old man, twenty-two hundred years ago. Today, even as I write, a man with two hearts lies in Grote Schure Hospital in Cape Town, South Africa, recovering from surgery apparently much like the one performed so long ago. Yet for us, today, it is a new, different approach to heart transplant.

Dotted throughout the nation are a number of home-grown preservation factories, coffin-sized freezers that will for a couple of thousand dollars tuck you into Arctic temperatures until a cure is found for the disease that has already killed you. You must be dead to qualify for freezing. Under our present technology there is no way of restoring to life an individual frozen to ice-cube hardness. The legal term, then, for freezing an individual while still alive is homicide, and the appropriate penalty presumably assigned.

The freezer program had its greatest impetus in 1966, when the plan, which had been a sort of cult idea, was finally and rationally spelled out in a book called *The Prospect of Immortality*, written by physics teacher Robert C. W. Ettinger. Admitting that the present-day state of the art offered not a form of suspended animation but "suspended death," Ettinger proposed:

After one dies a natural death his body could be frozen and preserved at a very low temperature—perhaps at absolute zero, the lowest possible temperature—to prevent any further deterioration for an indefinite period. The body will be damaged, by our current freezing methods, but it will not decay or suffer any more changes. One assumes that at *some* date scientists will be able to restore life, health, and vigor—and these, in fact, in greater measure than was ever enjoyed in the first place.

The heaven on earth that Ettinger goes on to depict is indeed blissful, removing even the possibility of pain from death:

> The tired old man, then, will close his eyes, and he can think of his impending temporary death as another period under anesthesia in the hospital. Centuries may pass, but to him they will only be a moment of sleep without dreams. After awakening, he may already be young and virile, having been rejuvenated while unconscious, or he may be gradually renovated through treatment after awakening. In any case, he will have the physique of a Charles Atlas, if he wants it, and his weary and faded wife, if she wishes, may rival Miss Universe. Much more important, they will be gradually improved in mentality and personality. They will not find themselves idiot strangers in a lonely and baffling world but will be made fully educable and integrable.

It is indeed a dazzling prospect, and Ettinger is wise enough to put it all into perspective:

> Clearly, the freezer is more attractive than the grave, even if one has doubts about the future capabilities of science. With bad luck some people will simply remain dead, as they would have in the grave, but with good luck the manifest destiny of science will be realized and the resuscitees will drink the wine of centuries unborn. The likely prize is so enormous that even slender odds would be worth embracing.

Ettinger's ideas were interesting, and anyone faced with the prospect of imminent death and possessed of the money to be properly frozen might elect to go into the freezer on the one-in-a-million chance that he will someday come out alive.

I ruled out the freezer concept as the method of immortality that might have been used to transport humanity across space. The technical requirements of vastly expanded life spans must have been met by those who crossed the void of space to get here. No matter how advanced their space travel capabilities, spaceships' storage capabilities are somewhat limited. Filling a ship with frozen colonists who would be stacked like cordwood in the afterhold somehow does not seem in accordance with the thinking patterns of beings who could solve the problems of interstellar travel. Rather, the same solutions we have found for weight reduction for space travel—microminiaturization—probably would have been sought by them. Nature had anticipated just that problem. As a point of fact, nature had anticipated every problem by programming the genetic structure of every organism. Every cell contains a complete set of instructions needed to create not merely that cell but every cell in the entire body—brain, toenail, eye color, antibodies—the entire complement needed to make and power a complete individual. The instructions are stored in a chemical molecule called DNA, deoxyribonucleic acid, which is inside the nucleus of every cell. The DNA molecule is a marvel of microminiaturization. All of the DNA in every cell of every living creature on Earth could be packed into one container no bigger than a pea. Thus it could be possible to ship to distant planets the distilled essence of entire colonies, stored in tiny packets. The DNA molecules need be activated only at the appropriate moment, thereby providing enormous savings both in shipping weight and in cost. A single cell from my body or yours will provide that DNA molecule, enabling us to be shipped across the void of space, hatched, and then begin life on a new world light-years from Earth. Is this then the form immortality took for those who came here, the form that may be possible for us? The question again brings me squarely up against a need for a definition of the word *immortality*. Would a cell from my body, grown out into a complete organism, be me? If I had died would my replica be considered a continuation of my life? If each time my body succumbs to illness or accident I reconstruct it according to the genetic instructions contained in my cells, will I have achieved immortality? The questions almost defy answers, for they lead me into complexities of spirit and science that inevitably boil down to individual beliefs.

Considering these questions, I came head to head with the nature-nurture controversy that has bedeviled psychologists for the last decade. Are we products of our environment or of our genes? A good case can be made for both sides. In fact, we are actually products of our experience, mediated by our genetic makeup. We react to an event because of the nature of that event and also because of our genetic capabilities to respond to situations. For example, a seven-foot-tall American boy will, in all likelihood, become an outstanding basketball player. A seven-foot-tall Masai herdsman will be a Masai herdsman. Both owe their height to genetic instructions to grow tall and to the environment, which provides food sufficient for them to respond to the instructions. Their professions depend upon their environment—the Masai herds cattle, the American plays basketball.

Let's go back to my lonely cell, which has been placed in tissue culture and is busily dividing into new cells. Each has instructions to ultimately grow out and become another Alan Landsburg. Something, of course, prevents it from doing that, a mechanism within the DNA structure that tells the cells to specialize—to be a toenail cell or a brain cell or a stomach cell and to go no further, to halt short of creating a new individual. But this possibility exists, and a bold new step across the frontiers of traditional biology has made a reality out of what was once merely a possibility. In the cells of man are the secrets of immortality, secrets that now are being unlocked and harnessed in the technique known as cloning.

3

How About the Clone?

Carbon copies of life, duplicating people: these are the catch phrases of the awesome biological technology we are now developing. The technical description, *cloning,* is a less dramatic term. Even in the original Greek the word *klon* means "twig." And that's where cloning began—with plants, or, more specifically, peas and carrots.

The peas, of course, were the experimental model used by Gregor Mendel, an Austrian monk whose twin hobbies of mathematics and botany eventually led to the discovery of the laws of genetics. In 1857 Mendel began to crossbreed pea plants and tabulate the results. From his meticulous observations over the next eight years he formulated a series of laws governing genetic inheritance that finally established heredity as a science and removed it from the realm of speculation, mystery, and superstition. Mendel found that specific characteristics, such as height, color, and size of blossom, were passed on to the new plant by its parent. Each of the characteristics was determined by mechanisms which Mendel called "factors," which we know as genes. He theorized that genes were transmitted as complete units and retained their individuality.

As I looked over the historical material on Mendel and his peas I began to have the feeling that we were investigating recipes for some sort of vegetable stew. To Mendel's peas I was now adding Steward's carrots, the first plant to be cloned experimentally.

19

At Cornell University in the early 1960s Dr. Frederick Steward began an attempt to force a single carrot cell to grow into a complete, fully grown carrot. Now, this might not seem like much of an accomplishment. After all, every spring we plant carrot seeds in the backyard. If we can keep out the neighbors' dogs and manage not to flood them with water or allow weeds to choke the struggling young seedlings, in a few months we have fully grown carrots.

In Steward's experiments the difference lies in the starting materials. We begin with the seed, which is the plant world's version of the fertilized egg. In the mammal that fertilized egg must be implanted in the womb for development to continue and a baby to be born. To the seed, however, the earth is the womb; once dropped in, its development begins.

Dr. Steward was beginning with a cell from the root of a carrot, a cell whose genetic instructions were equipped with a sort of stop button that prevented it from developing into a fully grown carrot and forced it instead to become what it was—a single, simple root cell in a carrot plant. To release this genetic brake Steward put individual root cells into a rich, nutritive solution and agitated them slowly on a mechanical shaker. Such techniques, and others, will cause an egg or seed to divide, but not a fully differentiated cell such as the root cells with which Steward was experimenting. With great patience, changing the elements of the nutrient solution, adjusting the rate of agitation, and other refinements of techniques, Steward eventually forced the individual root cells to form clumps which then began, astonishingly, to differentiate into other cell types. No longer were the clumps made up of root cells alone, but of stalk, leaves, flowers, and seeds. Steward had succeeded in growing out from the root cell a new carrot whose genetic instructions were identical to those contained in the root cell.

It was a remarkable breakthrough in biological technology and the implications for the future were enormous. As Dr. Willard Gaylin, president of the Institute of Ethics and Life Sciences, put it, "To a scientific mind, the leap from single cell to cloned carrot is greater than the leap from cloned carrot to cloned man."

Technologically it is a giant leap to go from plant cell to animal cell. That leap was first made in the mid 1960s by Professor John Gurdon, a biologist at Oxford University in England. Gurdon, a red-haired man with a ready smile, chooses his words with great precision. That same precision is apparent in the technique he developed to clone frogs.

A few years ago I went to Oxford to see John Gurdon and film his work. As I walked through the ancient streets of the town, redolent with the history of Empire and the great scholars who had studied here, I was struck by the incongruity of the ancient red brick buildings and the futuristic work being done under the microscopes in those buildings. John Gurdon's experiments were in a sense bringing the stars closer to Earth and stretching life to almost unimaginable lengths.

Inside the laboratory, which, save for fluorescent strip lighting, looked as medieval as the rest of the college, a huge aquarium stood on a black stone bench.

"That's it," said Professor Gurdon, waving his hand in the general direction of the aquarium. "That's what you have come to see, the clones."

"Of course," I said, looking more closely at the frogs. I had done my homework; I knew that Gurdon's experimental animal was the African clawed frog. I had expected to find one or two strange-looking creatures carefully isolated. Instead there appeared to be as many as one hundred of the creatures vigorously paddling about in the giant tank, staring back at me just as if they had been born in the ordinary way. I stepped closer and stared in earnest, trying to distinguish some difference, to see if I was being hoaxed, although the idea of this internationally renowned biologist wanting to hoax a journalist and filmmaker was patently absurd. Still, when confronted with something which one has been led to believe is impossible, the mind rebels and for short periods, at least, does not always perform rationally.

"They are identical, you know," Gurdon said, and at the same time implied that my reaction was no different from the reaction of others not working in the field. "They are wart-for-wart identical each to the other."

As he spoke the frogs continued their helter-skelter movements about the tank. The thought that they were all descended from and identical to the same, single parent was truly amazing. The reason became clear as Dr. Gurdon explained the great lengths to which nature had gone in order to prevent just such copycat forms of reproduction. For it is by sexual reproduction that nature ensures genetic diversity, a constant mixing and stirring of the entire population gene pool that guarantees the survival of the species. It makes available so many different genes that there are always some of just the right sort to defend against virtually any natural assault on the species. To accomplish this mix nature provides the sex cells—sperm in the case of the male and egg in the female—with only one half of the normal complement of genetic instructions. When sperm fertilizes egg, the two half sets of instructions combine to create a complete set of plans for one new and unique individual.

By cloning, Professor Gurdon has circumvented these carefully evolved plans. The sex cells contain only half of the genetic complement. All other body cells have a full set of plans; this is essential for the growth and development of the organism. By removing from a single body cell the genetic plans which are contained in its nucleus, it is theoretically possible to grow an exact duplicate of the individual who donated the cell nucleus. That is what John Gurdon did. He used a cell nucleus to provide the complete instructions to an egg whose own nucleus had been removed. The result: his frogs were identical copies of the single frog who had donated the cell.

At the time, Gurdon's was a remarkable, virtuoso performance. Almost no one else was cloning animals with anything even approaching the success achieved at Oxford, and those who were trying were using Gurdon's technique.

That was four years ago. Today a number of laboratories around the world are successfully performing John Gurdon's nuclear transplants, as the technique is called. I went to the University of Indiana to film on-going work in the field of cloning. Dr. Janice Brothers, a professor of zoology who was working on the nuclear transplants at the university, had told me that her experimental model was the salamander. I pictured them as small newts, one to three inches long, a dull, dark green, and photographically, at least, not terribly exciting. Still, I felt that the idea of cloning was the important thing, and so extremely interesting that actually seeing the process of cloning would more than make up for whatever it lacked in visual excitement.

That was my first mistake. When I found myself staring directly at Dr. Brothers' salamanders I felt that surge of delight that comes to a filmmaker when his subject is a "natural."

There were five shelves filled with ordinary goldfish bowls. Each held a creature about ten inches long. The one I was staring at was paddling slowly in a circle, his body coiling to match the curve of the glass. His skin was a shiny, gleaming gold. He looked for all the world like a prehistoric dinosaur, with tiny eyes placed deep within the saurian folds of his face. Most remarkable was the branched, feathered headdress that danced and floated about its head. I later learned that it was a common set of external gills.

I looked around at the other creatures swimming, for the most part lazily, in the bowls. In addition to the golden-colored ones there were pale whites and a spotted variety.

"They're called Axlotals."

I turned around and saw Dr. Brothers standing beside me. She had come into the lab while I was staring in fascination at these marvelously ugly creatures. It was time for my second surprise. A streak of male chauvinism had led me to envision the old movie stereotype of the woman scientist—horn-rimmed glasses, intense manner, and dumpy figure. What I saw was a pretty, dark-haired young woman who would grace the front of a camera as easily as she fit behind the microscope.

"They are named for Xlotal, the Aztec god of death and resurrection," she said. "When I discuss my work with nonscientists I generally say *salamander,* which of course they are, rather than Axlotal. It saves a lot of explaining. But they're ideal for our work."

The work began as soon as our cameras and lights were set up. First Dr. Brothers took what looked like a beaded necklace—in reality a string of eggs—from a bowl containing a white, female Axlotal. The eggs were then briefly exposed to a high intensity ultraviolet radiation, which destroyed their nuclei. They were now amorphous blobs—large, undirected single cells destined to be nothing but undifferentiated bits of protoplasm. The enucleated eggs were then placed under a binocular microscope that was surrounded by a beautifully machined armature. By manipulating the dials of that armature Dr. Brothers could operate tiny surgical tools that could perform the most delicate microsurgery on the cell. As we started to film she began the intricate task of nuclear transplantation.

There is something beautiful about watching a skilled professional at work. A transformation occurs; its the kind of change Joe Namath makes every Sunday from off-the-field playboy to on-the-field quarterback. The same change occurred as Dr. Brothers started demonstrating the cloning process. The very intensity of her concentration gave a glow to her face and seemed to infuse her hands with an ironlike steadiness.

First, from a newly formed embryo of a spotted Axlotal she cut free a number of cells. Manipulating the round knobs with deft movements, she brought a slender glass tube over the embryonic cells. Delicately she teased a nucleus from one of the cells and then touched another dial, which caused it to be sucked into the glass pipette. Now the tube, with its almost invisible nucleus, was maneuvered over one of the enucleated eggs that had been taken from the white Axlotal. The pipette descended and stabbed the egg. Dr. Brothers touched another dial and air forced the nucleus down the slender tube and into the egg.

Dr. Brothers looked up from the microscope. "That's it."

"Cut!" I called, and the camera stopped rolling.

"Now we'll go and call on Dr. Flaten," she said.

In filming the cloning of the Axlotal we had to somehow solve the problem of time, for after the transplantation had been done it would take some days for the egg, with its new nucleus, to develop from its initial one-cell stage to a fully formed tadpole, and weeks more to achieve adult size. Obviously we could not keep coming back to film the successive changes. The answer was to take advantage of a remarkable film made by Dr. Clarence Flaten, who had developed special time-lapse techniques and had filmed the developmental process from start to finish.

As I viewed his film, which showed the continuation of the process I had just seen, I marveled. Eggs began to divide over and over again, until they became a seething mass of thousands of cells. The divisions continued until we could no longer see individual cells. Remarkably, round cells began to elongate and fold in upon themselves, forming tubes in which spinal cord and digestive tract would develop. Suddenly I was looking at the classic embryo shape that all vertebrate animals assume—salamanders, chickens, fish, human beings—at this stage of their development.

On and on the developmental process continued; beneath the almost transparent skin I could see a heart begin to beat. Suddenly the embryos were transformed into tadpoles darting about the screen. The lights went up.

"Marvelous," I said.

"Thank you," acknowledged Dr. Flaten. "Now Dr. Brothers will take you back to her lab and you can film adult clones of the Axlotal."

"Fine," I answered, and we made arrangements for him to send me his remarkable time-lapse footage to be edited into our film. That was the last time I was to see Dr. Flaten, for unfortunately this remarkable filmmaker and scientist succumbed only a few weeks later to a massive heart attack. His talent will be sorely missed.

Back in Dr. Brothers' lab we began to set up our lights to film the cloned Axlotals. They swam lazily in a large tank, and at first they appeared no different from the normal Axlotals we had seen. Then I began to get the feeling that these clones were indeed different from the normal ones.

"It's their bodies," Dr. Brothers explained. "The clones are dumpier, the trunk of the body between the fore and hind legs is compressed. It's a mutation that occurs only in clones and so we presume it is one genetic change brought about by the nuclear transplant process itself. But it does not seem to have any effect on their life span or ability to function. In that regard they are very normal."

The implications to be read into these "normal" clones were staggering, and in fact have been the subject of great controversy among scientists almost since the day John Gurdon successfully cloned the Africa clawed frog. Among the possibilities were these summed up by John R. Platt, a biophysicist at the University of Michigan. Writing in *Science,* the journal of the American Association for the Advancement of Science, Platt offered the following possible uses of cloning:

For human beings, successful development of this method offers the possibility of giving babies to many couples who are unable to have children—babies which in this case could be genetic copies of the husband or wife. . . . It would also be useful to try animal-copying with the nucleus taken from one species and the egg in which it was implanted taken from another. Donkey and horse can be mated; will a donkey nucleus in a horse egg cell give a donkey—or something like a mule? This might teach us something about the developmental embryonic differences between species. If it would work, we might be able to save some vanishing species by transplanting their cell nuclei into the egg cells of foster species. Is the DNA that carries heredity destroyed immediately when an animal dies? If the meat of woolly mammoths locked for thousands of years in the Arctic ice is still edible, perhaps their DNA is still viable and might be injected, say into elephant egg cells, to give baby mammoths again. By some such methods, perhaps, we might achieve "paleo-reconstruction" of ancient Mexican corn, or of "mummy wheat," or even of the flies that are sometimes found preserved in amber. One man has devoted his life to reconstructing creatures like the ancient aurochs, by back-crossing modern cattle. May these other genetic methods of paleostudy also be worth trying? Success is uncertain, but the rewards would be great.

The possibility of actually cloning human beings has aroused the most controversy, and among the scientists doing nuclear transplants, the most fear. John Gurdon is absolutely horrified by the idea of cloning human beings, and even resists speculating on the idea. "My major concern," he says, "is with the on-off switching of the genes. I would like to know what it is that activates them, what is it that tells a cell to follow only part of the genetic instructions it contains and thus become a hair cell, for example, and not something else."

Dr. Brothers also told me of her firm opposition to cloning human beings. Cloning, she pointed out, creates a rigid mold that could stabilize one form, and that runs counter to the design of human creation and evolution.

As Dr. Brothers made her point I nodded agreement. As I looked at her "other world" Axlotals, each one spotted in exactly the same place, with a black pip of precisely the same dimension, I was reminded of a crystalline moment of revelation that I had experienced in the course of filming.

In an icy stream leading to an obscure Alaskan lake called Eva I witnessed the last leg of a salmon migration. The "pinks" were fighting their way upstream to reach their birthplace in the lake. Once there they would spawn new eggs and die. I was clinging to a tree root underwater at the edge of an eight-foot cataract, the toughest obstacle the salmon faced. Downstream, as far as I could see, fish clotted the water. Thousands of them waited their turn to try the course. All were of the same species, yet even huddled together each was clearly different from the other. Size, shape, and color tone set them apart. Perhaps most important of all, temperamentally they were different. One or two approached the falls and seemingly without hesitation made their leaps; others studied the problem, swimming in slow circles until they had the energy to try. There were those who could not make it on the first attempt but doggedly attacked the precipice time and again. Still others made one attempt, then gave up and allowed the current to drag them back toward the ocean and death.

I realized that nature had provided the salmon with a clear test of durability. Here, in the last moments of life, they faced their ultimate challenge. Only the strongest would survive to procreate, and only the genes of those who had passed the test would be carried to the next generation. The process had been ongoing for millennia. The fittest had survived, yet they were marvelously varied in their appearance. They had not stabilized into a single form, and therein lay the strength that variation supplies to us and our world.

As I looked at the Axlotals I understood Dr. Brothers' point about rigid molds being counter to human design.

Most scientists and other concerned laymen who are opposed to cloning of human beings take some comfort from the fact that it is still technologically impossible to perform nuclear transplants on the human egg. The difficulties involved are rather formidable, according to Dr. Derek Bromhall, a zoology department colleague of John Gurdon's at Oxford University. For some years now Dr. Bromhall has attempted to transplant the nucleus of rabbit skin cells into enucleated rabbit eggs. The rabbit eggs are almost exactly the same size as human eggs and the problems encountered are similar.

"The difficulties with working with mammals are enormous," Dr. Bromhall told me. "You're dealing with warm-blooded animals and so it's not like frogs, where you can put eggs in water and you can even put them on dry slides and do the nuclear transfers. A frog's egg is huge, and you can handle it very easily. But with mammals you've got the environment of the egg to consider. This egg was never meant to be exposed to anything other than the fluid that surrounds the sperm. You have to take the egg out of the animal with surgery, and you've got to have a lot of techniques all ready, and at the same time. You also need a lot of eggs. This is the difficult thing. With the frog you can do fifteen hundred transfers a day. If you get one percent of that, you've got something to work with. Now, I can do thirty to forty rabbit eggs in a day. Now one percent of thirty eggs isn't even one successful nuclear transfer."

There may, however, be a way around that problem. Experiments with cell fusion indicate that human egg cells might simply be fused together to form a single unit large enough to accept nuclear transplant without damage to the structures needed for development of the embryo.

The work is also being done at Oxford by Dr. Christopher Graham. He uses mouse eggs, which pose an even greater challenge, for they are extremely small —about half the size of the human egg. The idea, however, is relatively simple. Graham uses a virus to carry into the egg the nucleus of the donor cell. This eliminates the need for clumsy human hands to accomplish the actual nuclear transfer.

Normally a virus works by invading a cell and then somehow switching off the DNA machinery in the cell nucleus. The virus then hooks its own DNA into the system and the cell is forced to manufacture more viruses rather than parts of itself. Dr. Graham decided to take advantage of this viral technique of reproduction and chose as his carrier an influenza virus called the Sendai virus. When mixed with a solution of animal cells this virus acts as a sort of glue, binding together the cells and making both viral and animal cells respond to the genetic orders issued by the DNA of either one. Graham, however, first bathes the virus in ultraviolet light, which deactivates its own DNA.

Next, Dr. Graham takes several mouse eggs and washes them with a chemical called colchicine, which destroys the nucleus even though it is buried deep within the cell. He extracts adult spleen cells from another mouse and mixes them with a batch of the Sendai virus. The viruses stick to the walls of the spleen cells like raisins in rice pudding. To this virus-cell pudding

Graham then adds his enucleated mouse eggs and places the entire agglomerate under the microscope, where he uses a tiny glass rod to tap together an egg and a virus-covered spleen cell. Within three to eight minutes the virus fuses together cell and egg. Once this fusion has taken place, the nucleus of the spleen cell provides the genetic information for the egg to act upon. The egg begins to divide, just as if it had been fertilized in the normal way by a sperm. Unfortunately, these fused, dividing eggs do not continue to develop, and no cloned mouse has yet been born from this technique, but ultimate success is merely a question of time.

When the technique of cloning has been perfected, human beings carefully selected and genetically engineered will be cloned for specific purposes. At that moment the moral and ethical dangers will perhaps be the greatest mankind has ever faced, but so too will be the opportunities. I can foresee in clonal man not only danger but great hope, for he is our link with the stars and immortality. By cloning human beings, animals, and plants, each engineered and designed to fulfill a specific function, we would confer upon the clonal parents a form of immortality, extending their genetic "offspring" through time and space, where they will be implanted on other worlds throughout the galaxy. In just such a fashion the first clonal men may have come to Earth.

4

Engineering the Embryo

Just how difficult would it be to clone a few carefully selected human genotypes specially designed for space travel? Problems begin almost immediately.

Once the eggs are available for cloning, they will require something more than the petri dish needed by salamanders and frogs. For despite all our advanced technology we have not yet reached the "brave new world" where the test tube has completely replaced the womb. The possibility, of course, exists, and a "walking womb," such as the type we are now using, would offer some distinct advantages during space flight. The woman to whom it is attached, for example, could be an active, important contributor to the life and work of the spaceship. Her ability to intelligently perform many functions would provide her with a much higher weight/efficiency factor than that possessed by an artificial womb.

To preserve the genetic structure built into the cloned eggs, sexual intercourse for purposes of reproduction would not be permitted aboard ship. At the appropriate time, however—say within thirty years of planetfall—the female crew members would be implanted with cloned eggs. They, as surrogate mothers, would carry the eggs to term. Shocking, farfetched, impossible?

TEST TUBE BABIES BORN IN EUROPE. That headline screamed from newspapers all over the world in July 1974. Although no official announcement was made by any hospital or research institution, the report was traced to Dr. Douglas Bevis, a professor of obstetrics and gynecology at Leeds University in England. Bevis would give no details except to say that one baby in England and two in other western Europe locations had been conceived in test tubes during the previous eighteen months. The fertilized eggs had then been placed back in the wombs of the mothers and developed and were born normally.

Although scientists have been working on just such a procedure for some years now, the cries of shock and outrage that followed the announcement sounded as if such an event were not only a surprise but a biological impossibility.

"I am astounded that Professor Bevis would have made this statement," declared Dr. Patrick Steptoe of Oldham Hospital in England. "As far as I know, no one in this country or anywhere else has yet succeeded in this technique."

Steptoe's comments are critical for he, along with Cambridge University physiology professor Robert Edwards, have been working for years to devise techniques to fertilize a human egg in a test tube.

The idea of a test-tube baby has both fascinated and repelled people for some time now, but until recently no one had managed to actually fertilize an egg outside the human body. Edwards achieved this by placing premature eggs in a special solution made from the fluid contained in the Graafian follicle, the blister-like sac in the ovary in which the egg is stored until it is mature enough to be erupted into the fallopian tube and be fertilized in the normal manner.

After thirty-eight hours in the follicular fluid the eggs begin to divide, a process that normally occurs as an egg moves down the fallopian tube toward the womb. This initial division is a signal that the egg is ready for fertilization, and at this point Edwards added male sperm which had been stored in a special fluid designed to enhance their mobility.

The eggs fertilized in the test tube were never permitted to continue their embryonic development because the researchers felt that neither the techniques nor the need were available for continuing the growth of the embryo outside the womb. But the idea of implanting the fertilized egg in the womb of a woman who was infertile because of fallopian tube blockage had been paramount in the minds of many researchers, and sometime during 1973 the first successful implant was made. Or was it?

A few weeks after his startling announcement Dr. Bevis became unavailable to the press and has since refused to make any further statements about the initial report. It has been reported that he has ceased all work on the experiment.

It was an astonishing end to a remarkable story, yet I was more surprised by the premature publicity than by the fact that the first test-tube baby might have been born. For the technique of implanting into the womb the fertilized egg or embryo is so simple that it is now practiced with regularity by some animal breeders.

Not long before I read the Bevis story I was in Shrewsbury, Massachusetts, at the Worcester Foundation for Experimental Biology. Here the basic advances in biology that led to the birth control pill had been made, and here too was ongoing work that had obvious implications for space travel and longevity.

One group at Worcester was exploring the problems of cryogenics—freezing complex organisms and then restoring them to life without damage. Another was looking into a phenomenon known as delayed implantation. When a mammal gives birth nature adds to the offspring's ability to survive by guaranteeing maternal care for at least a short time. A complex sequence of biochemical events is triggered by birth, and a hormone is released in the mother's body which prevents any eggs which might have been fertilized from being implanted in the womb. The period of time varies in all mammals, depending upon the needs of the young. At Worcester, scientists have isolated that hormone in the mouse and can delay implantation for indefinite periods of time. Their interest, of course, is in gaining better understanding of reproduction and eventually developing a more efficient means of population control.

As I was introduced to their work I had the sense

that modern research was finding the techniques that another advanced technological society had perfected. I could now see one means of carrying future colonists into space and holding them in the fallopian tubes until needed. But there are other, perhaps simpler, ways of transporting fertilized eggs and embryos, and one of them had been pioneered by a gentle, humorous Chinese biologist who is today the head of research at the Worcester Foundation. Dr. M. C. Chang, with his merry, twinkling eyes and soft, gentle manner, might himself be the reincarnation of Confucius, I felt at our first meeting.

"You wish to see my rabbits?" he asked in a heavily accented voice. Dr. Chang had come to the United States to study soon after the conclusion of World War II. The convulsions of the Chinese civil war and the subsequent communist takeover had led to his decision to remain in America, where his brilliance had long been recognized.

"Yes," I replied, for in addition to the actual experimental work we had come to Worcester to film, I wanted to film Dr. Chang's rabbits; they were of great historic importance.

"You may have ten minutes, no more," he said, fishing a set of keys from his pocket as he led me down the corridor from his office to a locked door. Through the steel mesh and glass window that formed the upper half of the door I could see the cages where the rabbits were kept. The tumblers clicked, the door was pushed open, and I signaled frantically for the crew to move the equipment in.

"These rabbits," Dr. Chang said, "are the descendants of the original colony. Please try and disturb them as little as possible. They are very nervous." Then he added, "And so am I."

Dr. Chang had also agreed to an interview, in which he was to tell us the story of his rabbit colony. In 1952 Dr. Chang had taken fertilized eggs from his original rabbit colony in Worcester, put them into a thermos flask, slipped it into his vest pocket, and flown to England.

At Cambridge he opened his flask and implanted the eggs into the womb of an English rabbit. The eggs developed, grew to term, and the baby rabbits were born. Some months later he returned to Cambridge and reversed the procedure, bringing fertilized eggs back to Worcester and implanting them in his American rabbits.

He reached into one of the cages and took out a huge rabbit. "Here is a descendant of that original experiment," he said proudly.

"Using that same technique," he added, "it would be possible to ship embryonic human beings from one planet to another. Of course," he finished with a smile, "you would need an accommodating lady on that other planet to accept the embryo."

With that Dr. Chang unclipped the microphone. My ten minutes were up. His rabbits were restored to their tranquil solitude as he shooed us out.

Dr. Chang's original experiments have since blossomed into a sophisticated technology that today is used to ship all over the world entire herds of cattle, sheep, and other animals. The shipping container, however, is no longer the thermos flask; it has been replaced by the rabbit. In the rabbit womb hundreds of embryonic animals can be nurtured in transit for short periods of time. Just such a shipment was being made to the laboratory of Dr. E. S. E. Hafez at the Wayne State Medical School in Detroit.

"We are expanding and restocking our colony of research monkeys," he said as we arrived and began unpacking our equipment.

Dr. Hafez, who has been doing this sort of embryo transfer for a number of years and is no stranger to the media, almost took over the director's function. "If you will place your lights here and here, and your camera so, you will be in perfect position when we begin the transfer," he told the cameraman.

We set up, our lights kicking back flashes from the stainless steel operating table where the "action" was to take place. One technician draped the table with green cloths and another placed a large white rabbit on it. Hafez then walked out of the operating theater and into an adjoining room where a number of monkeys were kept. He looked carefully at the cages and then signaled, "That one."

A technician opened the cage, carried the monkey into the operating room, and placed it on a second table.

"Now," announced Dr. Hafez, "we are ready to begin. Is the camera ready?" he asked. Then without waiting for an answer, "So, we go. This rabbit was received here only yesterday from South America. Its womb is packed with two hundred embryos of research monkeys that are available in such large numbers only in South America. We shall remove those embryos and place them in the wombs of our own female monkeys and in a few months they will come to term and our colony will have grown by one quarter."

Dr. Hafez bent over the rabbit, made a small incision, inserted a tube. With it he withdrew what looked to the unaided eye like a very large drop of murky water.

"Can you see it?" he asked the cameraman. "Come in close now. I will hold it here for you. Have you got it? Good. All right, cut.

"Now we must go over here," said Dr. Hafez as he walked over to a bench on which rested a large microscope, "where we will examine the embryo and make certain it is undamaged."

Swiftly he slipped the tube containing the embryo under the microscope, made a few minor adjustments as he bent over to look, and then straightened up. "Perfect. We may proceed."

He picked up the tube and carried it to the second operating table, the one nearest the microscope. On it lay the female monkey. The tube was inserted into the vaginal canal and the embryo extruded into the womb. Here the process of implanting the embryo in the blood-rich wall of the womb would take place and it would grow and develop in its natural environment.

Throughout the entire procedure Dr. Hafez continued his instructions, his hands deftly performing their tasks while with equal skill he told the cameraman when to shoot and from what angles. For a moment after the filming had stopped we were half laughing and half marveling at Dr. Hafez's performance, for that is surely what it was, and then the significance of the work itself hit us. An entire troop of monkeys, enough to stock a very large research center—or a small jungle, for that matter—had been packed into a biological container the size of a small box, placed in an aircraft, and flown a distance of more than five thousand miles.

After what we had seen and filmed at Wayne State, Worcester Foundation, and the University of Indiana, it was not difficult to foresee embryos of very specialized genetic makeups being carried, either in living containers, in test tubes, in tissue culture solutions, or frozen, on spaceships hurtling through the galaxy. Only a handful of each type would be required, and when needed they would be cloned in the appropriate numbers to colonize worlds for which they had been uniquely adapted.

The technology for carrying such biological units across the vast distances of space and time is already developed, as are the techniques of cloning. But what of the genetic engineering required to build those chemical molecules that will furnish the precise genetic instructions needed to grow out these perfectly adapted human beings, plants, or animals?

The criteria for space travel, at least, have all been pretty well established. NASA follows a rigorously structured set of physical and psychological parameters in the selection of its astronauts. Might not these same parameters be computer-structured into a genetic profile which could then be built up from the DNA molecule to create the perfect "astrocolonist"? Might not this astrocolonist then be cloned to provide missions to the other solar systems in the galaxy with the sort of personnel best qualified to achieve success?

These were the questions I had been asking myself since leaving the cloning experiments at Indiana. It would not be a question of making basic changes in the human immunological system or brain size or skin color. Rather, we would look for such qualities as speed of reaction, superior eye sight, superb coordination, a physiology that responds better to low gravity, at least for the voyage out from Earth, and other physical and mental abilities that might provide the difference between success or failure, survival or disaster, for the mission.

I was beginning to stretch far beyond the limits of speculation acceptable to bioresearchers. I realized that the picture I had conjured of a space flight carrying some protoplasmic form of humanity to Earth violated the limits of most scientific sensibilities. But there are some investigators willing to consider the trail I was following and provide additional clues; one of them was Dr. Marc Lappe of the Institute of Society, Ethics, and the Life Sciences, located in Hastings, New York. He had just returned from a symposium on the social and historical implications of new discoveries in the field of natural science. As a member of the institute's staff, he was involved in the effort to expand the restrictive boundaries of thinking that often accompany research activities.

I don't mean to indicate that Dr. Lappe certified my being there in any way, but he was willing to suggest directions for me to pursue. I was on the phone with him, outlining some of my findings, when he brought up the fascinating work being done to unlock the "walled-off" genes.

"Genetic information," he said, "goes back for millennia, entombing genetic knowledge of previous lives. You can find genes that have been sequestered, locked up in some dark chamber of the nucleus. They are quiescent."

I began to wonder, as Dr. Lappe talked, at the possibility of walled-off genes suddenly popping up when needed to change the structure and perhaps even the function of an organism. He agreed that it was possible. I began to envision a genetic "time release capsule" that would at a given moment unlock a characteristic needed to ensure survival. I dove back into my books for more data on the process of genetic engineering.

The technology for tailoring genes is rapidly reaching a point where we shall be able to build genes that express specific characteristics. The problems still to be overcome are enormous. Although we can read the DNA code we have yet to understand the complexities that go into the multiple instructions needed for involved capabilities such as intelligence, hand-eye coordination, and longevity. Once understood, however, the technology required to carry these genes into the cell will be waiting.

To understand just how this can be accomplished I had to research the DNA molecule. DNA is chemical shorthand for deoxyribonucleic acid, a complex chemical molecule shaped like a spiral staircase. Its railings are made of sugar and phosphate and the rungs or stairs are composed of nitrogen compounds called bases or nucleotides. There are only four bases in DNA: adenine, thymine, guanine, and cytosine. The molecule is arranged so that A can link only with T, and G with C. But from this simple arrangement an infinite variety of coded combinations can produce the vast diversity of living things.

The order in which the bases are arranged determines the instruction that will be given to the cell. These instructions do not literally say "be a hair cell or a brain cell," but they might just as well, for they order the way in which the cell arranges amino acids. There are twenty amino acids that are basic to life, and these are structured by the cells to form proteins, which in turn are the building blocks of our hair cells and brain cells. As the code changes the sequence of amino acids in the protein chain is altered, so that— for example—a protein used to build brain tissue is not tailored to fit into a kidney. In this fashion all of the enzymes that power the body's chemistry and all of the cells that compose its structure are built, renewed, and multiplied. The question now is: How do we intervene in this elegant system to introduce the sort of modifications that may be needed to achieve man's ancient dream, immortality?

One recently discovered technique injects animal genes into bacteria. These genes are constructed from DNA bases culled from other genes and are thus called chimeras. Greek myths tell of the gods creating monsters, called chimeras, from many different parts, and the process here appears no different. But the chimeral DNA has a special quality: it reproduces itself inside the bacteria, independently of the bacteria's own DNA. This means that all the genes in the chimera replicate themselves—both the native genes and those culled from animals. The chimeral genes are then passed on to the offspring of the bacteria and in this way the chimeras are effectively cloned.

Given an understanding of the genetic code, we may build immortality and other qualities into the astro-colonists we shall send into space. Those same techniques might well have been used eons ago on worlds whose existence we are unaware of to design the DNA molecules that express the physical and mental traits we know as man.

The implications in these developing technologies are astounding and the speed at which they have come is even more remarkable. For it is less than 125 years since Mendel first began to study his pea plants. DNA was first discovered in 1944, and ten years after that the spiral stair structure of the molecule was uncovered. Now we are not only reading the code but altering it to suit our needs and desires. What might we be able to accomplish with another hundred years of DNA experience behind us?

Confronted by the advancements of modern science, I kept reeling back to discoveries I had made about the unwritten past. I recalled the Sculpture Garden of an ancient ruin high in the Andes. The city is called Tiahuanaco. Thirteen thousand feet up on the Peru-Bolivia border, we found the skeletons of a once great city. A row of stone sculptures is embedded along a surviving wall. They form a diverse collection of heads representing virtually every known race on earth and some that were unidentifiable. It appeared to be an anthropological museum. I knew that no one had been able to date Tiahuanaco. Estimates of its age ranged from 2,500 to 15,000 years. If, as we suspected, it was indeed the base camp of astronauts who had come to the earth thousands of years before, would not the technology that had brought them here be just as far advanced in biological areas? Could those heads, incredible as it seemed, be the record, frozen in stone, of genetic experiments conducted on earth by ancient engineers?

The thought is no more incredible than the report on genetic and embryonic engineering contained in this chapter. The difference is simply one of degree, not of ultimate capability.

5

Neurosurgeons in Peru

The plane was making dizzy circles over the mountains when it suddenly dropped like a rock toward the ribbon of concrete that was the landing strip. An instant later the wheels hit the ground and we rolled toward the arrivals building. CUZCO, ALTITUDE 11,444 FEET read the sign on the tower. Ground crews came running toward the plane and I was immediately struck by their appearance. Cuzco had been the capital of the Inca Empire, and these men with their curious tipped-forward, shuffling, half-running movement which was the typical gait in these high mountains were lineal descendants of the ancient Incas. Their bodies were marvels of adaptation to the high altitude: short, with low centers of gravity, and abnormally large chests housing oversized, powerful hearts that pumped such an astonishing quantity of blood that their skins had a purplish tinge.

As we stepped down from the plane I remembered our production manager's words in Lima: "Adapting to the altitude is easy if you do exactly what I say. Walk slowly, take deep breaths, drink the special tea, and lie down for at least one hour as soon as you reach the hotel."

I looked around at the rest of the crew. No one seemed to be bothered by the altitude, but of course we had just stepped off the plane. As is the case with camera crews wherever they travel, their sole concern was to see that the fifty-odd thousand dollars worth of

42

equipment in the hold of the plane was properly unloaded.

We finished counting the boxes, paid off the porters, and settled back in the two taxis that were to take us to the hotel. I pulled great draughts of the thin air into my lungs. Still no sign of the dread "sorocho"—altitude sickness—I had heard so much about.

At the hotel I ordered everyone to sit in the lobby and drink not one but two cups of the special tea. It had a thin, oily taste and left me with a slightly glowing feeling. The Indians called it "mate cocoa."

We scattered to our rooms and lay down, not for one hour but two. Cuzco was a major location for us. Sacsahuamán, that incredible stone fortress of the Incas, was just outside the city, while Pisac and other ruined temples hung from the peaks that towered over the city. Cuzco was also the jumpoff point for Machu Picchu and Ollyantaytambo, both important locations for us to film.

I woke up to the ringing of the telephone. I sat up, swung my legs to the floor, and reached down for my shoes. The floor suddenly spun wildly and the next thing I knew I was lying on it. I had blacked out for a moment or two, but aside from a slight dizziness I seemed to have recovered. I had suddenly gained a great deal more respect for the way high altitude treats the body.

Downstairs the crew was waiting; no one reported the slightest problem, so we left. The two cars climbed through the mountains up narrow, twisting roads that were little more than dirt tracks reaching up to the peaks. It took almost two hours to go a mere seventeen kilometers, most of it a series of serpentine bends on narrow ledges.

Then we stopped. The dirt track had become a footpath. "Up there," our driver said, "about a half hour's climb, is Pisac." Pisac was an ancient ruin atop a terraced mountain and was almost a replica of part of a stone model we had found some several hundred miles away. The model, carved from an enormous boulder, was thought to be either a map of the universe or a city plan complete with terraces needed for farming in the mountains. There were also temples, granaries, and fortresses. Nowhere is there a record of who carved the stone, or when, but the terraced fields that climbed the mountain slopes to the ruins of Pisac seemed to be the model come to life.

We began our climb, each of us carrying some of the equipment. We climbed for about twenty minutes and then were faced with a narrow ledge; it was no more than five feet wide. Below us the mountain fell away steeply some several thousand feet to where the terraces and the more gentle slopes began.

As we stepped onto the ledge the feeling of stepping onto the brink of eternity was unmistakable. I shivered and moved closer to the wall of the mountain, fearful of even approaching the edge of the ledge. Suddenly my head began to spin, just as it had earlier that day in the hotel. I pressed both shoulders to the mountain-side and waited for the spinning sensation to pass.

The others stopped and waited. "What's wrong?" asked Jeri, the cameraman. He is a wiry man with a neat beard and the strength and agility of a mountain goat. He had been climbing without stopping, holding a twenty-pound camera as easily as I held the two-pound lens case.

"I've got to stop. The altitude is getting to me."

"The light is going," Jeri answered. "Unless we get there soon we won't be able to shoot."

"Then go on ahead. Get me long shots, medium shots, and closeups of anything that looks interesting. I'll just lie here and probably die."

There was a good deal of joking about that but I really did feel terrible. "Go ahead, you can claim the body on your way back," I said in a feeble attempt at a joke, and they finally left, loaded like pack mules with camera, tripod, lenses, batteries, magazines, and film.

I slid down until I was seated, my knees upraised, my back against the wall. My world spinning like mad. My stomach then joined the spinning and I was now truly "sorocho"—altitude sick. I also began to feel terribly alone. There was, despite the wind roaring through the pass below me, a strange stillness and the feeling that I was the only person left in the entire world.

Some minutes later I heard a crunching noise, as if someone was walking on gravel. Then from below the ledge there popped a man's head. His shoulders appeared and the next thing I knew he was standing over me, his feet on the brink of the ledge, nothing behind him but the thin mountain air.

He wore a black, curving mustache and appeared to be at least six feet tall, about a foot taller than the Indians of the region. *"Que tal* [how goes it]?" he asked in Spanish.

"Not well," I replied in my own halting version of the language. The conversation limped along, he learning that I was an American, that I thought the mountains very beautiful, and that my head hurt and my stomach was upside down and that I was about ready to curl up and die.

" 'Sorocho,' " he said with sympathy. "I can fix that in a moment. Excuse me." He edged past and then scrambled up the face of the mountain and was soon about fifty feet above my head. He started pulling at some weeds growing in a cleft. A moment later he slid down and was beside me. "Here," he said, breaking and crushing the weeds he had pulled. "Breathe deeply."

I took the broken stalks and sniffed warily. "Deeply," he intoned. "Breathe deeply."

I did, pulling great gulps of air into my lungs. There was a distinct tang to the weeds, and whatever chemical had been locked within them was released by breaking and crushing; within seconds my head had cleared and after a few more moments of energetic sniffing and deep breathing my stomach was also restored to a sort of tentative equilibrium.

"Gracias, mil gracias [a thousand thanks]," I said.

"De nada [it is nothing]. Enjoy our mountains. *Buenos dias."* With that he left, following the track back the way we had come. To this day I have no idea who he was or where he came from. I had no time to wonder about it, however, for a few moments later there

was more crunching along the path; the crew was back. They weren't as lively as they had been when they'd left me—*abandoned* was the word I was later to use with them. Now they seemed crushed by the weight of the equipment. They were gasping and half staggering along. As they mounted the ledge and saw me they put down the equipment and dropped to the ground, backs against the mountain, exactly as I had.

"So, the mountain has gotten to you too," I said with less compassion than glee. "Here, I won't abandon you." I broke the remaining weeds into even smaller pieces and handed a bundle to each man. "Now, inhale deeply."

At first they looked at me as if I were crazy, then skeptically they sniffed and then were breathing deeply, pulling the tart, tangy odor deep into their lungs. When they were on their feet we started down to where our car waited, some twenty minutes' hike down the mountain. I asked the two drivers whether a man had passed and they said no, no one had been along, either up or down the mountain, since we had left.

The weeds, I later learned, were a traditional mountain remedy for altitude sickness, but—like the commercial—offered only temporary relief. The weed was also related to the cocaine plant from which the tea was made, which also explained the modest glow we had gotten after drinking the "mate cocoa." The experience, added to my interview with Dr. Cabiezas a few days later at the Cuzco Archaeological Museum, led to the feeling that there was far more than folk herbs to ancient medical practice. Rather, it seemed that a sophisticated medical science had existed and is in some cases only now being relearned by modern research.

From historians Craig and Eric Umland, whose speciality is ancient civilizations, come the idea that human sacrifice as practiced by the Mayas was a sacrificial rite only in the minds of modern archaeologists. "The Mayan physicians," they say, "were faced with unknown diseases, caused by microbes which were extremely lethal to the Mayas but relatively harmless to their neighbors." (*Mystery of the Ancients* by Eric and Craig Umland)

(Any group that has evolved without exposure to a specific disease organism will be gravely affected by a sudden exposure. The Hawaiian islanders were virtually wiped out when Captain Cook arrived and left the measles virus behind.)

"What do our own doctors do when the cause of death is uncertain?" continue the Umlands. "What do they perform when attempting to learn the effectiveness of different medications and vaccines? Are not dissections and autopsies common in such incidents, and should we not expect to find them being practiced by a highly sophisticated and superior race such as the Mayas?"

Even the most dramatic of modern surgical procedures might be only an echo of ancient techniques. Heart transplants began making headlines in 1967, when Dr. Christiaan Barnard performed the first successful one at South Africa's Grote Schure Hospital. The effect on primitive peoples of witnessing such procedures can only be imagined. The Umlands suggest that the Mayas were indeed practicing heart transplants and that these highly sophisticated surgical techniques were witnessed by the primitive Aztecs and Toltecs and were then copied by them and perverted into a bizarre religious rite.

"They assumed," say the Umlands, "that the Mayas must somehow be appeasing their gods with such strange practices, and so they attempted to appease their own with these sacrifices, hoping to become as great and powerful as the Mayas. Human sacrifice thus became a part of the Aztec and Toltec religions, and they copied as best they could the procedures of the Mayas. They tied the victim on a slab and cut open his chest with a stone knife and then removed the heart. Unfortunately for the patient, the Aztec and Toltec gods did not make their worshipers powerful enough to be able to transplant the heart once they had removed it. The antics of the Mayas' neighbors were similar to those of small children trying to imitate the activities of adults, having 'tea' and dressing up in parents' clothes. Comparing the activities of one group to the other, while amusing, will certainly not give a realistic understanding of either."

Since the calendar of the Mayas reaches back more than ninety million years, speculations have placed Mayan colonies throughout the world. A recent find in Siberia seems to indicate yet another Mayan outpost. The possibility is tenuous, based not upon any artifacts or cultural information but rather the bones of a number of prehistoric men. The find was made in 1969 and published as *Reports of the Marmajaijan Scientific Expedition in Soviet Central Asia in 1969 on Behalf of the Turkmenistan Anthropological Society*. The skeletons were estimated to be a hundred thousand years old, and several displayed evidence of successful thoracic surgery.

The Soviet scientists noted finding "traces of a surgical operation on the bones bordering the chest cavity." The report went on to detail the growth of the periosteum, the membranous covering of the bones, which revealed the degree of healing. "After the success of this major operation," the Soviet doctors reported, "the patient recovered and lived at least three to five years, as is shown by the thickness of the periosteum."

By contrast, the longest surviving heart transplant patient of modern times was Louis B. Russell, an Indianapolis schoolteacher who died on November 26, 1974, six years, three months, and three days after receiving a new heart.

Whether the Russians had actually found evidence of a hundred-thousand-year-old heart transplant is still an open question. Some experts have noted that the ribs that were cut are precisely those which correspond to the "cardiac window" used in our time by Dr. Barnard and his emulators.

The record of ancient transplants is firmly established in such ancient texts as the Indian Samhita, while the Roman historian Celsus reported that the Indians had developed the art of rebuilding from other parts of the body noses that had been sliced off in battle. Little attention was paid to Celsus's "tales" in the Western world until the sixteenth century, when an Italian professor of anatomy, Gasparo Tagliacozzi, read his account of the Indian rhinoplasty. The Renaissance had loosened superstition's stranglehold on science in Europe, and the time seemed right to attempt a procedure that was already millennia old. The need was great; syphilis disfigured thousands every year, while faithless wives and petty criminals were punished by removal of their noses.

Tagliacozzi did a tremendous amount of research, practiced on cadavers, developed a few refinements on the Indian method, and then accepted patients among the unfortunates of Bologna. His technique was far from painless, but apparently it was successful. His patients sat upright while he carved into the shape of the nose a flap of skin from the inner muscle of the upper arm. He stitched the flap to the forehead, just between the eyes, and down the inner surfaces of the cheeks. He left a slender strip of the flap attached to the arm to maintain a supply of blood and keep the tissue alive while it rooted on the face.

As a result, Tagliacozzi's patients were forced to remain upright, arm raised alongside the face and head turned in toward the arm. A bandage that rigidly encased the body, head, and arm kept them immobile during the two or three excruciatingly painful weeks of the healing process, but at its end a new nose bloomed where before there had been an ugly hole.

The operation was so rigorous that a judge ruled it was legal for a criminal who had paid with his nose to have it restored. "The procedure," he held, "was twice as painful as having the nose amputated in the first place, so the culprit was thrice punished." (*The Rebuilt Man* by Fred Warshofsky)

It was through the Roman historian Celsus that Tagliacozzi had first heard of the nose transplants of the Indians. It was the Romans who won the dubious distinction of introducing smallpox to the world. In 64 B.C. Roman legions invaded Syria, at that time a Greek colony. They swept through the countryside looting and pillaging. At a temple of Apollo, so the legend goes, they found a sacred box locked and sealed with a

potent spell. The Romans pried open the box and invisible seeds of pestilence leaped out and "suddenly
their faces grew livid with loathsome sores." (*Story of
Medicine* by Roberto Margotta)

The soldiers fled, carrying with them the germs of
smallpox. For the next fifteen years the entire Roman
world writhed in an agony of death and disfigurement
as one of the great pandemics on record swept the
Mediterranean world. At that time there already existed
a form of immunization that was even then several
thousand years old. In ancient China smallpox was a
disease of long standing, as was the means of its control. Chinese physicians routinely rubbed dried matter
from smallpox sores into the nostrils of their healthy
patients, thereby creating immunity against the disease.

The knowledge spread to India, where the Brahmans
altered the technique by rubbing smallpox crusts into
open scratches on the arm or forehead. This practice,
a form of inoculation, spread throughout Asia and into
Turkey. Europe, painfully struggling through the intellectual abyss of the Dark Ages, knew nothing of this
means of smallpox immunization.

Arrogant knights sallied out time and again to battle
the infidel in the Holy Land. The Crusaders returned
from the gates of Jerusalem bearing not booty but the
virulent virus of smallpox. Europe was laid prostrate
by the "black pox" which killed, maimed, and blinded
its inhabitants for centuries.

In 1716 Lady Mary Wortley Montagu, wife of the
British ambassador to Turkey, saw the ancient practice
of inoculation. On her return to England she introduced
the practice and aroused bitter storms of controversy.
Nonetheless, inoculation hospitals soon blossomed all
over Europe.

I was struck by this movement of knowledge from
east to west, delayed in some cases by thousands of
years. Historical forces, of course, had a great deal to
do with that delay, but it indicated to me that outposts
of the ancient astronauts were certainly not limited to
pre-Columbian America and the Near East. India
seemed to be a seminal font where not only evidence

of space colonies might be found but also where technical knowledge of a high order seemed to flow. We consulted an expert on the Rig-Veda (one of the volumes of the Samhita), Padrhasi Sivirammamurti, a curator at the National Museum in New Delhi. When he learned that we were interested in the ancient wisdom of India his nut-brown face, with the red caste mark on his forehead, shone with delight. "The Veda," he told us, "is perhaps the oldest organized source of wisdom we know—at least five thousand years old. It was handed down orally from generation to generation, and we have the Veda recited today almost as they were chanted thousands of years ago."

Mr. Sivirammamurti then rose, took us to a cabinet, and removed several scrolls. These he unrolled to reveal marvelously illustrated hand-lettered versions of the Veda. "Only recently," he said, "we have begun copying the Veda down in manuscript form for scholars to study."

"But these look quite old," I pointed out, for the caligraphy and illustrations rivaled those of the monks of Europe during the Middle Ages.

"Oh no," replied Mr. Sivirammamurti, "the oldest ones we have are only a few hundred years old. Manuscripts are so fragile, you see. The chanted Veda is far more reliable, for it is imperishable. They are, however, taken down meticulously and a record is made that this was recopied at such and such a time by such and such a king, so that it may not perish. Palm leaf and paper manuscripts cannot be expected to have that length of life, and so they are often recopied. The oldest that we have may go back only a few hundred years," he finished somewhat apologetically.

As we talked on, I learned that the Veda cover an entire range of technological knowledge that is breathtaking—aircraft design, spaceship engines, television, nuclear energy, all are discussed in great detail in a verbal encyclopedia known to be at least five thousand years old. Here was an outer space connection that simply had to be pursued for its relationship to immortality.

"What about medicine?" I asked after Professor Sivirammamurti had expounded on the technological aspects of the Veda. "Just how accomplished were the ancient Indian physicians?"

"You know, of course, about the Indian success with transplants. Well, that is but one aspect of Indian medicine. Many of the diseases we now consider incurable were in fact cured in ancient India with medicines which are now lost to us. One area of scholarship is exploring the ancient texts to see if we cannot uncover some clues to the formulations of those medications."

When we finally left the museum, we had a list culled from the *Sushutra* of surgical procedures that included instructions to remove anal fistulas and neck tumors; operations such as tonsilectomies, lithotomies, and amputations were also described. Listed too were 121 different surgical instruments, a diagnostic manual, and the etiology of a number of diseases not achieved by the Western world until the late nineteenth century.

The sophistication of some ancient medical knowledge is so great it seems impossible that it originated in a culture lacking the complex biomedical technology we have developed. Yet how can we explain the ancient Chinese texts that reach back to the beginnings of their civilization, five thousand years ago? The *Nei Ching*, the Book of Medicine written about 2650 B.C., contains this description: "All the blood of the human body is under the control of the heart and regulated by it. The blood current flows continuously in a circle and never stops; it cannot but flow ceaselessly like the current of a river or the sun and the moon in their courses."

It was not until the seventeenth century, or forty-two hundred years later, that William Harvey, an Englishman studying in Italy, described the circulation of the blood pumped by the heart throughout the body. This discovery revolutionized European medicine, which until then had thought that the liver was the origin of the circulatory power.

Even more remarkable is the Chinese concept of yin and yang, the two opposing forces of the body which have their origin in an astronomical concept of order. As spelled out in the *Huang-ti nei ching*,

The Yellow Emperor's Book of Internal Medicine: The principle of yin and yang is the basic principle of the entire universe. It is the root and source of life and death. Through the interactions of their functions, yin and yang, the negative and positive in nature, are responsible for diseases which befall those who are rebellious to the laws of nature. In order to treat and cure diseases, one much search into their origin.

The origin of yin and yang is found in the Taoist legend of creation in which chaos was overcome and order established on the basis of the two opposite poles, yin and yang.

Yang represents the positive pole: active, masculine, embodied in the sky, light, hardness, and warmth.

Yin, by contrast, is negative: passive, feminine, finding its embodiment in the moon, Earth, darkness, cold, and moisture. In the body yin is found on the right side and yang on the left side.

To the Chinese, yin and yang are the dynamics of existence. Together they guide the stars and the planets through the seasons, exerting their influence on every living thing in the universe. In the individual, illness is caused by an imbalance between yin and yang, and death occurs only when they become so wildly upset that they cease to flow. Immortality, according to these principles, is possible so long as the yin and yang continue to flow, maintaining a reasonable balance with each other.

The idea of yin and yang has been treated by Western scientists for the most part with jaded ridicule and dismissed as peasant superstition. Paul Libasi, in the New York Academy of Sciences' journal, *The Sciences,* says:

But suppose the human body is actually regulated by two opposing but complementary forces, two chemicals present in every human cell. When the level of one chemical rises, concentrations of the opposing substance drop; this allows one set of body functions to occur and inhibits others. Just the opposite takes place when the chemical seesaw reverses itself; processes inhibited by the first chemical are promoted by the second.

Yin and yang—the idea is no longer comic superstition, for now being uncovered in both the United States and in England is experimental evidence that two chemicals, found in virtually every human cell, may be modulating or controlling hundreds of functions on the cellular level by acting in opposition to each other. These two compounds have already been implicated in such diverse effects as how forcefully the heart contracts and whether blood clots and blood vessels tighten or relax to raise or lower blood pressure.

The chief investigator in this area is Dr. Nelson Goldberg, a pharmacologist at the University of Minnesota. Seeking a simple term to describe the way the two compounds, known as cyclic AMP and GMP, produce their opposing effects, he contacted an old friend at Brown University, Chinese scientist Dr. Sungman Cha. He told Dr. Goldberg of the principle of yin and yang and the way Chinese physicians prepared drugs to restore their balance within the body.

"I was fascinated by the idea," said Dr. Goldberg, "because I think that many of the body's 'on-off' reactions could be mediated through the actions of just these two compounds."

After reading Libasi's account of the Goldberg research I too was fascinated, by yet another idea. It seems to me that in our laboratories a great deal of what we are doing is relearning principles we have known but ignored for thousands of years, principles that may well have been brought here by those who came to Earth chasing the elusive quality of immortality.

There is some evidence that the secret of immortality may have been given to the Egyptians. Early in Egyptian history they developed a highly effective medical science which became so sophisticated that it was divided, much as our own modern medical practice, into specialties. The Greek historian Herodotus described Egyptian medicinal practice as follows:

The art of medicine is thus divided; each physician applies himself to one disease only and not more. All places abound in physicians; some are for the eyes, others for the head, others for the teeth, others for the intestines and others to internal disorders. (*History of Herodotus*)

But by the time Herodotus came to Egypt, in the fifth century B.C., Egyptian medicine had declined into a pseudoritualistic exorcism, clinging daily to the organizational forms of the past. Physicians cured their patients by ridding them of demons rather than seeking physical causes and cures. There is evidence that much earlier in Egyptian history medicine was based upon scientific knowledge rather than superstition.

The Edwin Smith Papyrus, found at Luxor in 1873 and thought to be some five thousand years old, is astonishing in that it is totally free of magical incantations and references to demons or religious beliefs. It is purely and simply a surgical textbook that begins with an essay on the heart and circulation. There follow forty-eight sections that deal with the treatment of wounds and fractures, arranged anatomically. Each section has five parts: the nature of the wound, examination of the symptoms, diagnosis, treatment, and prognosis: "An ailment which I will treat" (cure certain); "an ailment with which I will contend" (cure possible); "an ailment not to be treated" (certain death).

Another ancient text, the Ebers Papryus, describes a diagnostic procedure in this fashion:

In the case of a tumor affecting a vessel in the form of a callosity, which is stone-like to the touch, I would say it is a tumor of the vessels suitable for treatment by surgery. After surgery, cauterize the wound lest it bleed too much.

I was at the most frustrating point in accumulating the research for substantiating the outer space connection. Helpful scholars were providing details that opened new vistas. I was changing many of my initial ideas. Naive assumptions of how the connection was made were falling by the wayside and a second generation of thoughts were taking shape. The key remained immortality and its achievement. The Rosetta stone might show the heavily underlined parallels between practices of ancient medicine and modern scientific research.

I desperately wanted to find specific cases where rites practiced thousands of years ago originated from a technology that had found the secrets to immortality. The papyruses in the British Museum were impelling me to return to the Middle East for a second look at Egyptian medical practice. I wanted to go back to the time before the truly rational medicine of the Egyptians degenerated into a mumbo-jumbo of exhortation and prayer designed to drive out demons. With that degeneration the idea of immortality moved from the House of Life to the House of Death.

The treasures of the ancient Egyptian tombs, now housed in places like the British Museum and the Cairo Museum, include a large number of implements that are exact counterparts of the basic tools of modern surgery. There are forceps of various kinds, scalpels, and clamps, indicating that the ancient surgeons of Egypt had very sophisticated skills. Surgery which required opening the skull is also described in the annals of Herodotus. From the records of battles, listing the dead and the wounded, we have evidence that the Egyptian military surgeons knew how to stuff a wound with cobwebs to prevent infection—an ancient version of our modern-day penicillin?

But even with the array of medical skills that was taught to young physicians in the House of Life, the enormous teaching hospital of ancient Thebes, even with their vast knowledge of life-saving techniques, the Egyptians, when all medical and surgical skills had failed, passed through a place that would prepare their corpses for resurrection. They began their second lives from the great mortuary palace of ancient Thebes, the House of Death.

6

The House of Death

For all of time the Nile has meant life and death to
Egypt. Each year the great river rises to flood level and
innundates the delta and then recedes, leaving behind
a nutrient-rich layer of silt. By providing a natural
fertilizer the Nile made ancient Egypt among the richest and most blessed of nations. For the people of ancient Egypt the Nile also marked the border between
life and death. The east bank traditionally was the
land of the living. Even now people pursue the same
timeless rhythms of life that have existed there since
the beginning of Egypt. Within view are the great and
mysterious monuments of the past, pyramids that tower
across the river like great question marks. I stared at
these marvels, convinced that they held secrets of immortality, that the pyramids are marked by the influence of visitors from space. Like any other tourist, I
gaped, while around me the Egyptians pursued the tiny
movements of their lives. They bought, they sold, they
walked, they rode, they fetched and carried. In short,
they behaved like people all over the world, possessed
by the moment, only vaguely conscious of tomorrow
and oblivious to the past.

I have seen the same lack of awareness of the great
and historic in cities all over the world. There are
sophisticated New Yorkers who pride themselves on the
fact that they have never been to the top of the Empire
State Building or inside the Statue of Liberty, London-
ers who have never been in the Tower of London, and

Parisians who have never ventured to the top of the Eiffel Tower.

The Cairenes are no different from most other twentieth century people, but once, a few thousand years ago, the Egyptians who lived on the east bank of the Nile were far less preoccupied with the details of their daily lives. To them, life was but a temporary stopover. Death was not an end but a continuation of life in a different form. The ancient Egyptians wanted to take with them across the river into their second life all that was pleasant and enjoyable. So important was this desire that the Egyptian pharaohs lavished all the nation's energies, treasures, and intellectual talent on the construction of tombs, mortuary temples, and pyramids.

Why this preoccupation with death, this almost perverted twisting of the finality we have always associated with the word? To the Egyptians death was not an end but a beginning. It struck me that their belief might indicate that the Egyptians had uncovered the secret of immortality. An old burial ritual ends with this priestly promise: "You live again, you revive always, you have become young again, you are young again and forever." (*The First Great Civilization* by Jaquetta Hawkes)

Immortality and the universe are recurrent themes in ancient Egypt, visibly inscribed on the monuments of the Nile's west bank. The journey to immortality was a physical one, for it was only after making the trip across the Nile, to the Valley of the Kings, that the pharaohs became truly alive. The trip is in many ways merely an echo of a voyage into space. Shown in preparation for the trip are symbolic boats that will carry the individual through the twelve hours of darkness to the dawning of a new day, a new life. I cannot help but wonder if the boats of Amon-Ra, the sun god, are the spaceships that took the newly deceased into the realm of the gods, the world of outer space, where the dead were somehow imbued with new life.

We had arrived in Cairo only that morning and were scheduled to begin shooting the next day. I left the hotel alone and walked to the river. I stood on the east bank of the Nile, looking at the fiery orange disc that turned the river to molten gold. Around me the city moved and flowed as the three million people pursued their lives, but I was unaware of their movements. I strained my eyes, trying to see tiny points pricking the horizon twelve miles away. There, on a sandy plateau in the desert, stood the great pyramids of Giza.

"It is much more beautiful much more closer," said a man who had come upon me unnoticed. "I can show you secrets people do not see, things in the pyramids unknown to most."

I laughed. Twenty-five hundred years before, the Greek historian Herodotus, the father of history, might have stood on the desert's edge and been told "marvelous secrets of the pyramids" known only to the guide offering to tell them for a price. Herodotus, in his "History of Egypt" (*History of Herodotus*) records a number of tales told by guides and priests which have been questioned almost since the moment he wrote them. There was, for example, the story that Cheops, who built the Great Pyramid at Giza, was so strapped for money that he sent his daughter out prostituting to raise the funds needed to finish the project. Not to be outdone, the daughter, according to Herodotus:

. . . at the same time bent on leaving a monument which should perpetuate her own memory required each man to make her a present of a stone toward the works which she contemplated. With these stones she built the pyramid which stands midmost of the three that are in front of the Great Pyramid, measuring along each side a hundred and fifty feet.

"Okay," I said, "let's go." He led me to a rickety taxi, rattled across the bridge to the western bank of the Nile, and then headed north toward Giza and the pyramids. As they loomed ahead I felt the hairs on the back of my neck rise. Every so often, while filming *In Search of Ancient Mysteries* and *The Outer Space Connection,* we had touched history and an incredible feeling of deja vu had stolen over me. At that moment I felt a kinship with the people who had built these incredible structures. I sensed the master design, I could feel the texture of the stone, and I could see the sheer walls bathed in the glow of the setting sun, not as they were now—red and roughened—but as they were twenty-five hundred years ago when Herodotus looked upon them. For these incredible monuments—the Great Pyramid built by Cheops, as the Greeks called him, and the two lesser pyramids known as Chephren and Mycerinus, built by other kings, and the incredible half-woman, half-lion sphinx that lies in the sand and guards them—were as ancient to Herodotus as they are to us. His view of the Great Pyramid was of a huge, dazzling white structure capped by a golden point that shot shafts of light back at the sun.

The original facing, a pearly limestone, had been stripped off thirteen hundred years after Herodotus's time in order to build the Arab mosques and palaces of Cairo. What I was looking at was the bulk of the pyramid—2.3 million blocks of red sandstone carved from the very plateau on which it stands. The blocks themselves were enormous, weighing from two and a half to fifty tons each, fitted with a neatness and exactitude that even today still befuddles experts.

So it stands on a thirteen-acre base and soars 481 feet above the desert sand, encompassing more comparison, admiration, analogy, mystery, and unanswered questions than any other structure in the world. Consider the following comparisons compiled by Dr. I. E. S. Edwards, keeper of Egyptian antiquities at the British Museum in *The Pyramids of Egypt:* "It has, for instance, been calculated that the Houses of Parliament and St. Paul's Cathedral could be grouped inside the area of its base and still leave considerable space unoccupied. According to another estimate, there would be room for the cathedrals of Florence, Milan, and St. Peter at Rome, as well as for Westminster Abbey and St. Paul's Cathedral. It has also been reckoned that if it were sawn into cubes measuring a foot in each dimension and these cubes were placed in a row, they would extend over a distance equal to two thirds of Earth's periphery at the equator."

Not even Napoleon was immune to offering analogies attesting to the majesty and size of the Great Pyramid. One day during his Egyptian campaign Napoleon sat in his tent at Giza while several of his generals set out to climb the Great Pyramid. When they returned he announced that on the basis of his calculations the pyramids on the Giza plateau contained enough stones to build around the whole of France a wall ten feet high and one foot thick.

These numbers are only a small sample of the varied speculations the pyramids have aroused. Begin with its age. Most Egyptologists are in agreement that the Great Pyramid was commissioned by Cheops, or Khufu as he was known in Egypt, and completed about 2900 B.C. But in the year 1000 A.D. the Arab historian al-Masudi wrote that the Great Pyramid had been built by a pharaoh named Surid three hundred years before the Great Flood. Surid had been commanded in a dream to build a great structure to preserve for posterity all of the wisdom and scientific knowledge of the Egyptians that might otherwise be lost to the deluge. "In the eastern pyramid," wrote al-Masudi, "the king caused to be inscribed the celestial spheres, the chronicle of times past and future and of all that was to happen in Egypt." (*Timeless Earth* by Peter Kolosimo)

Little of Surid's chronicle remains, but from our vantage point at the base of the pyramid I could see a thin line marking the high-water point of the deluge. It proved that the flood was real, that thousands of years ago cascading water had caused unimaginable havoc. What remains to tell the story is a faint line etched on a pyramid. To one historian, al-Masudi, the flood accounted for the existence of the pyramid. For my part, I was sure that there was much more to the story of how and why the structures were built.

I stood at the base of the Great Pyramid and cursed the ravages of time and man that had obscured the true purpose of this unique masonry. As I approached the entrance each individual block of the base loomed well above my head. The massive granite blocks made me feel dwarfed; I pulled back at the entrance, a little reluctant to let all of that brooding intensity engulf me. A warm smile and a friendly arm reached toward me. "Come, sir, right up these stairs, and I will show you the inside of the Great Pyramid." I accepted the offer, shelled out the customary baksheesh, and allowed myself to be led inside the tunnel-like opening that serves as the tourist entrance to the pyramid. Abruptly the heat of the desert sun receded, along with the raucous cries of the camel drivers and automobile horns. The immediate interior of the entrance chamber was cool and quiet, the peaceful stillness of centuries broken only by the incongruity of fluorescent lights. I had barely had time to catch a glimpse of the three enormous granite plugs that were used to seal up the original entrance to the pyramid when suddenly the lighting flickered and went out. We were plunged into total darkness. Around me were mutterings of "Power failure!" a scratching of matches, and the beaming face of my guide appeared. "Not to worry, sir. We will go up by candlelight." Gripping our candles, we began the ascent into the pyramid. I was filled both with trepidation and with a tremendous excitement as I realized that I was seeing the interior of the Great Pyramid exactly as it may have been viewed by Herodotus himself.

The candle glimmered up a narrow wooden staircase built over an eroded stairway. It seemed to me that we were climbing up at a right angle, bent almost double because the ceiling was so low. Even with the coolness and lack of humidity inside the pyramid I was drenched with sweat from the exertion of the climb. We emerged from the cramped confines of the ascending stairway into the vaulted grandeur of the Royal Gallery. I unbent myself and stopped to catch my breath, only to feel another tightening of my chest as I looked around me. Even by candlelight the symmetrical proportions and lofty ceilings of the Royal Gallery were magnificent. Massive blocks of stone, smoothly faced, were constructed to form corbeled arches around the graceful sweep of another ascending staircase. Elegant wall carvings of ancient deities danced faintly in the light and accompanied us up through the gallery to an opening into the room called the King's Chamber.

Here I was gripped again by a sense of deja vu, of knowing this room, of having been here before. With practiced twists of a candle held in each hand, my guide illuminated a high ceiling chamber made of neatly dressed blocks of granite. At the far end of the otherwise empty room stood a giant lidless sarcophagus. I crossed the room with an urgent desire to place the palms of my hands against the walls and was somehow not surprised to find them cool and dry to the touch. A breeze fanned past my face and my guide explained that the King's Chamber had its own air-conditioning system—ventilating shafts that penetrated through several thicknesses of stone to the pitiless desert heat. The vents eliminated humidity in the pyramid's interior.

I wandered over to the sarcophagus, wondering for whom it was meant and how it was used. Had this monument truly been intended solely as the final resting place for an ambitious pharaoh, or was there perhaps another purpose for the some eighty pyramids that dot the deserts along the west bank of the Nile? To the best of all archaeological knowledge, the great tomb of Cheops at Giza is the only pyramid that contains within itself a burial chamber. In most other pyramids there are only burial pits dug several feet below the foundations of the actual structures. But speculations about the use of mysterious rooms in pyramids have come down to us from the records of Earth's earliest civilizations. I remembered reading the works of an Arab historian who had assigned great age to the pyramids. He referred to an inscription that purportedly says it was built "when Lyra was in the sign of Cancer, twice 36,000 solar years before the date of Egypt." That would make the pyramid of Cheops about 73,000 years old.

Roman historians prior to the fifth century A.D. quoted legends that the pyramids were Joseph's granaries used for storing corn during the years of plenty. This idea found its way onto the dome of St. Mark's of Venice, where it is emblazoned in gilt paint.

In 1859 London publisher John Taylor drew upon all of these ideas and wrote a book that shocked the historians and scientists of the day. Taylor claimed that the pyramids had been built by Noah, who had been directed by a race of superbeings from another world. The idea was at first laughed at and then dismissed out of hand until the Astronomer Royal of Scotland, Charles Piazzi Smyth, published figures that tended to support the idea of extraterrestrials having built the pyramids.

Smyth found a number of astronomical and mathematical correlations within the dimensions of the Great Pyramid. For example, the area of the base divided by twice the height equals pi, which of course is a major mathematical concept. Pi is the ratio of a circle's circumference to its diameter. The height of the Great Pyramid multiplied by a billion equals approximately the distance between the sun and Earth, and the base line divided by the length of one of the stones was 365 —equal, of course, to the number of days in the year.

For a century the mystics of the world constantly referred to the Smyth calculations to support their belief of visitors from outer space, but numerology is a shifting platform upon which to base so weighty a conclusion. In 1922 a German Egyptologist, Ludwig Borchardt, published a demolishing attack on the Smyth conclusions. Titled *Against the Mystical Interpretation of the Numbers on the Pyramid of Cheops,* Borchardt noted:

> If anyone takes the trouble to measure such a complex structure as the pyramid, he is bound to come across various "basic" measurements which he can apply at will to produce a desired conclusion. Given sufficient patience and versatility, he is sure to be able to arrive at figures that coincide with important scientific data and formulae. In fact, the quest could hardly be unsuccessful since it is not subjected to the discipline of any rule.
>
> Take, for instance, the height of the pyramid. Smyth multiples it by 10^9 (one billion) to obtain the distance from Earth to the sun, but this figure 9 is quite arbitrary. If no such simple multiple had met the case, Smyth could have chosen some other that would have given the distance from Earth to the moon or the nearest star, or any other known measurement. The only "discovery" of this sort that is somewhat harder to explain is that involving the value of pi. The Egyp-

tians may have used this ratio on purpose, but it is more likely to be the incidental consequence of a different plane of construction.

The validity of the Smyth theory was further shaken when one of his assistants found him sawing away at a projecting piece of granite in the royal antechamber in order to make its dimensions fit his numerology more closely. The final indignity seemed to have been provided by modern technology, which has shown that the pyramid measurements upon which Smyth based his theory were all wrong. They also reveal, however, that the sides of the base come to within seven inches of forming a perfect square. They are also oriented to within one tenth of a degree of true north, and the southern wall is aligned almost exactly along an east-west axis.

As a result of these numbers the idea has again been raised that the pyramids were constructed with the aid of a technology that employed lasers, computers, and antigravity devices. This idea has been reinforced by the two ultimate mysteries contained in the Great Pyramid. The first is obvious—how was this enormous structure built? It is not an easily dismissed question, for we have a truly accurate picture of Egyptian technology of the time and nowhere does it contain the elements necessary to build the Great Pyramid.

Neither the wheel nor draft animals were part of ancient Egyptian construction techniques. They had no knowledge of pulleys, block and tackle, winches, or derricks. How then could they erect such an enormous and almost perfectly proportioned structure with nothing more than stone and copper tools, crude surveying instruments, and their own muscle?

This question is made even more puzzling by the discovery of a piece of smelted iron, presumed to be part of a tool, found in the Great Pyramid centuries before the Iron Age began. A piece of smelted iron, an artifact out of its own time, the kind of object that Ivan Sanderson referred to as an OOPA, an acronym for an "out-of-place artifact."

When I consider the pyramids themselves, massive

triangular structures scattered over the empty, burning desert, they are equally isolated in time and space, a kind of gigantic OOPA. Again and again the question rises: Why were they built? Since the actual burial pits of pharaohs have always been found beneath the pyramids, it is quite possible that their use as tomb markers was not part of their original purpose. Dr. Patrick Flanagan, a California physicist and inventor, has spent most of his life investigating the nature of a phenomenon that he calls pyramid energy. As Sally and I researched our way through pyramid lore in the writing and filming of *In Search of Ancient Mysteries* we repeatedly encountered mentions of Dr. Flanagan and decided it was time that we met him.

Pat is an intense young man who told me that he believes his life has changed as a result of his pyramid investigations. As he settled into his chair he said, "Since I spent a night sleeping in the Great Pyramid I have discovered powers of which I was never before aware."

"Meaning what?" I asked.

"I am not altogether sure, but somehow my psychic consciousness has expanded. I have keener perceptions of people, a new consciousness of events."

"What would be your guess, Pat, about the origins of this new phenomenon?"

He smiled and said, "I guess it is involved with pyramid energy."

I told Pat that we wanted to discuss fully his concept of the strange energy absorbed by the pyramid form and how it affects life exposed to its forces; however, for the moment we wanted his opinion on the origins of the pyramid.

"It's very possible," he said, "that the Great Pyramid of Giza was constructed by a race of scientists having knowledge far superior to our own. The dimensions of the pyramid itself indicate this, due to the fact that the French meter, which is our own standard system of measurement, is supposed to be based on the dimensions of Earth as calculated by scientists. In the International Geophysical year in 1958, the exact dimensions of Earth were determined by satellite, and the French meter was found to be incorrect, but what was most amazing was that the Egyptian cubit, the unit of measure used in the Great Pyramid, was found to be exact. In other words, the cubit fit into the dimensions of Earth within five decimal places, and this is a rather startling coincidence. The fact that the Great Pyramid is level over an area of fourteen acres within one half of an inch and is the world's most accurately aligned building, true north, and the fact that it incorporates higher mathematics in its very design indicate that a superior race designed the Great Pyramid."

There was much more I wanted to know from Pat, and our interview lasted, in fact, for almost four hours. Later in this book I will report his findings concerning pyramid energy.

Pat had given me a clue that I wanted to investigate. I assembled all of the literature, ancient and modern, concerning the structure of the pyramids, and sorted through it to find the elements that pointed directly to an outer space connection involving the building of the pyramids.

A variety of explanations are offered to explain just how the Egyptians quarried the huge blocks and then dragged them to the site. The granite used to build the galleries and chambers inside the Great Pyramid, for example, came from as far away as six hundred miles, from Aswan. Stone workers were presumed to have chipped notches in the granite and then slipped in wedges of wood. The wood was then soaked and expanded until they finally split the blocks off from the main outcrop.

The blocks, so the reasoning continued, were then shaped and smoothed at the site and finally levered onto sledges, with the aid of wooden crowbars. Gangs of laborers then hauled the enormous blocks, some of which we know weighed at least fifty tons, to barges on the Nile. The way was greased for a sledge, argues one expert, by pouring milk—"the fat content of which makes it a better lubricant than water—on the ground before it." (*Ancient Engineers* by Sprague de Camp)

There is in all this guesswork an overweening sense of superiority, a modern inability to acknowledge a technology more advanced than our own, especially one that might have been used on Earth thousands of years before we split the atom and began our own adventures in space. And so we use milk to lubricate the way for fifty-ton sleds and use the comparative hardness of various minerals to find stone implements harder than the granite they were presumed to have chipped.

Yet the machinery needed to raise these enormously heavy blocks into place is not depicted anywhere in Egyptian accounts. Only Herodotus offers a crude description of the construction methods and machinery used to erect the Great Pyramid, and that has been discounted by historians and engineers who cannot accept the idea of the Egyptians possessing sophisticated machinery. Herodotus wrote:

The pyramid was built in steps, battlement-wise, as it is called or, according to others, altar-wise. After laying the stones for the base they raised the remaining stones to their places by means of machines formed of short wooden planks. The first machine raised them from the ground to the top of the first step. On this there was another machine which received the stone upon its arrival and conveyed it to a second step, whence a third machine advanced it still higher. Either they had as many machines as there were steps in the pyramid or possibly they had but a single machine which being easily moved was transferred from tier to tier as the stone rose—both accounts are given and therefore I mention both. (*History of Herodotus*)

To a man of Herodotus's time the idea of helicopter-borne winches, laser beams, and other advanced technological devices capable of cutting, shaping, moving, and raising the pyramid blocks are totally unthinkable and are thus reduced to the materials and technology of his time—"machines formed of short wooden planks."

Our own historians of science tend to see the machines described by Herodotus as simple levers worked by the brute force of slave labor. They point out that such simple devices could not have raised the large fifty-ton slabs and that to build the pyramid it would have taken far more than the twenty years Herodotus tells us were needed. When the Greek historian stood here, where I stood, twenty-five centuries ago, he saw an immense causeway sixty feet wide and half a mile long leading from the edge of the Nile to the Great Pyramid. Questioning priests and guides and using his own eyes, Herodotus gives us this account of the building of the Great Pyramid and its causeway.

A hundred thousand men labored constantly and were relieved every three months by a fresh lot. It took ten years' oppression of the people to make the causeway for the conveyance of the stones, a work not much inferior, in my judgment, to the pyramid itself. This causeway is five furlongs in length, ten fathoms wide, and in height, at the highest part, eight fathoms. It is built of polished stone and is covered with carvings of animals. To make it took ten years, as I said—or rather to make the causeway, the works on the mound where the pyramid stands and the underground chambers, which Cheops intended as vaults for his own use. . . . The pyramid itself was twenty years in the building. (*History of Herodotus*)

In the accounts of Herodotus the mysteries become magnified. The causeway took ten years to build, the pyramid twenty—a total of thirty years. Historians of the present day, however, note that Cheops reigned for only twenty-three years. If he died before the project was completed the likelihood of a succeeding ruler finishing it for him is remote. But there, of course, it stands, unquestionably a finished monumental achievement, undiminished even by the stripping of limestone from its face and cap. The ruins of the causeway or ramp are seen alongside the two other pyramids at Giza, but there are no remains leading to the Great Pyramid.

The condescending view held of ancient engineering techniques insists upon the construction of great earthen ramps over which the pyramid blocks were dragged into place. And there, the archaeologists say smugly, is the evidence, visible even today in the ruins of the ramps that lead to the other pyramids at Giza. But those ramps would have had to maintain a gentle upgrade to reach each course of stone. As the pyramid rose, the ramp would have to be raised and lengthened each time a new course of stone was added. Engineers have estimated that a ramp to service the pyramid of Cheops would finally have had to be a mile long, with a volume of masonry four times greater than the pyramid itself. Using only the energy provided by gangs of laborers, the engineers further estimate that Egypt would not have been able to supply enough men to build such a ramp more than halfway up the Great Pyramid.

"Even assuming such a ramp existed," points out one expert, "it would have had to narrow until, at the pyramid's apex, it was only three yards wide—not enough space for men to stand while dragging the last blocks to the summit. Even with platforms and scaffolding, engineers say, it would be impossible to place enough workers up there to heave the huge capstone into place."

Alternative solutions include a spiral ramp snaking up the pyramid's sides and greased wooden tracks up the pyramid's faces. Nowhere in Egyptian records—not in the tomb paintings nor on papyrus or other media—is there anything remotely resembling such construction techniques.

As a result, archaeologists are left with the unenviable task of accepting a technology far more sophisticated than anything known to have existed in the ancient world, a technology that utilized space-age tools and concepts; or an insoluble riddle that resists their best efforts at explanation. That mystery of the pyramids will remain unanswered so long as today's scientists look for primitive building techniques as the methods employed to construct buildings that call for space-age technologies.

Paradoxically, we have tried to employ some of those space-age tools to solving the other major mystery incorporated in the Great Pyramid: Where is the mummy of the man for whom it was built? Almost from the moment it was completed men have been prying into the Great Pyramid seeking the remains of the Pharaoh Cheops. Everything from stone sledge hammers to cosmic ray detectors have been used to pierce the veil of mystery that hides Cheops from prying eyes, and all have failed.

The first recorded attempt to enter the Great Pyramid was in 820 A.D., when the Arab Caliph of Egypt, Abdullah al-Mamun, learned of the secret scientific manuscripts hidden within it. While all of Europe wallowed in the intellectual and social morass we call the Dark Ages, the Muslim world was reaching the heights, producing great astronomers, mathematicians, and poets. From them al-Mamun learned of "strange metals that would not rust" and were hidden inside the Great Pyramid. Today's chrome alloys, stainless steel, and plastics might be described in just such a fashion, but these, of course, were unknown to the ancient Egyptians and ninth century Moors, but it did not deter them from searching for those treasures.

So cleverly disguised was the limestone door to the pyramid that al-Mamun never found it and was forced to tear his way into the Great Pyramid, tunneling into the stone a few feet above the sand. After his tunnel had reached a hundred feet into the pyramid it intersected the passage that descended to the subterranean burial pit. It was empty, but halfway up the passage the Arabs found an entrance to an ascending passage. It was blocked with huge granite plugs and the caliph's engineers took the easy way; they bored through the adjoining softer limestone, creating the alternate entrance that is used today. Ultimately this too was empty, and they resumed probing a room known as the King's Chamber. Here they found an immense, polished granite sarcophagus without a lid. It too was empty. Nowhere in the three chambers or the passages, galleries, and tunnels of the Great Pyramid did they find anything but dust and rubble. Not a flake of golden treasure, not a shred of papyrus, no statues, clothing, food, furniture, or any of the other burial goods always interred with a dead pharaoh were ever found in the Great Pyramid of Cheops. And of Cheops himself there was not a trace.

"This," points out one expert, "is incredible. Considering the immense treasure found in the tomb of Tutankhamen, an unimportant ruler who died at the age of nineteen after only nine years on the throne, the burial treasure that the mighty Cheops assembled during his twenty-three-year reign must have been several times as great. And to be of any use to him, it had to be interred with his body—which was also missing."

Since then other attempts, both government sponsored and highly illegal, have been made to find some shred of treasure in the Great Pyramid. Almost a thousand years after the al-Mamun assault on the Great Pyramid another passageway was discovered. It was a twisting, roughhewn vertical shaft two hundred feet long that led from the King's Chamber down around the blocked passageway and finally into the descending passage which led to the secret door. This passageway is thought to have been cut by workmen who otherwise would have been trapped after dropping the granite plugs in place. Using this passageway, archaeologists surmise, grave robbers might have entered the King's Chamber and emptied it of all of its treasure, including the gold-layered mummy of Cheops, which would have had to be broken into small pieces in order to fit down the narrow, roughhewn shaft.

But would they also have taken the huge, enormously heavy sarcophagus lid? Could they have broken up the granite into small pieces as readily as a mummy's bones? And why would they have taken the thousands of vases of dried food which the grave robbers of other tombs aways ignored? In each of those other rifled tombs the passageways and crypts are stuffed from floor to ceiling with thousands of jars and vases of dried grains. Yet not one kernel of food, not one jar or potsherd, has ever been found in the Great Pyramid.

Instead, there lies inside the King's Chamber a gapingly empty sarcophagus, the inner vessel meant to carry a pharaoh on his journey to immortality. The sarcophagus, at least what remains of it, was a disappointment to examine. The mortar was chipped and the empty pit reeked of urine deposited by less-than-considerate tourists. There was little to record on film, and as I set up the few shots I kept wondering why the pyramid had been built.

I began to lean very heavily on Dr. Flanagan's theory that it was a greenhouse for gathering and storing life energy. "The East Indians have called it Pranah," he explained. "It's been called the energy of Tantra, it's been called Manna, Odic force. And the Russians call this energy bioplasma. I have called the energy biocosmic energy, and these energies are those that surround living organisms."

"How does it apply to pyramids?" I asked.

"The pyramid appears to harness cosmic forces in much the same way a greenhouse harnesses infrared energy. A greenhouse is designed so that the sun's rays strike the walls at a right angle so you will attain maximum transfer of infrared energy to the interior of the greenhouse, although the rays can pass completely through the greenhouse."

"Funny. The greenhouse is pyramid-shaped, isn't it?"

Pat smiled. "Of course we may have learned about greenhouse construction from the pyramid. You see, the pyramid is designed so that it is properly aligned to Earth's magnetic poles so that cosmic radiation penetrating the pyramid at right angles to the wall will charge the pyramid with what we call biocosmic energy or pyramid energy."

"How would the energy affect living matter?"

Pat thought for a moment and then pointed out to me a rather unique fact. "Grains of five thousand years old found inside the Great Pyramid in containers or on the floor sprouted immediately. My own research indicates that, for instance, plants such as mung bean sprouts mummified in the pyramid were capable of growing after they had been rehydrated. So this indicates that the pyramid-energy phenomena maintain the actual life forces within the organism. This energy can alter the growth rate of plants. Plants grown in a pyramid develop three times faster than plants grown in control boxes of other shapes. Small human cells have lived, when placed in a nutrient solution inside of a pyramid, nine times their normal life span. There are people sleeping in pyramids, meditating in pyramids; they are treating their food in pyramids, growing their food in pyramids, treating cigarettes and cigars in pyramids. In fact, there is a whole international pyramid cult going on right now. I've even received letters from mainland China regarding the mummifying of bodies, which may indicate that they're interested in using the pyramids for mummifying the bodies of their dignitaries."

I went right to the heart of the subject: "Is there any possibility, in your opinion, that the bodies that are mummified in pyramids could be used as a basis for some form of cloning?"

"It's very possible that pyramid energy could be used to preserve tissues over extended periods of time, such as on long space flights, or for purposes of cloning for future cell regeneration. The pyramid's phenomenal ability, or the pyramid-energy ability, to mummify food so completely, with no destruction of the tissue, indicates that it would be a very valuable natural source of preservative energy for cloning purposes or for preserving anything, any cell structures, for an extended period of time."

7

Back to the Pyramids

I browsed through the dimly lighted exhibit halls of the Cairo Museum. Ornate cases housed centuries worth of artifacts from whose musty remains I hoped to exhume the next critical link in the chain leading to outer space. Another wrong turn, more pots and miscellaneous amphorae, more gritty cases, and suddenly there he was. He lay in state inside of yet another glass case, this one crisscrossed with masking tape and banked by sandbags to protect its sacred contents for the duration of the Middle East furor. The setting was incongruous; he'd been around for about four thousand years, and now he was lying there enigmatically, oblivious both to the tourists and to the bombs. His name is Ramses II, Pharaoh of the Two Truths, and I had traveled halfway around the world to try to penetrate the twin mysteries of why and how his body had withstood the decay of countless centuries.

The riddle of the almost perfect preservation of a human body for thousands of years had haunted me since my first foray into the ancient mysteries of mankind. I felt that if I could glean some concept of the technology that had solved the problems of mummification, I might discover some key to man's eternal quest for immortality.

"You live again, you revive always, you have become young again, you are young again and forever." This was the promise of the Egyptian priests at burial, a promise of immortality that far exceeded any treasure a man could hope to procure. It was a promise which, I felt, had its roots in space, in what was perhaps a dim, ancestral memory of another world.

"These words 'forever' introduce the great cosmological dream that lies behind the personal desire for resurrection, the dream that accounts for the Egyptian preoccupation with death," says British archaeologist Jacquetta Hawkes in *The First Great Civilization*. "Inspired perhaps in part by the regularities of the Nile valley and its seasons, their philosophers saw the maintenance of an eternal cycle, unchanging except within phases of the cycle, as the meaning and purpose of existence. This was what the gods had begun, what Ma'at presided over, and what pharaoh made available to his people. Yet the death of the individual appeared as an offense against the eternal order; it was a change, and an intensely painful change that was nonrecurrent and therefore meaningless. It can be said, with a rough kind of truth, that the concern with death was to defeat it, to counteract a meaningless outrage and see to it that the dead individual was in fact enabled to take his place in the cycle of the universe."

The ancient Egyptians chose to guarantee immortality by preserving the body itself in as lifelike a state as possible. To accomplish this they either developed or received instructions almost five thousand years ago in the technique of mummification. The Egyptians practiced it for twenty-five hundred years, yet today there exists only one major account of the procedure. It was recorded by the Greek historian Herodotus in the year 484 B.C., at least twenty-five hundred years after the Egyptians first began their efforts at preserving the body. Herodotus, however, could not gain entrance into the mortuary temple itself. According to his own report, the following details were given him by a friend:

> The mode of embalming, according to the most perfect process, is the following. They take first a crooked piece of iron and with it draw out the brain through the nostrils, thus getting rid of a portion, while the skull is cleared of the rest by rinsing with drugs. Next they make a cut along the flank with a sharp Ethiopian

stone, and take out the whole contents of the abdomen, which they then cleanse, washing it thoroughly with palm wine and again frequently with an infusion of pounded aromatics. After this, they fill the cavity with the purest bruised myrrh, with cassia, and every other sort of spicery except frankincense, and sew up the opening. Then the body is placed in natron for seventy days and covered entirely over. After the expiration of that space of time, which must not be exceeded, the body is washed and wrapped around, from head to foot, with bandages of fine linen cloth, smeared over with gum, which is used generally by the Egyptians in the place of glue, and in this state it is given back to the relations who enclose it in a wooden case which they have had made for the purpose, shaped into the figure of a man. Then fastening the case, they place it in a sepulchral chamber, upright against the wall. Such is the most costly way of embalming the dead. (*History of Herodotus*)

The entire affair was supervised by a priest wearing a jackal-headed mask. He was the living embodiment of Anubis, the god of the embalmers, who prepared the deceased for his journey to the Land of the Dead. Anubis was one of the gods who prepared Osiris, the son of Amon-Ra, for his resurrection to a second life. At this point the conjunction of space and immortality is made, for in the legend of Osiris there is the familiar spaceman theme of a god descending from the sky to give to an ancient, primitive people the tools and knowledge to rise above the animals. Osiris, the legend says, ascended to the throne of Egypt when Amon-Ra, his father, returned to the heavens. His first task was to abolish cannibalism and to teach his half-savage subjects the art of fashioning agricultural implements. He taught them how to raise grain and grapes and convert them into bread and wine.

Osiris brought wealth, contentment, and civilization to a savage people but was murdered by his brother Set, who cut the body into fourteen pieces and scattered them along the Nile. Isis, Osiris's wife, searched the river until she had recovered every piece of the precious fragments, save for the phallus, which had been devoured by a Nile crab, oxyrhynch, which Egyptians forever curse for this crime. Then, for the first time on Earth, Isis, together with Anubis, performed the embalming rites which restored to Osiris eternal life as ruler of the Kingdom of the Dead.

With the precedent of immortality established, the Egyptians began to treat death not as an end but a beginning, a doorway to a richer, fuller life in the hereafter. In the Egyptian art of mummification there is an echo of the modern-day preparations for space travel. The Egyptians believed that a man was protected during his life by three spiritual elements, only one of which left the body after death. Two of them, the *ka* and the *ba*, remained, and these were immortal, not merely in a spiritual sense but in a very real physical sense.

The *ka* was a man's alter ego. He was born with it, it encompassed his qualities and traits, and after death it remained with him in his tomb. The *ka* was thought to be a kind of double, an exact physical duplicate of some sort. Considered as such, the *ka* is a significant aspect of physical immortality and suggests the possibility of a clone or biological double.

The *ba* was linked to space flight. After death it traveled with the sun on its nightly journey through the underworld but returned to the body each morning. To the Egyptains these spirits were not abstract, disembodied ghosts but real entities, tangible, physical aspects of immortality, and as such they required a place to dwell for all time. That place was the body, and no effort was spared to render it habitable throughout eternity. Destruction of the body carried with it the loss of immortality, and so the techniques of mummification became so elaborate and expensive that at first only the pharaohs could afford it. But eventually high officials and then even the poorer classes were able to afford some form of mummification.

Indeed, Herodotus pointed out a dichotomy between the treatment of the bodies of the ordinary Egyptians and the preservation of the bodily remains of the nobility. Two other methods, in fact, existed, and they indicate that the average Egyptian, whether poor or rich, was embalmed by a group of professional corpse-tenders not to be confused with the funerary priests of the Per-nefer, the House of Mummification. These great mortuary temples are found in the immediate vicinity of the tombs and the pyramids in the great necropolis compounds of Egypt. But the ordinary, less than eternal modes of preservation were done on a mass-production basis in one great Temple of the Dead, located within the city confines.

Here the mummification procedure was quite different. Herodotus noted:

> If persons wish to avoid expense and choose the second process, the following is the method pursued: syringes are filled with oil made from the cedar tree which is then, without any incision or disembowling, injected into the abdomen. The passage by which it might be likely to return is stopped and the body laid in natron the prescribed number of days. At the end of the time the cedar oil is allowed to make its escape, and such is its power that it brings with it the whole stomach and intestines in a liquid state. The natron meanwhile has dissolved the flesh, and so nothing is left of the dead body but the outer skin and the bones. It is returned in this condition to the relatives without any further trouble being bestowed upon it.
>
> The third method of embalming, which is practiced in the case of the poorer classes, is to clear out the intestines with a clyster and let the body lie in natron the seventy days, after which it is at once given to those who come to fetch it away. (*History of Herodotus*)

Clearly these differences in the mummification process were based upon some qualification other than mere payment of money. Something took place within the Per-nefer that did not occur in the ordinary House of the Dead. Perhaps a knowledge of chemistry and physics was known only to the priests of the Per-nefer and forbidden to those embalmers who practiced in the city's House of the Dead. The idea of immortality has been in the minds of men ever since the Egyptians first began their complex mummification procedures. That secret of immortality has been pursued eagerly by grave robbers and scientists from the moment the first pharaoh was mummified. Grave robbing is a pursuit at least as old as the pyramids, and in them the defilers of the tombs hoped to find not only the gold and jewels buried with a pharaoh but his secret of immortality. The answer was thought to be wrapped up within the mummy itself. How else can we explain the fact that although thousands of noblemen and pharaohs were mummified in the Per-nefer over a period of twenty-five centuries, only a handful of their mummies remain? Indeed, even the inferior mummies of the poor, of which there were hundreds of thousands, no longer exist. The Cairo Museum, for example, possesses a total of only thirty-three royal and noble mummies, and fewer than twenty others are scattered about the museums of the world. What happened to all the other mummies?

They were, quite simply, consumed over a period of twenty-five hundred years by people seeking immortality. The Egyptian legends of immortality became, by a circuitous route, equated with an ancient medical cure-all—bitumen. This black mineral pitch was part of the folk pharmacopoeia and ancient physicians believed that it would cure most diseases. The only source of pure bitumen—which the Persians called *mummia*—was a mountain in Persia. So valuable was it to the ancient world that the bitumen was stored in the royal treasury and the mountain from which it came was guarded day and night by the king's own troops.

The resins and other chemicals used to mummify the pharaohs had the same color and glasslike consistency as bitumen, and the immediate connection between immortality and mummies was made. The word *mummy* in fact comes from the Persian word for bitumen—*mummia*. The demand for bits and pieces of mummies, ground into powders, chopped into pieces, mixed into potions, was insatiable. As the dark curtain of ignorance slowly lifted over Europe, the wealthy and noble there joined in the clamor for a piece of immortality.

Is there
a connection
between
outer space and
immortality?

Scenes from the movie and observations
from Alan and Sally Landsburg

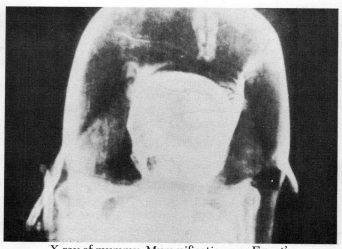

X-ray of mummy. Mummification was Egypt's
clue to the world of outer space.

They Have Been to Earth

On January 16, 1958, aboard the ship *Almirante Saldonha*,

and Left Their Mark...

this UFO was spotted off the coast of Brazil.

This UFO was seen on April 18, 1965,

A businessman in Melbourne, Australia, sited this UFO

near Albuquerque, New Mexico.

on April 2, 1966.

Does Immortality Depend

The Giza complex in Egypt: far right, Cheops; middle Chefren; left; Mycerinus. After spending the night in the pyramids, Dr. Patrick Flanagan believes that

on the Pyramid Shape?

enclosed in all pyramids is an energy field,
which he calls biocosmic energy. We believe this
could be a way to communicate with UFOs.

The biocosmic forces in pyramids act as a preservative. Here is a mummy with eyelashes.

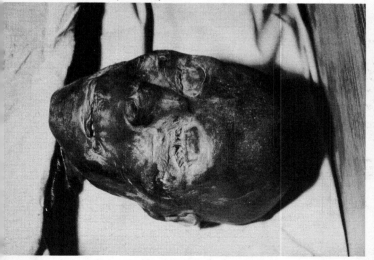

Ramses II had light skin and blond hair.
We think the Egyptians were trying to preserve
cell tissues for later cloning.

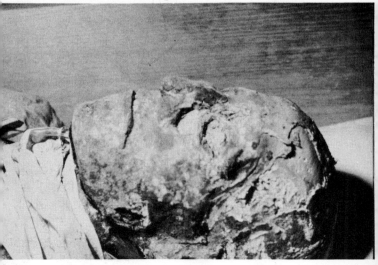

This sarcophagus with mummy reveals the a
that represents an exact record of every day spent o
earth—like a diary. Did the Egyptians thin
that reincarnation was possible if the body's cel
were preserved? The diary would then ser
as a coded memory for a new bod

X-rays of mummies indicate that the
Egyptians died much younger that we ever imagined—
in their late teens and early twenties.

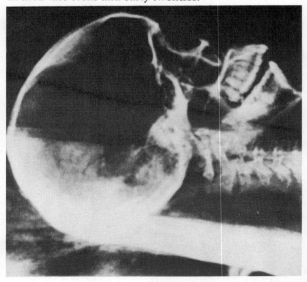

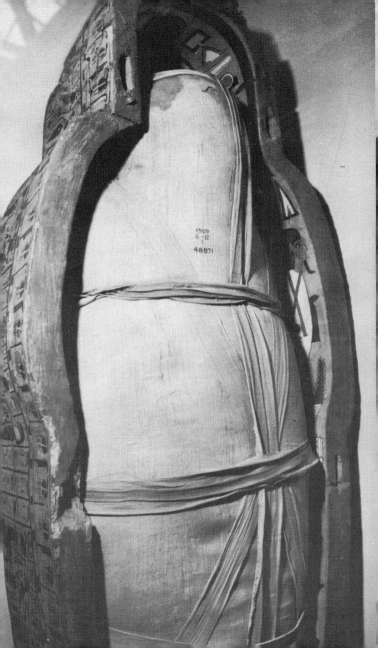

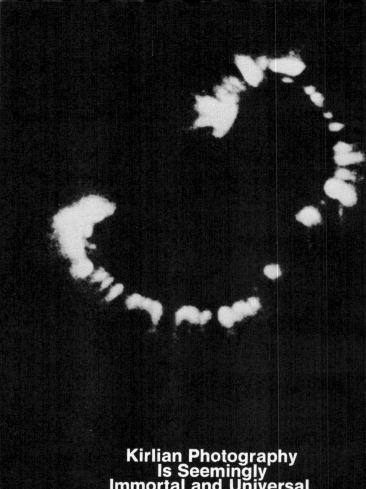

**Kirlian Photography
Is Seemingly
Immortal and Universal.**

At the UCLA Neuro-Psychiatric Institute, Kirlian photographer Dr. Thelma Moss photographed the fingertips of two volunteers before they kissed. Here is the aura from the two volunteers. *(Courtesy Dr. Thelma Moss)*

Kirlian photo of a strongly emotional person. *(Courtesy Dr. Thelma Moss)*

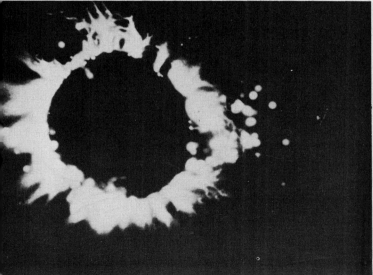

Kirlian photo of an emotionally mild person.
(Courtesy Dr. Thelma Moss)

Aura of a man under the influence of marijuana.
(Courtesy Dr. Thelma Moss)

The phantom leaf. Before the photograph
was taken the leaf was cut in half, but the aura is
of the entire leaf. *(Courtesy Dr. Thelma Moss)*

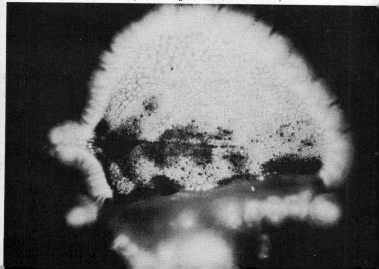

Was Embryo Transplant the Secret of Early Space Travelers?

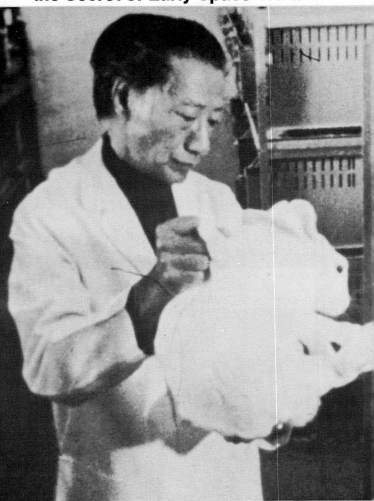

In 1952, Dr. M. C. Chang pioneered experiments in the embryo transplant of rabbits at the Worcester Foundation for Experimental Biology.

At Wayne State Medical Center in Detroit,
Dr. E. S. E. Hafez transplanted the embryo of a chimpanzee
into a rabbit. The rabbit becomes a living
container for shipping. When the rabbit has reached
its destination, the embryo is removed
and transplanted into a chimpanzee host mother.

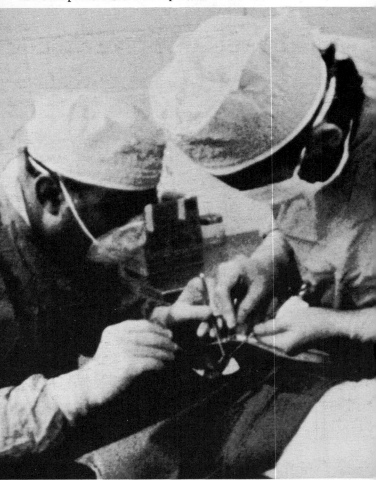

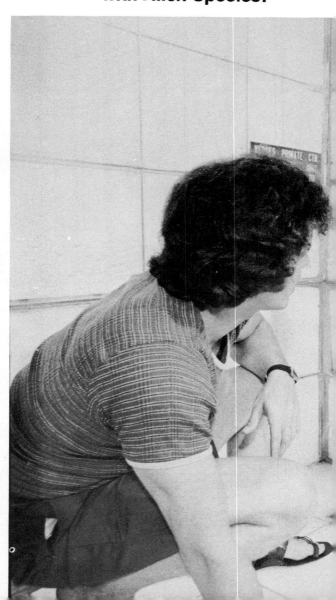

Lana, a chimpanzee, is taught language synthesis at the Yerkes Primate Center at Emory University, Atlanta. From Tim Gill, she is learning to operate a computer to form sentences which must be in perfect syntax before she is rewarded.

They Have Left Their Mark

Around the World.

A pyramid-shaped burial mound in Sillbury Hill, England. Pyramid forms, burial sites, and astronomical measuring devices are always found together.

The idea of travel off this earth had
reached England by 250 B.C. Wheels were put
on the grave for travel after death.

Ancient Greek medical instruments.
Modern technology has not improved much on
the design of these instruments.

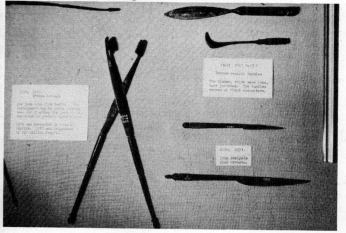

What Planet Did the Mayas Come From? Where Have They Gone and When Will They Return?

Mayan calendar glyphs. The Mayan calendar operates on a 5,000-year cycle. The most recent cycle will end December 24, 2011. We believe this is when the space colonists will return.

The prototype of all pyramids was built by the
Mayas. The Pyramid of Magicians (right) and the
Nunnery (left) is found at Uxmal, Mexico.

This ancient American Indian astronomical
calendar called the Medicine Wheel is evidence of what
might have drifted northward from the Mayas.
This calendar, found in Big Horn, northern Wyoming,
is unlike any found in the plains.

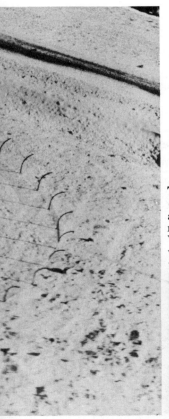

The remains of the House
of Death at Uxmal
are an unusual piece of
representational carving.
We think this is
where the Mayas did their
transplant work.

The Hope of Immortality Is Stored in the Nucleus of a Cell.

The eggs from a white axlotal lizard are gathered.

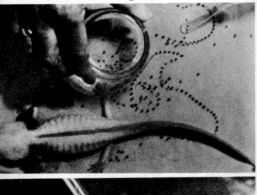

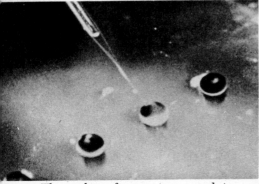

The nucleus of an egg is removed. A cell from a spotted axlotal is then inserted into the nucleus of a white axlotal.

The product is a perfect clone—a spotted axlotal.

Touching Immortality.

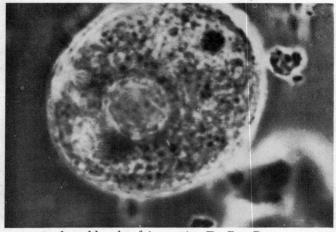

In the cold rocks of Antarctica, Dr. Roy Cameron
has found the oldest living thing ever to inhabit
the earth—a colony of bacteria reawakened in the
warmth of the laboratory 1 million years after
they came into existence. *(Courtesy Dr. Roy Cameron)*

Shakespeare considered it a magic ingredient in the witches' brew in *Macbeth*. Sir Francis Bacon, the great English philosopher of the time, prescribed it for every illness. The king of France, Francois I, nibbled on a piece of mummy whenever he felt ill, and anyone who could afford even the smallest fragment was prepared to do so for his chance at immortality.

As a result, for a period of more than four hundred years, from the thirteenth century to the seventeenth century A.D., the hunt for mummies and their secret of immortality became intense. The mummy sold in bits and fragments was far more valuable than the golden goods that accompanied it in the grave. Egyptian tombs were stripped of mummies and sold to those wealthy enough to afford immortality. Even the communal tombs of the poor, stacked like hives, with the "less than immortal" mummies of the House of the Dead, were looted and sold for vast profit.

And what of the mummies that remain? Do they contain the secrets of immortality? The question leads us back to Ramses II, who lies in his blackened and leathery state in his current resting place. The artifacts of other mummies, such as that of the fabled Tutankhamen, have resided from time to time in museums all over the world. The people of many nations have viewed with awe the treasures of gold, silver, and glittering jewels that were meant to establish his rank on his journey to the so-called Western world, the place of immortal residence. Elaborately carved and scrolled furniture, exquisitely wrought hangings, linens and textiles of excellent craftsmanship were entombed with him for his comfort in his new home. Personal possessions, including eating utensils, shaving gear, trinkets, and sometimes beloved body servants and favorites of the court—all the conveniences of a luxurious life-style—accompanied the Egyptian pharaoh on his journey.

I found myself staring at Ramses II, trying desperately to get a clear image of him and his world. Eight hundred lifetimes ago his body was committed to an exotic ritual known only to the priests. The mortuary temple in which the procedure took place was constructed very near the pyramids. The proximity could not have been accidental; there must have been some link between the two. I was sure that the pyramid, with its strange preservative forces, was somehow connected to the process of mummification. Certainly mummification was a part of the quest for immortality.

I could see the possibility of a relationship between Dr. Patrick Flanagan's theories of pyramid energy and the cloning experiments of Dr. Janice Brothers. To produce an Axlotal Dr. Brothers needs one viable cell and one available egg. Dr. Flanagan's research into pyramid energy as a preservative force indicated that a viable cell could be obtained if the living creature had been mummified using the effects of pyramid energy.

Now all the travel and investigation was beginning to pay off. A new perspective was emerging from the information I had gathered. I suddenly realized just how vital the connection might be between the mortuary temple and the pyramid shape. Every important site of ancient mysteries had both temple and pyramid close at hand.

At Tiahuanaco, in Peru, the sculpture garden with its many experimental skull forms was set within a hundred feet of the giant pyramid. At Uxmal, in the Yucatan, the so-called House of Death was less than a thousand yards from the Pyramid of the Magicians. At Chichen Itza the distance between the site reserved for the dead and the great pyramid was even less. In each of the civilizations there were priests who held extraordinary knowledge of medicine, mathematics, engineering, and astronomy. It was the priests who communicated with the world beyond. I began to wonder if the priests had held the secret of immortality, rendered to them from another world; if immortality actually had existed; if some act of resurrection took place long before the beginning of the Christian era. Then I could begin to understand the elaborate rituals that in the past accompanied the deaths of monarchs.

Food, dishes, and jewelry reflecting the station of the deceased are found in the grave mounds and tombs of almost every culture, historic and prehistoric. In some cultures not only were the wealthy dead equipped with every material necessity, but slaves, charioteers, ladies-

and gentlemen-in-waiting, and even the royal consort were buried, sometimes alive, to ensure that the honored person would be well accommodated on his journey.

In one Sumerian grave people were found interred with a woman obviously of high rank. Surrounded by every luxury in life, she certainly lacked nothing in death. Wandering through the Sumerian exhibit in the British Museum, I gaped at her intricate headdress, the remnants of her gown, and a caseful of exquisite jewelry and pieces of gold and silver household utensils. Her possessions include gold-trimmed musical instruments, game boards, and dice. Entombed with her were her personal wagoneer, along with a carved sledge and the oxen to draw it. She was accompanied to her final resting place by her ladies and slaves, all clothed as fashionably as she. But, while her personal belongings have withstood the ravages of time, the bodies of the woman and her retinue are mere skeletons.

On the Scythian steppes one powerful warrior king was found buried with food containers, wine jugs, pots that had held incense and oils, woven rugs, furs, and gold-trimmed weapons, mementos of an active military life. Carefully entombed with him were other human remains, probably members of his royal household and faithful assorted retainers. That in itself was not uncommon in the enormous graves of the ancient aristocracy. What was rather startling about this interment, however, was the inclusion of what appeared to be a royal honor guard of some sort. Ranged in a circle about the king and his court were twenty warriors dressed in full battle regalia, complete with helmets, breast plates, swords, and battle axes. They were mounted astride horses, in an upright position. The horses had been impaled on stakes to give the king's bodyguard a totally lifelike appearance. The entire diorama was then buried, to be stumbled upon and reconstructed approximately a thousand years later. Archaeologists find that the remains of these powerful monarchs, whose elaborate arrangements attest to their lust for life, are for the most part in a state of bones, rags, and time-encrusted metals, to be painfully cleaned and reassembled for us to speculate about their way of life and death.

According to Incan tradition, the dead were mummified in their own fashion but not always buried immediately. Persons of great importance had their mummified remains housed in their own palaces and continued to abide with the living. I learned that it was customary for members of the family to visit the mummy, seated permanently on his thrown, for a chat or perhaps some consultation on an important matter. The mummy of the Incan grandee was considered the legal head of his household as long as his mummy sat in state in his personal residence. Whatever fortune he had acquired in his lifetime was utilized in perpetuity for the expenses of an enormous number of dependents, including wives, mistresses, children, overseers, house servants, and slaves. The custom may have made life a little difficult for his heirs, who were expected to go out into the world and make their own fortunes, but it would seem a most effective method of preventing patricide and enabling the family to have a comfortable sort of relationship with death.

The fabulous wealth and mummification procedures of the nobility were considered merely legendary until recently. A few years ago, however, archaeologists began to locate some of the graves of the Incan nobility. Along with a great display of rich personal possessions, jewelry, beautifully loomed textiles, and exquisitely patterned lace, the discoverer might find pottery of highly skilled craftsmanship and carvings of rare artistry. But the state of preservation of the mummy itself, while still retaining its hair and bones, was not even vaguely comparable to that achieved in the Egyptian mummy.

Only in the fertile crescent of the Nile did the royal dead maintain a totally lifelike appearance. They are so perfectly preserved after two millennia that the details of their bodies can tell us a bit about their personal history.

Seqenere Tao, a seventeenth-dynasty ruler, could

well have died in battle. His mummy has a tremendous cleft on the right side of his face and his forehead contains a large hole. An X-ray of his head shows that he was wounded with a battle ax and hit on the head by some blunt instrument. It is assumed that Seqenere Tao died in battle. If he had survived his wounds the X-ray would also show new bone formation and healing.

The mummies of Yuya and Thuya, parents of Tiy, the consort of Amenhotep III, are most beautifully preserved down to the stubble of beard on Yuya's chin. Their long flaxen hair is intact and their gentle faces reflect only the calm repose of a healthy sleep.

The preserved remains of Queen Nojime, wife of Ramses II, evoke additional feelings of sentiment because of the packing of the face, lifelike eyes, and ornately braided hair. In death, despite the passage of time, she is almost doll-like in her appearance. But my most careful attention was reserved for the face that had given me the horrors since early childhood. The mummy of Ramses II was the prototype that was used to terrify millions of moviegoers in the era of "Frankenstein Meets the Mummy" films. I felt the same ambivalence between scholarly interest and childhood creepiness that many tourists must experience on their first glimpse of Ramses II.

I continued my perusal of the Cairo Museum, becoming more and more immersed in a fascination with the living dead. My interest in mummy lore was becoming a raging curiosity, an intense desire to solve the riddle of why it had been necessary to preserve these royal bodies so perfectly that they withstood for several thousand years the ordinary putrefaction of death.

I went back through my notes on research on mummies, and found one bit of information that now seemed especially vital. Mummy tissue had been studied to determine the extent of preservation of various parts of the body over several thousand years. The examination showed, among other things, that the skin cells of large areas of the mummies were in a state of perfect preservation.

Interesting data, but of no particular significance at the time; put into another frame of reference, however —the combined fields of cytology and genetics—that interesting fact might be the single most valuable clue to the possible relationship between the classic mythology of the Egyptians and contemporary scientific experimentation.

Recent work in molecular biology has led to a theory that cells are neither living nor dead, only intact or not intact. This means that the DNA molecule, with its genetic blueprint for a complete organism, is also intact, and lacks only the materials to organize the structures and enzymes needed to continue life. But if these were supplied the genetic blueprint would be followed, and a living, breathing pharoah would arise from his own mummified tissues—the immortal embodiment of the Osiris legend.

Perhaps that explains the Egyptian preoccupation with death and burial. The purpose of the rituals that accompany it was to guarantee the resurrection to life in another land, and they are described in detail in the ancient Egyptian Book of the Dead. Innumerable papyrus copies of the Book of the Dead, with its detailed descriptions of the afterlife, have been found in the linen wrappings of the royal mummies. Were the dead expected to wake at some future time in a new place and need a guidebook to facilitate their lives in alien territory? I am beginning to wonder.

8

Book of the Dead

The white walls of ancient Memphis shimmered in the blazing sunlight. I stood before the first of all pyramids, the step pyramid of Saggara, actually a series of square tombs called mastabas, laid one on top of the other. I wanted to investigate the original pyramid more closely but my guide was urging me toward a desolate pile of rock, vaguely pyramidal in outline, that stood some distance away. Puzzled but intrigued by Mr. Abu's excitement, I allowed him to lead me into the musky tomb beneath the tumbledown pyramid. As my eyes adjusted to the dim light in the crypt of King Unas, I saw the Book of the Dead for the first time.

Greenish hieroglyphics covered the walls of the chambers and sprawled into the passageways. I recognized a few of the more familiar symbols— the ankh, ☥, sign of life; three wavy lines, ≋ representing water; three small flags, 𓊃𓊃𓊃, meaning the gods; the twisted spiral, 𓏲, signifying eternity.

I was seeing the individual symbols, but the content and meaning of the text were lost to me. From the pyramids of Sakkara to the tombs of Luxor to the Cairo Museum I went, and the more I traveled the more the hieroglyphics became part of the seemingly unchanging background.

All of the gods of the underworld greeted me from endless walls and papyri; the same gathering was always present to conduct the deceased to his new abode: Osiris, Anubis, Isis and Thoth, arm in arm with ancient pharaohs, carrying out rituals and ceremonies whose meanings are lost in the past. I saw representations of the ceremony of opening the mouth so that the deceased could take nourishment, the ceremony of teaching the deceased to learn to breathe in the underworld, the rituals of mummification, the preservation of the mortal remains for a trip into eternity. I knew that although all other entrails were removed in the mummification process, the heart was carefully left in place. I came back with a start to the voice of another guide.

"The scarab was the sign for immortality," our guide said. "That is why inside mummies you will often find the heart intact, banded in gold with a scarab attached. Scarabs are very difficult to destroy. You cannot burn, bury, or crush them." With each comment he attempted to snuff out the life of a scarab he'd picked up off the ground, but after every assault the creature popped up intact. Long ago, I thought, someone probably observed the scarab's seeming indestructibility and made him a symbol of immortality. It seemed an object lesson in the origin of mystic concepts. Again my interest wandered back to the Book of the Dead.

The title "Book of the Dead" is a misleading description. It has been applied to all of the inscriptions found at burial sites. Essentially, these texts were renditions of what we think of as religious burial services. At one time there were many Books of the Dead; each was tailor-made to the immortal needs of the deceased, detailing extensive biographical information as well as instructions for getting to the land of the Dead. The more important the person, the more detailed and individualistic was the Book of the Dead prepared for him. No one knows when the original so-called Book of the Dead was composed. It has been difficult, if not impossible, to trace the changes that have filtered down through time until a more or less fixed text began to appear.

I came back to the tomb of King Unas. The walls around me were literally covered with hieroglyphics. I spent hours staring at the symbols, trying to imagine the moment when they were inscribed. I envisioned Egyptian priests gathering to compose the proper instructions for committing King Unas to the beyond. Bits of information borrowed from the past were mingled with prayerful entreaties and warnings of danger. In essence, the Book of the Dead was a handbook compiled in order to ensure the immortality of the sovereign. Great care was given to the words used in the ceremony so that the king would find safe passage to the heavens.

I wondered again if the entire process had been an imitative rendering of a long-forgotten event? Was it possible that a group of select individuals had once been assigned to service on Earth? Assume that extra-terrestrials had established a colony, and after one tour of duty—for argument's sake, say seventy years—individual members of the expedition were sent home. Whatever steps needed to ensure the continuation of their life force were taken, and then it was time to leave Earth. If, as Dr. Flanagan has suggested, mummification by pyramid energy would produce a skin cell that would remain viable over hundreds of years, a suitable tissue bank for innumerable clones would have been established. It is possible that, in the ancient past, surveying parties from another galaxy used the cloning process to prepare individuals for the extended journey into space after their period of service on earth? And one fine day, when their explorations were completed, quietly packed up their equipment and went home? What would have happened?

For a while the preparations for space travel would be remembered. In time, however, they would become simply another part of folklore. Sitting in the tomb at Saggara, I had a feeling that the ritual burial of great personages in Egypt could have been inspired by space voyages made in the distant past. To substantiate part of my fantasy trip I had to carefully examine the Book of the Dead. I owe a great debt to E. A. Wallis Budge, a nineteenth century Egyptologist who dedicated years to the translations of one of the most complete papyri of the Book of the Dead, the funerary relic of one court scribe named Ani. In his work, *The Egyptian Book of the Dead,* Budge explains that no single text exists. A number of lengthy renditions of the ceremony have been found on papyri on tomb walls dating back five thousand years. The chapters are in no particular order and sometimes one chapter may be repeated in two or three variations.

I studied the catalog of ceremonies in the Book of

the Dead and found a peculiar hodgepodge of elements. In some cases it included concepts that were so old that no trace of their origin has yet been found. Evidently even the priests of that time did not understand the exact meaning of their own words. Other parts of the ceremony contained standard references, and still others were newly composed to suit the special needs of the particular voyager.

With each succeeding generation the rituals became more formalized, until finally, near the end of Egypt's golden ages, the Book of the Dead degenerated into a litany with blank spaces left for the name of the deceased. I concentrated my research on the remaining texts of the early versions. Somewhere in the evolution of the Book of the Dead the concept arose that the human being was composed of separate entities. Each part was supposed to have a function in carrying the individual on his journey to the new life. To me there was a fascinating correlation between the description of the trip that would be taken by deceased Egyptian nobility and what we know today of space voyages.

One of the entities described in the Book of the Dead is the *khat,* the mortal structure of the deceased. In the Book of the Dead's first mention of it, the body had already been encased in linen swathing. The last task involved in the preparation for the mummy's voyage concerned the necessity of ensuring a proper flow of food, air, and water to the dead. In short, it seemed reminiscent of the final details of dressing a modern astronaut. The precountdown ritual that became so familiar during the television coverage of space shots in the late 1960s was, I felt, echoed in the Book of the Dead.

References to other parts of the human entity took me further into the wealth of remarkable parallels between the experiments of modern science and the beliefs outlined in ancient lore. I began to see a multitude of possible genetic experiments.

The *ka* mentioned in the Book of the Dead was thought of as a physical counterpart or double. The description of the *ka* encompasses all of the traits we ordinarily associate with genetic characteristics. Included were the image, physique, emotional attitude, and mental capabilities of the deceased. Every trait of the *ka* drew on genetic material, but did not take into account environmentally caused deformities. A genetic blueprint was indicated suitable for producing a cloned double.

The *sahu* was thought of as the next body, and there were fascinating descriptions of its emergence. According to the Book of the Dead, "I germinate like the plant. My flesh germinates. I exist, I exist, I live, I live." The words that seemed to leap out at me were "my flesh germinates." Perhaps the *sahu* was a condensation of the concept of cloning based on the DNA material cloned from a single skin cell. Where had the idea originated? Why had a specific attribute of a person's skin become the source of new life? Examining the *sahu* further, I learned that it was capable of ascending to heaven and dwelling with the gods. The indication was "gods," not the singular God, creator of all, mentioned in other parts of the Book of the Dead. The ancient Egyptian texts make constant reference to one God to be totally differentiated from the colony of lesser gods who raced around the known world displaying the behaviors, both productive and destructive, of any ordinary mortal. But they had one characteristic that sharply separated them from a common man, the ability to live, seemingly, forever. The pantheon of gods, along with those aristocratic Egyptians who were permitted to join their ranks, were privileged to live millions of years. They were granted immortality. In the Papyrus of Ani, the royal scribe questions one of the gods with, "How long have I to live?" The god answers, "Thou shalt exist for millions and millions of years, a period of millions of years."

Khu was still another part of the departing body. This *khu* was described as a shiny or translucent casing covering the body. Once a *khu* surrounded the body, it remained with the person entering the new life. Religious art of medieval times still bears the traces of the Egyptian *khu,* the emanating light or halo around an important figure. Today we have begun to study the possible relationship of electronic, pulsating halos emitted by the body. We don't understand what the emanations are or how they function, but we do know that they exist. The *khu* might have been a reference to the cosmic energy employed in the mummification process. Where did the Egyptians learn of its existence?

Finally, there was *sekhun,* which was a basic form, a featureless mold containing all rudimentary life forces. I had been fascinated by the idea that extraterrestrial explorers might have been trying to colonize suitable planets. I had wondered what they might have carried with them to fulfill this goal. One possible item would have been a "basic model," a schematic alignment of genetic possibilities for survival in many different environments. Once a specific set of requirements became known, adaptive genetic mechanisms would then have been added, more or less like accessories for various models of cars. It was the vision of the basic model that came to mind when I read about the *sekhun.*

After spending days reading the Book of the Dead, it was a relief to return to the monuments on the west bank of the Nile. More than anything else, the temples, the tombs, and the pyramids themselves seemed to certify the ancient Egyptians' profound belief in immortality. An early text etched in the pyramid showed the process of resurrection of the natural body. It was a conviction that dated to the dawn of the Egyptians.

As Mr. Budge comments in his book, *The Egyptian Book of the Dead:*

> There is no doubt that from first to last, Egyptians firmly believed that besides the soul there was some other element of the man that could rise again. The preservation of the corruptible body, too, was in some way connected with the life in the world to come and its preservation was necessary to insure eternal life; otherwise the prayers recited to this end would have been simple and the time-honored custom of mummifying the dead would have had no meaning.

Why had so much massive paraphernalia been constructed over thousands of years to support the singular conviction of immortality? Where had the belief originated? What had inspired it?

The Sumerian and Babylonian cultures, which predated Egypt, were possible sources. I looked again at the increasingly enigmatic pyramids. According to Herodotus, the pyramids were supposed to contain the sum of all knowledge. I was able to divine some tantalizing information. The creation myths inscribed on the wall, for example, hint at a knowledge of the human evolutionary processes. They show a determined attempt to explain the origins of life and man; they echo the theory of Directed Panspermia that was once explained to me by Dr. Leslie Orgel. He had said that all life forms possess the same basic structure. We have no evidence of competing or different life forms. He concluded, therefore, that one way to account for this condition was to assume that life was sent here from another planet.

In the hieroglyphic pyramid texts I found a general description of creation. The Egyptians believed that the germ of all things, male and female, arose from an embryonic bit of primeval matter, which they portrayed as water. An egg was supposed to have been formed from the "matter." In the actual story of creation this tale was told:

> I, the evolver of the evolutions, evolved myself, the evolver of all evolution, after many evolutions and developments, which came forth from my mouth. No heaven existed and no earth and no terrestrial animals or reptiles had come to be. I formed them out of an inert mass of watery matter. . . . None other worked with me. I laid the foundations of all things by my will, and all things evolved themselves therefrom. I united myself to my shadow and I set forth Shu and Tefnut out from myself; thus from being one god, I contained three and Shu and Tefnut gave birth to Nut and Set, and Nut gave birth to Osiris, Horus-Khentan-Maa, Sut, Isis and Neththys, at one birth. One after the other, and their children multiply upon this earth. (*The Egyptian Book of the Dead*)

The origin of the text remains unknown. Whoever was responsible for the thought, however, could take credit for blazing trails that we have been following for eons. Firstly, the story contains the principle of monotheism, a creator God. Secondly, it indicates an understanding of evolving life, beginning with a single cell and in time becoming a complex organism. I returned to my original premise that somehow a real event had been the Egyptians' inspiration. It seemed possible that a colony of extraterrestrials bearing responsibility for the life forms of Earth might have been modeled for the text, perhaps the later pantheon of gods departing to the far reaches on an immortal journey home, as it is written in the papyrus of Ani: "I grow young in my cities, grow young in my homestead. . . . My nest is not seen and I have not broken my egg. I am lord of millions of years. I have made my nest in the uttermost parts of heaven." (*The Egyptian Book of the Dead*)

The passage seemed to me to describe the return voyage of an immortal. The references to an egg and a nest indicated to me that Ani was in control of his own life forces, a race that had mastered problems we were just beginning to understand. My interpretations of the writings in the Book of the Dead differed considerably from comments made by Egyptologists who represented a wholly romantic view of a mysterious and still baffling body of literature.

There is strong opinion that the origins of folk myths were traceable only to our ideas of how ancient cultures might have lived. Gradually we have realized the possibility that knowledge, understanding, and technological advancement has been anything but lineal. We have assumed a strict building-block theory that projects a primitive creature gradually acquiring a civilized mien. We have written off as aberrant digression periods like the Dark Ages of medieval Europe. Finally, we have accepted the dogma, ignoring pieces of evidence that seem to cry out the existence of science and technology far beyond the abilities we ascribe to ancient civilizations. The vast knowledge and technology of the Sumerians, Babylonians, Egyptians, and Mayas have been dismissed because the existence of such advances destroys the magic spiral called progress. I have chosen one possible interpretation of the evidence I have found; there are other explanations, but I find them unsatisfying. For example, there are scholars who believe that all mysteries are due to religious fervor. J. Eric Thompson made this note in his work *The Rise and Fall of Mayan Civilization:*

> Why, one wonders, did the Maya use the corbeled vault instead of thatching their temples? Or covering them with flat beam-and-pole roofs, so much simpler to construct and permitting much wider rooms . . . The answer must be that no effort can be too great in building to the glory of God or of gods: man's creations are sanctified by overcoming difficulties.
>
> . . . It is remarkable that the intellectual successes of the Maya were not (from our point of view) practical; they were the outcome of spiritual needs. The Mayan astronomers strove for knowledge, not as an end in itself but as a means of controlling fate, a kind of astrology. There was, they felt, an orderliness in the heavens to which the gods conformed; once that was learned, they could predict the future through exact knowledge of which gods held sway at any given time, and influence it by knowing when and whom to propitiate.
>
> The great ways were not built for practical ends, for the Maya had no beasts of burden or wheeled vehicles; they were surely for spiritual purposes—as a setting for great religious processions. The corbeled vault was not employed for utilitarian purposes but almost sheerly as an embodiment of sacrificial effort. Even the Mayan blue pigment was primarily for painting murals to the glory of the gods. In the field of everyday living I can think of no discovery of a practical nature attributable to the Mayas.

Where the shoe does not fit, it is not worn. No, I believe there is far more to the Mayan intellectual achievement than religious fervor, as I believe my interpretation of the Egyptian Book of the Dead had given substance to the theory I was shaping. In search of immortality, I moved deeper into the legends of the past.

9

Myth as History

I have spent a lot of time in museums both for work and for pleasure. I have watched the idle crowds that wander through; they look, nod, and smile, and for the most part appear only politely interested. Teachers drag in young schoolchildren, grateful to be out of the classroom for a day, and the children, just as pleased, quickly lose interest in the dusty, dry exhibits and begin racing up and down the galleries, sliding on the marble floors, occasionally provoking a slight smile from a bored guard.

The scholar immerses himself in the museum, reading in the painted design on a potsherd the customs of a people, finding in the form of a statue the aspirations of a society. In filming *The Outer Space Connection* museums were absolute-must locations, treasure troves of the smaller pieces of evidence, all stored, cataloged, and displayed. I have found that these museum exhibits supply a framework that helps us to understand the myths and legends of our history. Our oldest written records go back a mere six thousand years, yet we know that the history of modern man on Earth reaches back at least fifty thousand years to the cave paintings of Cro-Magnon man. Depending upon the evaluation of very recent discoveries, man and his less evolved ancestors may have antecedents that go back as far as four million years.

The record for most of that fifty-thousand-year period is an oral one, handed down through a thousand generations, embellished by time, bent by forgetfulness, limned by hyperbole. Cast as myth and legend, it has for the most part been discounted, seen only as vague shreds of some universal truth, a glimpse of the past in metaphor, a primitive concoction of tales to scare children. Eminent scholars have in the past dismissed myth as old wives' tales, legend as fairy tales, and sought only the truth of the written word. But man and his experiences are far older than writing, and so it was in myth and legend that I began to look for some truths about our past. None is more pervasive and more ubiquitous in ancient cultures than that of the Flood.

> And the Lord said unto Noah, come thou and all thy house into the Ark. . . . For yet seven days I will cause it to rain upon the earth for forty days and forty nights; and every living substance that I have made will I destroy from off the face of the earth. And it came to pass after seven days that the waters of the flood were upon the earth. In the 600th year of Noah's life were all the fountains of the great deep broken up and the windows of heaven were opened. (*Bible,* Genesis)

I was intrigued by the story of the Flood, a myth found in virtually every early culture on Earth. I was fascinated by its chief protagonist, Noah, who, according to the Bible, was six hundred years old when the waters covered the earth. Noah and the other biblical patriarchs combined vastly extended life spans with continual references to visitors from outer space. It was an area I was to pursue in connection with immortality.

We waited in a large, empty room in the British Museum to get confirmation of the Flood itself, proof of a persistent myth that was an actual account of a very real and terrible event. I found it impossible to believe that this was simply another legend conjured up by an old storyteller on a dark night; rather, I felt that it was an eyewitness account of a disaster so terrible that it was remembered only as a punishment from above.

The proof was soon brought in by a tall, thin,

brown-haired man, an assistant curator. We had been waiting for twenty minutes, locked and guarded in a large room, forbidden to look elsewhere in the museum "until your arty-facks arrive." This was no public gallery, but a sort of staging area where new exhibits were set up before being placed on view and where old exhibits were broken down. On tables and shelves about us were the pieces and bits of a dozen different civilizations, representing as many different exhibits at the British Museum over the last several years. The museum authorities had kindly given us this room where we could film undisturbed, and to this room they were bringing our "arty-facks," as one of the guards had put it.

I was quite surprised at the way it arrived, one of the world's oldest and most priceless records. The man who brought it carried it in a cardboard shoebox and was as testy as a salesman who had just spent an hour showing every shoe in the shop to a woman who simply would not buy anything.

"I do hope you appreciate the trouble you've caused me," he said with a sniff as he placed the box on the table. I looked in at a pale orange clay block. Once rectangular, it had been broken on one side and was now classified as a fragment. Into it had been dug a series of wedge-shaped marks; it looked as if a flock of birds had formed ranks and marched back and forth on the clay, leaving their tracks. This was my first glimpse at the cuneiform text that held the earliest known account of the Flood.

He lifted the tablet out and placed it on a black velvet cloth on the table. "I'm terribly pressed for time so you must hurry, please."

I nodded to the cameraman, who began swiftly to light the tablet, making certain that the deep cuts that formed the strange writing would show up, but my mind was winging back through time as I stared at the clay remnant.

The tablet, not kept on display, normally was reserved for viewing only by scholars equipped to read and translate the cuneiform writing. To my knowledge, only two men in all history had done that with this particular tablet. The first was Berossus, a Babylonian priest who served the great god Marduk. In the year 275 B.C. Berossus wrote a history of his nation, using thousands of clay tablets which filled the Temple library of King Ashurbanipal. Almost twenty-five hundred years ago Berossus held the tablet in his hands and translated the cuneiform script from its original Assyrian into Greek. His history covered the story of Babylonia from her very beginning—the creation of the world—to her liberation by Alexander. Within that history Berossus told the tale of the Flood, a mighty deluge that had covered the earth in ancient times.

Twenty-two centuries later, in 1853, a team of British archaeologists uncovered fragments of the same tablet, along with a thousand other broken pieces that had formed the great Temple library of Ashurbanipal. These fragments, excavated from the ancient city of Nineveh, were brought to London, where they lay for another twenty years before their true significance was discerned.

Finally, in 1873 George Smith, a banknote engraver turned scholar, was given a cardboard box containing the clay fragment we were filming. The tablet, which had only just been cleaned, despite its twenty-year residence in the museum, contained an account of the Flood. When Smith, "the first man to read that after more than two thousand years of oblivion," as he put it, realized what he had just read, he immediately put down the tablet. Then "he jumped up and rushed about the room in a great state of excitement and to the astonishment of those present began to undress himself." ("The Babylonian Legend of the Flood," pamphlet from British Museum)

Smith's excited behavior belied his scholarship, which fortunately soon reasserted itself, and a few months later he delivered a paper describing his findings of the Babylonian account of the Flood.

Other tablets and fragments have been discovered over the years and all add to the Flood story, but Smith was convinced and subsequently proved that his text and all the others that were found could be dated about the eighth century B.C. and were actually themselves translations of much earlier accounts written in the strange language Sumerian.

Although we can translate Sumerian we are unable to relate it to any other known language on Earth. In the British Museum pamphlet "The Babylonian Legend of the Flood," there is this startling statement: "Akkadian is a Semitic language cognate to Hebrew, Arabic, etc; Sumerian, on the other hand, is an unclassified language which has so far resisted all attempts to relate it to any known living or dead language."

The Sumerians are among the most mysterious people in the history of Earth. They appeared suddenly in the fertile crescent that is the Tigris Euphrates valley, which had been inhabited by Neolithic farmers and villagers and Semitic nomads. They bore no racial resemblance to the other Indo-European ethnics of the area. Moreover, in cultural and technological development the Sumerians were virtually light-years ahead of the people indigenous to the area. They built great cities, established vast libraries, and created magnificent gold vessels, beautiful jewelry, and ornaments. They demonstrated an astonishing grasp of higher mathematics—dividing the circle into 360 degrees, the hour into sixty minutes, the minute into sixty seconds. And, unlike the crude pictographs that passed for writing throughout the world at this time—perhaps seven thousand years ago—Sumerian writing is highly sophisticated, totally unlike and unrelated to any other known form of writing.

That writing was unearthed on clay tablets found in 1914 by a German-American archaeological expedition that dug up the ancient Babylonian city of Nippur. From these tablets scholars deciphered the Sumerian account of the Flood, an account which George Smith was convinced was accurate.

The discovery of the Sumerian account of the Flood at first caused consternation among Fundamentalists, who interpret the Bible as literal truth. In detail and degree the Sumerian writing described a biblical event that seemingly predated the Bible. Was the Bible, then, recounting even older stories in the same manner that

Smith's tablet was based upon the accounts of earlier civilizations? There seems little question that the biblical Noah is patterned after a Sumerian hero named Utanapishtim, who had been warned by his god, Ea, of an impending deluge that would destory all living things on Earth. And just as God commanded Noah, so Utanapishtim was directed by Ea to "tear down thy house, build a ship; abandon wealth, seek after life; scorn possessions, save thy life. Bring up the seed of all kinds of living things into the ship; the ship which thou shalt build. Let its dimensions be well measured."

The parallels between the Sumerian tablets and the Bible are astonishing. "And Noah went in and his sons and his wife and his sons' wives into the ark, because of the waters of the flood. Of clean beasts and of beasts that are not clean and of fowls, and of everything that creepth upon the earth. There went in two and two unto Noah into the ark, the male and the female," as God had commanded Noah.

The Sumerian account of Utanapishtim says:

"All that I had I loaded, of the seed of all living things. I brought into the ship my whole family and kinfolk. The cattle of the field, the beasts of the field, all craftsmen—I made them go up into it." (*The Epic of Gilgamesh* trans. by N. K. Sandars)

Of the Flood itself the Bible says:

And it came to pass after seven days that the waters of the flood were upon the earth. . . . And the flood was forty days upon the earth and the waters increased. . . . And the waters prevailed exceedingly upon the earth and all the high hills that were under the whole heaven were covered. And God remembered Noah and made a wind to pass over the earth and the waters assuaged. The fountains also of the deep and the windows of heaven were stopped, and the rain from heaven was restrained. And the waters returned from off the earth continually and after the end of the hundred and fifty days the waters were abated. And the Ark rested in the seventh month on the seventeenth day of the month upon the mountains of Ararat. (Genesis)

The last line, giving the location of the Ark, has for centuries spurred men to seek some remnant of the vehicle that preserved life on Earth. Mt. Ararat lies in eastern Turkey close to the borders of Iran and Russia. The peak towers to a snow-roofed summit of 16,000 feet. Somewhere between the 13,500- and 15,000-foot levels of the peak, buried under thousands of tons of ice and snow, lies Noah's Ark. At least that is what many biblical conservatives believe, and every summer at least one group applies to the Turkish Government for permission to search for the Ark.

Ark hunting is an old and popular occupation; it dates back perhaps three thousand years. Josephus, the Jewish historian, and Berossus, the Babylonian, mention the Ark as being in existence, and the Armenians, who for three thousand years have lived on the slopes of Mt. Ararat, have always maintained that remnants of the Ark have been sighted by their shepherds over the centuries.

In 1833 a Turkish expedition set off from the Armenian village of Bayazit to find the Ark. Shepherds from the village guided them to what they described as the wooden bow of a ship which was sticking out of the south glacier. In 1876 Sir James Bryce, a British scholar, after intensive research on the subject, climbed Ararat and found at thirteen thousand feet a large piece of hand-tooled timber which he believed came from the Ark.

In 1892 Father John Nouri, the archdeacon of Jerusalem, climbed the mountain and upon his return told of seeing a ship wrecked in the ice. "The interior was full of snow, the outer wall was that of a dark red color." (*Adventure on Ararat* by John D. Morris)

The scientific age of Ark hunting began during World War I when a Russian aviator named Roskowitzki returned from a sortie across the Turkish border and reported sighting "the remains of wreckage of a fair-sized ship" on the southern slope of Mt. Ararat. Czar Nicholas II, despite his troubles on the battlefield and at home, immediately dispatched a search party, which reportedly located the Ark, entered it, and photographed it. Before they could present their evidence to the czar, however, the October Revolution broke out; the soldiers scattered and the photos disappeared.

More reports were made between the wars, and World War II produced several aerial sightings. On two occasions the Russians took aerial photos which purported to show the Ark sticking out of the ice. The most reliable findings came from the expedition headed by French explorer Fernand Navarra in 1955 and again in 1969. He brought back from the first trip an L-shaped beam of wood, dark in color and hardened to an almost fossilized consistency. The UCLA isotope laboratory, using radio carbon dating techniques, estimated that the beam was 1,250 years old and the wood samples found in 1969 were between 1,500 and 1,600 years of age.

Experts in Europe, however, considered the UCLA dating in error, due to possible contamination of the samples, and conducted their own laboratory tests. Their conclusion: the wood was of "great antiquity," possibly five thousand years old.

Fired by these results, other potential expeditions have been formed, but the Turkish Government has been reluctant to allow aliens to wander over its mountains. The recent war with Greece, over Cyprus, has made the Turkish Government wary of giving permission to foreign explorers. The conviction remains that Mt. Ararat holds the remains of the Ark. In February 1974 U. S. Senator Frank Moss, chairman of the Senate Space Committee, announced that the Earth Resources Technology Satellite had sent back a photo taken from 450 miles up. On it, said Senator Moss, was a formation "which appears to be foreign to other materials on the mountain. It's about the right size and shape to be the Ark," he concluded.

Whether the ERTS has indeed photographed the Ark remains to be proven. There is still some question as to whether the Ark even rests upon Mt. Ararat. If the Bible reports upon the same cataclysmic flood as the Sumerian tablets describe, then still another site is possible. For Utanapishtim says: "I opened the window and the light fell on my face. The ship lay upon

Mt. Nisir. Mt. Nisir held the ship and allowed it not to move." (*The Epic of Gilgamesh*)

Moreover, the old Babylonian cuneiform writing describes with great precision the location of Mt. Nisir. It lies between the Tigris River and the Zab River among the rugged Kurdistan mountains of Iran. No one has searched Mt. Nisir for the Ark, and the question of whether the Bible and Utanapishtim describe the same flood remains unanswered. The Sumerian account is particularly vivid and distinguished by a reportorial quality that is often found in eyewitness accounts. Said Utanapishtim of the Flood: "Six days and nights raged the wind, the flood and cyclone devastated the land. When the seventh day came, the cyclone, the flood, the battle was over. The sea became calm, the cyclone died away, the flood ceased. And all mankind had turned to clay. The ground was flat like a roof." (*The Epic of Gilgamesh*)

Excerpts from *The Epic of Gilgamesh* seem to indicate that Utanapishtim had delivered nothing less than an eyewitness account of an incredible flood, one that is echoed on a far smaller scale by the cyclones and accompanying floods that lashed the Bay of Bengal and Bangladesh and caused such vast destruction just a few years ago.

Such events are considered analagous evidence. They indicate that phenomena such as flooding on a massive scale can occur. They do not offer proof of a universal deluge or vouch for the accuracy of an account written more than seven thousand years ago. Yet this myth of the Flood, this legend that has been disparaged as a fairytale told by a primitive people in the Bible, has found support in accounts written by a very sophisticated people in a language unrelated to any other known tongue. There is further evidence, solid testimony in the strata of the earth itself, which provides a geological example of a world covered with clay untill "the ground was flat like a roof."

One hundred and twenty miles north of Basra, on the Bagdhad Railway near the Persian Gulf, is a small station called Ur. Beyond the tracks and the small station house lies the desert. It is a vast, flat expanse, broken only by a massive red mound. Today it shelters the bedouins during sandstorms or draws them to the sparse grass that blooms around its base after the infrequent rains. Four thousand years ago the huge red mound was a vast square tower of brick, one hundred twenty feet long on each side, seventy-five feet high, topped by a golden roof. Around it great fields of corn and barley and groves of palm and fig trees stretched away to the horizon, all served by irrigation canals from the Euphrates River. These fields were above Ur, one of the mightiest and richest cities of Sumer.

Abraham set forth from Ur to seek his God, and it was in Ur that a great archaeological discovery removed the last shred of doubt concerning the authenticity of the Flood story. The great Tower of Ur is but a stump now, torn apart by Englishmen seeking treasure in the form of suits of armor and by Arabs who carted away the bricks of the tower for their own building purposes. The bricks once bore the imprint of Ur-Nannu, the man who ruled over Ur some five thousand years ago. The clumsy treasure hunters and scavengers of the nineteenth century who destroyed the Tower of Ur knew little of its past. It was, until 1923, only a site to be plundered, but then an Anglo-American expedition under the leadership of Sir Charles Woolley began to dig into the mutilated base of the tower. For six years they dug, finding the remains of five temples dating back thirty-eight hundred years. Outside the temple area a city emerged, streets, buildings, squares —the city of Ur. It was an incredible city, rich, sophisticated, and worldly. Woolly wrote:

> The houses reveal comfort and even luxury. We found copies of the hymns which were used in the services of the temples and together with them mathematical tables. On these tables were anything ranging from plain addition sums to formulae for the extraction of square and cube roots. In other texts the writers had copied out the old building inscriptions to be found in the city and had compiled in this way a short history of the temples. (*Gods, Graves and Scholars* by C. W. Ceram)

Woolley's team continued to dig in a mound near the temples and uncovered the tombs of the Sumerian kings. They had been buried in stone vaults surrounded by golden drinking cups, jugs, vases, mosaics, jewelry, silver, helmets, harps, lyres, combs—a stunning array of treasures that made the grave goods of Tutankhamen and Nefertiti look like a beggar's hoard. Each of the kings was surrounded by a retinue of servants, animals, and footmen, all buried with their masters to tend the teams of oxen and great wagonloads of furniture that accompanied him.

These "Graves of the Kings," as Woolley had dubbed them, were at least a thousand years older than the Egyptian pyramids. Woolley was convinced that they were "upper level" finds—they covered the remains of a still older civilization. The workers plunged shafts through the stone tombs and into the earth below. In straw baskets they pulled bits of rubble and dirt to the surface Wolley wrote:

> Almost at once discoveries were made which confirmed our suspicions. Directly under the floor of one of the tombs of the kings we found in a layer of charred wood ash numerous clay tablets which were covered with characters of a much older type than the inscriptions on the graves. Judging by the nature of the writing, the tablets could be assigned to about 3000 B.C. They were therefore two or three centuries earlier than the tombs. (*Gods, Graves and Scholars*)

Like a bloodhound maddened by the scent, Woolley kept on digging. The shafts drove deeper and deeper. Pots and bowls were hauled to the surface, layer after layer was uncovered, and still more pottery was sent to the experts for examination. They were astonished. Each layer represented hundreds of years of elapsed time, and yet the pottery from each layer was identical in design and construction. Sumerian civilization, therefore, had remained remarkably stable for centuries and, moreover, had reached an extremely high degree of development very early in man's history.

The shafts were sunk deeper and deeper until one

day the baskets hauled to the surface contained a type
of clay that could only have been left by water. But
water from where? Woolley's first thought was that it
had been deposited by the Euphrates, which had
passed by the doorstep of Ur four thousand years ago.
He soon reconsidered. "I saw," he wrote in his diary,
"that we were much too high up. It was most unlikely
that the island on which the first settlement was built
stood up so far out of the marsh." (*Gods, Graves and
Scholars*)

There was no answer, and so Woolley decided to
keep digging. Down deeper and deeper he went, three
feet into the layer of clay, five feet, amost ten feet deep,
and the baskets were bringing up nothing but clay.

What happened then is perhaps best described by
Werner Keller in his famous book, *The Bible As History*.

The next baskets that came to the surface gave an
answer that none of the expedition would have
dreamed of. They could hardly believe their eyes.
They had expected pure virgin soil, but what now
emerged into the glaring sunshine was rubble and
more rubble, ancient rubbish and countless potsherds.
Under this clay deposit almost ten feet thick they had
struck fresh evidence of human habitation. The appearance and quality of the pottery had noticeably
altered. Above the mud stratum were jars and bowls
that had obviously been turned on a potter's wheel;
here, on the contrary, they were handmade. No matter how carefully the contents of the baskets were
sifted, amidst increasing excitement, metal remains
were nowhere to be found. The primitive implement
that did emerge was made of hewn flint. It must belong to the Stone Age.

That day a telegram from Mesopotamia flashed
what was perhaps the most extraordinary message
that had ever stirred men's imaginations: "We have
found the Flood."

Woolley's announcement was well founded. The ten
feet of clay contained just one type of foreign body—

the shells of tiny marine creatures that had died thousands of years ago. They could only have been left behind in the mud left by a vast deluge—a flood.

By counting back through the layers of his dig Woolley was able to compute the time when the waters of the Flood had receded and "all mankind had turned to clay." It was four thousand years ago and the account of the flood as told to Gilgamesh fit in every detail the incredible story found in the wedgelike writing baked into the clay tablets I was filming in the British Museum. Moreover, the original story had been told to a man, Gilgamesh, who immediately gave up all other pursuits and set out on his own quest—for immortality.

10

◆◆ ◆◆ ◆◆

Methuselah Was 969 Years Old

I looked across the steep, narrow valley at the keyhole-shaped entrance of the caves of Khirbat Qumran. Behind me was the east bank of Israel's Dead Sea; around me were the ruins of a tiny settlement where Hebrew asetics had taken refuge from persecution and practiced the rites of Abraham's religion. The scrolls bearing the word and the law by which they lived were their most precious possessions. When sentinels warned of impending attack, members of the band secreted the scrolls in earthen jugs and carried them into hiding. From the village it was barely a thousand yards to the cave, but the entrance was hidden and the cave itself protected by a precipitous climb from the valley floor. Fewer than one hundred men and women had occupied the settlement, somehow finding sustenance in the blast-furnace heat of the desert that surrounds the Dead Sea.

I imagined what the end was like for that small group of people. Knowing that they could not withstand assault, they must have hidden their scrolls in the cave and then awaited the inevitable final encounter. Perhaps they, like the defenders of Masada, had chosen mass suicide rather than face a life where they would be banned from practicing the ancient religion of their fathers. What they left was a precious record, the oldest known written account of the Bible.

The Dead Sea scrolls gave scholars an opportunity to see how details of the biblical accounts were changed by the passage of time. At the Jerusalem Museum I looked at the fragments on display. What surprised me most was the physical beauty of the writing. The carefully blocked letters looked as if they had been printed by a press. As I examined them I remembered the explanation I was given for the fact that Semitic script was written right to left: Early writing was engraved on stone with a form of hammer and chisel. A great majority of people are right-handed, so it was assumed that the hammer was held in the right hand, the chisel in the left. The most natural way to handle the tools is to tip the chisel toward the right; as each character is tapped out, the scribe would move from right to left.

What a marvelous moment it must have been when some ancient Leonardo Da Vinci discovered that etching the letters in soft clay was much easier than carving in stone. Because carving was such an arduous task, only the most critical details of daily life were recorded. An event had to be of monumental importance to warrant the time and effort needed to record it. It was a thought that plagued me as I returned to the examination of the tablets of Utanapishtim.

If we are to believe what is written, Utanapishtim not only survived the Flood, he became Earth's first immortal. His name in Akkadian, the language used by the early Babylonians who adopted the story from the Sumerians, means "I have found life." In the original Sumerian tongue Utanapishtim is known as *Zi-u-sudra,* which translates to "life of long days."

His immortality was conferred by the greatest of the Sumerian gods, Enlil, who boarded the Ark after it had grounded atop Mt. Nisir, touched Utanapishtim and his wife upon their foreheads, and said, "Hitherto has Utanapishtim been mortal. Now shall he and his wife be like the gods; and they shall dwell in the distance at the mouth of the rivers."

References in ancient legends to gods and their actions could have, I felt, been inspired by astronauts whose technologies were so advanced that to primitive Earth men they would appear capable of performing miracles.

The older tablets, which carried accounts of the Flood in the Sumerian language, identified Utanapishtim as Zi-u-sudra. The description of Zi-u-sudra attaining immortality seems to be told more in terms of events inspired by outer-space visitors than the later Akkadian and Assyrian translations indicate. The Sumerian account says:

> Anu and Enlil cherished Zi-u-sudra. Life like a god they give him, breath eternal like a god they bring down for him. Then Zi-u-sudra, the King, the preserver of the name of vegetation and of the seed of mankind, in the land of crossing, the land of Dilmun, the place where the sun rises, they caused to dwell. (*The Epic of Gilgamesh*)

The accounts of encounters with gods and/or spacemen that are woven through the myths of most cultures are, of course, subject to individual interpretations, but the evidence overwhelmingly supports the event of the Flood in Utanapishtim's story. The tale can be derived from more than sixty thousand tablets and fragments that have been unearthed over the last hundred years. Many remain untranslated, but even now there appears a determined effort to be truthful in those that have been translated.

Writing was thought to be a gift from the gods and, as such, too precious to be wasted on unimportant events or accounts. This was true not only of the Sumerians but of all the early cultures. British archaeologist N. K. Sandars points out:

> The majority of ancient texts are commercial and administrative documents, business archives, lists, and inventories. The recent decipherment of the so-called linear B script of Bronze Age Mycenae and Crete has revealed no literature. A huge library discovered at Kanish in Central Anatolia is entirely made up of records of business transactions and apart from a solitary text—and that a curse—there is not one of a literary kind. The importance of the excavations at Nippur, Nineveh, and other great centers of early civilization in Mesopotamia is that they have restored a literature of high quality and of unique character. (*The Epic of Gilgamesh*)

As I read the translations of the tablets there appeared to me an almost desperate attempt to prove that what I was reading was truth. Part of my feelings came from the colophon, the scribe's note at the bottom of the tablet. He usually gives his name, title, and other particulars, giving modern scholars invaluable information. For example, from the Atram-hasis, the Akkadian version of the Flood, I found this colophon translated by the British Museum in the "Babylonian Legend of the Flood":

> 2nd tablet. When the gods man. Its total 439 (scil., lines) HAND OF Ellit-Aya, the junior scribe. Month of Shabbat, 28th day, year in which Ammi-saduqa, the King, built Fort Ammisaduqa at the mouth of the Euphrates.

British Museum scholars explain that colophon as follows:

> It tells us not only the name of the scribe who wrote down this copy of the epic toward the end of the eleventh year of King Ammisaduqa's reign (1692 B.C.), but also that this tablet, of which only some 50 lines are left, originally had no less than 439 and

was the second of the composition which began with the words "When the gods man." Works were identified simply by quoting their first two or three opening words. "When the gods man," or, in Akkadian, *inuma ilu awilum*, were therefore the first three words of Tablet I of the epic, both the beginning and end of which are now broken away.

By using such notes, made in this case almost four thousand years ago, scholars have for the past hundred years been painstakingly assembling the broken bits and fragments into a single, coherent history of Sumer. From the standpoint of our search for immortality, the most significant fragments were those containing the Sumerian King-list, a catalog of all the kings who reigned in Babylonia before and after the Flood.

Scholars consider the King-list historically accurate, but they are astonished and confounded by the number of years assigned to each king's reign. The King-list reads:

After kingship had descended from heaven, Eridu became the seat of kingship. In Eridu, Alulim reigned 28,800 years as king; Alalgar reigned 36,000 years—two kings reigned 64,800 years. Eridu was abandoned and its kingship carried off to Badtibira.

In Badtibira, Enmenluanna reigned 43,200 years; Emmengalanna reigned 28,800 years; Dumuzi, the shepherd, reigned 36,000 years—three kings reigned 108,000 years. Badtibira was abandoned and its kingship was carried off to Larak.

In Larak, Ensipazianna reigned 28,800 years—one king reigned 28,800 years. Larak was abandoned and its kingship was carried off to Sippar.

In Sippar, Enmeduranna reigned 21,000 years as king. Sippar was abandoned and its kingship was carried off to Shuruppak.

In Shuruppak, Ubar-Tutu reigned 18,600 years as king. . . .

Total, five cities, eight kings reigned 241,200 years. The Flood then swept over the land. . . .

How accurately the King-list relates to what we know of Sumerian history and what we have managed to uncover in the stones and rubble of Nineveh, Nippur, and the other ruined cities of Babylon was supported by British Museum studies:

Zi-u-sudra is listed as the last antediluvian king. He is said to be the son of King Ubar-Tutu and is given a reign of 36,000 years, a not abnormal figure by antediluvian standards. His capital was Shuruppak, a city which German excavations have identified with the site of Fara, some ninety-five miles southeast of Baghdad, and forty miles northwest of Ur as the crow flies. All this is consonant with the Flood story as told in the Epic of Gilgamesh, where Zi-u-sudra is addressed by the god Ea as "Man of Shuruppak, son of Ubar-Tutu." ("The Babylonian Legend of the Flood")

The astonishing longevity of the pre-Flood kings of Sumer was not continued after the waters receded. For Utanapishtim, who had become immortal, was supplanted by a succession of twenty-three kings, each of whom reigned for less than a thousand years.

After wars and other causes had moved the Sumerian capital to Erech, monarchs reigned and presumably died after very short periods of time, the longest being 420 years, the shortest a mere 8 years. A total of twelve kings reigned during the postdeluvian period for 2,310 years. Among them was a king who became the most important hero of Sumer and old Babylon—Gilgamesh, for he is the first man in recorded history to actively search for the secret of immortality.

He was the twenty-eighth Sumerian king to rule after the Flood, and he reigned for 126 years in the city of Erech. Here, in what is now the city of Warka in southern Iraq, archaeologists have found the oldest clay tablet ever to be discovered, dated 3100 B.C., or 5,100 years old. It tells in part the Epic of Gilgamesh, who after many adventures sought out Utanapishtim in the hope of gaining from him the secret of immortality.

Utanapishtim tells Gilgamesh in great, almost paralyzing detail the story of the Flood and finally agrees to share with him the secret of immortality:

> Gilgamesh, I shall reveal a secret thing, it is a mystery of the gods that I am telling you. There is a plant that grows under the water, it has a prickle like a thorn, like a rose; it will wound your hands but if you succeed in taking it, then your hands will hold that which restores his lost youth to a man. (*The Epic of Gilgamesh*)

Gilgamesh finds the plant, but it is stolen by a snake, who immediately eats it and sheds his skin, thus rejuvenating himself. It seems that Utanapishtim may have played somewhat loosely with the truth. Gilgamesh was disposed of by being given the secret of rejuvenating, not of immortality. No matter, Gilgamesh, who wanted to restore eternal youth to himself and the elders of his kingdom, failed and ultimately died.

The Epic of Gilgamesh, in its transit from the Sumerians and then later the Babylonians, suffers because the tablets are broken and pieces are missing. The story has been derived from many different sources, each subject to changing nuances of meaning and interpretation by their various copyists, translators, and analysts. More important, it seemed to me that the epic had been recast from some other, far more technical and advanced form into a simplistic "legend." What remained of the tale was geared to the intellectual level of the Babylonians, toward whom it was ultimately directed.

It seemed probable that the narrative's simplicity caused historians to dismiss as mere legend the idea of immortality. The truth of the story told in the Gilgamesh epic rests in part upon the bedrock—or rather the clay strata deposited by the Flood waters at Ur. The Flood deposit is not the only evidence. At the mound of Al-Ubaid, near Ur, Sir Charles Woolley found a temple dedicated to the Sumerian goddess Nin-Khursag. One of the oldest buildings ever discovered, it had a wealth of artifacts, including a golden bead on which an inscription clearly identified the builder of the temple—a man named A-anni-paddi.

The name meant little until a few weeks later, when Woolley uncovered a limestone tablet in the temple foundation. On it was a cuneiform inscription, a dedication of the temple by a "A-anni-padda, King of Ur, son of Mes-anni-paddi, King of Ur."

Mes-anni-paddi is inscribed in the King-lists as the founder of the third dynasty after the Flood, which begins with the movement of the kingship to the city of Ur. Thus, the golden bead and the temple inscription provide tangible archaeological evidence that at least one of the Sumerian kings whose existence was thought to be pure myth was in fact a real, living person.

I started to enjoy the Charlie Chan-ish endeavor of sorting out the evidence that supported the reality of myth. I drew on many sources, knowing that the myths were many thousands of years old and suffered from the patina of time, which tends to obscure meaning. The King-lists, with their record of incredible longevity, were inextricably entwined with the Flood legend, which found physical corroboration in the ten-foot-deep layer of clay and other eyewitness accounts. The most important, of course, is the Bible, wherein Utanapishtim is replaced by Noah.

Were Noah and Utanapishtim the same man? No one can say, but another of the towering biblical figures, Abraham, came from Ur, and some of the Old Testament seems to have its roots in Sumerian legends. Great controversy, however, surrounded the Flood account. Some scholars claim that both the Bible and the Epic of Gilgamesh report the same event from two different vantage points. Others feel that the biblical account is simply a later version of the Sumerian tale. Similarly, the biblical lists of the patriarchs following Adam bore a striking resemblance to the Sumerian King-lists. Were they a Hebrew echo of the Sumerian culture carried by Abraham out of Ur?

I found no supported answer to that question and no agreement among scholars. But suppose the legends of Sumer and the tales of the Bible were, as one school suggests, eyewitness accounts of the same events recorded by two different peoples. Suppose, further, that a small cadre of spacemen, gods in the parlance of the legends, had been assigned to each group—Sumerians and Hebrews. The Sumerians, who seem to have come from nowhere, were suddenly possessed of a technology far superior to that of their neighbors. They created a written language that apparently has no connection with any other language on Earth. The Hebrews, a nomadic people, were led by a patriarchal chief called Abraham, who claimed to have come from Ur, a Sumerian city. The Hebrews were no different from the dozen or so other nomadic shepherd tribes, with one notable exception: they owed their allegiance to a fierce god who came from the sky and insisted that they follow a moral code very different from the common practice of the region. Their beliefs marked the practitioners apart from all other human beings of that time.

The Sumerians and the Hebrews had other similarities that seem to connect them with extraterrestrials. Both cultures abounded with tales of gods descending from the skies. Time and time again I came across careful and detailed descriptions in *The Epic of Gilgamesh* and the Bible of "spaceships" and accounts of persons being carried aboard, taken on journeys, and then returned to Earth. Finally, both the Sumerian King-lists and the Old Testament contain records of incredibly long-lived peoples.

The Book of Genesis does not elaborate on the longevity of the patriarchs but, like the Sumerian King-lists, merely catalogs their ages, beginning with Adam, who died at the age of 930. Moreover, they were particularly vigorous old men, siring sons long after the age of reproduction is past for modern men. Adam fathered Seth when he was 130 years of age. Seth lived to be 912, and at the age of 105 had a son named Enosh, who lived to be 905. Enosh was a comparative youngster, just 90, when his wife was delivered of Kenan.

And so the record continued, Kenan dying at 910 but siring Mahalel at the age of 70. Mahalel lived to be 895, and at age 65 had a son, Jared. Jared, who at 162 fathered Enoch, died when he was 962.

Enoch died at the age of 365, a relatively short life span in the record of patriarchs, but at age 65 he fathered Methuselah, whose name was to become synonymous with longevity.

"And all the days of Methuselah were nine hundred sixty and nine years; and he died." (Genesis)

The accounts continued through Lamech and Noah, who—unlike his Sumerian counterpart, Utanapishtim —did not become immortal and died at the age of 950.

Most scientists feel that the longevity of the patriarchs as reported in the Bible is not accurate. Isaac Asimov, the noted science writer and biochemist, sums up the prevailing scientific opinion in his *Guide to the Bible:*

> These patriarchs cannot be associated with any historical personages, and nothing is known of them beyond this bare biblical mention. They seem, however, to be a reflection of Sumerian legend. At least the Sumerians had lists of nine or ten kings who reigned before the Flood, each of them living for many thousands of years. One was listed as having reigned nearly sixty-five thousand years. The writer of this portion of Genesis, far from imposing on credibility by making use of extended life spans, apparently took legendary material and did his best to cut those ages down to reasonable size.

Despite Asimov's skepticism, I found it intriguing that even if the writer of Genesis was reworking Sumerian legends, his idea of "reasonable" age was still twelve times longer than the projected seventy-year life span of today's average American.

Other scholars attempt to explain these great ages by examining the calendrical basis used when the Bible was written. Like many primitive people, the Jews of the Old Testament used the lunar calendar and some experts have therefore "corrected" the ages of the biblical patriarchs by dividing them by twelve. The theory works quite well if the primary concern is bringing the ages of the patriarchs more into line with contemporary life spans. Dividing Methuselah's age by twelve makes him a mere eighty-eight years old when he died. It also means that he would have become a father at the age of fifteen, admittedly not an impossibility. Applying the same rule of division to the other patriarchs, however, makes them remarkably sexually precocious boys; Enoch would have been only five years old when he fathered Methuselah, and Seth would have become a father at the age of eight.

I had begun my perusal of the Bible seeking substantiation of the possibility that the knowledge and methodology required to achieve immortality had once existed on Earth. My proofs seemed negative and tangential. For the most part, I was confronted with interpretations of the Bible that reduced it to mere myth and allegory. Obviously there was enough substantive material to support the theory that the Bible is history. I had made the Flood the center of my research. The records were fragmentary and filled with gaps but offered enough evidence to tantalize me with questions of what life might have been like in those antediluvian days. There was, for example, a marked reduction in the life span of the Sumerian kings after the Flood. The same is true of the patriarchs and prophets of the Old Testament; life spans, after the Flood, were more in keeping with those of modern-day men.

I turned to a more certifiable record of longevity. I kept thinking of a strange statement made by noted marine biologist Dr. Walter Starck. He told me that he thought he might like to investigate the possibility that pure-salt-water fish *never* seem to die of natural causes, that in fact they may be immortal. Predation and severe environmental shifts, in his view, caused salt-water fish to die.

I assembled lists of long-life phenomena found in modern medical literature. Recent records listed only a comparative handful of people who lived for more than 100 years. Among the most famous was Thomas Parr, an English farmer who died in the year 1635 at the age of 152. His obituary said:

He died not from the disease or decay of a single organ but from too great fullness of blood caused by more than usual indulgence in eating and drinking. He had led an active country life and enjoyed country air and exercise but was invited to London where luxurious eating and drinking soon finished him. (*Secrets of Long Life* by George Gallup and Evan Hill)

Parr had been brought to the court of King Charles I as a curiosity, but life at court proved to be too much for him. King Charles's physician, the famous William Harvey, performed an autopsy and stated that Parr's muscles, intestines, and brain were in an excellent state of preservation.

There were other recorded instances of long-lived individuals: Henry Jenkens of Yorkshire, England, 169; Joseph Surrington, Bergen, Norway, 160; Flora Thomson, Nashua, North Carolina, 150; Christian Drackenberg, Denmark, 146. Most of the centenarians died in the seventeenth, eighteenth, and nineteenth centuries. Actuarial tables quoted in 1974 *Guinness Book of World Records* indicate that only one 115-year life can be expected in every 2.1 billion lives. This means that with the population of the Earth approaching 4 billion people, two among us might reach 115 years of age.

Confounding the actuarial tables, however, were the oldsters who lived in three widely separated parts of the world—in the Russian Caucasus, in the Andean village of Vilacabamba, Ecuador, and in Pakistan's Hunza province. Each of these places boasted a disproportionate number of centenarians. Vilacabamba, a Catholic community, produced church baptismal certificates to validate the ages of its old people, and a 1971 census showed the tiny village to have 9 people out of its total population of 819 over the age of 100. By contrast, the United States had about 3 people over the age 100 for every 10,000 of its total population.

Hunza, a rugged, mountainous area in northern Pakistan near the Chinese border, has forty thousand people but no written language, so it was almost impossible to pinpoint the number of centenarians. Dr. Alexander Leaf, Jackson professor of clinical medicine at Harvard University Medical School, has made a study of the old people in all three areas and reported, "I was not able to confirm exact ages in Hunza. Yet I had the definite impression of an unusual number of very vigorous old folk clambering over the steep slopes that make up this mountainous land." (*National Geographic,* "Every Day Is a Gift When You Are Over 100")

Russia seems to have the most centenarians. According to a 1970 census, in the mountainous villages of the Caucusus there were five thousand people over the age of one hundred, making it an astonishing sixty-three centenarians per hundred thousand people.

What accounted for such extended life spans (extended, that is, when compared to modern life spans but not those of the predeluge lives)? Dr. Leaf believed that it was a combination of genetics, diet, and a vigorous life-style. "There is no known gene for longevity," points out Dr. Leaf, "only the absence of bad genes—those that increase the risk of fatal disease."

The centenarians seemed to eat far less than the average American, and their diets contained far less animal protein than our diets.

Dr. Leaf noted:

Whether slim or not, the old people of all three cultures share a great deal of physical activity. The traditional farming and household practices demand heavy work, and male and female are all involved from early childhood to terminal days. Superimposed on the usual labor involved in farming is the mountainous terrain. Simply traversing the hills on foot during the day's activities sustains a high degree of cardiovascular fitness as well as general muscular tone. (*National Geographic,* "Every Day Is a Gift When You Are Over 100")

Dr. Leaf's conclusions were those of an extremely competent scientist, and they offered a clue to ways in which we might extend by several decades modern man's life span. Even if we doubled the seventy years now considered the statistical norm for Americans, we still would be very, very far from the great ages achieved by the Sumerians and the biblical patriarchs. Why? What has happened to us between the time of the Flood and today to make us age so rapidly? These were questions I began to ponder with increasing urgency, for the prospect of immortality seemingly was snatched from man a thousand generations ago. Could it be restored? Was there an answer in space, a clue to the secret of immortality we might once have possessed and then lost?

11

Old Age: A Curable Disease?

"Death is unnatural. . . . Theoretically, man is quite immortal. His body tissues replace themselves. He is a self-repairing machine. And yet he gets old and dies, and the reasons for this are still a mystery." (*Extended Youth* by Prehoda)

The speaker was Dr. Linus C. Pauling, a world-renowned chemist, winner of two Nobel Prizes, and one of the most original thinkers of our time.

"If we kept throughout life the same resistance to stress, injury, and disease that we had at the age of ten, about one half of us here today might expect to survive in seven hundred years' time," said Dr. Alex Comfort, director of research in gerontology at University College, London.

"Someday," added Dr. Bernard Strehler, a biologist

at the University of Southern California, "we may live almost indefinitely." (*Newsweek*)

I was in the cutting room leafing through research notes when I found the statements of these three distinguished scientists. I compared their comments to the record of the immortality achieved by the ancients. Then I began to ponder what it was that we had lost. Comparatively speaking, modern man's sentient being lasts oh-so-brief a time. Why do we age? What is there about our bodies, our metabolism and physiology, that turns us from healthy, active, alert men and women into sagging, senile, sick old people? A great deal of research is now underway to answer that question. One of the early heartening results is the idea that aging as a physical process is no longer considered an inevitable event but rather a wasting disease that can be cured.

If we consider aging a disease, then the symptoms are representative of a biological war taking place within the body. The results of that war can be seen in many cases and measured in others. The skin dries and wrinkles, hair falls out and is dusted with gray. Our sensory organs begin to fail: the lenses of the eyes thicken and lose their crystal clarity; our hearing mechanism degenerates and loses its acuity. Fat accumulates around the torso and the butt. Muscles shrink and grow slack. Joints stiffen and swell.

In old age the body's life-supporting organs suffer because the heart pumps blood less effectively and the vessels through which it travels lose their elasticity. Lungs remove less and less oxygen from the air we breathe; kidney and bladder functions drop sharply. The flow of hormones—the chemicals that control many of our body's functions—is reduced. The brain, man's crowning achievement, shrinks each day by more than a hundred thousand cells.

Aging is a cumulative weakening process, rendering the body vulnerable to the many degenerative diseases such as cancer, cardiovascular ailments, diabetes, etc. If these diseases don't kill, the body finally dies from the sum total of ills we call "old age."

Throughout history men have sought immortality, hoping to slow, prevent, or arrest the aging process.

In ancient India tiger testicles were used in the treatment of old age. Achilles supposedly ate the marrow from the bones of young bears. King David was treated by the ancient practice of geracomy—sleeping with young virgins in the hope that their body heat and breath would restore youthful vigor to the aged. Into his bed came Abishai the Shunammite, but the treatment apparently failed, for, the Bible says, "He knew her not," and soon thereafter King David died.

Geracomy was not, however, without its successes. The tombstone of one noble Roman reads: "To Aescalapius and health—L. Claudius Hermip—who lived one hundred and fifteen years and five days with the aid of the breath of young women to the surprise of physicians. Lead your life accordingly."

In his book *Men Against Age* Robert DeRop points out:

Hebrews and Syrians bathed in and drank the blood of young people, hoping to recapture their youthful vigor. Romans in the arena would lap the freshly shed blood of gladiators. They also favored the practice of sucking blood mixed with milk from the breasts of young slave girls, a procedure revived in part by Marsilio Ficino in the fifteenth century. "He should find a young, healthy, gay, and beautiful girl and attach his mouth to her breast when the moon is becoming full and then he should eat powdered fennel with sugar." If that failed to produce results, he should suck her blood "like a leech." What the girl thought about all this is not recorded.

Blood sucking gave way to blood transfusions in the fifteenth century when Pope Innocent VIII lay dying in Rome and physicians from all over Europe hurried to his side. Only one, an unknown surgeon, offered the slightest hope. In an attempt to gain immortality for the Pope, Church officials eagerly agreed to let him try the radical treatment he proposed. The doctor, whose name is, with good reason, unrecorded, argued that an infusion of young blood would rejuvenate the Pope. Moreover, if the treatment was repeated each time he became ill, he would continually be cured. The cumulative effect was immortality.

Unable to resist such a glittering promise, Church officials condoned the treatment; the blood of three boys was injected into the Pope's veins. The boys were bled to death. The Pope died too, and the physician fled.

Today, blood transfusions are a common medical procedure but no physician views them as a potential source of immortality. Some doctors believe that a technique called cellular therapy offers great hope for the rejuvenation of aged bodies. This treatment is based upon an injection of cells taken from lamb fetuses. Developed more than forty years ago by Swiss surgeon Dr. Paul Niehans, it became the beacon that drew many of the world's aging celebrities and leaders to his clinic on Lake Geneva. Among his patients were Somerset Maugham, Noel Coward, Winston Churchill, the Duke of Windsor, Konrad Adenauer, Bernard Baruch, Thomas Mann, Hedda Hopper, Charles DeGaulle, and many others. They came to Clinique la Prairie, as the Niehans clinic is known, to have the cells of a lamb fetus injected into their buttocks. After the injections they returned home, usually professing to have been rejuvenated. Niehans used cell therapy not only to cure old age but as a treatment for the specific diseases of old age—heart disease, anemia, diabetes, hypertension, impotence, even cancer.

"Cell therapy," he said in an attempt to explain how his process works, "is a selective form of treatment which aims at developing underdeveloped organs or organs which are not capable of regeneration themselves." (*The New York Times* magazine) Just how cells taken from animal fetuses and injected into human beings could fulfill the promise he failed to say. One measure of cell-therapy effectiveness was Niehans himself, who died at age eighty-eight. Many of his famous patients, such as Churchill and Adenauer, reached their nineties. Ninety *is* old, but it is far from immortality, especially when compared to the ages recorded for Sumerian kings.

Cell therapy remains a popular treatment for those

who can afford to pay for what may be temporary relief from the symptoms of aging; to me, however, lamb-fetus injections seemed a dead end in the search for immortality.

Many researchers believe that the secret of arresting or even curing old age will be found *inside* the walls of the cell. Many of the experiments now going on in laboratories throughout the world seek to understand the aging process on the cellular level. A number of important mechanisms have been uncovered. The body contains about 50 trillion cells, each in a constant state of growth and reproduction by division. Protein is the key both to growth and to division. The cells use their DNA blueprints to construct the specific proteins needed to build essential structures such as cell walls, cytoplasm, and other components. Eventually the cell reaches a stage when it must divide, and half of the DNA blueprint is passed into each of the two new daughter cells created by the division. The new cells must then construct the missing half from available components within the cell. After several generations of such reproduction the DNA templates, or blueprints, may become blurred and "noise" creeps into the message. After several more reproductions the errors multiply and a faulty protein is manufactured. The cells then divide less frequently; they begin to deteriorate. In short, they age.

This multiplying of cellular mistakes is a theory of aging called "error catastrophe." It was devised by Dr. Leslie Orgel, the brilliantly imaginative biologist at the Salk Institute in La Jolla, California. Dr. Orgel, who along with Nobel Laureate Sir Francis Crick, is the author of another theory called Directed Panspermia, which postulates that Earth might have been seeded many thousands of years ago by an intelligent extra-terrestrial life form. I had interviewed Dr. Orgel about that theory for the film *In Search of Ancient Mysteries,* and I went back to him for a more thorough explanation of "error catastrophe."

"If a factory that produces machinery utilized by a second factory makes inferior machinery," he explained, "the second factory will produce poor products. If the product of that second factory is machinery utilized by a third factory, the second factory's product will be poorer than the first's, and the third factory's products are certain to be even poorer than the second factory's. And so it goes."

"In other words," I said, "we are doomed by the passage of time to produce poorer-quality cells which in turn will lead to the breakdown we call aging."

"I used to think so, but now I'm not so certain. While error theory is by no means dead, it's not as strong an explanation for aging as I once thought it was."

I was still intrigued by the error-catastrophe possibility. It seemed to be a reasonable explanation of the body's aging process.

Perhaps the theory explains the wide gap between pre- and post-Flood life spans. The generations of man, in their continual reproduction, could have been subject to error catastrophe on the reproductive-cell level just as it might have occurred on the body-cell level. Over thousands of generations the errors could have blurred the perfectly balanced combination of genetic instructions that seem to add up to immortality.

According to another theory, catastrophe itself could produce genetic mutation. Did the Flood and its aftermath induce a mutation that became a dominant factor in the human gene pool, and did that mutation rob man of his chance for immortality?

I turned back to the film we had accumulated for *The Outer Space Connection*.

"Let's look at Medicine Wheel again," I said. "Maybe we missed a significant point." A primitive culture might have left some indication of how a catastrophic event possibly had affected mortality, and this is what I was seeking.

We found Medicine Wheel nine thousand feet up in the Big Horn Mountains of northern Wyoming. An archaeo-astronomer, Dr. John Eddy, had led us to the site. As Eddy explained, "Medicine Wheel is a monument in stone that has long been a mystery to archaeologists. It's unique because apparently it's prehistoric and was left by the Indians of the Great Plains, who were not builders. They were the nomadic tribes of the plains. Medicine Wheel is unique because these people moved about, they didn't leave things behind. They were believed to be a very simple, uncultured group. But in spite of that, this structure stands on a high mountain far above usual civilization, above water, above the timberline."

Flying over Medicine Wheel, the landscape of the "badlands" was laid out before us. At the top of a grim, inhospitable peak we could see the outlines of a circle some ninety feet in diameter. The ring was made up of piled stones, and twenty-eight spokes radiated out from the center.

"It's unlike anything else that's been found on the plains," Dr. Eddy told me, "and it's always been kind of a mystery. It doesn't seem to fit in with the archaeological knowledge of the Plains Indians."

"What is the Medicine Wheel?" I asked, and Dr. Eddy explained his own theory.

"It was a calendar in stone, and therefore it is fair to say that it's like the other kind of monuments of Mezzo-America, Central America, and South America. I think one of the most exciting things about it is that most people are loath to believe that the Plains Indians had that kind of culture. He was a guy with dirty fingernails, didn't have anything written. In fact, it's very crucial that the Indian left no writs and records, so things like this become very valuable in marking out what was his past. It was his way of telling us something about his life. I think that, interestingly, Medicine Wheel was probably used only by a few—by medicine men."

"Could it have marked some catastrophic event in the tribe's history?"

Dr. Eddy said that that was possible. But his main concern was that responsible interpretation be given to the monument. From his point of view, Medicine Wheel was an unusual astronomical calendar, not unlike Stonehenge. He felt that it was a striking attempt by a primitive culture to cope with their environment. By marking one solstice the medicine men of a prehistoric plains tribe could predict the seasonal changes. But why, I wondered, was only one medicine wheel found, and why was it isolated on a mountain peak pointed heavenward?

I began to feel that Medicine Wheel was a reminder of a catastrophe that had affected tribal life. Somehow it seemed to signal a radical change that threatened survival in their environment.

I have seen the evidence of catastrophic destruction at Jericho, where, the Bible reports, the sun stood still in the heavens as Joshua's trumpets caused the destruction of the wall. If the sun stood still, the walls would have fallen, trumpets or no. We can only guess at what might have caused the sun to stand still. For some reason, apparently, day did not follow night. What was being reported was a calamitous event. Its shock waves would have profoundly altered the nature of the environment. Such changes help account for peculiar adaptations made by many forms of life.

We know, of course, that we are the sum total of our genes and our environment. Our lives are mediated by both. At this point in man's development we can control the environment far better than we can control our genetic makeup. The twentieth century has produced better sanitation, improved food handling to eliminate pathogens, and developed pesticides and antiseptics to eliminate insects and germs that cause disease. The result has been a greatly increased life expectancy. But we have been unable to find a gene that controls aging, or to manipulate all of the other genes that jointly contribute to our ability to withstand disease and the collective degeneration of the body's systems that we call aging.

The ultimate answer to aging, I think, will be found in the genetic blueprint. We must control the role played by each cell and determine how long it will continue to play that role. One man who feels that the ultimate answer will be found in the genes is USC's Dr. Bernard Strehler. Speaking to the American Association for the Advancement of Science's Symposium on the Biology of Aging, Dr. Strehler attempted to pull together under one biological umbrella all of the differing theories on aging. He explained:

Nearly all of the special theories and research on biological aging that appear to be quite different from each other are united by a common fact. They ultimately reflect a decreased ability of one or another body system—immune, neural, hormonal, etc.—to maintain an optimum state because the genes required for such maintenance are in a switched-off state.

During human development there are obviously certain things that must be turned off. Brain size, for example, can't increase indefinitely because the skull is a cage of limited dimensions. The evolutionary process has resulted in an optimum body-size ratio so that all our organs can function efficiently in concert. (*Newsweek*)

As long as the genes are active—switching on for growth of individual cells and then off when the optimum size has been achieved—life is a vigorous, healthy process. When the genes turn off for longer and longer periods of time, however, the supplies available for the cells' production of crucial components shrink. The cells then deteriorate and finally die. When enough cell systems are affected in this fashion the body begins an irreversible aging process that quickly ends in death.

Strehler believes that aging can be arrested simply by reactivating the turned-off genes. *Simply* is of course the wrong word. Achievement of this is a Herculean task that at the moment remains far beyond our grasp but not beyond our reach. "The whole nature of genetic on-off switches can undoubtedly be understood if the effort is made," he says, "and it can be done within five to ten years. Once we have learned to reactivate switched-off genes, even if it is only temporary, lost functions could be restored to many tired old cell systems." (*Newsweek*) Here, then, might be the means to circumvent a system that seems to have been built into the cell to limit its ability to be immortal.

Genetic limitation of immortality seemed to be the inevitable conclusion of research done by Dr. Leonard Hayflick, professor of medical microbiology at Stanford

University. He found that the cells of our bodies are seemingly not programmed for immortal life. In his lab Dr. Hayflick grew human fibroblasts, the protein bricks used to build the structure of most body tissue. He found that the cells divided rapidly for a time, then slowed down, stopped multiplying, and died after their fiftieth population doubling. After many more experiments he finally came to the conclusion that approximately fifty population doublings were the limit of human life, meaning that man's biological clock is wound for a life span of about 115 years. Even that brief time is beyond the endurance of most people, but it seemed an absolute limit to life and a complete denial of the prospect of immortality.

Dr. Hayflick's idea seemed incontrovertible until another series of experiments created another possibility. Using cells originating from the line of human fibroblasts Dr. Hayflick developed for his experiments, these experimenters reported 117 population doublings. The work was done at the University of California at Berkeley by Drs. Lester Packer and James R. Smith. They added vitamin E to the fibroblast cultures and more than doubled the life span of the cells. Those 117 population doublings represent, in terms of the human bioclock, a possible life span of 269 years. Better, but still far from immortality or even the longevity of the biblical patriarchs.

The success of vitamin E in increasing the cells' ability to continue to reproduce is an example of what we are learning about cell function and breakdown. It seems that as every cell grows older it develops an increasing number of molecular fragments that break free of various structures within the cell. These fragments, called "free radicals," bang about within the cell and eventually cause so much damage that the cell breaks. The effect has been compared to pouring sugar into an automobile gas tank or sand into machinery gears. Butter turns rancid due to the effect of free radicals. Radiation causes much of its damage to living systems by breaking off fragments within the cells and creating free radicals. Vitamin E retards aging of cells by inhibiting the production and movement of free radicals.

In systems more complex than tissue culture, vitamin E treatment has been encouraging in some species and ineffective in others. Fruit flies and roundworms have had greatly increased life spans when fed vitamin E; mice have not benefited at all. At present we do not know just why this is so, but it seems that the more complex the system, the more difficult it is for vitamin E to reach the bio-clock that ticks away within it, causing aging.

Researchers are not even certain of just where that bio-clock may be, but some seem to feel that it is in the hypothalamus, which controls most aspects of human development. Buried deep beneath the cortex of the brain, the hypothalamus represents only about one three-hundredth of the total bulk of the brain, and yet it has a disproportionate share of tasks to perform. It appears to be the master control of the body's metabolism, temperature regulation, appetite and thirst, sleeping and waking, emotions such as anger and pleasure, and, of course, growth. Perhaps the single most important control task of the hypothalamus is to oversee the function of the pituitary gland. This is often called the master gland of the body, for it regulates the body's output of hormones through its control over other glands such as the thymus, the adrenals, and the reproductive glands.

From the moment of conception hormones play a vital role in the processes of growth and aging. Hypothalamus, pituitary gland, and hormones all come into focus in the most dramatic single aging event we know of—menopause.

Menopause, which occurs in women, is often a physiologically as well as psychologically trying time. The flow of estrogen—the hormone that makes a woman female—slows to a trickle and finally halts. All of the tissues dependent upon estrogen wither and atrophy. Bone cells fall away, the arteries, for some reason protected from hardening in premenopausal youth, lose their elasticity. The ovaries cease releasing eggs every month, menstrual flow stops, and a woman's reproductive days end, the first indication of a hastening of the aging process.

Although estrogen comes from the ovaries these organs do not seem to be the cause of menopause. Nonfunctioning ovaries transplanted from aging female rats into younger ones soon resume their hormonal secretions. Later these same ovaries once more put forth eggs, and when fertilized the eggs give rise to healthy offspring. The ultimate control of estrogen production goes back to the function of the hypothalamus. For many reasons, it seems possible that the secret of aging is contained within the hypothalamus. In a startling experiment recently conducted at Michigan State University, Dr. Joseph Meites succeeded in restoring ovarian function in a menopausal rat by stimulating its hypothalamus with a tiny tickle of electricity—one one-thousandth of a volt.

Was electrical stimulus part of the antiaging armory of the Sumerian kings? Again, a question we cannot answer, but consider this discovery by German archaeologist Wilhelm Konig. In 1938, while on a dig near Baghdad in what was once the land of Sumer, he found several small earthenware jars. Inside the jars, iron rods encased in copper cylinders protruded through the asphalt-covered cylinder necks. To Konig the jars resembled electric batteries, but the idea of a two-thousand-year-old electric battery was too fantastic to be accepted.

There matters remained, for the world's interest had turned from archaeology to war. It was not until after World War II that a General Electric Company engineer reproduced the Sumerian battery, filling it with an electrolyte. Incredibly, it worked. Moreover, subsequent digs in the region indicated that certain materials had been electroplated two thousand years before the Konig battery had been built. That would mean that the Sumerians had batteries capable of generating enough electrical current to stimulate the hypothalami of their kings.

I wanted to shout "Eureka!" when I made the connection between Dr. Meites' experiments and the Konig battery. The battery was an "out-of-place artifact" that had been reported in many journals of the "believe it or not" kind. Although no attempt was made to divine the reason for its existence, an effort was made to relate the battery's presence to extraterrestial influence. By examining the possibility that a knowledge of immortality had existed on Earth eons ago I had stumbled into the relationship between two disparate discoveries. It was not an enormous leap, for along the way I had found only bits and pieces of corroborating evidence. I had before me a cabinet full of sophisticated medical instruments used by Egyptian doctors. I had the skulls of Peruvian noblemen bearing signs of very successful brain surgery. Finally, I had a list of Sumerian kings reported to have lived for thousands of years. My question was, did the antediluvian Sumerians solve the problem of immortality by electrically stimulating the hypothalamus? Does this, then, account for their incredible longevity? We again have posed a question for which we simply have no answer, but we do know that there exists a number of strange life forces, inexplicable sources of energy that seemingly have the power to preserve, to rejuvenate, and to create life.

One of the places I wanted to visit was Azerbaijan, in the Ukraine. It was one of the centers that Dr. Leaf had studied when he compiled the data on unusual centenarians. What impelled my desire was a report that near the city was a deep well possessing a strange electrical phenomenon. A blue sparklike glow was said to have been evident at night, and folk legend contended that the longevity of the resident population was due in part to water drawn from that well. I wanted to see the strange emanation but I found it extraordinarily difficult to arrange a filming trip into the Soviet Union. I did, however, find a possible explanation for the fiery ring around Azerbaijan's well, and I found it on my doorstep.

12

Strange Life Forces

The lab was a small room with a row of windows along the back wall. A large collection of surreal photographs, looking like flaming suns, burning red, yellow, and orange, covered the other walls. The rest of the room was dominated by what looked like an enormous floor-to-ceiling box.

"This," Dr. Thelma Moss said to me, indicating the box, "is where we do our photography. It is absolutely light-tight."

She swung open the door and I could see that it was at least a foot thick and rimmed by heavy sponge-rubber gaskets. It seemed to me an odd way to shoot film, in complete darkness. As a director, fully half of my problems have always been caused by light—usually there is not enough of it. Years of rising before dawn on location to take full advantage of the sun made this looming, dark box the very antithesis of everything I knew about filming.

We had come to film a very strange form of photography, a system that recorded not the image of objects themselves but rather the strange, glowing emanations, or force fields, given off by the objects. It was called Kirlian Photography, after Russian electronics expert Semyon Kirlian, who had discovered the technique in the late 1930s.

In Kirlian's technique, the object to be photographed was placed on photographic film and then sandwiched between two metal plates. A small electric current then passed through the plates and left an illuminated glow on the film. Living objects produced the most varied flaring glows.

Of his early experiments Kirlian wrote:

> In living things we see the signals of the inner state of the organism reflected in the brightness, dimness, and color of the flares. The inner life activities of the human being are written in these "light" hieroglyphs. But to read them, we're going to need help. . . . (*Time* magazine)

That help has been coming from the United States only recently, in large measure from Dr. Thelma Moss's work at UCLA's Neuropsychiatric Institute. And that is where we now were, our crew and equipment as well as half a dozen volunteer subjects filling all of the available space in the laboratory and spilling into the hall outside. Dr. Moss, a medical psychologist, is probably the foremost researcher in the field. She has taken more Kirlian photographs and done more experiments with it than anyone else outside Russia.

"We use a slightly different technique," she told me, leading me into the box. There, on a table, stood a glass plate and a control box. A wire ran from the box to the plate. "Kirlian's metal sandwich was replaced by this glass electrode. The object to be photographed was placed on the plate like so," she said, putting the ball of her index finger on the upright glass pane, "and photographed on motion-picture film.

"When the door is closed," she went on, "the experimental chamber is in total darkness, and the only light that can possibly form an image on the film is that produced by the object subjected to the Kirlian effect."

We had brought with us a number of objects to test the theory ourselves. Through the kindness of the L. A. County Museum of Natural History we had been loaned some very old fossils—a trilobite, an ancient marine creature that had died some 450 million years ago; a mastadon tooth that was about 10 million years old;

even a mummy's hand, which was 4,000 years old. We also had some objects that had never known life—a piece of jade and an artificial gem.

We moved our camera and lights into the box. We would film the object as it appeared in the light and then pull the plug, plunging the room into darkness. Whatever was to happen next would be filmed by another camera, set up directly in front of the glass plate.

Paul Desatoff, our cameraman, began to film the process.

Dr. Moss flipped a switch on the control panel and immediately there was a buzzing sound; it wasn't very loud but it was easily distinguishable from the faint hum of the camera, which was the only other sound in the eerily quiet chamber. For in sealing out all light, all of the ambient sound of the laboratory was also screened out. Dr. Moss waited only an instant, then picked up the jade and placed it against the glass.

I told the electrician to pull the plug, and suddenly it was as if we had been plunged into a sea of black ink. But I soon forgot the darkness as my eyes dilated to allow whatever light there was to come in and flash the image onto my retinas. And what an image. Wherever the jade touched the plate it glowed with a green fire.

Dr. Moss withdrew the jade from the plate and we were once again plunged into total darkness. "Lights," I called, and we blinked as the hot floods seared the room. Once again our eyes made the adjustment, this time from total darkness to blazing light. My eyes, however, still burned with an after-image of green fire.

"That was an inanimate object," Dr. Moss said. "It is dead and doesn't produce a changing aura. Let me show you something alive and you will see the difference."

Once more she threw the switch that sent current into the glass plate. We started rolling the film in the second camera and killed our lights. Just before they went out, however, I saw Dr. Moss place the tip of her index finger against the glass plate where the jade had been. Then it was dark, and then it wasn't. The glass blazed with a shooting fire that leaped and danced. I closed my eyes to be certain that I was not seeing an after-image of our movie lights, then opened them, and the same blazing fire was on the plate. Spikes of blue, white, and purple danced about in the shape of the ball of a fingerpad.

The lights went back up and Dr. Moss explained, "That is the difference between things that are alive and objects that are not. In living things, the aura is constantly varied. The Kirlian effect is produced by some energy force that is associated with life. Let's just say that there are about six different words we can use to describe this effect, depending on who you are. If you are a conventional physicist, you will call it an electrical emanation caused by the current and the voltage going through the object. Some people who are more inclined to the occult or to the mystical call it an aura. They will point out that in famous paintings, whether it's of Buddha or Jesus or Muhammed, or anyone else, there are these auras circling around the head. They would like to believe that what we are photographing with this electrical photography is a representation of that aura. Something invisible to the eye but which exists in and around the body. But I prefer to call it an emanation or some outpouring of an energetic thing. The Russians call this energetic thing by a technical name, bioplasma. . . . Whatever it is, though, I'm interested because it reveals enormous differences in energy states in individuals and thus may have practical applications for treating diseases."

She was growing impatient. She wanted to expose to the Kirlian effect the museum pieces we had brought. They were the remains of what had once been living tissue. The fossils had been frozen by time into a stone cast of the original creature. The trilobite was placed against the plate. It sparked rather than flamed. Unlike the steady glow of the jade, it winked at us, flickering and dancing—definitely not the avid flaming of a living finger, but neither was it the quiescent glow of an inanimate mineral. To me it meant that something of the life force remained; something was still embedded in those ancient fossils millions of years after the creatures supposedly had died. Was that life force eternal, immortal? Did it persist as part of the universe, a cosmic

entity that ensured the propagation of life throughout
the heavens?

There was more evidence for this kind of thinking.
Dr. Moss left the chamber and came back with a leafy
potted plant which she called a Creeping Charlie. Of
all the effects in Kirlian Photography, the experiment we
were about to see was the most intriguing. Dr. Moss cut
off one of the leaves and held it to the plate. After we
had again plunged the chamber into darkness the outline of the leaf left no doubt as to the vigorous life that
flowed within it.

The lights went back on and Dr. Moss removed the
leaf from the glass plate. Then she cut it in half, and
again the lights went out. The half leaf was placed
against the glass and began to glow and flare. For a few
moments the flaming halo outlined half a leaf. Then, as
we continued to watch, the other half of the leaf—the
half that had been cut off and was lying on the floor
at our feet—began to glow on the plate. Its aura was
less distinct, it sparked and sputtered rather than flamed,
but it was unmistakably there.

"We call it the phantom leaf effect," Dr. Moss said.
"It demonstrates that the Kirlian effect is very real, that
there is an energy body, a duplicate of the physical body
made of a far finer substance that we can now capture
and hold on film. Ultimately," she went on, "we hope
to learn how it can be utilized."

Kirlian Photography, we were told, had been used
to explore acupuncture, and while no conclusions could
be drawn there seemed to be an uncanny relationship
between the two. Kirlian photographs of the entire
human body show certain points that radiate light flares
more vividly than the areas around them. These points
correspond exactly to the 741 acupuncture points
mapped out by the ancient Chinese. To test this relationship and capture it on film Dr. Moss had arranged
for Dr. Richard Konig, a skilled acupuncturist and a
professor of medicine at the UCLA Medical Center, to
be present. He would demonstrate how acupuncture
treatment changed the glow emanating from a subject.
I volunteered.

"I'm going to stimulate the nerves running from your

hand to your shoulder," the doctor said. "We should be able to see the effect of the stimulation in the Kirlian photograph of your thumb."

First we examined the aura of my finger without the acupuncture needles inserted. I pressed my thumb against the plate and felt the slightly vibrating electric current. In the darkness the tip of my thumb was like a top view of a gas-stove burner. An irregular circle of blue flame sprouted from a darkened central core.

The acupuncture procedure then began. A needle slipped painlessly into a point at the base of my thumb, not on the palm side, as I had expected, but on the top of my hand. The doctor twirled the needle gently, and a tingling though not at all painful impulse raced to my shoulder.

The stimulation continued for a minute or so, with the now-familiar shooting sensation terminating at varied points along my arm.

"Now this may cause some discomfort, so be prepared," the doctor warned as he began to vigorously manipulate the needle. A hot fire pulsed from my elbow to my shoulder, then suddenly it stopped. With the needle still lodged in my hand, the doctor suggested we wait about ten minutes before taking the Kirlian photograph, so that the treatment would take effect.

I was fascinated by the study of acupuncture. "Will this treatment cure my tennis elbow?" I asked.

"It might. Actually we've had marked success treating tennis elbow, but the procedure we use is different from the stimulation you're experiencing tonight. Dr. Richard Konig was engaged in a serious research program to determine the limits and practicality of utilizing acupuncture to deal with various illnesses and diseases. He talked cautiously about the possible benefits to be derived from intensive study of one of the oldest known forms of medical treatment."

A question was preying on my mind. Less than a month before the filming my father had been admitted to this very same UCLA hospital. Surgery revealed metastasized cancer, beyond treatment, fatal. I said goodbye to my dad with an irreparable sense of loss and I cursed human mortality. Like millions of others, I wondered why we couldn't solve the problem of a virus gone berserk.

"What about acupuncture, could it have helped save my father?"

"No," the doctor replied, "nothing indicates that acupuncture is a miracle-working tool. We've had some possible success with isolated forms of cancer but not anywhere near enough to justify holding out any hope for a cancer cure."

I began to ponder the process by which acupuncture was learned. Was it a gradual accretion of medical knowledge developed by the practice of medicine in the Orient? Or was it ordained by the knowledge of an existing life force brought to Earth by extraterrestrials? Was the halo—the aura, the glow—a part of our heritage from space?

The ten minutes were up. I pressed my thumb against the Kirlian plate and was startled by the appearance of the glow. Great tongues of flame leaped up from the perimeter. Hot, red points flickered on and off. I was feeling no after-effect of the stimulation, but the aura from my thumb clearly suggested the change that was taking place. I had witnessed directly an accurate picture of a life force produced in Kirlian Photography. All sorts of possibilities occurred to me. I wanted to know if emotion produced an aura. To demonstrate that it did, Dr. Moss called in two of our volunteers, Arlene and Fred. Dr. Moss asked if they would mind kissing passionately while we photographed their fingertips.

The kiss began, the lights went out, and as Dr. Moss viewed the Kirlian plate she began a running commentary on the interaction produced by the embrace.

At first Arlene seemed to be enjoying it a lot more than Fred, but as he relaxed the two auras began to reach for each other. As the passion of the volunteers grew the glow increased until, at the very center, between the fingertips, a red, hot burst of light blazed bright orange. We had literally watched them being "turned on." The lights came up then, and somewhat reluctantly Fred and Arlene ended their long kiss.

I suddenly realized that Kirlian Photography may give us a clue to the way ESP works. The interaction of the glow coming from the fingertips was unmistakable. The life force evident in the pictures exists in *all* living things. Is it possible that we are subconsciously sensitized to the auras of all forms of life? If so, can it be that we are connected to events that occur in distant places through a network of different living things, plants as well as animals? After all, what I had just seen was an electronic pulse that could instantly travel immense distances. I wanted to explore the idea further to verify the possibility that those premonitions of danger that twins experience when the one is in jeopardy in some distant place might be traceable to the biocosmic life force we all possess. Do psychics have the power to channel this energy? There were a dozen ideas tumbling through my mind.

Dr. Moss answered all of my questions noncommittally: "It's possible, but we still have a great deal to learn about what we are seeing."

By this time we were eager to see the final museum object, the mummy's hand. Placed before the Kirlian apparatus, we witnessed the extraordinary phenomenon of a four-thousand-year-old remnant of humanity still clinging to the fire of life.

Later, over coffee, we discussed long-range applications of Kirlian Photography.

"There may be some practical applications for this photography," said Dr. Moss. "In some preliminary work we're doing with rats, photographing their tails, cancerous rats show a different pattern than do healthy rats that do not have a tumor. We've experimented with perhaps three hundred rats, and generally we get this kind of cloudy effect from the cancerous rat, whereas we get the bright, brilliant, clear emanations from a healthy rat. Whether this will hold up over thousands of trials, which we will need, of course remains to be seen."

I then asked Dr. Moss if she felt that the Kirlian effect is a universal phenomenon—"universal" in an astronomic sense.

Dr. Moss found the prospect interesting. "We've had various inquiries in our lab from very strange sources, and one of the sources that has come to speak to us is

NASA. Their particular interest in this photography is very, very serious; they want to know if in outer space, when we get to Mars, when we get to Venus, we will be able to distinguish living materials from dead materials. In other words, is our universe aligned with other planets rather than this one? They're hoping that they will be able to take on board the Mars probe one of these devices so that they will be able—with television equipment—to look at micro-organisms that they might pick up, or anything that their instruments can pick up with probes, and photograph it to see if it luminesces the way we expect living organisms to light up with this technique. I would very much like to see the Mars probe take along a device like the Kirlian apparatus, and wouldn't it be fascinating if that was the clue that would tell us that there are other kinds of life in the universe?"

Is Kirlian Photography part of the outer space connection? We began with the idea that life is not unique to Earth, that it must be present on many of the other worlds in our galaxy, and that there is an underlying theme of immortality threaded through it.

Man too is part of that thread, and the more we examine the rhythms of nature that manipulate the connection, the more we appreciate the truth of John Donne's concept that no man is an island. Psychologists Dr. Marvin Karlins and Lewis Andrews note:

> Man is not just a clock within himself, he is a part of a much larger timepiece called the universe. His abilities, moods, and even thoughts are influenced by the ebb and flow of celestial mechanics: the slow spinning of Earth around its axis, the elliptical swing of the moon, the pulsating flares and electromagnetic energy from the sun. Our ancestors knew intuitively that man was a reflection of his environment. The ancient Greeks defined physical health as being in harmony with nature. (*Biofeedback* by Marvin Karlins and Lewis Andrews)

Nowhere is that desire to remain in harmony with nature more evident than in India, where among the freely wandering cattle I found starving people and incredible filth. I saw fakirs walking through coals, lying on nail beds, and performing equally astonishing feats that have long been put down by Western science as beneath their attention, unworthy of investigation. No longer. The ability of the Indian fakir to control visceral behavior—that is, his heart, lungs, blood, intestines, glands, and other internal organs—has become the focus of serious scientific study. The result has been the astonishing revolution we call biofeedback. Beyond the toys and rip-off items sold to the gullible as alpha-wave generators, and other biofeedback devices that have little if any value, is the increasing body of medical application being found for biofeedback.

If a man or woman can learn to increase or decrease his blood pressure, heart rate, respiration, and other visceral functions by biofeedback methods, then obviously such techniques could be used as a specific treatment for high or low blood pressure and a number of other disease states. Simply by exerting his own will man might be able to "cure" many of the diseases that deny him a chance at immortality.

In the face of medical tradition this idea is not merely heretical, it is preposterous; however, a number of major medical institutions, including Harvard, UCLA, and others, are now treating patients, or rather the patients are treating themselves, with the techniques of biofeedback.

Much of the new knowledge about biofeedback is the product of years of dogged research by a distinguished experimental psychologist, Dr. Neal Miller of Rockefeller University in New York. Miller had some radical notions about the human nervous system, which led him to explore the manner in which they were controlled. Actually there are two human nervous systems: the central nervous system, which governs our conscious, voluntary functions, and the autonomic nervous system, which regulates the body's unconscious, involuntary functions. The voluntary nervous system directly controls all of the skeletal muscles via the brain, spinal cord, and nerves. Every movement—from lifting a fifty-pound weight to wiggling the ears—is learned under the direction of the brain's conscious volition and is controlled by it.

The autonomic, or involuntary, nervous system services the glands and visceral organs of the body, usually through hormonal secretions regulated by the deep, primitive, unconscious regions of the brain. The name *autonomic* means, literally, "independent of brain and spinal cord." It has always been believed that this system and the organs it serves is the body's own mysterious business, outside the control of consciousness.

In classic psychological training an animal or human learns through trial and error and gets a reward when he does what the experimenter deems correct. This process, involving the brain and muscles and affording enormous possibilities for variety, has been assumed to be the exclusive domain of the voluntary nervous system.

Only in unusual instances, such as Pavlov's famous dog experiment, was the autonomic nervous system thought to be involved. Pavlov's method was simple. To condition a dog he would ring a bell just before feeding time. Eventually the dog learned to salivate at the sound of the bell, whether or not there was any food. This type of conditioning was considered quite involuntary; the dog, once conditioned, simply could not stop himself from salivating.

In apparent contradiction of this separation between the two nervous systems, yogis have for centuries been demonstrating remarkable abilities that control their heart and respiration rates. Generally it was thought that deception was involved; it was assumed that the yogis, by some clever trick, were using their skeletal muscles to produce an effect on the heart or lungs.

Dr. Miller was far from convinced that there had to be two different types of learning, one to go with each nervous system. It seemed inefficient and illogical. "I've always been impressed with the similarities rather than the differences between classic conditioning and instrumental learning," he explained. "That is, the laws they follow are more alike than different. This led me to challenge the idea that the autonomic nervous system was beyond voluntary control."

The problem was to devise an experiment to demonstrate the similarity without having the animal cheat. The method finally adopted involved paralyzing with curare the muscles of ten rats, so that they couldn't cheat by using their bodies in any physical way, and then offering them a special reward for learning. The reward was ESB—electrical stimulation of the brain's pleasure centers—a reward that has proved more attractive to laboratory animals than eating, drinking, sex, or anything else.

The brain of the rat has been thoroughly mapped, and Miller knew precisely where to place his electrodes. But there was a major problem in keeping the rats alive after they had been given curare; the drug paralyzes all of the skeletal muscles, including the ones in the rib cage, needed for normal breathing. In large animals the scientist simply punches a hole in the windpipe so that air can be automatically pumped in and out by a respirator. Laboratory rats are small and their windpipes demand delicate surgery—too delicate, in fact, for experimental purposes. The solution was to use a small balloon as a face mask for the rat. The narrow mouthpiece used to inflate the balloon was cut off and slipped over the rat's snout. The other end was cemented to a hollow cork through which a tube was connected to a pump respirator.

To teach the rats to increase their heart rate Dr. Miller set up a timing device that counted heartbeats. Every time the heart rate exceeded the normal four hundred a minute he sent a mild electric jolt to the rat's brain's pleasure center. Other animals were given a safe jolt whenever their heart rates slowed.

The rats performed brilliantly, learning to raise or lower their heart rates by five percent. This was a remarkable amount since the heart rates of rats under curare are extremely regular. In later experiments the changes reached up to 530 beats a minute or down to 230. In addition, after only forty-five minutes of training the rats had learned their lessons so well that they remembered how to do it after three months' vacation.

Encouraged by this performance, Dr. Miller turned

to other organs of the rat's body. Soon the lab animals began to master an entire repertoire of internal controls. They could increase or decrease the rate of urine formation, raise or lower the amount of blood flowing to the stomach walls or to the tail, boost or limit the amount of gastric secretions, and even raise or lower blood pressure.

It became obvious that if a rat was capable of exerting such control, a man certainly should be. It's just like learning to ice skate, Dr. Miller thought. "You may have some idea of what you're doing right and can give yourself direct commands to do it, but a lot of it is just automatic. You do this, you move along better. You do that, and you fall down.

"If you get somebody on ice skates and try to tell him exactly how to do it, you won't succeed very well. A lot of our learning is automatic this way. I think that this is exactly what visceral learning is, although we may discover more about it as we work with people."

The studies have been going on in a clinical environment for five years now. Patients at New York Hospital, Baltimore City Hospital, UCLA Medical Center, Harvard, and elsewhere are controlling their blood pressures, heart rates, and respiration rates through the visceral-control techniques of biofeedback. The secret is to know what the rate is—thus, blood pressure, for example, is monitored and when the patient has succeeded in lowering it to any measurable extent he is notified by a tone. Most patients have no idea how they achieve the desired effect, but once they have mastered the technique they are, in effect, using their own life forces to treat the disease that threatens their lives.

Other energy forces are generated all around us, on Earth and in space. Radiation is but one example of the background energy that permeates the universe. Radio signals given off by distant stars have been traveling through space since the universe began; X-rays and cosmic rays rattle through the void like the balls of some cosmic pachinko game, scarcely slowed by their passage through Earth and other planets. With this universal phenomenon in mind, Dr. Luis W. Alvarez, a Nobel Prize-winning physicist from the University of

California, went to Egypt in 1966 in hopes of finding hidden chambers within the pyramids of Giza.

Alvarez set up cosmic-ray detection in the chamber beneath a pyramid built by Cheop's son, Khafre. By recording the direction and speed of the cosmic rays as they penetrated the stonework from space and feeding the readings through a computer, an X-ray picture of the pyramid's interior was formed. No hidden chambers were found before the 1967 war halted the work, but other experiments have shown that something happens to cosmic rays when they penetrate the walls of a pyramid.

Thirty years before Alvarez set up his cosmic-ray detectors a Frenchman named Bovis began exploring the pyramids. In the King's Chamber of the Great Pyramid he found a garbage can stuffed with small dead animals. There were dogs, cats, rats, and mice who, the guide explained, were constantly wandering into the pyramid and losing their way in the vast structure. Eventually they would starve to death, be picked up by the guides, and dropped into the garbage can. When the can was filled its contents would be buried in the sand outside the pyramid. The process had been going on for thousands of years.

Bovis noticed something quite strange about the can: it did not smell. The dead bodies, which obviously had been collected over a period of months, had not begun to decay and thus did not give off the foul odor of putrefaction. Bovis looked more closely and picked up one of the dead animals. It had been perfectly preserved, mummified after it had starved to death inside the pyramid.

Asking both the local guides and the experts at the Cairo Museum, Bovis could get no logical explanation for the strange phenomenon. Why should the animals be mummified simply because they had died inside the pyramid? What force had accomplished this remarkable preservation effect? It was not simply the process of desiccation, because the pyramid interiors trapped what little moisture there was and consequently were much more humid than the surrounding desert.

Upon his return to Paris, Bovis built a plywood

pyramid with a three-foot base. Inside it he placed a
dead cat. A week later the cat was completely mummified. He was elated with the result and began a series of
experiments, with appropriate controls. Bits of food
that spoiled readily, such as eggs, liver, brain, and
hamburger, were placed inside the pyramid. The same
foods were placed on plates outside the structure. The
foods inside the pyramid remained moist and edible for
weeks. After only a few days, however, the controls
smelled so badly that they had to be thrown out.

Bovis published his startling results but few people
took him seriously. Most of the curiosity came from
scientists living behind the Iron Curtain, but the best-
known investigator in the United States is, of course,
Dr. Patrick Flanagan.

In his latest work Dr. Flanagan has uncovered the
possibility of applying pyramid energy toward a study
of immortality. "We've had cells taken from the human
body," Dr. Flanagan told me, "live in a nutrient solution
inside a pyramid shape nine times their normal life
span."

I was drawn back to Dr. Hayflick's experimental
work on human fibroblasts. He had found fifty population doublings to be the limit of cellular life. Other researchers had simply added vitamin E to the nutrient
solution and more than doubled the life span of the
cultures. Now cosmic rays trapped inside the walls of a
pyramid had succeeded in extending that life span nine
times. The links of the theory were coming together.
Immortality and outer space seem inextricably connected by a thread that is woven throughout a universe
that teems with life.

13

◆◆ ◆◆ ◆◆

Afterlife: The Journey to The Heavens

The ruin was silhouetted against a leaden, prehurricane sky. The dome was crumbling; time had hammered away at chunks of masonry, breaking the gracefully arched line of what once had been an astronomical observatory. Standing on the veranda of my room in a modern tourist hotel located in amid the ancient Mayan citadel of Chichen Itza, I could not take my eyes away from the ancient structure. If the brickwork was spruced up and the backdrop changed it could have been mistaken for the observatory at Mount Palomar. The building, Mayan in origin, was constructed probably about seven hundred years ago, yet there was the modern-looking dome, the slotted roof, and the observation balcony. It was uncanny, but then I realized that many past civilizations had been obsessed with the heavens. I was reminded of the observatory at Lahore, India; almost exactly half a world away, the Indian observatory stood on the same latitudinal line as Chichen Itza. Both the Indian and the Mayan civilizations had accumulated vast libraries of knowledge about the sky and the space beyond. In the *Veda,* the spoken encyclopedia of eastern India, space travel was an accepted fact. The Mayas recorded planetary movements in the solar system and other astronomical events that could not have been witnessed by the naked eye, yet as far as we know they had no telescopes. Where did they learn that a year on Venus was 584 days long? Our modern computers placed the Venusian year at 583.82 days.

149

They predicted the Martian year with equal accuracy. Nothing I found in the observatory helped answer the question. Almost five hundred years of defacement had stripped all the artifacts of possible value, leaving only a graffiti record of little worth.

Pathetically little remained of the vast body of work which summarized the knowledge of the Mayas. Scholars had only three documents to study as they searched for information about this strange Central American civilization. To draw any conclusions from this slim skein of data would be equal to analyzing American society based on a single verse of the "Star Spangled Banner."

Ruins still exist, and perhaps their study will yield clues. For me, the destroyed citadels heightened the mystery of the Mayas. Settlements of surprisingly sophisticated engineering and architectural design exist on the Yucatan Peninsula and in Central Mexico. Some were within a hundred miles of one another. No roads were built to connect them, yet the Mayas were expert at building roads. In one settlement a wide boulevard had been constructed across a two-mile stretch of marshland. If they did not build roads, what mode of transport carried commerce between the citadels?

Perhaps the answer lay in Palanque, one of the oldest Mayan cities. A complex of pyramids and temples were centered around one of the most remarkable tombs ever constructed. Thousands of stone blocks were carved from nearby mountains and moved to the ceremonial center of Palanque. Mounted on six huge slabs was a massive stone sarcophagus, its interior hollowed out in the shape of a giant womb. It weighs twenty-five tons. Above the sarcophagus a stepped pyramid was built. A second pyramid was constructed on top of that, and finally above all there soared a temple. Inside the temple, I followed an inner staircase that plunged downward through the pyramids to the burial chamber.

I eased my way down the steep stone steps to stand before the tomb of Halach Uinic, a Mayan title that means "The True Man." At one time The True Man was the ruler of Palanque and at his death he was interred here, in this incredible stone tomb that offered an even more astonishing story. Covering the sarcophagus was a heavy granite slab etched with hieroglyphs, but in the center was a figure of a man. I had found on the tomb of a dead man a picture of his undeniable belief in immortality. Death was left behind as he himself departed Earth for a journey into space. My surmise that his ultimate destination was outer space seemed to be borne out by the glyphs that surround the figure in the capsule. They provide dates beginning with his birth, on a day known as 8 Ahau on the ritual calendar, and his death, which is inscribed on both the ritual and the popular calendar.

The popular calendar marks the solar year and is as accurate—within seventeen seconds—as our own calendar. It shows that The True Man was born in the year 655 A.D. and that he died on December 19, 694. But the ritual calendar, called the Tzolkin, is quite different. Composed of thirteen months of twenty days each, it added up to a year of 260 solar days. Such a calendar was useless to a primitive agricultural people. It could not keep track of the seasons, could not mark the times of planting and harvest, and could not be used in astrological computations. Why then did the Mayan priests keep not only a solar calendar that tracked Earth's days with remarkable accuracy, but a calendar that obviously did not mark the passage of time on Earth?

The answer appeared to lie in outer space. The Tzolkin calendar of the Mayas probably marked the yearly passage of a planet other than Earth about a star that is not our sun. Was this the destination of The True Man of Palanque, or does the tomb merely represent a desire on the part of all men to reach the stars in their search for immortality?

In posing questions about the Mayas we had inevitably come upon dead ends, but all of the signposts that led us there contained tantalizing hints of space travel and immortality. The number system of the Mayas, for example, is designed to cope with the immensities of space flight. Our own present-day astronomers have developed numerical concepts to deal with the vastness of space. The distance between stars, for example, is measured in light-years; the space between galaxies is often measured in parsecs, a unit composed of 3.26 light-years.

Similarly, the Mayas devised units that incorporated unwieldy numbers into simple terms. A *kinchiltun,* for example, was equal to 57,600,000 days, an *alautun* to 23,040,000,000 days, or 63,123,000 years. Of what possible use could simple farmers and hunters make of such mathematical units? The answer, of course, is none. They would be of absolutely no use to a people concerned only with the cut-and-burn agriculture practiced in pre-Columbian America. Obviously the Mayas were more than simple farmers. They were, in fact, a people obsessed with time.

Such enormous numbers are used not only to measure distances in space but time as well. For distance is a function of time, and time can be expressed in many ways. Were the Mayas measuring the distance to a planet somewhere in outer space, a planet they had left millenia before arriving on Earth? Or did the Mayas require such great numbers to tick off the passing of the years that mark a life that reaches out toward immortality?

The keepers of Mayan numbers, the men who possessed the so-called secret language of the Mayas, were priests. At least we have given the name "priests" to the most important decision makers in the kingdom. I noted earlier that some experts on the Mayan culture believe that all advancements were based on religious fervor, so it is natural for modern writers to apply the title "priests."

One account drawn from a surviving Mayan text indicates that an important religious functionary was charged with the role of communication with the gods and then rendering decisions to the public at large. The assumption has been made that he called upon some form of mystical vision to fulfill his duty. When I read the account I wondered whether an alternative explanation was some form of man-made communication device from which he received instructions. Such a radio probably would not have been beyond the grasp of the Mayas.

There was one other strange and unexplainable

mystery about the Mayas that seems to link them with outer space and the concept of immortality. Genetically, the Mayas were unlike any other human race. Isolation of their gene pool might account for part of that difference, but there is one physical trait that was so outstanding, so obvious, that it forever set them apart from all other human beings. The Mayas are short and stocky, with, insofar as we can tell, absolutely no variation. There was absolutely no record either pictured or in a readable glyph of a tall Maya. No one Maya was more than an inch or two taller than any other. In most races there are occasional variations, such as the seven-footer in a population that averages a height of five feet 9 inches.

There was one other characteristic associated only with the Mayas—their remarkable sloping foreheads. This was a genetic trait. To maintain their physical uniqueness the Mayas accentuated it by tightly binding a board across every baby's head. In this way the sharply sloping forehead would be defined even more clearly.

The vast relief portraits of the Mayas called to mind a remark Dr. Brothers had made during her discussion of cloning. In experiments with the Axlotal she pointed out that the cloned lizards acquired a genetic trait that set them apart from normally born animals. The bodies of the cloned lizards were always stumpier than the normally reproduced Axlotals. The Axlotals at the University of Indiana were cloned for experimental purposes. The goal was to learn more about the way cells differentiate and genes express themselves in the dividing egg. Men might be cloned for some future space mission that might take them light-years beyond Earth. So, too, might an arriving spacecraft have carried its colonists to Earth as clones, each possessed of the identical genetic blueprint to be executed when the target planet was reached.

Similar journeys through space and away from death were the goal of many ancient cultures. In fact, all men hoped to make a journey to the stars when death temporarily ended their life on Earth. The idea was firmly rooted in the minds of ancient man.

Socrates, just before taking the hemlock, says: "There comes to mind an ancient doctrine which affirms that the souls of men after death go from hence into the other world and returning hither are born again from the dead." (*Plato's Dialogue of the Immortality of the Soul.*)

That doctrine, already ancient in the fifth century B.C. when Socrates was brought to trial by the frightened Greeks of Athens, is one we cling to even today. The hope of life after death is, according to Freud, "the oldest, strongest, and most insistent wish of mankind. In his unconscious," he wrote, "every one of us is convinced of his own immortality." (*Immortalist* by Alan Harrington)

In the death rituals of the Egyptians and other great civilizations I found a determined effort to lay claim to immortality. Death becomes not an end but a beginning that launches a journey to the stars. In the myths of many cultures around the world, the phoenix was the symbol of life ending and then rising again from the ashes of the pyre. The phoenix was a giant bird of great beauty, sleek and slender, and when it died—after a life that lasted from five hundred to six hundred years—it burned itself on a pyre and then rose from the ashes in the freshness of youth to live through another cycle of years.

The legend of the phoenix is so widespread that it was reported by the ancient Irish, who gave it a life span of at least six hundred years before its resurrection ritual. The Japanese possessed a myth of the phoenix called Kirin: the Turks called their phoenix Kerkes and it lived to a thousand years old. Herodotus, that ubiquitous traveler of the ancient world, noted that the phoenix is one of the sacred birds reproduced in Egyptian hieroglyphics. The Persians knew of the phoenix as the *Sigmorgh* and saw in its fiery end and rebirth the revival and renewal not only of man but of Earth.

The ancient Hebrews, too, had a phoenix in their desert-hardened folklore. "The Rabbis speak of an enormous Bird, sometimes standing on the earth and sometimes walking in the ocean while its head props the sky," wrote Dr. E. V. H. Kenealy in *The Book of God: The Apocalypse of Adam-Oannes*.

Suppose we read "rocket" for "phoenix"; we would then have a vehicle that would carry the dead into the sky on a blaze of flame, to be reborn in the stars.

Rebirth, resurrection, is the obverse side of the immortality coin. Death certainly plays a role in the complex ecology of a life-support system as large as Earth. Death invariably provided the means for renewal of life in future generations of all living things. Is man the individual also renewed?

There was a vast body of belief and evidence that said he is. The ancient Egyptians, of course, demonstrated their total belief in the concept of immortality through resurrection in their mummification procedure and in the words of their priests. I have noted how passionately the Egyptians believed in reincarnation. Egyptologist Dr. Margaret Murray, who wrote *The Splendor That Was Egypt*, underlined the thought:

> Herodotus is very definite on this subject and his statement is fully borne out by the Egyptian evidence. . . . The ka-names of the first two kings of the Twentieth Dynasty show this belief clearly; Amonemhat I's name was "He Who Repeats Births," and Senusert I's name was "He Whose Births of Births," and it was by this epithet that he was addressed by the god Amon at Karnak.

From the Nile delta to the towering mountains of Tibet is a journey halfway across the world and from sea level to the roof of the world. But here, in the breath-snatching altitude of the Himalayas, lives the reincarnation of the Tibetian god known as Chenrezi. The Tibetans believe that their gods come down to Earth from space and enter the bodies of certain men who are known as incarnation lamas. Chenrezi, the most important god, enters the body of the greatest incarnation lama—the Dalai Lama. When the Dalai Lama dies his spirit enters a Tibetan child and Chenrezi is reborn. In 1933 the thirteenth Dalai Lama died, and the

Tibetans were faced with the urgent problem of finding his reincarnation in a little child.

The burden of proof was tremendous, for a child was expected to remember and select the personal belongings of the dead Dalai Lama, to bear a physical relationship to him, and to demonstrate a concept of the involved Tibetan theology. A number of mystic signs guided the lamas to the child who was supposed to be the reincarnation of Chenrezi. He was called Lhamo Tondrup and had been born to a peasant family in the village of Amdo two years after the thirteenth Dalai Lama had died. The search party of lamas brought the young boy the drum, rosary, and walking stick of the dead Dalai Lama. They also carried exact duplicates of those objects, which the dead Dalai Lama had never touched. The two sets of possessions were placed on the floor of the cottage and the boy was told to keep the ones he picked.

In his biography of the fourteenth Dalai Lama, Lowell Thomas, Jr., described the scene as the seeking priests and the awed parents looked on:

Only a Tibetan can feel to the full the tension of that moment. The child's parents watched breathlessly, overwhelmed with the idea that their son might turn out to be the incarnation of the great god Chenrezi. The officials and lamas too were breathless. The fate of Tibet hung in the balance. The nation would be in jeopardy until they could formally announce that the god had returned to Earth. The Lamaist religion would be without its most important lama until the monks in the monasteries could be assured that the Dalai Lama was back in the Potala. The search had been on for two years. Should this child fail in spite of all the omens, there would be nothing to do except to go on looking and there was no assurance how long this interim period would be. They knew the Dalai Lama was somewhere—but where? Here, perhaps? In this house?

The tension eased considerably when the four-year-old selected the objects that had belonged to the Dalai

Lama. He picked up each one, hugging them to his chest as if they were long-lost toys.

Then the searchers questioned the boy about Lamaist theology. "Since the Dalai Lama is the principal theologian of Tibet, as the reincarnation of the great god should be, he must reveal even in infancy the ability to think truthfully about religion," noted Lowell Thomas, Jr. And so questions about the transmigration of souls, reincarnation, immortality, the nature of the gods, the duties of the Dalai Lama, and so on were asked by the priests. The answers given by the child were deemed correct.

The physical test removed any doubts the searchers may have had. Luck might have played a role in the child's selection of the dead lama's possessions and he might have been coached on his answers to the questions on theology. But the god Chenrezi was supposed to have had four arms. His reincarnations have always in the past had the vestigial traces of an extra pair of arms—definite marks on the shoulders where Chenrezi's arms had been joined to his body.

The questing lamas removed the boy's robe. There, on his shoulders, were the unmistakable marks. The space god Chenrezi had once more descended to Earth, reincarnated in a four-year-old boy named Lhamo Tondrup.

The Dalai Lama is merely the most famous and most carefully documented account, but there are literally thousands of other reports of reincarnation. They all echo the idea that immortality in one form or another is attainable.

For the most part reincarnation as a form of immortality is an Eastern idea which has only recently begun to penetrate the mainstream of modern Western thought. The idea that immortality is possible is the theme of a number of recent books and is becoming an important philosophical idea in Western intellectual circles. Philosopher Alan Harrington summed it up:

Death is an imposition on the human race and no longer acceptable. Man has all but lost his ability to accommodate himself to personal extinction; he must now proceed physically to overcome it. In short, to kill death; to put an end to his own mortality as a certain consequence of being born. (*Immortalist* by Alan Harrington)

Just how successful we are in killing death, in grasping our own immortality, depends upon learning the secrets that lie in outer space. Space is the birthplace not only of man but of all life. In space death is banished and only the seeds of life are propagated. So strong has this idea become that it has engendered a number of probes designed to reach out to those other civilizations in space across the void of time and distance where the only common denominator is life.

On Saturday, November 16, 1974, a message was beamed from the giant radio antenna at Arecibo, Puerto Rico, toward a distant cluster of stars known as Messier 13, at the edge of the Milky Way. There are more than 300,000 stars in the Messier 13 cluster, and some of them are thought to have planets similar to Earth. The message beamed at them is traveling at 186,000 miles per second, the speed of light, and will take twenty-four thousand years to arrive. It can be converted into a television picture which will explain to the watchers that elsewhere in the galaxy is a planet called Earth, which is dominated by a species called Homo sapiens, whose genetic construction is mediated by the chemical molecule known as deoxyribonucleic acid—DNA. The message contains other information as well, including a request for a reply.

When I examined the "message" I had an eerie feeling that I had seen it before. And I had, many times, in many places on Earth. I had seen it at Toro Muerto in the Andes, scratched on a rock fourteen thousand years ago. It was so simple that it could have been a child's drawing. I immediately made the assumption that it was a primitive man's celebration or recording of a crucial event. Why else would he have taken the trouble to carve it in stone? On the rock were the stick figures of two men, arms upraised, saluting a round disc held upright on four legs. It was a crude drawing of some form of space vehicle not unlike our lunar landing module.

Launched from a mother ship orbiting the planet, the lander might have carried a party of explorers to probe the environment of Earth. When I saw the carving I paid little attention to another symbol placed about six inches from the capsule. I had seen the same figure often in so-called primitive drawings. It was a jagged spiral reaching upward, which is the form of a DNA molecule. When I looked at the 1974 signal of our existence to the universe I was reminded of Toro Muerto and the jagged spiral that represented the DNA molecule. The same drawing was repeated on dozens of boulders. On some there was an extra added attraction. Staring out was a face represented by a bull's-eye pattern of circles. At the top of the head were two lines extending upward, then turning at opposite ninety-degree angles. At the tip of the projecting lines were two orbs that I fancied were the antenna of a space helmet. And perhaps they were. If we sent a cryptic message to outer space, encompassing our essence in a few signs and mathematical symbols, was it possible that some arriving explorer left his own very clear imprint on the Toro Muerto plain? It was the representation of the DNA molecule that set off the question.

We have a handful of physical "laws" that are recognized by scientists. These laws are valid only if they operate in exactly the same manner under all conditions. Once found, the laws become the building blocks of a broad range of scientific endeavors. The operation of the DNA molecule is in all cases primary to the creation of life. We have only recently discovered DNA's existence, learned its function, and understood its universal application to known life forms. Our message to Messier 13 included the fact that we are the product of DNA construction. Since we know no other basis for mediating life, we have assumed that Earth's singular characteristic is truly universal. I feel that there is reason to be awed by the existence of that DNA message in hundreds of simple drawings etched on open rock faces and cave walls. Perhaps they are greetings left behind for us in terms which the visitors thought we might be able to understand.

The modern message to space presumed that the

progress of civilization and the development of technology of some distant planet have paralleled our own. There were reasons to believe that this premise was correct. We may assume that in environments similar to ours the adaptive process of evolution will operate in the same way it has on Earth. It has been estimated that in the universe there are at least fifty thousand planets (and that is a very conservative guess) with environments matching Earth's. There may be as many as one million such planets. How might our rudimentary characterization of Earth be accepted in space by a society more highly advanced than ours? In the past century we have made remarkable progress toward the realization of many dreams. We have applied our understanding to the construction of a world shaped by our immediate needs and desires. No wish is as fondly held as immortality. In one form or another, we have found that that hope may be realizable, and if we can achieve immortality we will have the power to finally weld the outer space connection to our own existence. We will be here to receive the return message from Messier 13 fifty thousand years from now. We will possess the ability to travel to other worlds, to join a community of worlds already in deep communication with one another.

My one uneasy feeling as I traveled and filmed was that the first gestures of communication with other planets have already occurred, that the quantum leaps of civilization in the past were made by those who had been affected by the outer space connection. I wondered finally if we ourselves were not the product of seeds left here to germinate by visitors in the distant past.

Epilogue

I had been working for almost three years. I had traveled hundreds of thousands of miles. I had talked to more than four hundred people, each an expert in a specialized field. Time and time again during the course of discussion a number of questions popped up, and I wanted to set down the answers to those questions as I prepared to sum up my findings.

One inevitable query was, "What's all this for?" I measured out my answer very carefully because I never knew what response could be forthcoming. Each time I had the feeling that I was dropping a live hand grenade. My reply went something like this: "I'm trying to find evidence that there is a direct connection between us and outer space." And then I waited. On some occasions my statement brought wrathful thunder. "You're going to use this interview in a cock-and-bull story like that?" This rhetorical posture often was followed by a determined, "Not on your sweet life!"

I explained that I would treat the information I received in exactly the context from which it came. I promised not to distort the individual's efforts, not to make it appear as if the researcher fully supported my point of view. On occasion I found interested and sympathetic response, but most of the experts were highly skeptical, if not downright antagonistic. "Don't associate me with *that* idea," was a frequent comment.

I hope I have not violated that order. If I have done so in the course of reporting, then I would like to correct the impression. The research I have noted, the experiments I have reported, were not intended to prove an outer space connection. The conclusions are mine, based on what I saw of the work of others.

There were other reactions to my investigation. At

times I was waved aside with a skeptical, "Oh, you're doing that von Daniken stuff." Yes, I was. I owe a debt to Eric von Daniken. When I became involved in the film based on his book *Chariots of the Gods?* my curiosity was piqued and I began my own journey into the past. I have taken a separate course in search of the possibility that life on Earth has been influenced by extraterrestrials. Von Daniken's subsequent explorations have followed a path different from mine. Inevitably we will disagree, but that only makes our ventures more interesting.

I have encountered many other generalists in pursuit of answers to old mysteries, the inexplicable events of the past. I have shared ideas and experiences with them. As a group they possess inquisitive and investigative minds and are unwilling to take any fact for granted just because "it has been written." With traditionalists my arguments never centered on facts that were reported, but on the basic premise which the information supported.

I should point out that once the cameras stopped and the recorders were turned off, the conversations with even the most diehard opponents of the basic thesis became much more gentle. Off the record, men and women who pursued research careers in varied disciplines were willing to join in considered speculation about the concept of an outer space connection. I have found their comments thought-provoking and sometimes more helpful than any part of the direct interview. From time to time I have cited their comments as those of unnamed experts mainly because they wished to remain anonymous.

There were moments of great clarity inspired by their comments. Often one bit of information cracked open a new area of investigation. Dr. Marc Lappe had mentioned to me a study of the walled-off gene. For all I knew at that moment, he might have been talking about the chef at New York's Waldorf Astoria Hotel. But as he explained the portent of the idea—that there are time capsules in us that may go off at critical junctures—I knew I had a fruitful course of research to pursue. The key phrase was "the walled-off gene."

The walled-off-gene principle is a simple one. I have already described the process by which the genetic blueprint sets the course of our lives. I had always assumed that every gene passed on to us by our parents played a role, whether dominant or recessive. The suggestion of a genetically transferable characteristic being walled off from utilization was startling. Is it possible that we carry in our cells for generation after countless generation information that is waiting only for the proper signal before emerging? And what would that signal be? When I followed the theory that the intent of man's nature is survival and all the mechanisms of his body were designed to furnish the means for survival and procreation (the one form of immortality we *know* exists), then I found a place for the walled-off gene. The constant battering of an environment weighted against survival may be the signal for the walled-off gene to emerge. We know that mutation exists and think of it as an aberration of form. When the so-called mutation provides a characteristic that enables the species to survive in a new form we call it a beneficial mutation. Much of the modern theory of evolution leans on the appearance of the mutant as a better-equipped unit.

I moved a step further with the concept. I made reference earlier in the book to the possibility that there exists a basic model of man. It was a thought inspired by an Egyptian text that told of starting a new life with every body part derived from a god. The description was a somewhat mystical rendering of a possible truth. It would be accurate if there were a "basic model" containing a genetic blueprint of a generalized yet highly sophisticated form of life. For ease of description I likened it to the Model T Ford. In all respects the model was functional. A series of accessories, a kind of broad scale contingency plan, was simultaneously drawn to account for survival factors in varying environments. It was something like a list we would make of supplies needed on a camping trip. The Model T, the basic model, was then seeded into the universe. Under any circumstances it was a working model. Cloned from a central seed, it seems likely that it was manufactured on an assembly-line basis. The customizing of the form was then left to the forces that surrounded the individual model when it reached the "field." Was it too farfetched, I wondered, to carry the idea still further, and speculate that the working models were placed on Earth in our past? Would the "arrival" then begin to account for the mysterious centers of civilization that flourished tens of thousands of generations ago? Does a patrol return from time to time to check the progress of the human Model T and see how it has fared?

I thought of the places I had been where civilization had sprouted unaccountably, and I focused in particular on the Mayas. They had an infinite view of time, in fact were obsessed with it. They were a strange people with marked physical characteristics and a record of extraordinary and virtually incomprehensible achievements.

One item of Mayan folklore ran through my mind. It was noted that somehow every five thousand years a civilization ends and a new one begins. What was the meaning of that precise measurement? Did it relate to the replacement of the basic models? Did something occur in the basic model's genetic refinements that was degenerative in effect and demanded the release of new basic models to alter the stock? Is that why the Mayas carefully measured the beginning and end of each cycle? In fact, they marked the very date when the current cycle will end. The cycle began in 3113 B.C.; it will close in the year 2011 A.D. And the date? December 24. That's right, Christmas Eve, 2011 A.D.

Welcome to the outer space connection?

Bibliography

Asimov, Isaac. *Guide to the Bible,* Volumes I and II. New York: Doubleday, 1968.

Basham, A. L. *The Wonder That Was India.* New York: Grove Press, 1959.

Bloch, Raymond. *The Etruscans.* London: Thames and Hudson, 1961.

Blum, Ralph and Judy. *Beyond Earth: Man's Contact With UFOs.* New York: Bantam, 1974.

Brugsch, H. *Zwei Pyramiden Mit Im Schriften Aus Ben Zeiten Der VI Dynastie.* AEG Zeit, 1881.

Budge, E. A. Wallis. *The Egyptian Book of the Dead.* New York: Dover Publications, 1967.

————. *The Mummy.* New York: Collier Books, 1972.

Campbell, Joseph. *Masks of God: Occidental Mythology.* New York: Viking Press, 1964.

Ceram, C. W. *Gods, Graves and Scholars.* New York: Alfred Knopf, 1967; Bantam Books, 1972.

Claiborne, Robert and Samuel Goudsmit. *Time.* New York: Time-Life Books, 1966.

Coe, Michael. *The Maya.* London: Thames and Hudson, 1966.

Coedes, George. *Angkor.* Hong Kong: Oxford University Press, 1963.

Collis, Marcel. *Cortes and Montezuma.* London: Faber and Faber, 1963.

de Camp, Sprague. *Ancient Engineers.* Cambridge: M.I.T. Press, 1970.

DeRop, Robert. *Men Against Age.* New York: St. Martin's Press.

Edwards, I. E. S. *The Pyramids of Egypt.* Baltimore: Penguin, 1961.

Eliade, Marcea. *Shamanism.* Princeton: Princeton University Press, 1964.

Ettinger, Robert. *Man Into Superman.* New York: St. Martin's Press, 1972.

————. *The Prospect of Immortality.*

Flanagan, G. Pat. *Pyramid Power.* California: Pyramid Publishers, 1974.

Frazur, Sir James. *The Belief in Immortality,* Volumes I and II. London: Macmillan and Co., 1913.

Gaster, Theodor. *Myth, Legend and Custom in the Old Testament.* New York: Harper and Row, 1969.

Gallup, George and Evan Hill. *Secrets of Long Life.* New York: Bernard Geis.

Harrington, Alan. *Immortalist.* New York: Avon, 1970.

Harris, James and Kent Weeks. *X-Raying the Pharaohs.* New York: Scribners, 1973.

Hapgood, Charles. *Maps of the Ancient Sea Kings.* Radnor, Pa.: Chilton Books, 1966.

Hawkes, Jacquetta and Bernard Bothmer. *Pharaohs of Egypt.* New York. Harper and Row, 1954.

Hawkes, Jaquetta. *The First Great Civilizations.* New York: Knopf, 1973.

Hawkins, Gerald. *Beyond Stonehenge.* New York: Harper and Row, 1973.

Herodotus. *History of Herodotus.* New York: AMS Press, 1924.

Homet, Marcel. *Sons of the Sun.* London: Neville Spearman, 1963.

Irwin, Constance. *Fair Gods and Stone Faces.* New York: St. Martin's Press, 1963.

Karlins, Marvin and Lewis Andrews. *Biofeedback.* New York: Lippincott, 1973.

Keller, Werner. *The Bible as History,* translated by William Neil. New York: William Morrow, 1956; Bantam Books, 1974.

Kenealy, E. V. H. *The Book of God: The Apocalypse of Adam-Oannes.*

Kolosimo, Peter. *Timeless Earth.* New York: University Books, 1974; Bantam Books, 1975.

Lockyer, Norman. *The Dawn of Astronomy.* Cambridge: M.I.T. Press, 1964.

Margotta, Roberto. *Story of Medicine.* Golden Press, 1967.

McWhirter, Norris and Ross. *Guinness Book of World Records.* New York: Bantam Books, 1975.

Mendelssohn, Kurt. *The Riddle of the Pyramids.* New York: Praeger, 1974.

Morris, John D. *Adventure on Ararat*. San Diego: Creation Research, 1973.

Murray, Margaret. *The Splendor That Was Egypt*. New York: Praeger, 1973.

Neugebauer, Otto. *The Exact Sciences in Antiquity*. Providence: Brown University Press, 1957.

Prehoda. *Extended Youth*. New York: Putnam.

Santillana, Georgio and Heartha von Dechand. *Hamlet's Mill*. Boston: Gambit, 1969.

Schure, Edoard. *From Sphinx to Christ: An Occult History*. New York: Rudolf Steiner Publications, 1970.

Stephens, John. *Incidents of Travel in Central America: Chiapas and Yucatan*, Volumes I and II. New York: Dover Publications, 1969.

Thompson, John Eric. *The Rise and Fall of Mayan Civilization*. Norman: University of Oklahoma Press, 1966.

Thompson, William Irwin. *At the Edge of History*. New York: Harper and Row, 1971.

————. *Passages About Earth*. New York: Harper and Row, 1974.

Tompkins, Peter. *The Secrets of the Great Pyramid*. New York: Harper and Row, 1971.

Umland, Eric and Craig. *Mystery of the Ancients: Early Spacemen and the Mayas*. New York: Walker, 1974.

Velikovsky, Immanuel. *Worlds in Collision*. New York: Doubleday, 1950.

von Daniken, Eric. *Chariots of the Gods?* New York: Putnam, 1970; Bantam Books, 1971.

Warshofsky, Fred. *The Rebuilt Man*. New York: Crowell.

————. *The Control of Life*. New York: Viking Press, 1969.

Anonymous. *The Egyptian Book of the Dead*, translated by E. A. Wallis Budge. London: Routlidge and Kegan Paul Ltd., 1960.

Anonymous. *The Epic of Gilgamesh*, translated by N. K. Sandars. New York: Penguin Books.

Anonymous. *The Tibetan Book of the Dead*, translated by W. Y. Evans-Wentz. New York: Oxford University Press, 1957.

PERIODICALS AND PAMPHLETS:

Baity, Elizabeth Chesley. "Archaeoastronomy and Ethnoastronomy." *Current Anthropology*, October 1973.

Eddy, John A. "Astronomical Alignment of the Big Horn Medicine Wheel." *Science,* June 7, 1974.

Ferris, Paul. "The Fountain of Youth Updated." *The New York Times* Magazine, December 2, 1973.

Gaylin, Willard. "We Have the Awful Knowledge to Make Exact Copies of Human Beings." *The New York Times* Magazine, March 5, 1972.

Hall, Alice. "A Lady from China's Past." *National Geographic,* May 1974.

Hare, Burt. "Mummies: Man's Drive for Immortality." *Science Digest,* December 1969.

Leaf, Alexander. "Everyday Is a Gift When You Are Over 100." *National Geographic,* January 1973.

Libasi, Paul. *The Sciences* (New York Academy of Science's Journal), Volume 14, No. 10, December 1974.

Plato. *Plato's Dialogue of the Immortality of the Soul,* translated by Theobald. New York: AMS Press.

Platt, John, R. *Science* (American Association Journal for the Advancement of Science).

Sollberger, Edmond. "The Babylonian Legend of the Flood." London: British Museum, 1962.

Strehler, Bernard. *Newsweek,* April 16, 1973.

Tompkins, Calvin. "Thinking in Time." *The New Yorker,* April 22, 1974.

Watson, James D. "Moving Toward Clonial Man." *Atlantic Monthly,* 1973.

Anonymous. "Can Aging Be Cured." *Newsweek,* April 16, 1973.

NAVY SEAL PROTECTOR

Bonnie Vanak

HARLEQUIN® ROMANTIC SUSPENSE

Recycling programs
for this product may
not exist in your area.

ISBN-13: 978-0-373-40232-8

Navy SEAL Protector

Copyright © 2017 by Bonnie Vanak

Printed in U.S.A.

www.Harlequin.com

New York Times and *USA TODAY* bestselling author **Bonnie Vanak** is passionate about romance novels and telling stories. A former newspaper reporter, she worked as a journalist for a large international charity for several years, traveling to countries such as Haiti to report on the sufferings of the poor. Bonnie lives in Florida with her husband, Frank, and is a member of Romance Writers of America. She loves to hear from readers. She can be reached through her website, bonnievanak.com.

Books by Bonnie Vanak

Harlequin Romantic Suspense

SOS Agency

Navy SEAL Seduction
Shielded by the Cowboy SEAL
Navy SEAL Protector

Harlequin Nocturne

Phoenix Force

The Shadow Wolf
The Covert Wolf
Phantom Wolf
Demon Wolf

The Empath
Enemy Lover
Immortal Wolf

Visit the Author Profile page at Harlequin.com.

For Frank, my hero. I love you, always.

Chapter 1

No one was kicking her out of her home, even if she had to work double shifts until she dropped.

Shelby Stillwater swiped a hand across her sweating brow, righted the white cowboy hat on her head and then watched as the bartender poured another frosty pitcher of golden beer. Friday night at the Bucking Bronc Steak House. Tips should be good tonight, as long as she could avoid the ungentlemanly slurs and smile, smile, smile.

Brown curls bobbing as she walked and the white fringe at the hem of her short skirt swaying like reeds in a hard wind, she carried the pitcher to table fourteen. The gray-haired geezer with a belly spilling in a waterfall over his silver belt buckle tried to squeeze her bottom, but she danced away.

"C'mere, sweet thang," he called out in a slur. "Lemme take another look at you."

Look at this, she silently fumed, tempted to flip him her middle finger. Instead, she headed for another table, pad in hand, her back and feet feeling as if twin weights were dumped on them. The group of ten businessmen from Nashville had ordered enough food to feed a small country. Their bill was solidly into the triple digits and they might give her a triple-digit tip if she could avoid the octopus with the wandering hands.

A big tip meant a store-bought cake instead of home-made for Timmy. His sixth birthday was in a few days and she planned to celebrate it in style.

Shelby bustled through orders, patiently allowing a patron to switch tables three times "because the lighting isn't good here," and returned a steak when a grumpy woman said it was rare, even though the woman had ordered it extra rare. She generally liked waitressing and most guests were well-mannered locals who treated her well. But with the big country-music convention in the next town this weekend, the out-of-town guests were taxing her patience.

Shelby returned the credit card to table fourteen. Waterfall Belly belched, signed the check and the men left, talking loudly.

She peeked at the bill and stared at the tip.

A measly twelve dollars for a three-hundred-and-fifty-dollar bill? Anger simmered, but she refused to surrender to it. Already skating on thin ice with Bill, if she ran after the customers and told them what she thought of their "tip," then...

Instead, she shoved the check into her apron and pushed on.

Later, she'd kick off the white cowboy boots, put up her feet and have a glass of white wine while watching *Steel Magnolias*, a favorite comfort movie. Gone were the days when her mother, in a rare moment of sobriety, would cuddle up next to her on the sofa and they'd watch the movie while munching on a tub of popcorn. Mom had named her after the tragic Shelby in the film. This Shelby preferred to think she was more the Ouiser type, tough and pragmatic.

I'm more like a tin daisy. But I've had it worse.

Living in her family's car when they were evicted because her daddy couldn't hold down a job was worse. Going to school in ragged clothing that she'd mended herself because Mama was sleeping off a hangover was worse.

But eighteen years ago, when Silas Anderson gave her father a job at the Belle Creek Ranch, things started to turn around. A sudden bout of grief made her pause and catch her breath. Silas had died last week. Funeral tomorrow. She'd felt genuine sorrow for the man's passing. Silas had been more of a father to her than her drunken dad.

She'd put her own money into the ranch, reducing her salary for the job she did as the ranch bookkeeper, and paid for small repairs when things got broken. Lately, lots of things had been broken. Shelby would do anything to keep her little apartment above the garage. The Belle Creek was home. Silas and Dan, his nephew and the ranch manager, had allowed her to live rent-free for the past ten years.

Even though the ranch could face foreclosure, she felt confident things would work out with her help.

Timmy loved the ranch, more than he adored cake. *I'll make Timmy the biggest, best birthday cake with his favorite cinnamon icing. Maybe add sprinkles—he's crazy about colored sprinkles…*

Out of the corner of her eye, she saw a grizzled, silver-headed man sit at a booth in her section. He wore a faded olive drab jacket decorated with many patches. Old Vern,

who'd served many tours in 'Nam. Shelby forgot about
the lousy tip. With a big smile, she headed for him.

"Hi, Vern. How are you?"

The elderly man brightened. "Right as rain, Shelby."

For a few minutes she listened to him talk about everything from the weather to his grandchildren. Vern
came in every Friday, probably for the company. He lived
alone, and she knew he had little money. So every Friday, she paid for his meal on the sly, telling him they had
a "special" for vets.

Seeing her manager frown and start toward her, she
promised Vern to put in his order straightaway.

After doing so, head pounding from the grinding
country music pumping through the speakers, her feet
hurting, Shelby decided to steal a five-minute break. She
headed into the back room that served as the employee
quarters. Rows of steel-gray lockers lined the walls,
where the women and men could safely stash valuables.
There was a painkiller calling her name right now and…

Shelby ground to an abrupt halt.

The padlock on her locker hung open. Someone had
snipped it clean through, probably with bolt cutters. Same
as last Friday night.

Blood pulsing through her body, breathing ragged,
she whipped her head around. No one about. Not even
the lingering odor of cigarette smoke that hung in the air
when Ann sneaked back here to take a few puffs.

Who could have done this?

She had to find out. If someone stole her purse, her
one credit card that wasn't already maxed out…

Or worse.

Shelby inched toward the locker, eyes pinned to the
dangling padlock. With a hand that shook, she removed

the lock and set it down on the bench seat. *Please, don't let it be like last week...*

One, two, three!

She flung open the door and stepped back.

A nauseating odor slammed into her and she gagged. Shelby blinked hard, looking at the top shelf and the cause of the noxious smell.

A dead rat.

Shelby grabbed her purse where it hung on a hook inside the locker, her fingers fumbling for the clasp. Sure enough, just like last week, a white note with typed letters was stuffed inside it.

Leave the Belle Creek before we make you leave.

Shelby dropped her purse. Bile rose in her throat, but she forced it down. Had to get rid of the rat before some happy customer came tripping back here in search of the restroom, freaked and called the county board of health. If Bill saw this, he'd fire her. Last week someone had dumped a dozen dead cockroaches into her locker. Bill had seen those and written her up. The manager had been on her case because Natalie, the new owner, had disliked Shelby ever since high school.

Shelby found a black plastic garbage bag and gloves. The dead rat was out the door and into the Dumpster shortly after. As she washed her hands in the bathroom sink, Ann sauntered into the ladies room.

Ann stopped short and gave her a quizzical look. "You okay, Shel? You look like you've seen a ghost."

No, a dead rat. "Just tired."

Her friend dabbed on fresh lipstick and touched up her

hair. "Well, I've got something to put the spark back in your tank. Sexy-guy alert, table nine. Panty-melting hot."

"Takes a lot more than sexy to dissolve my underwear," Shelby joked back.

"You need a life," her friend said with a good-natured grin. "Or don't wear panties at all. Want to grab a drink after work at the Tipsy Cowboy?"

Ann had a brazen attitude, bleached blond hair and wore her skirts too high, but she was the best friend Shelby ever had.

"Rain check. Dan's wife is babysitting Timmy as a favor and I don't want to be late."

Ann patted her shoulder. "You work too hard, hon. Let me know if I can help in any way."

The kindness nearly made her dissolve into tears. Ann had boarded her horse at the Belle Creek, giving the ranch much-needed income, even if it was only rough board and not full. Shelby smiled. "You've already done enough, hon. I'll be fine."

As her friend left, Shelby realized the dull throbbing behind her temples had turned into a fierce headache. She stashed her purse behind boxes of sanitary napkins in the employee lounge and headed back onto the floor. Maybe the rest of the night would be uneventful. *Please let it be calm, please...*

The devil himself sat at table nine.

She forgot to breathe, forgot the dead rat in her locker. Forgot who she was. Good thing she wore a brass tag with her name on it. Time rolled back in a fog.

That kiss, those sinfully sexy eyes, smoldering at her as he lowered his mouth to hers...

You never forgot your first kiss. And no woman who still had a pulse ever forgot Nick Anderson.

Dark blond hair curled at the ends as it rested against the collar of his black shirt. He wore it longer now, and he was thicker in the shoulders and chest. He was a man now, instead of the teenager he'd been when she'd sobbed and told him to get out of her life. Still had the same languid grace as he relaxed back in the imitation-leather booth, his dark gaze scanning the restaurant with the same cool, searing intensity displayed ten years ago. Nick looked hungry, as if he needed a good meal…or a bad woman.

Already the dynamic inside the Bucking Bronc had changed. Female waitstaff sashayed instead of scurried and the men stood a little taller. No one here could best Nick's six feet three inches. Or his mouth…

Two men stopped by his table and chatted. Nick's heroism as a former Navy SEAL was a source of pride in these parts. She overheard a few invite him to sit with them and pay for his dinner, but Nick politely refused.

He must be back for his dad's funeral. She'd been so busy trying to find ways to save his father's ranch, she'd almost forgotten he existed.

Almost.

Shelby took her order pad from her apron. Tonight she had to have a steel backbone. Forget the honey-sweet flower attitude. The man deserved pure vinegar.

Be courteous. The pencil nearly snapped in her tight grip. "May I take your drink order?"

He turned. Soft light from the overhead lamp put the angles of his face into sharp relief. Shelby bit back a gasp at the jagged scar carved on one angular cheek. It looked as if a vicious animal had torn his skin apart.

It made him no less handsome; indeed, it made him look more ruthless and dangerous.

Nick dropped the guarded expression, replaced it with a heavy-lidded assessment. "Shelby Stillwater. You are a lovely sight for weary eyes like mine. What are you doing here, darling?"

At sixteen, the compliment would have thrilled her. Now she was older and wiser to his charms. "I'm working. And you?"

Nick's gaze shuttered and a slight tension rippled through his muscled body. "I returned for the funeral."

His Deep South accent was barely noticeable. And this Nick was different. Still charming and suave, but something lurked beneath the surface. Not the scar—Shelby dismissed that, for she'd never let such superficial markings bother her. But shadows lingered in his dark eyes.

"Nice of you to finally come home. Too bad you were too late to say goodbye to your father."

His expression darkened. "Soon as Dan found me and contacted me, I was on my way back here. I dropped everything because he was sick."

"I'm sorry for your loss," she said in a gentler tone. No matter if Nick didn't care when Silas fell ill, the man was still his father.

He gave a rough nod.

"Where are you staying?" She didn't want to be polite to this man, who'd broken her heart ten years ago when he'd pushed her aside like the boys in high school who called her "trailer trash." But Nick was Silas's son, and for the sake of honoring his dad, she'd mind her tongue.

Long as he didn't kiss her again. *Your tongue wouldn't mind that, huh?*

Shelby told her dancing female hormones to get lost and mentally recalled the dead rat. Worked wonders for lowering a libido.

"At the ranch." Nick stretched an arm along the booth as he watched her.

She managed to conceal her surprise. "I'm sure your cousins will be happy to see you."

Nick's gaze turned hard. "Doubt it. Dan and Jake won't want me around long."

She blinked in surprise. "You're always welcome, Nick. You were the one who left."

Everyone in town knew how Silas and Nick had clashed like two stubborn bulls in an arena, while Dan and Jake got along with the old man just fine. Shelby didn't understand how Nick could leave home and only return for his father's funeral.

Her parents had been drunks, and when they left town, Shelby barely noticed. But Nick came from a long line of solid, upstanding Barlow denizens. Andersons had served on the town council for as long as anyone could remember, and the Belle Creek had been an icon in the community for years, sponsoring 4-H competitions and Little League teams.

Something flickered behind his dark gaze. "I'm ready to order. Why don't you sit a minute, take a load off? You look as if you've been running ragged."

Pride struggled against the need to do exactly as he said. Weariness won. Shelby perched on the edge of the booth and put her pad on the table. Best not to show how much her hands shook, let him know his raw animal heat could still affect her, like a blast furnace. "Thanks."

"Where are you laying your head at night these days, darling? Apartment in town?"

Nick's deep, smoky voice made the question sound sinful and inviting. Shelby tapped her pencil against the battered order pad. "Silas converted the space above the garage into an apartment for myself and Timmy."

The scar on his cheek turned white as his jaw tightened. "Timmy?"

"My nephew. My sister and her husband are living overseas in Iraq. He's an engineer—got a very lucrative twenty-four-month contract."

Nick's mouth thinned, and he shook his head. "You couldn't pay me enough to live there. Did three tours in Iraq. Managed to survive, despite all the suicide bombers."

She knew this, knew it every day, and worried one day her sister and brother-in-law might not return home. "It's why they left Timmy with me."

"Still the same Shelby, living in the same place, taking care of everyone," he murmured, his gaze never leaving hers. "Darling, are you ever going to leave the Belle Creek? That old place has been trapping you there for years."

Shelby bristled at this truth. She'd given up her dream of traveling in order to care for Timmy. It was a reality she'd cheerfully accepted, but hearing it from his sexy mouth made it hurt. "My sister and her husband couldn't pass up this chance to make good money. They're moving back here when they return, and they promised I could live with them to save money for travel. Now, are you ready to order?"

"I'll have sweet tea, salad with raspberry vinaigrette, the chicken, baked potato and carrots."

"You like breasts or thighs?"

His eyes moved in a slow caress over her body that made all her hormones sing. "Both look good to me."

Damn that color rising to her cheeks. Nick chuckled. "Breast meat. Grilled."

After scribbling down the order, she stood. "Be right up."

He smiled, a genuine smile that added tiny lines to the corners of his chocolate-brown eyes and dimpled his right cheek. A bedroom smile that she suspected had lured many women into his arms. "It's good to see you again, Shelby. You're the one person in this town I like seeing again."

She wished she could say the same. The sooner Nick Anderson left, the better for her. The man had a habit of disarming her, shaking up her world. In a world that was already pretty rattled, she liked the idea of stability.

After she brought his food, Nick didn't dig in right away, but kept looking at her, as if she was steak and he was starving. "It really is good to see you again, Sweet Pea Shelby."

The nickname caught her off guard, and coaxed an uncertain smile to her mouth. "No one's called me that in years." Not since her parents had become more interested in alcohol than their daughters.

"Too bad," he said softly.

For a moment she stood looking at him, her heart pounding like a war drum. Nick still had it. And damn her, she still wanted it.

Shelby hurried off to take another order. She stopped by to check on him ten minutes later. As she went to take his salad plate, his fingers brushed against hers. A tingle rushed down her spine and he stared at her.

Shelby became aware of her too-rapid pulse, the knot of desire centered low in her belly.

Vern waved at her and she turned, but Nick laced

strong fingers around her wrist. "Wait," he said softly. "Isn't that Vern Dickerson?"

"He comes in here every Friday." Her heart beat triple-time at the hint of steely strength restraining her, and yet his grip was gentle. "I think he's lonely."

Nick nodded. Without ceremony, he picked up his meal and glass, and walked over to Vern's booth, sliding in opposite him. "Hi, there, sir. I'm Nick Anderson. Mind if I sit with you? I hate to eat alone. Don't want to bother you, so I'll leave if you wish."

Vern beamed. As she left to take care of another customer, Vern began regaling Nick with stories of his time in 'Nam, Nick listening intently. Her heart softened.

When Vern excused himself to the restroom, Shelby stopped to refill Nick's sweet tea.

"Sweet Pea, give me Vern's check. A man who has served like he has shouldn't have to worry about his next meal."

"Already taken care of," she told him. "And thank you."

Nick blinked. "For what?"

"For spending time with an old man who is absolutely thrilled to sit with the hometown hero."

His expression darkened. "He's the real war hero."

Vern returned, and Shelby left them alone. A few minutes later, the elderly veteran waved her over and asked for the check. Shelby went into her usual dialogue about the special veterans plan. Vern thanked her, then the two men stood and shook hands.

"Been a real honor to spend time with you, sir." Nick nodded at him.

Beaming, Vern saluted him. "Same here, sailor. You

ever need someone to jaw with you about the service, I'm your man."

Vern left, his shoulders a little less stooped, his gait a little less unsteady.

Shelby began clearing the table of Vern's dishes as Nick sat down and asked for his own check.

"That was so nice of you," she told him.

"You're the nice one, Sweet Pea. Vern knows."

"Knows what?"

"That you pay for his dinner every Friday. Thank you, Shel."

Her gaze met his dark one and in the depths, she felt something stir. Not mere desire, but something deeper, and more lasting.

"Shouldn't you be working instead of wasting the customer's time?"

Shelby stiffened. The honey-sweet voice hid the acid behind those words. She didn't need to turn around to know that the owner stood behind her. The woman had been in the kitchen an hour ago, barking orders and giving the evil eye when Shelby asked the head chef about a cake recipe with cinnamon.

With her cascading wispy blond curls, big blue eyes and stylish clothing, Natalie Beaufort caught many male eyes in small-town Barlow. Big Chuck Beaufort, her wealthy dad, spared no expense on his youngest daughter. Natalie boarded her show horse, Fancy, at the Belle Creek, so Shelby had to force herself to be polite. The ranch needed the fees to survive. It was no secret Big Chuck coveted the ranch's lush four hundred acres for some pie-in-the-sky amusement park called Countryville. The man had been bragging around town about his latest plan.

Maybe Nick didn't care about the land that had been in his family for five generations, but she did. The thought of seeing the rolling hillside, the duck pond where she'd gone swimming on many a hot summer day, the horse pasture, the faded red barn and the rambling outbuildings turned into a tourist trap made Shelby nauseous. And furious.

Natalie slid into the booth across from Nick, pretty as you please, pushing Shelby aside. "Well, hello, stranger," she cooed. "Nice to see you again. And what are you doing here at my restaurant?"

"Leaving." Nick gulped down his tea and slid out from the booth, his gaze centered on Shelby. "I'll see you later, Shelby."

Silently laughing, she nodded at Nick.

He dropped several bills into the check folder and then looked at her with those sleepy bedroom eyes, now sharpened, as they centered on her mouth. He touched her cheek and she startled, the contact sizzling between them like a crackling electrical line. Nick gently stroked a thumb over her trembling lower lip.

"Maybe I should have stuck around ten years ago and finished what I started with you."

Whistling, he jammed his hands into his jeans pockets and strode off.

Natalie pouted so much she looked twelve instead of twenty-six.

"Get back to work," Natalie told her in a sullen voice.

Humming, Shelby cleared the table and dumped the dishes in the wait station near the bar. The recent troubles came back to haunt her. Nick was staying at the ranch. He'd been away for ten years and had no idea of what he was waltzing back into on the Belle Creek.

As she headed into the kitchen, a dreadful thought struck her. Nick returned for the funeral, but what if Silas left the entire ranch to his son?

Impossible. Dan had faithfully remained on the ranch as foreman, aiding his uncle. Silas and his only son, Nick, had been estranged for years.

Silas would never leave the Belle Creek to Nick, the man who wanted nothing to do with the ranch and would probably sell if it was his.

And if he was the new owner of the Belle Creek, she faced a real possibility of being homeless once more.

Chapter 2

Nick had never wanted to set eyes on the Belle Creek Ranch again.

Ten years ago, he'd thought the same about Shelby Stillwater, and not for the same reasons.

Sweet Pea Shelby. Damn, the girl had turned into a woman, and what a fine-looking woman. One night, upset over yet another fight with Silas, he'd come home and saw her sitting in the cabin, where he'd gone to sleep off the Jack Daniel's. He hadn't cared she was barely sixteen and he was old enough to know better. She looked so lost, as forlorn as he'd felt, so he'd kissed her. Her mouth had been warm and sweet, and the kiss had seared him to his very bones, so much that his dick had turned as hard as stone in his jeans and he knew if he'd stayed, he'd have done something very, very wrong.

Shelby was too nice for his brand of wicked.

And now she was legal. Very legal. With those big green eyes, thick brown curls with a hint of honey and sunshine spilling past her shoulders, all those curves and that spark in her eye, she made him think of hot, wet kisses in the night, and things men wanted to do to women who roused them to the point of madness. Long, slow sex. Fast, hard sex.

When he'd touched her, the past rushed back like a tornado. Her skin felt warm and soft as satin, and her mouth...

Nick pushed Shelby out of his mind. Tomorrow was the funeral, and then he'd be gone again, this time never coming back. He'd never return to Shelby or the ranch. Odd, he'd thought the old man would live forever, for Silas Anderson was one tough bastard.

Not too tough for the pneumonia that rattled his lungs and ultimately claimed him.

Nick parked his Harley in the curved driveway of the two-story white farmhouse and adjusted his backpack. Two elegant carriage lights tastefully accented the front porch, with its rows of white wicker rocking chairs and baskets of flowers. House...? Hell, this was a mansion compared to some places he'd slept.

He whistled. When he'd left, last time for good, the farmhouse had weathered paint, finicky plumbing and heat, and wood floorboards that creaked when you tried to sneak up the stairs. This kind of renovating took plenty of money. He knew, too, because over the past year since he'd left the teams, he'd found odd jobs doing construction and flipping houses.

His gut curling into a knot, he walked up to the double doors with the half-moon windows above them and rang the silver bell. Soft chimes sounded inside. Even the doorbell had changed from the sharp, annoying buzzer. He half expected a butler named Jeeves to open the door.

Instead, his cousin Dan did, and stood for a moment silently assessing him. Nick did the same. Five years older than Nick, Dan looked a little thicker around the waist than last time, and there were threads of silver in his dark hair. No welcome in his blue eyes, either. Once they'd been close. No longer. Not since the day Nick packed all his things and left for good. *Abandoning the family*, Dan had called it.

Survival, Nick termed it.

In a starched white shirt, black trousers and polished loafers, Dan looked more like a banker than a cowboy. Nick became aware of his shabby jeans, the faded black T-shirt beneath his collared chambray work shirt.

"Hi, Dan. Good to see you."

"Nick. You're here, finally."

Dan engulfed him in a hug that felt stiffer than a new board. Nick hugged him back a little more enthusiastically. He wasn't going to be a jerk, even if Dan wasn't exactly rolling out the welcome mat.

"Come on in. You can hang your things in the hall closet. Felicity doesn't like jackets strewn about the house."

Nick shrugged out of the frayed backpack containing all his worldly goods and then removed his leather jacket, placing it on a padded hanger in the closet. A black Stetson with a turquoise band sat on a shelf. Nick removed it and stroked a thumb along the brim.

"I remember this well," he mused. "Bought it at a rodeo when I was sixteen."

The remark made Dan thaw a bit. "You used to wear it in school."

Nick grinned. "Wonder if my head has shrunk since then."

Dan's smile faded. "Felicity doesn't like hats worn inside the house. But you can take it with you upstairs to your room and wear it on the ranch. Come, I'll introduce you to my wife and children."

The hallway was lined with white marble, and elegant framed paintings hung on the cream walls. The entry to this house wasn't stacked with boots caked with mud and horse droppings. The antiseptic atmosphere made him feel as if he should have wiped his feet more before entering.

Dan led him into a living room with overstuffed brown leather furniture, a stone fireplace and gold lamps. A pretty but brittle blond woman dressed in a severe navy-blue dress was perched on the edge of the sofa. Next to her were two young boys with buzzed-cut brown hair dressed in neatly pressed trousers and white shirts.

Dan introduced the woman as his wife, Felicity, and their two sons, Mason, eight, and Miles, six. The little boys looked solemn.

Nick shook Felicity's hand, which felt as damp and listless as the Southern heat. He sat on the leather chair opposite them.

"Thanks for letting me bunk here tonight," he told her.

She gave a desultory wave of one hand. "It is your home as well, Nicolas."

Dan stood by the sofa, as stiff as his starched shirt. "Did you eat dinner yet, Nick?"

"I ate at the Bucking Bronc earlier. Didn't want to impose."

Felicity seemed to sit even straighter. "It is no imposition. We already ate, but there are leftovers. Breakfast will be ready at seven o'clock sharp tomorrow. The funeral home requests family be there at nine thirty. We arranged to have two limousines. You may ride in one, unless you would rather provide your own transportation."

"I have my bike," he offered.

Her nostrils flared in apparent distaste. "You may ride in the second car, then. We expect promptness and we must respect the funeral director's wishes. The services will begin at eleven sharp. We have a few house rules. No shouting, running, hats worn inside the house or jeans at the dinner table. We dress for dinner, which is six o'clock sharp. Boots with spurs are worn outside only."

With all this "sharp" grating sharply on his last nerve, Nick wished he'd booked a room at the local motel. Then he remembered there was a country-music convention in town and there were no rooms. Maybe the barn. Might be a tad warmer sleeping with the horses than in this cold house.

He glanced at the dusty Western boots on his feet. "This is still a farm, right, Felicity?"

Felicity blinked. "Of course it is. But we are civilized people, and we must adhere to the rules in order to act as civilized people, not wild hooligans."

A dull flush crept up his neck. Damn if she didn't sound like old Silas himself, with the rules and the "hooligan" accusation. Maybe the old man had rubbed off on her. Or he'd died earlier and his ghost possessed this woman.

"I won't be much in your way." He gave her a pointed look. "After the funeral, I'm gone."

He'd think the idea would have pleased her. Instead, she kept twisting her hands together. What was wrong with this woman?

"Where's Timmy?" he asked. "I saw Shelby at the restaurant and she said you're babysitting."

Felicity sat straighter. "He's downstairs in the recreation room."

Recreation room? Dollar signs began pinging in his head. He wondered how much money Silas had sunk into this house. Unease gripped him. The old man had always been frugal, but this house cost money. Maybe the rumors he'd heard of the ranch being in debt were more than rumors.

Not your problem.

Dan stood and gestured to him. "I'll show you to your room."

He thanked Felicity again, and followed Dan up the sweeping staircase to the second-floor landing, his boot heels stomping firmly on each step.

At the hallway's end, Dan opened a door. Nick blinked. Once this had been his room. No longer.

The bedroom had been converted to a guest room with a white queen-size bed, a pink ruffled spread, pink walls, white girlish furniture and a white rocking chair with bright pink cushions by the window. Nick gave a rueful shrug.

"Felicity thought you might like to be in your old room." Dan shoved his hands into his pockets. "Except we did some redecorating, thinking you'd never come home again."

"No worries," he said easily. "I'm not staying long and I've stayed in worse places. Maybe not as pink, though."

Dan flashed a brief smile at the joke as Nick dumped his pack on the white carpeted floor.

"Bathroom is through that door." Dan pointed to a connecting door. "No one else is on this floor, so you don't have to worry about interruptions."

"Just my boots," Nick joked.

Dan jammed a hand through his short hair. "Ah, about the boots, don't worry about it. Felicity makes the rules mainly for the staff, who come into the house to use the office downstairs. Not family."

Am I still family? The question hovered on the tip of his mouth, but he only nodded.

"Where's Jake?" he asked.

"He's at his girlfriend's, but will meet us at the funeral home."

Lucky bastard. Maybe his girlfriend had a spare room for Nick. A room with less frills and less Pepto-Bismol decor.

"I'll need a suit for the funeral," Nick told him.

"Already taken care of. You can wear one of Jake's—you're about the same size. Felicity hung it in this closet."

As his cousin made to leave, Nick sat down on the pink chair. He was twenty-nine now, no longer the rebellious teen who looked up to his older relative for advice. "Stay a minute, Dan. Tell me what's been going on. All I heard was rumors about the ranch having financial trouble."

Dan stood by the bed. "There's been a lot that's happened since you left, Nick. Maybe if you had stuck around, if you had cared enough, things would be different."

Tension squeezed his guts. Once he and Dan had been close. No longer, for the cold anger flaring in his cousin's eyes told him everything. "I couldn't."

No use getting into the past, how Silas had browbeat him until Nick felt smothered, and how if he hadn't left, he'd have either turned into a ghost of himself, or he'd have gone mad. The old man had kicked him out when he was only sixteen, telling him to "learn to straighten out and you can return."

Nick survived six months being homeless, living by his wits, until the bitter cold weather drove him back, humiliated and ashamed, to his father. He remained at home another three years and then joined the navy.

No one knew the real reason he stuck it out. He preferred to keep that reason private.

Still, Dan should know his decision wasn't capricious. "You remember that day when I was fourteen and I found the puppy by the roadside? How I begged Silas to keep it?"

His cousin nodded. "Always thought it was a bad deal that the dog was so sick you had to put it down. Tough call, but Silas said it was for the best."

Nick gave his cousin a level look. "The dog was fine. I secretly brought him over to the vet to have him checked over. He didn't need anything more than a deworming, Dan. Silas wanted me to shoot it because he said I needed to grow a set of real balls, and not get all 'female' over a damn stray dog."

Dan blanched. "Silas would never do that."

Nick gave a grim smile. "Oh, he would never do that to you. But me, he did crap like that all the time. Guess you'll never understand. But before you go judging me for leaving here, understand I had my reasons."

His cousin looked away, but not before Nick caught a flash of guilt on his face. "Silas could be tough, yeah. But if he didn't take us in after my dad died, we'd have been really bad off, Nick. I guess that's why I could forgive anything he did."

"You had your reasons for staying, just as I had mine for leaving." Nick stood and went to his pack, then unzipped it. "Thanks for letting me stay here."

Dan started for the door. "Like Felicity said, it's your

home, too. I'll be downstairs if you need anything. Make sure to lock your window before you go to sleep."

Lock his window on the second floor? Nick looked up, but his cousin was gone.

Nick went to the closet and opened the door. A black silk suit hung there, the dry-cleaning plastic still encasing it. He tore off the plastic and then tried on the suit. A little tight around the shoulders, but it would suffice.

He hung it up and then went into the adjoining bathroom to shower. When he emerged, in clean jeans and a gray T-shirt, the two boys stood in the doorway. Nick waved them in. They entered, their big blue eyes wide.

They watched him as he unpacked and rummaged through his clothing.

"Daddy says you're a hero. You're a Navy SEAL," Mason said.

Hero? The thought soured him, even as he appreciated his cousin's compliment.

"I was a Navy SEAL." Nick hung a hat on the bed's post.

"Mommy doesn't like hats on the bed," Miles informed him.

Wonder if Mommy likes anything on the bed, he thought, and sighed. The boys stood opposite him, so stiff that they resembled wooden bookends.

He wasn't good with kids, except his best friend Cooper's family, and these boys looked too wary, too uncertain of this stranger in their home.

Their home, not his.

Nick dug into his knapsack. He removed his one good white shirt, wondering if Felicity had an iron he could borrow. Judging from the woman's attitude, she probably kept a dozen.

The gun case was stashed at the bottom. He removed it and stared at the pistol encased within.

He'd have to keep his SIG Sauer locked up and wondered if Silas still kept his shotguns and rifles in the downstairs study. Ah, hell.

Bracing his hands on his knees, he felt a bout of piercing grief at what had been lost between himself and the old man. Silas had taught him how to shoot when Nick was ten. Took him hunting in the mountains, and had pride in his first kill.

The old man showed him how to be an expert marksman. Insisted he take care of his weapons, clean them and make sure they were locked up, away from curious fingers.

It was one of the few areas they had in common and didn't clash about.

"Is that a gun?" Miles asked.

Nick nodded, replaced his sidearm in the backpack.

"Can we see it?" Mason said, his voice growing excited.

Giving his cousin's son a long look, Nick shook his head. "Hands off. I never let another man handle my sidearm."

The boy pouted a little until hearing the word *man*.

"Dad wants to take me hunting, but Mommy says guns are dangerous," Mason said.

"They are, if you don't know how to use them. Maybe your dad can convince your mom to let you go hunting next year, when you're a little older."

"Daddy keeps a gun under his pillow," Miles told him, but clammed up when Mason frowned at him.

Odd. Dan had always been a bit squeamish around guns. Necessary on a ranch, but his cousin let Silas do the shooting. Why would he feel the need for home protection with a gun, especially with vulnerable children living here?

Next he removed a small black velvet box and opened it, studying the gold winking in the lamplight.

"What is that?" Mason asked.

Nick removed the pin and showed them. "That's my Budweiser, my Navy SEAL pin. Only real Navy SEALs get these."

The boys examined the pin with avid interest while Nick went to the window. He lifted the curtains with the back of one hand, peering into the darkness at the twin carriage lights on the garage. Shelby lived out there. Cute, curvy Shelby, who had turned his world upside down ten years ago with that killer kiss...

"If you're sleeping here tonight, make sure to lock your window. We all have to make sure the house is locked tight before we go to bed," Mason told him.

Nick recoiled. He glanced down at the ground two stories below. "Why?"

"So no one breaks in, like they did last month."

Crime, here at Belle Creek? "What happened?"

"Someone went into Mommy and Daddy's bedroom." Mason looked troubled.

Nick squatted down by the solemn little boy. "What happened?"

"Daddy says not to talk about it outside the family," Miles told him.

Nick smiled. "I'm family. You can tell me."

Miles seemed to consider. "Someone stole Mommy's favorite pen."

"Pin," Mason amended. "They went into our parents' bedroom and took Mom's jewelry. Her favorite pin. It had

a silver horse with emerald eyes. It was right a.
when Readalot died—"

"Daddy was real upset," Miles interrupted.

"I'll tell it, Miles." Mason looked at Nick. "Readalot
was our champion jumper. He won lots of competitions.
Shelby went into the stables and Readalot was dead in
his stall. He was our champion jumper. Hank, the ranch
hand, say the horse was healthy as an ox. Someone killed
him."

He needed to find out what the hell was going on
around here. Then he remembered he didn't live here
anymore.

Nick ruffled the boys' hair. "Don't worry about it.
Do as your mom and dad tell you. I'm sure things will
be fine."

But they stared at him with those big eyes. "Will you
stay here? Maybe if we have a real Navy SEAL stay here,
the bad things won't happen."

Tightness formed in his chest. Bad things happened
all the time, and he couldn't do a damn thing to prevent
them. But these were young, innocent kids, and while
they didn't deserve lies, they also didn't deserve adult
worries. "We'll see," he said vaguely. "I'll do everything
I can while I'm here, okay?"

The words were more BS than the droppings in the
pasture, but both boys looked relieved.

"Now, go downstairs to your mom. I'm sure she's worried about you being up here with big, bad cousin Nick."
He winked at them and they grinned in pure male cama-
raderie of doing something they shouldn't.

When the boys left, Nick fingered his SEAL pin. Hell
of a price paid for getting it, but not as much as his brothers
in arms, who had paid the ultimate price with their lives.

The pin meant everything to him. But he'd left the teams after his hospital discharge, when he knew he couldn't perform up to par, knew he would never be at the top of his game again.

And now he felt more lost than when he'd stormed away from the ranch and Silas's iron grip when he was nineteen, never looking back.

No reason for him to stay now. But as he gazed out the window, he saw a car pull into the driveway by the garage. Light from the dual carriage lamps showcased a woman climbing out—a woman with dark hair and a gentle sway to her hips.

Shelby. The mouth-watering, kissable Shelby.

He watched her walk across the drive toward the house. Nick checked his appearance in the mirror, finger-combed his hair and went downstairs as the doorbell rang.

Miss Shelby Stillwater. His blood surged, hot and thick. He thought of that kiss and how it had made every cell inside him alive and aware.

Maybe it was time to stay. At least until he could figure out what the hell was going on around here.

Chapter 3

The funeral had been a quiet, dignified affair. No one shed a tear, except her.

But as she'd stood by the graveside, watching the others throw flowers on the casket, she saw Nick rub his eyes. Maybe he and Silas had been on bad terms, but the man was his father.

Shelby had sidled over to Nick, who was standing alone and looking lost, and clasped his hand. He'd looked startled, and then a little grateful.

Now, as they sat in Silas's downstairs study in the farmhouse, Nick looked neither. Guarded, perhaps. No... wary. And quite uncomfortable, as was she. The last thing she wanted to do, after the emotion of the funeral and the strain of helping to host the reception at the house afterward, was to listen to the reading of the will. She only wanted to collect Timmy from the downstairs rec room, where he was playing with Mason and Miles, then go to her apartment. Maybe take Timmy riding on his pony later.

Lord knew they needed to return to some form of normalcy.

Normal certainly had not been last night, when she'd gotten Timmy from this house. Nick had been in the hallway, leaning against the staircase, his long, muscled body looking hot as sin as he'd hooked his fingers through the loops of his belt hoops. He looked ready for sex.

It had taken all her willpower to murmur a polite greeting and tear her gaze away from him instead of ogling him like a schoolgirl. Fortunately, Felicity had been in a hurry and practically threw Timmy into Shelby's arms. She'd made a quick introduction of Timmy, and then fled with her nephew as if a blond devil was on her heels.

Today's somber occasion reminded her that Nick was only here temporarily. Shelby was certain he'd leave right after this. Perhaps even faster than the last time he'd gone away, leaving only the angry rubber of his tread marks on the front drive.

Silas's lawyer, Kurt Mohler, had gathered them together in this room. Shelby sat straight in the leather chair, trying to keep her nerves from jumping like water on a hot skillet. She doubted Silas had left her anything in his will, but her main concern was keeping her little apartment above the garage, at least until Heather and Pete returned from Iraq.

On the leather sofa, Dan and Felicity and Dan's younger brother, Jake, looked attentive.

She and Nick perched on the wing chairs near the sofa, while Kurt, who seemed restless, paced before the fireplace. Finally the lawyer turned.

"Silas made his last wishes very plain and clear. Daniel, I want you to know that as the family lawyer, if you wish to contest his will, you have the right to do so. However, it will be a lengthy court battle, which is something I'm sure you can't afford."

Her stomach clenched in tight knots. This wasn't a good start.

Dan frowned. "Why would we want to do that? Uncle Silas was always good to us."

Kurt removed a gold pen from his suit pocket and began fiddling with it. "As you know, the ranch is deeply in debt."

She watched Nick frown, his gaze sharp as he scrutinized the attorney. Judging from his reaction, Nick had no idea how bad things were around here. Having done the books for the ranch, she thought she knew. But Silas also liked to handle the family's personal bills himself and there was the matter of the ranch mortgage.

He'd never let her know the exact amount, only muttered that he'd take care of it.

"How much in debt?" Nick demanded.

Dan stiffened. "That's not for public knowledge."

Without his gaze leaving the attorney's face, Nick snapped, "I'm not the public."

"All parties in this room need to know what liabilities Silas faced, as well as the assets he owned," Kurt assured him. "It's why I asked all of you here."

The attorney looked at Nick. "Silas took out an equity loan on the house to pay for repairs, using the ranch as collateral. His estate owes the bank two hundred and fifty thousand dollars on the mortgage. I'm afraid he fell behind in payments."

Dread curled through her. Two hundred and fifty thousand dollars! She'd known it was bad, but not that bad. Silas had been nonchalant when he'd mentioned he owed money. No wonder he always looked so pinched and worried.

"What about the assets?" Felicity asked.

The woman had a poker face. If she had shed a single tear, Shelby hadn't seen it. Felicity hadn't always been this cold and brittle. Not until all the mysterious incidents started around the ranch, and Silas had mentioned that money was tight.

Secretly Shelby wondered about the odd coincidence of the sabotage happening concurrently with Silas's announcement. Dan managed the ranch. He knew Silas owed money, and maybe he'd mentioned it to his wife. Felicity had high standards. She'd insisted on the elaborate renovations to the house. Was she also behind the vandalism as well, acts designed to make Silas sell the ranch?

"The assets are the ranch and the house and all the outbuildings, a life insurance policy, a policy to pay for the funeral and all associated costs only, and a very small investment account." Kurt stooped and looked at them grimly. "There is a very good offer on the table for the ranch, and the house, from Chuck Beaufort. More than enough to pay off the loan, with a nice sum to purchase a new house in a good part of town."

Dan looked uncertain. Felicity reached over and squeezed her husband's hand. "What does Mr. Beaufort plan to do with the ranch? He's a developer, not a farmer."

Kurt's gaze was impassive. "He has plans for a theme park, which will bring in plenty of tourists and new business to town. The view of the mountains is splendid from the pasture."

Clenching her teeth, Shelby fisted her hands in her lap. Chuck Beaufort would take the serene pastures and the wild, overgrown forest, with its tangle of brush, and bulldoze everything. The Belle Creek had been in the family for generations. Maybe she didn't have any kind of family connection to the place, but it had been the only real home she'd ever had.

How could the lawyer propose they sell? Had he ever ridden over the lush pastures at dawn in spring, fresh dew beading the grass, the leaden sky bursting into gold as the sun peaked over the mountaintops of the Smokies?

Had he ever hung on a fence railing, listening to the wind sweep over the hills, watching the children play in the yard as the horses peacefully cropped the grass? The air was so pure and fresh here, it hurt her heart to think of the ranch turning into a concrete playground for wealthy people.

Her hands clenched tighter. Barlow was a sleepy community, a typical small town, except for when the country-music convention came to town. It offered nothing to her. She planned to leave for the bright lights of Nashville when Heather and Steve returned from Iraq. Heather promised they'd all get a place in the city big enough for Shelby while she pursued her dream of traveling to Paris to learn art.

But she'd always imagined the Belle Creek would be here if she ever wanted to visit. She couldn't imagine Barlow without the sprawling ranch.

She also couldn't imagine it without Silas. He was the heart of this place. Fresh grief made it hard to swallow past the thick lump in her throat.

A deep frown touched Nick's face. "The ranch always made money in the past. What happened that the old man got into such debt?"

The question was directed at Dan, who avoided looking at Nick. When Nick swept his gaze around the room, the lawyer also didn't meet his eyes.

"This is a good working ranch with a reputation for producing excellent studs and show horses." Nick leaned forward, his gaze hard. "The Belle Creek always had at least two dozen horses boarded here to provide a steady monthly income and we won hard cash in equestrian jumping competitions. Silas was a hardheaded business-man who pinched pennies. There's no reason for it to be operating that much in the red."

Silence draped the room. Jake grinned, but it looked forced. "We have only three boarders left, Nick. Things are not always as they seem, cuz."

His brother ignored the statement and gestured to the room. "Mr. Mohler, I'm not selling the Belle Creek. Uncle Silas told me five years ago when he named me as his trustee that I should never sell the ranch, no matter what. It had to stay in the family."

Relief swept through Shelby. She found it oddly ap-pealing that Dan was a champion of the old man, when they'd clashed over managing the ranch in the past.

Nick rubbed a hand over his chin. He looked uncom-fortable. Shelby felt a dash of pity for him. Even though he had abandoned his family, it had to hurt, knowing his father had overlooked him in favor of a cousin.

The lawyer cleared his throat. "I have here a letter from Silas to you, Nick."

As he handed over the envelope, Nick looked at the letter as if it was a snake.

"I suggest you read it in private, when we are done here. I'll want to meet with you soon in my office down-town, Nick."

Felicity frowned. "What does Nick have to do with

any of this? We know Dan is the trustee. Silas told us he was leaving everything to Dan, with provisions for Jake."

Kurt looked uncomfortable. "Silas came to me six months ago to update his trust and his will. There is a small provision for Dan and Jake, amounting to a total of twenty thousand dollars to be divided evenly. That provision comes from the life insurance policy, so that is solid cash. Both of you will also receive a few acres of land each."

Shelby's stomach did a flip-flop. She had a bad feeling about this.

"Then who gets the house and the ranch?" Jake demanded.

Kurt looked right at Nick, the man who couldn't care less about any of this, who hadn't been home in ten years. "The will states that Silas left almost everything to Nick. The house, the ranch, the horses, all the assets. It is his to do with as he pleases. Including the investment account, which I'm afraid only amounts to ten thousand dollars."

"What?" Felicity shrieked.

Dan looked pale and Jake laughed. Nick said nothing, but went very still, his hands curling around the letter, as if he wanted to crush it.

Or crush Silas.

"Well, at least the old man's funeral is paid for," Jake joked.

"That isn't funny," Felicity snapped.

She didn't dare breathe. She wasn't mentioned at all in this family drama. For a moment she wondered why the lawyer wanted her here.

Didn't Silas remember her at all?

As if he'd heard her thoughts, Kurt turned to Shelby.

"Miss Stillwater, there is also a provision in the will for you."

She waited, nails digging into her palms.

"Silas arranged to give you the apartment over the garage. It's yours to occupy as long as the ranch remains in the family. You can't sell it, of course, but you're free to live there and he made it clear no rent will be charged as long as you occupy it."

A little of her tension fled. She managed a tight nod. "Thank you."

The lawyer nodded. "Silas always thought highly of you. He loved you like you were his daughter."

She warmed a little to the man. And then he added, "But you are not family, only an employee of the Belle Creek. Silas made it clear that only family is to have what funds he left. I don't blame him, as I know your family's history with the ranch is circumspect, specifically your father and how he left here owing money."

Talk about a dose of ice water. Holding on to her pride, she sat straight and managed a tight smile. Nick, however, wasn't smiling.

"That's not necessary, Mohler," he said in a quiet, dangerous voice. "Shelby is not her father. Show her some respect."

She didn't need Nick defending her. Her smile grew tighter. "Nick, he's right. I'm not family."

Shelby locked gazes with the lawyer. "I'm also not my father. Or my mother. I've been employed by the Belle Creek for ten years and in those ten years, I've paid back every cent my daddy owed. I'd appreciate it if you would not confuse me with my parents."

As the lawyer started to stammer, she gave him a singularly sweet smile. "Are we clear on that, Mr. Mohler?"

He nodded and fumbled with his papers. Nick gave her a winsome grin. She ignored it, far too upset inside. Well-mannered Southern girls did not speak back, especially not to wealthy attorneys. But she was so damn tired of people in Barlow bringing up her parents, as if they waited to see if she'd pass out cold in her home from drinking too much.

Not that she really had a home. Her home depended upon the whims of what the family did with the ranch.

Shelby's troubled gaze flicked back to Nick. Not family. Silas's only son, Nick. He was the sole owner of the ranch now.

Nick stared back at her, the scar on his cheek turning white. "The will states Shelby can live here as long as I keep the ranch. What if I decide to sell?"

"Then she, along with everyone else, will have to leave." Kurt didn't look at her.

Felicity was rocking back and forth now, her jaw clenched so tight it could pound nails. The woman looked ready to rake her claws over Nick. Or scream. Or do both. But unlike Shelby, Felicity was a well-mannered Southern lady and she would not say a word.

Not until she was alone in her bedroom with Dan. Shelby didn't envy Dan for that.

Jake leaned forward, his hands on his knees. "How much did Uncle Silas owe? He never told any of us about this." His glance went to Shelby. "Not even Shelby here, who kept the books. Uncle Silas was very private about that."

"He was very far behind in payments, and the loan had a balloon due four months ago. The bank already started foreclosure. The total amount needed to prevent this is fifty-nine thousand, seven hundred and fifty. The bank needs this by the end of the month."

They had one month to come up with nearly sixty thousand dollars. She glanced at Nick. No, he had that time to come up with that cash.

"The ranch is worth much more than the mortgage, Nick." Kurt handed him a white business card. "Come and see me first thing Monday morning and we'll go over everything, including Chuck's offer to buy Belle Creek. He's offering nearly a million in cash. I can help set up a meeting. Chuck is a business associate."

Shelby couldn't think, could barely register what had just happened as Nick stood and shook the man's hand. The lawyer exited, and Felicity almost ran out of the room, her heels clicking on the hardwood floor as she left the Oriental carpet, her hapless husband trailing her. Jake looked stunned for a minute and then shrugged. He slapped Nick's shoulder.

"Welcome home, cousin. What a sly trickster that Silas is. Let me know if you're going to sell and I'll move my stuff in permanently with Lynn, not just my toothbrush. Maybe see about getting on with a horse farm in Kentucky." Jake grinned and left.

She was alone with Nick. He stood and went to Silas's big mahogany desk. How many times had she seen the old man sit there, dusty boots sprawled across the faded Oriental rug, frown lines denting his forehead, much as they were denting Nick's now? Silas had always brightened when she'd entered these hallowed quarters, inviting her to sit and talk.

He'd made her feel comfortable and at home, not like the hired hand she had been. Silas would insist on brewing them a little tea, and they'd sit, as fancy as if they were sipping tea in the queen's parlor. She'd tell him all about how Readalot performed his paces that day with Jake, and then how the horse kept nosing in her shirt pocket for the apple he knew she'd hidden as she curried him. Silas had listened to her, really listened, as his tired blue eyes met hers over his teacup.

The thought that he wouldn't be around anymore to listen to her talk about her day, ask in his deep, gravelly voice how she was doing, caused an unbearable clench of grief.

Nick turned from the desk, with its neat piles of papers and files. His gaze was bleak. He lifted a hand to her and she saw he had the letter.

"Shel…"

Frozen in shock, she could only stare as a kaleidoscope of disastrous possibilities whirled through her mind. Nick was now in charge. Nick, who had kissed her and left, making her feel as abandoned as a shelter dog. Nick, who fought hard with Silas and didn't care about the ranch's legacy, or his heritage.

"I didn't want this," he said, and the letter shook a little in his hand, as if a breeze caught it. "I need time to sort things out."

Time? "You have less than a month, by the look of things." She tried to make her voice light, but an undercurrent of bitterness laced her tone. "The bank looks to foreclose if they don't get sixty thousand dollars by then."

His eyes closed, and his long, dark lashes nearly swept over his elegant cheekbones. Such a handsome man, even with that sinister scar. It was a shame a man had such great lashes. No mascara for him.

She realized she felt slightly hysterical.

He opened his eyes, and a determined glint shone

there. "You'll always have a home here, Shel. You and your nephew."

"Sure." Now there was no disguising the anger in her voice. "As long as the ranch remains in the family. Because as the lawyer said, I'm not family."

No longer could she remain here, trying to be civilized. Emotion boiled in her stomach and she walked out of the room, not bothering to close the door. Only when she reached the privacy of her apartment over the garage did the tears come. She let them flow. Grief was better than the haunting thoughts about the future stabbing her mind.

Would Nick do as the lawyer suggested and sell the ranch? She couldn't even entertain that possibility.

Because if Nick decided to sell the ranch, it would be the worst for her. She and Timmy would be homeless, with no money, and nowhere else to go.

Chapter 4

Alone with the past.

Nick sat in the big leather chair behind Silas's desk, staring at the paneled walls of his father's study. He'd always hated this room. It was here that Silas lectured him, yelled at him and then finally shook his head in disgust, announcing that Nick was useless.

The day he ran off to join the navy, he never felt more determined to prove the old man wrong. He'd sweated, strained and broken bones to become a Navy SEAL.

And swore he'd never return to this room. Well, here he was, the echo of his father's voice bouncing off the walls, a ghost from the past.

Nick fingered the letter the lawyer had given him. There had to be a reason why the old man gave him everything and dissed Dan. To torment Dan like Silas had tormented Nick? Only one way to find out. With grim amusement, he looked at his hands as he took the brass paper opener to slit open the envelope. Hands that had held a weapon steady while facing insurgents were now trembling.

The old man certainly could be as scary as a terrorist at times. His psychological methods of wearing you down had honed Nick's stubborn streak to never give up. Never quit.

Unfolding the letter, he read the first two paragraphs. Unable to stomach more, he crumpled it up, his palm now shaking with anger, and threw the paper toward the empty fireplace. His father's portrait, stern and stately, hung over the mantel.

"Damn you to hell, Silas," he said hoarsely to the painting. "Damn you."

Clever bastard knew Nick would not accept the ranch, and would sign his birthright over to Dan and leave nothing behind but dust in his wake. Except Silas hit on the one thing he knew would guarantee Nick would stay— challenging him not to fail.

You are the only one who can save the Belle Creek from foreclosure or development, Nicolas. I leave this world counting on you. Don't disappoint me and fail at this one thing I ask of you.

All his life, the old man warned Nick would become his biggest disappointment. Never once did Silas say he was proud of Nick. Or even that he loved him.

Eyes wet, he stared at the portrait. "Why couldn't I ever be good enough for you?"

All the medals he'd won, the missions he'd accomplished, the work he'd done with the teams, and Silas never said a word. Never reached out to the son who'd stormed out of here, angry at a father who thought him useless.

Until now.

Too late.

He should call the lawyer, tell him he didn't want the ranch and arrange to have Mohler deed it over to Dan. Dan and his ice-cold wife could have the place and decide to sell. Nick retrieved the letter and fished out his phone, ready to contact the man. And then a face stabbed at his brain.

Shelby. If he did this, Shelby would be homeless. He wasn't certain if Dan would let Shelby and Timmy stay at the ranch, rent-free.

Nick smoothed out the paper and glanced at the letter again.

I'm counting on you. Things are very bad at the Belle Creek.

How bad was bad? The ranch never failed to earn money.

For the next half hour, he sat at the desk, ruminating over the tremendous responsibilities Silas had saddled him with. Nick took out a piece of paper and a pencil, and began jotting notes. Seldom one to make snap decisions, he called Dan on his cell. Minutes later, his cousin joined him in the study. Face sullen, Dan crossed his arms at the chest and didn't look at him.

He leaned forward, keeping his voice low and earnest. "I'm sure this comes as quite a shock, Dan…"

"I've worked here for years, and Belle Creek is my home," Dan snapped. "How do you think I feel? Silas shut me out again. He never listened to me, or agreed to implement the ideas I had to make the ranch more child- and family-friendly. He was stuck in the past. And now everything I've poured into the ranch is about to go up in smoke. If you sell, I'm left with nothing. Nothing!"

"I haven't decided yet about selling."

"This is my home," Dan said tightly. "My family's home. More than yours. But it's said and done. You going to sell?"

Loaded question. "I need to evaluate all the angles." Nick studied his cousin, seeing the worry lines denting his face, the purple shadows beneath his eyes. It wasn't right. Dan had managed the ranch for years, and for Silas to cut him off entirely had been cruel. No matter what his father's intentions, Nick knew he had to win his cousin's loyalties first.

"I'll make you a deal." Nick tapped the pencil on the desk. "First thing Monday, I'll go into town, see Kurt Mohler and draft a legal agreement. You and your family stay here at the Belle Creek, with you as manager of the ranch, and as soon as the bank is paid back, I'll increase your salary by fifty percent and give you twenty-five percent of the ranch's profits as soon as its operating in the black."

No tension left those rigid shoulders. "And if you sell?"

"You get ten percent of the cash left over from the sale, after the bank is paid." He thought of Jake and Shelby. "I'm offering similar deals, with less percentages, to Shelby and Jake."

Dan blew out a breath. "That's a sweetheart agreement for you. I get a much smaller percentage if you cut everything and sell."

"It's more than fair. Call it an incentive to keep the ranch operational. But the agreement also includes stipulations." This was the hard part, and he wasn't certain if Dan, who had run the ranch as he'd pleased, would agree. "Your salary goes into a fund to help operate the ranch and that includes paying the salaries of the stable hands. You'll still live at the house, rent-free, and you'll have an allowance for food, spending money and necessities. It's the only way I can corral the expenditures until we come up with a way to pay back the bank. I'm going to trust you to help the ranch get back on its feet, but you have to trust me, too."

His mouth flattened as Dan leaned back. "You just returned, Nick. Why should I trust you won't sell and run off?"

"The legal agreement. It will bind us both here. First, tell me why Silas had no money. He was never one to carry debt. What happened?"

His cousin didn't meet his eyes. "Who knows? It's expensive to run a ranch these days. If that's all… I have to talk to Felicity about all this."

Dan pushed away from the chair, clearly finished with the conversation. He left, but in a considerably better temper than when he'd first walked into the study.

Nick watched him leave, his mind clicking over the facts like a well-oiled machine. Now was not the time for emotions, and Dan's were running high after the funeral.

He had savings. But not even close to sixty thousand dollars. And Dan and everyone else seemed loathe to provide any information about why the ranch had slid into such dire straits.

Tucking his phone away, Nick left the study to change his clothing. He took the letter, hoping to get answers from the one person he knew would tell the truth.

She knew he'd come knocking at her door someday. All the years since he'd been gone, Shelby kept telling herself Nick would return. Now he stood on the landing outside her apartment, a big man taking up half the front window Silas had installed when he'd renovated the place ten years ago.

Why did he have to do it when her eyes were swollen and red from crying, and her hair a frizzy mess?

He's not here to seduce you, she warned herself. Shelby crumpled up the tissue and threw it in a wastebasket, then opened her front door.

Tall and leanly muscled, he wore a clean black T-shirt and blue jeans. Gone was the somber funeral attire. Somehow she liked this better. It was a clear reminder of the cocky man he'd been, the one who had almost coaxed her into sex all those years ago. A wicked-looking pistol was tucked into a holster at his leather belt.

He was carrying and the sight of the weapon comforted her a little. With all the vandalism at the ranch, it was good to have a man around who knew the business end of a pistol. Dan was hopeless when it came to guns and Felicity was too squeamish. Jake knew how to shoot, but he joked he was a lover, not a fighter.

Shelby's hungry gaze traveled down from the flatness of his stomach and the muscles rippling beneath the tight T-shirt to the polished brass buckle with a bucking bronc on it. Her gaze traveled a little lower to the interesting bulge just below...

Did I just look at his crotch? Oh, stop it, Shel!

Fortunately, he didn't appear to notice. Nick's expression was all business. "Shelby, I'm sorry to bother you, but I need answers about the ranch."

She stepped aside as he walked in. Typical Nick. Direct, no dancing around, but clearly stating his intentions.

Except when he kissed you, a little voice inside her head nagged.

With a desultory gesture toward the tiny living room,

she perched on the wing chair that had been a real steal at a garage sale. Nick sat on the blue-and-white-striped sofa with the stain on the back that she'd hidden by pushing it against the wall.

He gazed around at the landscape paintings on the bright yellow walls and the vase of daisies she'd placed on a round table by the front window.

"Place looks real good, Shel. You've made it into a home." His glance landed on the art easel and the board upon it, tucked into a corner. Nick pointed to the landscapes. "Did you paint those?"

She nodded, folding her arms across her chest. Painting had been a favorite pastime, but with the long hours she worked lately, it had to be set aside. Keeping her home mattered more.

A home she could easily lose, depending on his whims. "What do you want, Nick?"

He opened his palm, showing a piece of crumpled white stationery. "What's happened at the Belle Creek that it's losing so much money, Shel? Silas wants me to save it from foreclosure…or a sale to Beaufort."

Honest, direct. Relief calmed a little of her jangling nerves. She took in the bleakness on his face, the firm set of his lips.

"Come into the kitchen and I'll make us coffee."

He squeezed into one of the two chairs in the postage-stamp kitchen, his big frame seeming to suck up all the space. Nick pushed a hank of dark blond hair away from his brow with an impatient gesture as she measured the grounds and started the coffee.

Too shaken by his nearness to sit, she leaned against the sink. "What exactly did Silas say in that letter?"

Nick shook his head. "Tell me what's going on around here."

"Same old Nick. Always your needs first before anyone else's," she countered.

He leaned forward, locking his intense brown gaze to hers. "No, Shel. I put your needs first ten years ago. 'Cause if I hadn't, I wouldn't have walked out of here leaving you a virgin."

Old hurts surfaced, needling her. "Maybe I needed to lose my virginity back then, hotshot. Did you ever think to ask?"

Intent flared on his face. "No need, darling. If I'd made love to you, I would have been inside you so deep that no matter who took you after that, the memory of me would always linger," he said softly.

A furious heat crept up her chest, to her throat, warming her cheeks. Shelby hoped he'd think it was anger.

"Is this why you're here, Nick? To taunt me with our past?"

Regret touched his face. "No. But I swore I would go to hell first before following through on what I wanted to do to you. Not what I had to do."

As an apology, it sucked. Made him look noble and self-sacrificing while leaving her looking like a horny teenager eager to explore her newfound sexuality.

"You don't have to worry about me anymore," she said coolly. "The coals of that particular fire got stamped out long ago when you turned around and ran, never looking back."

Now it was his turn for his cheeks to turn ruddy. Nick's guilty gaze darted around the kitchen. Damn if he didn't look like he did ten years ago, all adorable and contrite when he'd kissed her and confessed that he had condoms in his back pocket.

Condoms he'd never used with her.

She gestured to the paper. "What did Silas say to you?"

He shook his head, rubbed a hand over his chin. "It's private. I need to know exactly why the Belle Creek is losing money. Miles and Mason said there was a break-in and Felicity's jewelry was stolen right after Readalot died."

Nick had been gone a long time. He didn't know the troubles they faced. "I found Readalot in his stall. He was young, only eight, but he died during the night. The vet said it was natural causes. Maybe a heart attack. That was the first suspicious incident. He was very healthy. About two days later, someone broke into the house and stole Felicity's jewelry. A couple of gold bracelets and her favorite sterling-and-emerald pin. Jonah Doyle and his men dusted, took notes, but found nothing."

His gaze widened. "Jonah Doyle? He's working for the sheriff?"

"He *is* the sheriff now. There have been other incidents as well, small things that are frustrating, but when you run a ranch, it all adds up. Fences broken, a horse trailer that was in perfect working order and suddenly had two flat tires. Stuff like that."

Leaning back, Nick frowned. "Who is threatening the place? Why are almost all the rental stalls vacant? I did an inspection and the security system isn't the greatest, but it works. So what's going on?"

The coffee machine pinged, indicating it was ready. Shelby remained motionless, her heart hurting and her throat tight.

Nick lowered his voice, the deep, gravelly tone sexy

and yet oddly soothing. "I want to make it right, Shel. I'm not back to hurt you, or anyone else. But I want answers. Now."

Take-charge Nick. Maybe he could save the ranch. She pushed a hand through her unruly hair.

"Sabotage. I have no idea who is doing it, or how they gained access to the ranch, but it has to be someone very familiar with the workings. The security system…" he suggested.

She sighed. "It's fake. Silas had me stop paying the monthly fee over a year ago to save money. It's pretty bad, Nick."

A low curse tore from his throat. "Tell me everything."

"Beaufort isn't the first developer to make Silas an offer. There have been others. He's offering the least money, though. Silas refused. He said the ranch has been in the family for generations, and it would remain that way."

"Stubborn," he muttered.

She gave him a calm look. "Like someone else I know."

Shelby fetched two cups, adding cream and sugar to hers, and added a sprinkle of cinnamon to Nick's cup from the container on her spice rack.

"You remembered."

He offered a smile that erased the hardness in his eyes, and made her lady parts ache with yearning. Same killer smile that could coax women into his bed, same charm that tamed the wildest horse.

Stay immune to that charm, Shelby. He's dynamite.

She sat at the table, turning the cup around in her hands, the familiar tightness squeezing her stomach. This time, it was as much Nick's nearness as her anxiety over the ranch's failing business.

"Tell me exactly what your role is at Belle Creek," he ordered Shelby.

"I handle the accounting, deposits, invoices and data entry for the farm. And payroll. Everything but the family's personal finances." Shelby sighed. "And the mortgage. I had no idea Silas had the ranch that much in debt."

"How much did Silas pay you for that?"

Shelby shook her head. "Nothing, as of the last year. I stopped taking a salary and living off my waitressing job when I saw the income was dropping. I wanted to help save money."

Nick stared at her. "Are you a saint?"

Anger surfaced, but she struggled with her temper. "No, I'm pragmatic. Silas gave me a place to live, rent-free. It was my way of paying him back."

"I have a new offer to make."

She listened intently. Maybe she wouldn't get tossed out after all. Nick offered her a real salary, with a ten percent increase once the ranch operated in the black, and a five percent share in the profits. If he sold, he'd give her a flat cash fee of fifteen thousand dollars after all debts were settled. He intended to draft the agreement to have them work together to make the ranch solvent.

Jake would get the same offer.

"Jake might not like it. He's family, and he's the one who runs the stables and handles the horses. I'm only the bookkeeper."

Nick gave her a wry smile. "I doubt it. I suspect you run this ranch more behind the scenes than Dan or Jake."

Warming to his praise, she hid a smile. Very perceptive of him.

"When did the losses start?" he asked.

"We started losing boarders about eight months ago,

right after three Realtors first approached Silas about
selling some of the land to him for development. This
section of Tennessee, with its main artery only forty-five
minutes to Nashville, is prime real estate for those wishing to commute to the city."

"The ranch has a solid rep. What happened to Jack?"

At the mention of the ranch's top-notch trainer, she
shook her head. "He moved back to Kentucky. Someone
made him a lucrative offer at a very big stable. And then
the social-media posts began."

She fetched her laptop from the bedroom and opened
it on the kitchen table, then navigated to the ranch's business page on social media.

Nick narrowed his eyes as he scanned the posts. She
winced as he came across the most recent, virulent posting.

Don't board yer horses here. They kill them for
dog food.

"I don't need to see more."

She shut the lid, glad to switch off the ugliness of the
words. That posting had been mild compared to others
that accused them of stealing money.

"The posters create anonymous social-media accounts
and then shut them down by the time we notify Facebook.
No one seems to be able to track them down."

"I can."

Hardness filled his gaze, making her shiver. She'd
never seen this side of Nick before, dangerous and pur-
poseful. Small wonder he'd been a SEAL. Pity the enemy
who ran into him.

Maybe Nick was exactly what the Belle Creek needed to pull through this mess.

"Someone hacked into our social-media sites and said that Belle Creek was letting its horses starve. There were horrible photos of starving horses, probably photos stolen from animal-rescue sites. Rumors spread, and soon no one wanted to board their horses here. The reviews on travel sites have been much, much worse. Anonymous posters saying that we deliberately beat the horses and never muck out the stalls. Business was starting to taper off before, and now it's positively at a standstill. The only two boarders we have left are Chuck Beaufort's daughter Natalie's mare, Fancy, and my friend Ann's horse."

He studied the liquid in his cup, the dusting of spice floating on the top. "Someone was trying to make Silas sell. Small wonder the old man didn't capitulate."

Loyalty to his father surfaced. "It would take more than vulgarities on social media and a few threats to bring him down when he was alive."

"No, it took his own damn stubbornness. Why the hell didn't he see a doctor when he was that sick?" A pulse ticked at the side of his neck.

Fresh tears threatened. She sipped her coffee, ducking her head to hide them. "Doctors are expensive and he said home remedies worked fine for him. He said that up until the EMS came to take him to the hospital."

He slid his hand across the table as if to comfort her, but she drew back. The less skin contact they shared, the better. Nick gave a rough nod.

"I'll stay, for now. If you agree to work with me on finding out who the hell is doing all this."

His voice lowered. "It means working close with me, Shel. Can you manage?"

At her little nod, the tension left his broad shoulders.

"I'll find whoever is doing this. And they'll pay." He lifted his mug in a salute. "To you, Silas. Wherever the hell you are, I hope you know you roped me into this place good."

Tipping back his mug, he took a large swig of coffee.

And coughed violently. Liquid sloshed over the cup's side as he slammed it down.

"Sweet Jesus," he gasped, still choking.

Nick raced to the sink, twisted the tap and grabbed a glass from the dish drainer. He chugged the water and then set down the glass.

"It's cinnamon, just as you used to like in your coffee." Bewildered, she stared at him.

"That's not cinnamon," he muttered. Nick strode straight to the small spice rack on the counter and began pawing through the bottles. He found the cinnamon, uncapped it and sniffed.

"Someone isn't just messing around with Dan and his wife, Shel." He held out the bottle.

Her eyes watered and her throat closed up as she inhaled a whiff. Shelby coughed violently. Nick fetched her a glass of water.

"Drink," he ordered.

She did, and the tightness eased in her throat a little. "What is that?"

"Cayenne pepper." He studied the little glass container clearly labeled Cinnamon. Shelby's heart dropped to her stomach, and her pulse raced.

Whoever was threatening her at the restaurant had followed her here as well.

The implications slowly dawned on her. "I don't have cayenne pepper in the house. I threw out that bottle that came with the spice rack. I was going to make Timmy a cake for his birthday. With cinnamon frosting."

"Who knew this?"

Her shoulders sagged. "I don't know. I asked at the restaurant if someone had a recipe…"

And Natalie had been there, in the kitchen, looking things over, claiming that her father wanted to make sure everything was up to par. Natalie, who must have overheard Shelby talking about Timmy's allergies and how cayenne pepper was dangerous to him. Shelby shivered, remembering how Timmy liked to lick the frosting off the spoon…

"Timmy's allergic to cayenne pepper. It could have sent him to the hospital."

Nick settled his hands on her trembling shoulders. "That's it. I'm moving in with you until we clear this up."

Oh, hell no. She waved a hand. "I'll have the locks changed."

"And whoever did this will break inside again. No protests, Shel. I'll sleep on that couch. It's a foldout, right?"

"You can't. What about Dan? You have your old room at the main house…"

Nick's mouth twitched in a ghost of a smile. "Felicity turned it pink with flounces. If I stay there, I'll start singing soprano and want to paint my nails."

Not taking chances, she marched the spice out of the house and tossed it into the metal can by the garage door, making sure to clamp the lid down tight. As she trotted back up the stairs, her head pounded. Timmy could have been badly hurt with the cake she'd planned to make him. If he'd gone to the hospital, she had only catastrophic health insurance coverage. The bill would wipe her out.

Not to mention how sick her nephew would have been.

"C'mon, Shel. It'll be okay. I promise." Nick held her shoulders, his thumbs stroking in soothing circles. The caress sank through her wool sweater and suffused her entire body with heat.

It took her back to years ago, when he'd done much the same the night he saw her crying in the cabin over the loss of her dog. Silas had put him down because Rex had grown old and feeble and could barely walk. Silas had been gentle and compassionate, but firm.

And losing her pet, who had been her best friend, who had seen her through her parents leaving her, had crushed Shelby.

But no longer was she the softhearted teenager with stars in her eyes each time Nick Anderson drew near. Shelby jerked out of his embrace.

"I'll be fine. If it means checking out all the spices, my refrigerator and packing a loaded pistol under my pillow like Dan does, no one's going to get to me. Or Timmy. No one is breaking in again at the house or your place."

She spread out her hands helplessly, frustration biting her. "Jonah said without the security cameras recording who goes in and out, the person would be hard to catch, with the staff traipsing in and out of the house."

Rubbing the nape of his neck, Nick frowned. "Jonah Doyle can be a jerk, but he's right in that. Anyone could have gotten into the bedroom. First thing we do, get those security cameras back up."

Shelby shook her head. "Silas owed the alarm company a lot of money."

"No need for an alarm company. I'll set up a new system to monitor them from here." His mouth compressed. "I'll wire them myself."

"Fine. I can show you where the cameras are." Her

jangled nerves made it feel like ants were crawling beneath her skin. "But you're not staying here. My apartment is too small and that couch has a thin mattress."

Nick shrugged. "I've bunked in much worse, and tighter spaces. It's my skill set."

But not around her. Never around her. It was hard enough breathing the same air as him. How could she sleep with him in the next room?

Then her gaze fell to the pistol hanging on his belt. Timmy's welfare came first. She could control her raging libido for her nephew's sake. Shelby walked away, hugging herself as she stared out the front window.

"So what if I haven't had sex in eight months?"

"Been that long, huh?"

Shelby whirled to see his wide, Cheshire cat grin. "You heard."

Nick tapped his ear. "Another skill of mine. I know how to listen, darling."

Making a note of that, she gave him a pointed look. "Okay. You can stay here. But this is my house and my rules. You sleep here." She pointed to the sofa. "You'll share a bathroom with Timmy, not me. I have my own and plan to keep it that way. And no flirting and suggestive remarks or cussing. My nephew is only five."

Nick spread his hands out in a gesture of innocence. "I'm innocent."

Right.

He stood close enough for her to count the bristles on his chin. Nick had shaved in a hurry, neglecting one spot. Memories assailed her. Sixteen years old, scraping her fingers over his chin and then kissing that one particular spot.

Shaking free the memory, she glanced at her watch.

"Felicity wants us all to dine together at the main house. Six o'clock sharp. Wear something more civilized than jeans. She likes to dress for dinner."

He considered. "I have some black silk boxers that are formal. That do?"

Flushing, she scowled at him. "Stop it, Nick."

Then his cocky grin dropped and his gaze turned serious. "You'll be safer with me here, Shelby. I'm not going to leave until I find out who's been doing these things and threatening you and the ranch. I promise you, I will catch them."

With a nod, he headed out the door. "I'll bring my things over later. Need to have a look around the place first."

Watching him walk down the steps, a warm tingle raced down her spine. Not from his quiet words, or the relief they brought, but the awareness of him as a man and the unspoken intent lingering in his eyes, a sensual promise that could lead them straight down the road where they'd left off ten years ago.

And straight back into hell.

Chapter 5

Shelby. Soft, warm body, mouth that would tempt a monk.

Nick tried to keep the image of her at bay as he took the golf cart on the trails winding through the ranch. What he saw so far dismayed him. Barbed wire fence broken in places, posts that leaned or were too weathered to hold anything back.

Easy enough to infiltrate the property. Why had the old man slipped? Never had Silas been this lax while Nick was living here. He ran a tight ship. Maybe having Dan as the ranch manager had meant things got sloppy.

His cell phone rang. Stopping the golf cart, Nick glanced at the number and answered it.

"Nick. I'm so sorry about your father. We only found out today from Jarrett. You okay?"

His buddy Cooper sounded concerned. Jarrett Adler, former Navy SEAL lieutenant, was an octopus when it came to keeping up with his former teammates. The man could find anyone. Married now to the pretty daughter of a former US senator, Jarrett was living the good life after the navy.

Nick sighed. "Fine. I would have told you, but I didn't want to drag you and Meg away from the farm. The funeral was quick. I barely made it home in time."

He told Cooper about the inheritance, and briefly mentioned the financial cloud hovering over the ranch.

"You need a loan? Want us to gather a group of guys to come down there and help get things back in shape?"

The same self-reliance that guided him through life after leaving home filled him now. He didn't need help. Even if his good friend meant well. "No thanks, man. I can handle it."

"Nick, you helped save Meg. I never forget a debt. I mean it. If you need me..." Cooper's voice dropped. "Or Jarrett—don't let that damn pride of yours stop you from calling. You know Jarrett. He's always willing to help out, and he's looking for guys for Project SOS."

"I will. Gotta run. My love to Meg and the fam." He thumbed off the phone and kept driving, wondering what other bad news he'd find on the trails.

He came to the outcropping of forest where he'd once played as a child—to escape Silas—then parked the golf cart and got out. Nick rested a hand against the thick magnolia tree that guarded the entrance to these woods for decades, perhaps centuries. Searching through the gnarled bark, he found the initials.

SS + NA

Grinning, he traced the faded marks, remembering the day he'd first encountered Shelby carving them into the tree. She was only eight and declared Nick had to marry her since their initials were formally engraved on "their" tree, the spot where they'd played tag as children.

Little minx even swiped his favorite Boy Scout knife to make the mark.

Nick rubbed the initials. He wasn't a Boy Scout anymore, and she had a body made for hard loving at night. Sleeping only footfalls away from her would test his endurance. But hell, he was a former SEAL who had pushed his body to the limits. He could handle the close proximity to pure temptation.

Nick closed his eyes, remembering her mouth, soft and warm upon his. How she'd been eager and inexperienced as he'd tutored her in how to use her tongue, and how her hands had skimmed up his back beneath his skirt, exploring his body.

Hands off. She's not for you.

Shelby was home and hearth and he was…what?

Needing to leave, as soon as things were settled. Already he felt the pinch of yearning to hit the road again. Ever since leaving the teams, he had fierce wanderlust.

Nick continued his patrol, avoiding the thick woods where the old cabin stood. No more memories of Shelby, and the kiss they'd shared. Instead, he drove back, parked and walked away from the view of the jagged purple mountaintops shrouded in mist, toward the stables and barn. Horses cropping grass in the pasture didn't even glance up as he passed.

When he reached the red barn, the door was wide-open. Nick scanned the perimeter, saw nothing odd, but someone was inside.

The barn was an open space, with rafters reaching to a loft. Here, Silas had stored the wagon used for autumn hay rides, the winter sleigh, the two tractors and other equipment. The wood building still had stalls once used for horses before Silas had built the much larger, more modern stables. Bales of hay stacked to the loft made it an excellent place for hiding. He grinned as he walked across the wood floor, his soft-soled shoes making no sound.

Behind one of the stalls, a towheaded boy sat on a bale of hay, playing a video game. Beeps blared from the tablet he held. Nick grinned.

"Hi, Timmy."

The kid jumped, nearly dropping the tablet. Guilt crossed his face.

Nick jammed his hands in his pockets, not wanting to scare the kid further. "I'm Nick. Visiting for a while."

"I know," the boy said with aplomb. "We met."

He rubbed his chin. "Are you supposed to be in here without an adult?"

Timmy picked up the tablet and waved it. "Aunt Shelby told me to play. She didn't specify what to play."

Smart kid.

Nick pointed to the hay. "Mind if I join you?"

Timmy made a gesture much like his aunt had made in her living room. Nick sat.

"Uncle Silas was your daddy." Timmy's gaze swept him up and down, as scrutinizing as Shelby's had been. "You left here a long time ago. I heard them talking."

I bet. "I'm back now, for a while. I'm moving in with you and your aunt."

Blue eyes rounded. "You're supposed to live in the big house."

Suppressing a snort, he lifted his shoulders. "The

house is too stuffy for me. I'd be more comfortable with you and Shelby. If it's okay by you."

Timmy considered. "If Aunt Shelby says you can, then I guess it's okay."

The boy gave him a long look. "Is that your motor-cycle parked in the driveway?"

Nick nodded. Timmy's eyes lit up. "It's nice. Nicer than my trucks."

Chuckling at the thought of his Harley being compared to toy trucks, he wondered if Timmy liked hanging out here. Nick had as a child. The soothing smell of the bales of hay provided a seat, and there were no prying eyes to see how hurt he'd been at Silas yelling at him to shape up.

"You come here often, Timmy?" At the nod, he went on. "See anything odd?"

"Like the stuff that's been happening around here?" Timmy shook his head. "I like to hide in here because no one ever looks for me here."

"Especially when you've done something you shouldn't have?"

Timmy's lower lip jutted out, a startling resemblance to his aunt when Shelby was much younger. "I told Aunt Shelby I'd clean the paint off the wall. I didn't mean to splatter it."

At the boy's chagrined look, Nick grinned. "No worries, Tim. I did the same when I was your age. Good place to hide when my daddy wanted to spank me."

He shook his head. "Aunt Shelby's nice. She would never spank me. It's only Uncle Dan I like hiding from."

Odd. "Why? Does he threaten you?"

"No, but he yells sometimes. He gets all worried and his face scrunches up. I don't like it."

Nick didn't, either, but considering how much financial trouble the ranch was in, he couldn't blame his cousin. He stood, nodding toward the door. "Let's get out of here before someone discovers you've left."

Timmy joined him as Nick walked to the nearby stables. The boy chattered as he clutched his tablet. When they reached the stables, Timmy ran through the opened door to a stall at the end.

"Hey, Macaroni pony!" He reached up as a pony stuck its head close to the bars in the stall. Timmy climbed onto a bale of hay and stroked the horse's nose.

"This is my pony, Macaroni. Well, he's not really my pony, but Macaroni likes me more than Mason. Mason doesn't like horses, so Miss Felicity said I can ride Macaroni and care for him. Aunt Shelby will only allow me to come here with an adult."

Nick gave a pointed look around the stables. Timmy flushed. "Today's different, because of the funeral."

"Listen to your aunt," he said mildly. "You shouldn't be here in the stables alone or the barn alone with all these strange things happening. You're too young."

Timmy frowned. "I'm almost six years old. I'm not a baby."

He really liked this kid and his sass, which reminded him so much of Shelby. "You're with me now, so it's okay."

The child sat on the bale of hay and began toying with his tablet again. "I like you, Nick. You're nice. Dan yells at me all the time when I'm in the barn or the stables. Uncle Jake's okay. He doesn't mind me hanging here. Mario, one of our stable hands, is usually here but he got the day off because of the funeral. He likes Aunt Shelby. He brought her flowers last week."

Jealousy pinched Nick. Silly. He hadn't been in Shelby's life for years. Why shouldn't she date?

"Is Mario her boyfriend?"

Timmy shook his head. "He just likes her because she helped him with his English lessons."

"Does Aunt Shelby have a boyfriend or any other guys who visit her?"

Timmy's gaze sharpened. "No. Why?"

Nick gave a grudging laugh. Very smart kid. Small wonder, with Shelby raising him. "Wondering who else might come on the ranch. I need to account for everyone."

"Uncle Jake's seeing Lynn. He brings her to dinner sometimes, but Miss Felicity doesn't like her because she dyes her hair pink and snaps her gum."

Nick liked the rebellious Lynn already.

"Do you like pink hair, Nick?"

He thought of sable-soft hair, slipping through his fingers as he fisted it in his hands, his tongue moving deep inside a wet, warm mouth. "I prefer dark brown."

He investigated the stables, leaving Timmy to his video game. At least here he could see evidence of money well spent. Silas had upgraded the facility, installing new sliding doors and heaters. The stalls were roomy. But with few boarders, what good was it if the stables didn't pay for themselves?

He came to a stall occupied by a curious filly, who came over to greet him. Timmy abandoned his tablet to join Nick.

"That's Fancy, Miss Natalie's horse. She doesn't want her out in the pasture with the others because she's afraid she'll get bitten. Or mounted." Timmy frowned. "What's mounted? I asked Aunt Shelby and she just stammered something about what horses do."

Hiding a grin, Nick looked at the horse, who blew softly at him as he stroked her nose through the bars. "They do at that," he muttered, thinking of how he'd enjoy doing the same to Timmy's aunt.

Down, boy.

"Miss Natalie said that she wouldn't board her horse here unless she got preferential treatment and Silas installed new heaters for the winter." Timmy looked at the horse. "I heard Silas say it cost a pretty penny. But he wanted her business."

Interesting. Why would Natalie board her filly here when Chuck Beaufort had stables of his own? Maybe she had a particular reason for visiting the Belle Creek…or she wanted an excuse to get on the grounds.

"Does Miss Natalie come here often to ride her horse?"

Timmy nodded. "She was supposed to come today, even though Aunt Shelby said no visitors at the ranch. Miss Natalie said she wasn't a visitor, that she paid plenty of money to keep her horse here and didn't need special visiting hours."

Sounded like the snobbish Natalie. Nick looked down at Timmy. "When was she here?"

"She was here just before you arrived. Her car's still parked outside."

So that was the fancy Jag he'd spotted on his walk. Natalie had been a high-stepping and snobbish filly back in their school days and it seemed little had changed. Perhaps she'd noticed something in her daily visits to the stables. He'd chat her up, coax information from those glossy lips.

Not his type. No, he preferred natural mouths with plump lower lips that trembled when he stroked his thumb across the soft texture...

Time to go, before he started daydreaming again about the boy's aunt and developed a condition Timmy was too young to understand. A stable hand entered the stables, nodded at him and began dishing out oats for the filly.

"Hi, Hank!" Timmy waved at the man, who nodded back at him. "Hank is always here, so I'm never really alone," he told Nick. "I usually leave when it's time to give Fancy her oats."

More expenses. Miss Natalie's horse had tastes as expensive as her owner's.

"I'll walk you back to the house," Nick told Timmy.

Timmy grabbed his tablet and began chatting about school and his birthday. He'd wanted a store-bought cake, only to please his aunt, but he really preferred Shelby's because she let him help, and lick the spoon.

Nick smiled. "Frosting's the best part."

They cleared the stables and started on the pathway snaking through the grass that led to the main house.

Out of the corner of his eye he saw movement by the stables and something sail through the air toward his head. Nick automatically ducked, then pushed Timmy to the ground and covered his body. Withdrawing his sidearm, he waited.

But all he heard was the wind rustling through the nearby trees and the whinny of the horses in the nearby pasture. Nick eased off Shelby's nephew. "You okay?"

Wide-eyed, Timmy stared at him. "I'm o-okay. Wh-what was that?"

"I don't know. Someone threw something at me." He gestured to the ground. "Stay here and stay low!"

Nick ran to the stables and saw the hired man still feeding Natalie's horse. "Has anyone been by here?" he asked sharply.

Hank shook his head. "Only Miss Natalie a few moments ago. Not here now. Said something about going to get her car."

After checking out the stables and the perimeter, he saw nothing. Nick headed back to the scared Timmy and saw something in the grass nearby. His blood pressure skyrocketed.

It was a small cloth bag, tied at the end with a cord. Suspicious bags in his world could mean an explosive device. Memories hammered at him, the sinking feeling as the Humvee rattled over the road, the terrible bang and right after, the horrid pain in his leg and the burn as shrapnel sliced open his left cheek...

"Timmy, go back to the house right now."

"But—"

"Now!"

Not until the boy had reached the house safely and was inside did Nick stoop to examine the bag. He listened. Nothing ticking.

Nick walked away, found a rock and lobbed it at the bag.

Ping! The rock hit the paper, but nothing exploded.

With extreme caution, he approached the bag and then very carefully sliced the cord with his pocketknife. He opened it.

Nothing but rocks inside. Whoever did this had wanted to hit his head, but not injure him badly. The rocks were more for weighing the bag down than to cause real injury.

But something else was there as well. A glint of white paper. A note?

He pulled it out. The bold, black lettering was clear, along with the intent.

Welcome home, loser. Now get out of town. We don't need no failures here in Barlow.

Chapter 6

Nick kept quiet during dinner that night. He didn't want to talk, only observe. Someone didn't want him here, and he was determined to find out who it was. Fortunately Timmy hadn't seen the bag, or guessed what the contents were.

Harmless as threats went. Except the note's nasty words jerked his chain as effectively as if Silas himself had penned them. How well he remembered his father leaving him notes around the ranch as reminders to finish his chores. Notes that lacked any affection, but were as stern as his father's voice.

Loser.

Failure.

I'm neither. I became a SEAL and left all that behind.

But deep inside, the hurt little boy he'd been still remembered how painful it was to hear Silas lecture him, and shake his head in fatherly disapproval. How old had he been when the first lectures started? Eleven, maybe. Shortly after his mother died, and his father became more sullen and angry, and turned his scrutiny to Nick. Nick had sorely missed his mom, who showered him with love and kisses. The day she'd died, he'd taken one of the ranch ATVs out on a joyride, and ended up turning over in the creek bed. He'd cried and cried.

Silas hadn't comforted him. Instead, the old man caned his ass. The ATV was valuable farm equipment.

Nick tucked that sour memory back into his mind, focusing on the present. Silas was dead, and all his disapproval went with him. The note was a nasty trick left by someone who didn't like the prodigal son returning home.

He hadn't seen the elusive Natalie, either, but as he'd left the stables, a sleek black Jag had pulled away, gravel spitting beneath the tires. It could have been Natalie who tossed the bag at him. Until he questioned her, he didn't know.

Or it could even be someone sitting at this table.

He had less reason to suspect Natalie, unless she was vindictive and didn't like the way he'd rejected her last night. But Nick never had been one for fancy, polished women.

His gaze shot over to Shelby. No, his tastes were singular, running to sassy, pretty brunettes with kind hearts.

Felicity had insisted on everyone dining together "in honor of our dear, departed Silas." Even Shelby and Timmy sat at the polished inlaid dining table in the formal room. Candles in silver holders flickered as light from the crystal chandelier overhead glinted on the gold-rimmed china.

He'd grown up with wealth and privilege, but Silas had been more a practical sort, especially after Nick's mother died. Meals were usually taken in the smaller kitchen, and formal dinners were for holidays. Nick suspected Felicity wasn't the same.

After leaving Shelby's apartment, Nick had dug around the barn, looking for answers. Hank told him they'd found Readalot, their champion jumper, dead one morning. Nothing suspicious. The horse had simply died. Maybe it was colic. Dan had filed a report and the insurance company paid up.

But Nick knew there were ways of killing horses that would make it look natural. Electrical shock, for one. Insurance claims had been paid out, a pretty sum of fifty thousand dollars. Not enough to pay down the debt on the ranch, but no chump change, either.

His gaze whipped over to the diamond hanging around Felicity's neck.

"That's a very pretty necklace, Felicity. A gift?" he asked, then sipped his red wine.

She preened. "Dan gave it to me on our tenth wedding anniversary last month."

Nice gift. Dan's wife had expensive tastes. What if the saboteur was Dan himself? Or even Felicity? Quick cash, instead of waiting for the next horse competition or for stud fees? Readalot was the ranch's prized possession. When he died, there went their chances of income. It would nudge Silas closer to selling.

Felicity sipped wine from the crystal goblet. He noted Shelby had left hers untouched. Shelby never touched a drop of alcohol. After growing up with two drunkards for parents and being the one to care for her younger sister, he understood.

Dan's wife turned to him. "Nicolas, if you're headed to Kurt Mohler's office Monday, you can borrow one of the ranch vehicles. It has a GPS. Kurt's office is difficult to find downtown. I'm sure you will want to sign the papers to sell the ranch and then be on your way."

All eyes swung over to him. All but Shelby's. She stared at her teacup as if trying to divine the leaves.

"I'm not selling."

Three words that drained the blood from Felicity's face. "But, but…"

Dan covered his wife's hand with his own. "Enough, Felicity. The ranch belongs to Nick now. It's his to do with as he pleases."

Jake brought a forkful of green beans to his mouth and chewed. "Damn straight. The man can do as he pleases, Felicity."

"Don't talk with your mouth full, Jake," she snapped. "It's a bad influence on the children."

"Yes, ma'am." Jake winked at Timmy, who giggled as he sipped his milk.

Whee. If dinners together were this much fun, he'd spend his meals eating in town. Nick watched Shelby pour Timmy more milk from the pitcher. She was good with her nephew, had a real motherly streak.

His thoughts drifted. What if he had explored beyond that kiss ten years ago and they'd made love? Would he have made her pregnant? Silas would have forced him to marry Shel, not that Nick would have minded her in his bed for the rest of his life. But any time Silas wanted him to do something, Nick resisted.

But what if he hadn't resisted? They'd have at least two kids by now…with sparkling eyes like hers and that sassy lil grin…

He shook free the thought. He was a wandering man, not inclined to settle. Not even for the temptation of Shelby's lush body beneath his every night.

She fit into this life, this world in Tennessee. He no longer did.

Then where the hell do you fit in?

Dan asked Nick about his travels around the country. Nick told him about the nomadic lifestyle he'd lived since leaving the teams, doing odd jobs and then moving on to explore a new town. Shelby's eyes lit with interest, while Felicity merely looked bored.

Nick directed his attention to Shelby. "New Hampshire's real sweet this time of year. Bite of fall in the air, the apples are crisp and the colors so sharp they explode."

She sighed. "I've always wanted to travel. Paris would be my dream destination, where I could study art, but I'll take anywhere out of Barlow. When my sister and her husband get back, they said we'd live together in Nashville."

He lowered his voice. "Nashville is not out of town, Shel. Why don't you pick up and leave when Timmy's parents return?"

For a moment wild hope ignited her gaze. Then it shuttered as she stabbed her vegetables with more effort than required.

"It's not as simple for a woman as it is for a man," she muttered.

"Nothing's ever simple, Shel. You have to make it happen."

A loud *pop* exploded outside. Nick jumped to his feet as Felicity yelped.

Timmy's fork clattered to his plate as Shelby looked alarmed, but calm. His gaze immediately whipped over to Dan, whose expression was guarded.

"What was that?" Jake demanded.

Nick wasn't going to wait to find out. He raced outside, followed by the others.

A brown bag was on fire on the front stoop. Dan

stamped on it, and his shoes came away covered in horse droppings. Mason laughed.

"Daddy stepped in horse doodie!"

Felicity hushed her son as Dan removed his shoes. Nick frowned, looking at the now extinguished horse droppings. As a prank, it was juvenile. But considering what else had happened on the ranch...and this happened while they were inside having dinner.

Maybe whoever did this planned something much more sinister and this was a diversion. Lure everyone outside so there would be a clear target...

"Get back inside, now!" he warned them.

Fortunately, Dan must have concluded the same, for he herded his wife and children into the house, Jake and Timmy following close behind. Nick withdrew his weapon and cocked the slide. If someone was watching, they'd see he was armed.

He noted Shelby had remained outside. "Shelby, go back inside before you become a target."

"No. This is my home, too. I need to catch the bastard who's doing this." That stubborn little jut of her lower lip and the line denting her forehead warned he'd have a hard time convincing her otherwise.

Nick didn't care. Someone had already gone after him. He wasn't about to let Shelby become a target, too.

"Get inside," he ordered.

When she stared at him in mute defiance, he didn't hesitate. Nick swept her into his arms, took her inside and gently deposited her on the living room sofa. "If you don't promise to stay there, I'll tie you up, Shel. I'll handle this. Now, you going to stay put, or do I get the rope?"

Anger glinted in her gaze, but she nodded.

Nick headed outside again.

The motion-activated lights switched on as he prowled over to the western half of the house. Using his cell-phone light, Nick circled the house and then headed for the garage and Shelby's apartment. He didn't like that the garage sat alone, unprotected, like a bull's-eye. Good thing he was sleeping there tonight.

He finished a preliminary search and found nothing. And then in the distance, he heard it.

A truck motor turning over. Squeal of tires. Someone using the back road, leading to the dirt road and the highway.

Damn it. Nick wished he had his NVGs. The night-vision goggles were perfect. Too damn dark to see who it was. He listened instead. Pickup truck, lightweight, with a bad muffler. But how the hell did he dump the manure and then get away on foot? No tracks. Maybe he'd been too busy looking down, when he should have looked up...

Remembering the magnolia tree that he always used to climb to get in and out of his old bedroom, Nick glanced skyward. The branches hung over the porch. No one had trimmed it in a long time. Near the trunk, he found the faint outline of a footprint. Nick climbed the tree and went out onto the thick limb near the porch. Perfect place to hide after dropping the bag, fire a shot to grab attention and watch everyone's reaction when they rushed outside.

Cursing softly, he climbed back down. Whoever did this was very familiar with the ranch, and the house. They'd have to know that the magnolia only had one strong limb that touched the house.

Frustration filled him. Nothing. Whoever did this was either very clever, very fast or both.

Or perhaps they were closer than anyone realized.

Nick dropped down from the tree, landing on his feet as the door opened. Shelby walked outside.

"I told you to stay inside."

"Whoever did this—" she pointed to the extinguished bag "—is gone. Did you hear that truck?"

He nodded. "Anyone you know needs a muffler repaired?"

Shelby sighed. "Half the guys in town."

"Tell me about the ranch hands Dan hired. Any of them drive a light pickup with a bad muffler?"

"No. They all have cars. There's three to help with the horses. Jake's now head trainer and gives lessons, since Big Jack left us."

"Where do they sleep at night? On the ranch?"

"No. They quit around six, but Dan asked them to stay a little longer to feed and bed down the horses because of the funeral."

So any of the ranch hands could have tossed that bag at his head and sneaked out here to leave a calling card of horse droppings. It made no sense, though.

Nick mounted the porch steps and squatted down by the burned bag of manure. In Dan's haste to extinguish the fire, no one had noticed the second, smaller bag sitting nearby. It was a plain paper bag. With extreme care, he opened it.

Inside was a crumpled T-shirt that stank to high heaven and a note.

Shelby's cute nose wrinkled as she peered into the bag. "Ugh. What is that? It smells like someone used it to clean up the stables."

Someone did. Nick gingerly lifted the note from the bag. It crackled as he read the big, black letters.

You stink at life more than flaming horse apples, Nick Anderson. Leave before someone discovers your secret.

He balled up the note in his hand and shook his head. "Kids playing around. Nothing more. Go inside. I'll clean up this mess."

"I can help—"

"No."

When Shelby left, he found a shovel and began working on the mess on the porch, his stomach twisted in knots. Someone was out to taunt him, make him leave. Someone knew how to push his buttons, knew that he'd pulled such a prank in childhood at old lady Whipple's house. Silas had discovered it and stuffed his favorite T-shirt into the manure pile.

And then forced him to wear it to the widow's house to apologize.

Except Silas hadn't driven him to the widow's house, but had gone to his friend's home, where all his best buds had gathered to play video games.

Nick never forgot, or forgave that humiliation. Never set flaming horse apples before someone's door, either.

Someone else hadn't forgotten, either. And they wanted to make sure he knew it and got the hell out of Dodge before something else happened.

The stress of the funeral and the day's events took their toll. As they headed back to her apartment, Shelby felt stretched tighter than piano wire. She forced herself to keep calm for Timmy's sake. Nick followed her up the stairs and after they went inside, he locked the door and drew the shades.

Timmy tugged at her hand. "Aunt Shelby, if my mama and daddy die like Uncle Silas, will you stay with me forever?"

Stunned, she crouched down. "No, honey, your parents will be fine."

She hugged him tight, wishing she could dispel all his fears. Parenting was a skill she hadn't managed yet, but she tried her best. And each day brought new challenges.

Timmy pouted. "I want to play trucks. Aunt Shelby, will you play with me?"

Nick glanced at her. "Sit down, rest. I'll handle him."

Grateful for the reprieve, for she'd spent many hours with Felicity arranging for the luncheon after the funeral, Shelby sat on the chair by the window and picked up a library book to read, but she was too tired. Soon she heard noises coming from Timmy's bedroom.

Curious, she headed there. At the opened door, she paused and her heart turned over. Nick, playing trucks with Timmy on the floor. His face scrunched up as he pushed a dump truck toward a stack of Legos. He might have been a big, bad Navy SEAL, but now all his concentration was centered on a very needy little boy.

I could almost love you for that. Her smile dropped. *Don't go there.*

Shelby knocked on the doorjamb. Both of them looked up. "I was going to make tea. And warm milk for you, Timmy."

"I'm not thirsty," the boy protested. "Warm milk is for babies like Mason."

"I drink warm milk all the time," Nick told him.

Timmy's jaw dropped. "You? You're a Navy SEAL."

"Warm milk is the preferred drink of SEALs." Nick winked at him. Then he looked at Shelby. "Bath time?"

At her nod, he continued, "Want me to supervise?"

Grateful for his help, she nodded again. "I'll heat the milk."

Leaving her nephew in Nick's capable hands, she went into the kitchen. The comfort of routine soothed her as she set the kettle on to boil. She wondered what Nick thought of what he'd come home to. He'd been so quiet after the flaming-manure incident, and acted odd when she'd tried to help him clean up. Nick hadn't let her see the note, either.

Shelby suspected it was targeted at him personally, and he didn't want her knowing it. Too many other odd things had happened for her to question him about it. Right now she wanted the soothing ritual of routine in her kitchen.

Nick came into the kitchen. "Timmy's getting dressed. Thought I'd help out."

Nick's big body seemed too large as he stirred the milk she'd poured into a saucepan and put on the stove. His hip brushed against hers and she tingled from the brief contact.

"You know, if we were married, we'd be doing this for our kids at night," he murmured.

Shelby's mouth quirked in a faint smile. "If we were married, I'd be doing this alone for our kids."

"How many?"

"How many what?"

"Kids would we have?"

She considered. "Two, maybe. How many do you think we'd have by now?"

"Five."

At his charming grin, she nearly dropped the two mugs. "Five kids! Do you know what that would be like?"

Nick grabbed a mug from her hand, his fingers brushing hers and sending currents of awareness shooting through her. "With you, it'd be an adventure."

He winked again as he poured the milk into the mug. "We'd have to have that many, considering how often I'd let you leave our bed. It would be great fun making them."

Nick's babies. She softened inside thinking about five golden-haired cherubs at their knees. Maybe three boys and two girls. And then she caught his grin and realized he didn't meant anything by it.

Nick was only making conversation. Her last nerve snapped like a rubber band.

"Stop it, Nick. Just stop it." She banged the mug down on the counter with a thud. "You're not here to stay, and you're never going to stick around, so stop teasing me."

Two lines dented his brow. "I told you I was sticking around for a while."

Men! How could such an intelligent guy be so dumb? She switched tactics. "Are you going to sell the ranch after you find out who the saboteur is?"

His expression shuttered. "I don't know, Shel. I promised I would give it one month to see if we can come up with the money."

Timmy appeared in the doorway, clad in his *Star Wars* pajamas. "What if you don't find the bad man by then? What will happen to the horses if you sell? To Macaroni?"

Shelby's heart twisted at the hurt expression on Timmy's

face. Lord, he loved that pony, even though he knew it wasn't his.

Before she could say anything, Nick squatted down to Timmy's eye level. "Tim, I'll find out who's doing this. And I promise, Macaroni will have a good home, no matter where he goes."

"With lots of oats? More than Fancy?"

He smiled and patted his shoulder. "As much oats as he wants."

They sat at the table with their mugs. Timmy asked Nick about the places he'd seen. Without revealing too much, Nick regaled him with tales of adventure, G-rated, of course, until the boy's eyelids drooped. Nick picked up Timmy very gently and carried him to bed, and Shelby tucked him in. They returned to the kitchen, but Shelby paced the tiny space, looking agitated.

"I wish you wouldn't do that, Nick."

He blinked. "Put him to bed?"

"Tell him your grand tales of your travels. You get him all starry-eyed, wanting to travel and be a Navy SEAL."

Nick's gaze flattened as he sipped his tea. "There are worse choices for a career."

"Not for him!" She whirled, her long hair flying out. "He's spent the past year wondering if his mom and dad will come home. I've curtailed his watching the news, but I can't supervise everything, especially when the kids at school tell him how bad things are in the Middle East. I promised his parents I'd take care of Timmy. That means not stuffing his head full of dreams about adventures. They want him to be an engineer, with a nice, safe position in tech, not a hot dog."

He inhaled sharply. "SEALs aren't hot dogs, Shel.

We're highly trained, and each op we take on means even more training."

Nick's keen gaze probed her, as if he could see inside her. "What's the real problem? You saying these things about Timmy because you're afraid he'll have the chance to dream, and explore the life you've denied yourself?"

He always did push her buttons. How could he cut straight to the heart of what really troubled her? "I haven't denied anything."

He softened his voice. "Then why are you planning to move in with your sister after she returns? All your life you've taken care of your family. Your parents. Your sister. And now your nephew. When is it your turn to see the world?"

Shelby's lower lip wobbled precariously. She pushed at the long fall of her hair, feeling her emotions unravel.

"It's not too late. Paris can be more than a dream."

Hope flared inside, and then she stared at her china mug. It had a small crack on the cup's edge.

"I can't do that. I have work. It's a long way off and I have responsibilities."

"Excuses," he murmured.

Shelby glared at him. "What about you, Nick? Hopping around the country from job to job, no real place to call home, no settling down. You were a SEAL. When are you going to live your dream? Why did you quit?"

Nick set down his mug carefully. "I would have stayed in the teams if I hadn't been injured."

Her voice softened. "What happened?"

Nick stared at the table as if it held all the answers to the universe. "My teammates and I met up with a little explosion while on patrol. Two men were killed. I survived and so did the guy I saved. I spent time in the hospital and then was released. After that, it was obvious."

"You were too injured to stay a SEAL?"

"No. The leg functioned, with intense therapy. My CO wanted to assign me to a special training unit for cyberterrorism."

"Why did you quit?"

His dark gaze narrowed. "I didn't quit. I didn't re-up."

Shelby's brow wrinkled. "Why? You had a great career with the navy. Everyone back here kept talking about you, how you risked your life to drag your injured teammate to safety. What have you done after you left?"

Innocent question, but anger tightened his face. "It's over. Done. Don't want to talk about it." Nick pushed back from the table. "I'll get my gear from the house. Lock the door behind me."

Shelby stared after him as the front door slammed. She sensed her questions had touched a sensitive issue. But she didn't understand. How could Nick, who'd once written to Silas that his life was the navy, and everything was the navy, leave the navy, the one thing he loved most?

Nick couldn't sleep. Shelby's innocent question taunted him like the long-ago school bully who had beaten him up when Nick refused to surrender his lunch money.

Why did you quit?

He pulled the sheet up to his chin and shifted to his side, avoiding the spring that stuck out in the pullout sofa's middle. Coming home was hard enough. Coming home to that hometown-hero label was even tougher. The navy had called his father after Nick had almost bought it in Iraq. When he'd been shipped Stateside to Walter

Reed Army Medical Center, Jarrett had called Silas personally to tell him.

Silas never showed up at Nick's bedside. Since Nick was stabilized, there was no need. When he was finally released, Nick didn't make the mistake of asking the old man for a place to lay his head while he got his act together.

When had he ever done anything right in Silas's eyes?

The IED nearly killed him and a bullet punctured his leg, while another nearly kissed his head as he struggled to lift his teammate from the wreckage and carry him. He was alive. Yeah, that mattered. But the man who stood tall and proud the day he received his SEAL pin wasn't the same. He'd promised to give his all, be the best.

Do everything his father said he could never do—be a winner, not a quitter.

When the IED exploded, it sent him to the hospital. When he emerged, he couldn't run as fast. Be as strong as before. Oh, he still had his brain, but something died inside him the day he lost two teammates and could have lost his leg. He didn't re-up, much as his CO kept nagging him. Didn't want to train other SEALs.

Silas's words echoed in his mind. *You're a quitter.*

SEALs never quit.

You did.

Loser.

He drifted into sleep, and suddenly he was back in the Hummer. An explosion, his eardrums ringing as he struggled with panic to lift Vinny out of the Hummer... But instead of tango bullets, his father was there this time, laughing and shaking his head. "I knew you'd never amount to anything. Some hero you are, Nicolas. Loser."

Silas laughed again, then grabbed the weapon out of Nick's hands and tossed it aside. It landed on the ground with a bang.

Nick sat up with a start.

No longer overseas, in the Hummer. No, he was in Shelby's apartment, and that noise wasn't coming from his head, but downstairs.

Nick pulled on his corduroy jeans and slipped into the soft-soled shoes he'd left by the sofa bed, then pocketed a slim flashlight he'd placed on the side table. He slid his SIG Sauer from under the pillow and glanced out the window. The twin carriage lights over the garage were out. He'd made a point of leaving them on.

He opened the front door and stepped outside, then quietly padded down the porch steps, holding his pistol out. Gravel crunched in the distance, as if someone was running away. Nick raced down the steps, squinting in the darkness, but saw nothing. And then he heard a motor turning over and tires squealing as the driver raced away.

Too far away to pursue. He took out the penlight and swept it over the ground outside the garage. Nothing. But someone had removed the light bulbs to the carriage lights, leaving the area totally dark.

All the vehicles on the ranch, including the two ATVs and Nick's motorcycle, were locked inside the garage. Shelby's older model truck sat outside, all four tires slashed. Nick rubbed the bristles on his chin. Someone had made a point of incapacitating Shelby so she had no vehicle to drive. It was more than a malicious act. He suspected whoever did this wanted to warn her to stay out of ranch business.

Tomorrow, he'd fix the security cameras and add two

Chapter 7

Sunday mornings were church mornings around the Belle Creek for everyone but Shelby. For her, it was the one time of the week when she had peace and quiet, and the place to herself.

While Timmy was at church and Sunday school, she'd catch up on paperwork and balancing the books. Not today.

Not today.

After Felicity and Dan picked up Timmy for church, she'd phoned the sheriff and Jonah Doyle promised to send someone over later to investigate. Next she called repair shops near Nashville to replace the four slashed tires on her truck. Not one of them could give her a price she could afford on her slim savings.

Depressed over her truck, knowing she had to now find a ride to work, she went to the stables to talk with Nick.

Jeans riding low on his narrow hips, his Western shirt loose and untucked, he looked natural and at home in the barn as he forked fresh hay into each horse's stall.

new ones to this area. With a little luck, he'd catch the perpetrator.

And then there would be hell to pay.

Joining him, she began the familiar routine. They worked in tandem for a while, Nick asking about the horses and their health. The mundane conversation eased the tension between them. When the horses were all fed and watered, they released them into the pasture.

Shelby dusted off her hands and began mucking out the stalls as Nick brought the wheelbarrow to deposit the manure. She'd use it later as fertilizer for the garden.

"Any luck with replacing your tires?" he asked.

She shook her head. "The truck is old and barely running. I can borrow Dan's when he doesn't need it and get a lift tonight to work with Ann."

"Anyone who has a grudge against you who'd want to do that to your truck?"

"Only Natalie Beaufort. She can't stand me. I think she's looking for a good reason to get rid of me, but so far, I haven't done anything at work that warrants her firing me."

He frowned as he removed the work gloves. "Shel, I need to show you something."

When they were inside the tack room, he pointed to the nearest bridle. "When I came into the stables this morning, I found this."

Alarmed, she examined the leather. The straps were cleanly cut, as if someone sliced them with a sharp knife.

"Oh, no." Shelby looked at the others. All of them had been cut in half. Ruined. Without the tack, they couldn't rent out horses for trail rides.

"Whoever slashed your tires may have done this. How much will it cost to fix this?" Nick fingered the broken bridle.

Her heart sank. "More than we have right now. I have a group coming in tomorrow, a big group staying at the

Huckleberry B and B. Ten people who wanted a trail ride, and two more groups later this week. I was counting on that money to help meet payroll for the month."

"Things are really bad if you need trail rides to pay the staff." He looked around the neatly organized room. "I'd bet my bike that whoever did this didn't leave prints, either."

"The sheriff might be able to catch whoever did this. Put the person in jail."

Nick's gaze hardened. "Shel, when I catch who's pulling all this crap, I'll deal out my own sense of justice. No one messes with me and mine."

A shiver raced down her spine. He looked like the fierce warrior everyone in town had talked about, the Navy SEAL who risked enemy fire to save his buddy from death. Shelby was glad Nick was on her side.

"I don't know how we can get new tack before tomorrow." She shoved a hand through her hair.

Nick frowned. "Doesn't the ranch still have an account with Grant's Western Tack? I could call in a favor. I was good friends with Tyler, Grant's son, in the navy. Showed him the ropes, watched his six. He could loan us tack until we get ours fixed."

Relief filled her. "That would be wonderful if he could. I don't want to turn down the group because they're with a tour from Miami and it's our first time offering them trail rides. Repeat business will give us a nice cash infusion."

"Who has access to this room?" Nick walked around, his boots clicking on the concrete. "Door wasn't locked when I came in this morning."

Anxiety churned in her stomach. "It's always been locked. Spare set of keys hangs in the kitchen in the main house. But the ranch hands have been careless lately, always coming and going to get ready for the fall season."

"No longer," Nick said firmly. "No one gets in or out without you, myself, Dan or Jake. If one of the hands needs something from in here, we'll unlock the door for them."

Shelby nodded. Bad enough to have their tack ruined, but if the saboteur cut up the borrowed tack, they'd really be in trouble.

When they left the room, locked, the key in the back pocket of her jeans, Nick walked her out of the stables, his boot heels clicking on the concrete floor.

"What are you doing the rest of the morning? Need a lift into town to look for new tires? I'm headed there later to buy security cameras to install over the garage doors."

She hesitated. Surely he wouldn't laugh at her. "No. Sundays are my only days when I have free time in the afternoon. I'm looking for Henry's lost treasure."

Nick scratched the bristles on his firm chin. "That old fable? You believe it?"

"Why not? People have talked about it for years. It's part of the ranch's history."

"I figured Silas made up that history to get people to go on trail rides, looking for the lost gold." He gazed at the meadow, and the sun shining in the bright blue sky. "Damn, I forgot how pretty it is here."

They went to the fence and climbed up on the railing, sitting to admire the view. Indigo clouds scudded over the jagged mountaintops. A cool wind rustled the gold and red leaves in the nearby trees. Shelby sighed. Taking time to enjoy the scenery at the ranch always gave her a sense of peace she'd found hard to capture elsewhere. Certainly she'd never gotten this kind of serenity at the roach-infested, tiny, cramped trailers where she'd spent the first seven years of her life.

Her parents had seldom held down real jobs. Both of them usually passed out in the morning when she'd crept out to the living room to get into Heather's room so she could help her baby sister dress. Little mama, Silas had called her the day they'd come to live at the ranch. There they had a real trailer, not one propped on concrete blocks. A real job for her daddy, who struggled to overcome his addiction to drink and make the most of the opportunity Silas gave him.

At the Belle Creek, she'd learned what it was like to have warm clothing in the winter and a full belly. Silas had ordered the housekeeper, Candace, to help care for Heather and he'd personally driven Mama to the first few AA meetings so she could stay sober. For the first time in her life, Shelby knew affection and kindness from Silas Anderson. She owed him everything for trying to help her parents straighten up, and giving them all a chance at a real life, a real home.

Her thoughts drifted back to the reality of the present. An oriole that had not flown south yet for the winter warbled in the trees and the notes played a lovely melody to the symphony of colors dancing in the sky. As an adult, she had learned to cherish the quiet beauty of her home, and the wonder of a fresh, new start.

Her hand grasped Nick's. He startled, and looked down at her.

"You should see it out here at sunrise. It's like nature puts on a new show every morning. You can be whatever you want to be because the sun is rising and it erases all the mistakes of yesterday," she murmured.

A muscle ticked in his jaw as he squeezed her hand.

"Sometimes those mistakes take a lot more than a night to erase."

She wondered what he meant by that.

Nick pointed to her boots. "If you're exploring the woods, best to wear sneakers or hiking clothes. Let's go back to the apartment, then meet me by the hitching post."

Shelby laughed. "You have hiking boots? You brought only a backpack."

"My old clothing and boots are still in the basement. Silas said when I left he would burn everything, but he didn't." Nick studied his clipped nails. "Silas never got rid of them."

Judging from his quiet tone, it was a sore spot with him. He'd left this life behind, but his father had waited for him to return. Waited for Nick to swallow his pride and come home to take over the ranch.

He'd died waiting. She knew about parents, how you could spend your life trying to earn their love and never succeed, no matter what you did. But Silas was different from her folks. He was a good man, who was tough but fair to all.

Loved and respected by everyone.

Except his son. Why?

An hour later, they set out for the beaten path by the creek.

Silly of her to think she could find Henry's gold, but the same little thrill raced through her as she and Nick navigated through the woods. Silas had woven tales about a treasure that had been lost during the Civil War. His ancestor, Henry, had squirreled away five hundred gold ingots on family land. No one knew how old Henry got the gold, Silas told her. Some said Henry had stolen it. Others more loyal to the Anderson clan said Henry earned it working at the mill house from dusk to dawn. Fact was, no matter how Henry earned the gold, he'd vowed to keep it away from Yankee hands when the war started.

"The war of Northern aggression," Silas had told her in his crackly voice, rocking in his chair by the fire.

"The Civil War," she'd corrected, sitting at his feet, fascinated by the tales of the Anderson clan.

"That's what the history books say. But here we call it differently."

The Yankees came and burned down the farmhouse, but they never got the gold. Henry died of a bullet wound at Gettysburg and Matty Anderson, nine months pregnant with Silas's great-grandfather, had gone on to rebuild and work the land herself to make it a profitable horse ranch. When times got tough, she sold two hundred acres to pay for the ranch's upkeep, but she never gave up the prime pasture.

Horses were in Anderson blood, Silas told her. And that gold was sitting somewhere on the two hundred acres, just waiting for an Anderson or some lucky devil to discover it and get rich.

As a child, she'd combed through these woods, eager to find the gold and buy her parents a real house like the one Nick and his family claimed. Silas said whoever found the gold could keep it. She took him at his word. Only if she found it, Shelby would save the ranch.

The loamy smell of freshly turned earth hit her as they walked through the pasture. In his camo pants, gray hoodie and hiking boots, Nick cut a fine figure as he accompanied her. Sweat pooled low at the waistband of her jeans. Shelby told herself it was from the exercise, not closeness to the man who managed to make her pulse skip a beat.

Nick stopped for a minute to survey the sweep of pasture. "Looks like some ploughing going on here. Dan planning to plant crops at this time of year?"

Unease bit her. "Dan let Chuck Beaufort run a dozer through this section of pasture to see how rocky it was, and how much work it would take to clear it."

His jaw tightened. "When did he let that bastard onto my family's land?"

While Silas was sick in the hospital the first time. Shelby didn't want Nick railing at Dan. Things were tense enough after the funeral. "A while ago. He's not come back since. Silas forbade it. He said the land belongs to the family, and no one could pry it from him."

"But my cousin thought he could sell." Nick scowled. "Dan was ripe to sell, while Silas wasn't. Add that to all these incidents of vandalism and anonymous commenters leaving bad online reviews of the Belle Creek, and it makes my cousin look very suspect."

Shelby hastened to assure him. "Dan wasn't trying to coax Silas into selling the entire ranch, just this section of pasture. It's fallow, and we never use it. Haven't for years. But it has access to the road."

Nick adjusted his pack and scanned the area. "Land's still good. Need to work the soil, that's all. No one's paid attention to it."

He talked as if he planned to stay, coax some life into the soil. "Now you're talking like an Anderson," she teased.

He shrugged. "No. I'm talking like someone who's been saddled with a six-figure mortgage who's trying to find answers on how to pay for it. Leasing the land for pasture won't do. Too late in the year and not enough income."

His sensual mouth thinned out and tension radiated from him. Shelby put a reassuring hand on his arm. "We'll figure it out, Nick. Silas may have left the ranch to you, but this is my home, too."

With a gruff nod, he gestured to the trail. "Let's go. I want to get to that cabin."

A little hurt by his reaction, she remained quiet as they continued. Maybe Nick didn't like the idea of her calling the ranch home. Made it more difficult for him to sell the place, cut his losses and move on.

He'd mentioned Paris. Perhaps that's why he'd talked about exploring her dreams. If she was gone from here, it would be easier for him to clear his conscience about selling.

"Don't sell," she blurted.

Turning, he stared at her, a frown denting his forehead. "What?"

"If you came with me today to survey the land to see how much you could squeeze out of Beaufort, then turn around and walk back, Nick. Your father never wanted to sell this land. It's been in your family for years and it's an institution—"

"Shel—"

"Do you really want to see a theme park built where your ancestors used to ride their horses, farm the fields, where history walked? Maybe you don't appreciate your family's past, but I do, and the idea of them tearing down the trees and running dozers over this land... I would work my fingers to the bone to save the ranch because this isn't only a place to live, it's—"

"Whoa." Nick lightly clasped her forearms, his dark

gaze serious. "Cut me some slack, Shel. I only found out I inherited the place yesterday. I'm not making any quick decisions. I promised I'd stick it out for a month, find out who's damaging Belle Creek. Okay?"

Shelby nodded, but mixed in with the relief was the ever-present worry. By month's end, Nick might not have a choice.

He gave her arms a quick squeeze, his deep chest rising and falling. "No more talk about selling. I want to see the cabin again. It's been years."

It was a clear day, the gray mist covering the land beginning to dissipate beneath the sun's warmth. The path snaked through the pasture into the woods.

"You really believe you'll find old Henry's gold after all these years?" He clasped her hand as she scampered over a rotting log blocking their path.

"Why not me? I need it the most."

Nick shook his head. "Yankees found that gold and Henry was too proud to admit it. Or his widow used it for upkeep of the ranch to pay the taxes the carpetbaggers heaped on the land."

"That's not what you thought all those times you sneaked out of the house to search with me."

A wide grin touched his face. "Maybe I was looking for a reason to spend time with you."

A thrill shot through her. Shelby tried to control her rapid pulse. He didn't mean anything by it.

"I bet I can still beat you to the woods," she taunted.

Barely had she spoken the words when he took off, running for the forest.

"Hey, that's cheating! You had a head start," she yelled.

They raced to the edge of the woods, Nick easily beating her. Shelby gasped for breath and sat on a rock as

Nick pulled a bottle of water from his pack. He drank, his strong throat muscles working. The man was so hot. Finely put together, a rugged specimen of pure maleness that sent her lady parts throbbing. Shelby wiped her brow with the sleeve of her sweatshirt, well aware that she was overheated not merely from their race.

How many times had she traipsed through these woods with Nick when they were younger, looking for berries to munch on in the spring? Searching every rock and incline for clues to the hidden treasure?

They pushed on and arrived at the creek spilling over the rocks. Nick studied the stones set into the water.

"Still here," he murmured. "Remember when we found them and rolled them into the creek because the bridge washed out? Silas said we'd have to wait for a new one, but that didn't stop us."

"Or slow us down." Shelby placed a foot on one stone and continued on, carefully navigating each one. "He never did rebuild the bridge."

They kept to the path, a narrow ribbon snaking through the tall yellow grasses of the pasture seldom used by the ranch. Nick sniffed the air.

"Always thought this would make a great place to build a cabin. Guess that's why Henry rebuilt the original cabin in the woods years ago." Mischief flared in his gaze. "I think he wanted a private place as a secret love nest."

Shelby laughed. "More likely a private place for his wife to get away from Henry's love nest. She bore him eight children."

Nick's gaze turned warm as he turned to look at her. "Eight's a good number."

She flushed as they continued on, wind sweeping over

the grasses and rustling the leaves in the trees. It was a cool, clear autumn day, perfect for such an outing. If not for the sheer desperation driving her to find the lost treasure, she'd thoroughly enjoy herself. Sun dappled the ground as they made their way back into a thicket of trees. Large boulders sprouted up here, outcroppings of limestone that made the going tricky.

"They fought a fierce battle here in the Civil War," Shelby murmured, fascinated by Anderson family history. "These very rocks sheltered rebels as they took a stand against the Yankees."

"I always thought this land was haunted," Nick confessed, stopping to examine a small red mark on a tree trunk. "It would make a great place to scare people, all this history of the war. Hey, the trail mark is still here. Shortcut to the cabin."

The county preservation society had wanted to purchase the land and turn it into a park. Silas balked, promising to never have the land leave the family. He'd kept to that promise.

He gazed around at the red and yellow leaves ablaze on the trees, the sweep of meadow. "Ever do more than trail rides here?"

"What else would you use this trail for?"

"A wagon, pulled by a tractor," he mused. "Halloween is coming up, hay rides, pumpkins…"

She'd seen that spark in his eyes before, when Nick got an idea. "What are you thinking?"

"Just thinking. Let's push on."

After leaving the thicket of woods, the land began to slope down gently toward the stream. They came to a small clearing. Large rocks jutted out from the ground, as did thick tree roots, making navigation a little tricky, but she knew each one, and wended through them as sure-footed as a billy goat.

Shelby quickened her pace, nearly running now. Protected by thick brush and trees, the two-room cabin came into view. Nick stood behind her as she gazed at the structure. Awe filled her. Here was where the first generations of Andersons had lived, fought, loved, birthed babies and died.

Nick's family had such a rich history, while she didn't even know if her grandparents were alive, much less where they hailed from.

A bucket sat by the stone well out front. Nick walked over and squatted down. "All still here, and in good shape."

"Silas insisted on preserving everything. Each spring he'd send everyone out here to clean up, get rid of any rat nests or other creatures that spent the winter. He painted the inside, but left the outside same as it was back in 1845, when your great-great-grandfather settled here."

Bracing his hands on the lip of the well, he peered down. "Good. Silas finally sealed it. It's too dangerous to have open with kids around. Though I doubt Felicity would let Miles and Mason come out here."

"For a long time I thought the gold was buried at the bottom, but Silas hired a man to check it out before he sealed it for good. And your father stood by the entire time, making sure that camera was operational and the man wasn't lying and planning to come back later."

Nick grinned. "Trust never came easily to Dad."

Finally he'd called him Dad. Nick always referred to his sire by his first name, as if preferring to distance himself from his parentage.

Shelby walked up the steps to the front door, then

stood on tiptoe to get the key. Nick came behind her, his body curving into hers, and he reached it first. The hardness of his body snug against hers made her all too aware of him, the slight spice of his cologne and the woodsy smell that was all Nick.

Remembering what happened last time they were here, she flushed and stepped aside to let him unlock the door.

Shelby understood why Nick's ancestors settled here. With the abundance of land, the sparkling creek providing plenty of water and the tall trees, it was a perfect spot for a couple getting their start in life. Henry's father had been a farmer, and he planted corn in these fields that were too rough to sustain anything else.

The cabin was rough-hewn logs. Henry had built it shortly before the war, expanding the two rooms and adding a loft for his growing family. The cabin was actually two cabins joined by a chimney.

A mill had been erected by the stream, but it had long fallen into disrepair, and Silas's father tore it down when it became too dangerous. Near the cabin was the stone foundation of the original barn, where Henry stabled his cows and horses, and began experimenting with breeding Tennessee walking horses.

Dust motes danced in a stray sunbeam let in by the bank of windows on the far side of the room. Silas had wanted to preserve the cabin's historical integrity, but when Nick was a child, he'd gotten lost in the woods during the winter and would have frozen, but for the cabin. After that Silas moved in a table and chairs against one wall, and a trundle bed with a thick down quilt. An oak cabinet that once stored food was stocked with canned goods in case of emergencies.

"I remember how this place saved my sorry butt when

I was ten," Nick murmured, gazing around the darkened room. "Damn blizzard made me lose my way. I would have frozen to death if not for Henry's cabin."

"Good thing you learned how to build a fire during those Boy Scout sessions," she teased, wanting to erase the solemn look on his face.

The cabin must remind him of all the times he'd come here with Silas, when his father taught him how to hunt and live off the land. Shelby suspected those skills honed Nick's abilities as a SEAL, though she doubted he'd give credit to Silas.

In one of the last letters he'd written home, Nick told his father he became a SEAL on his own merit. She understood that, but never understood how he felt he had to take full credit on his own. Hadn't Silas been a good parent to him?

He walked across the cabin floor to the chimney that divided the homestead into two rooms. He squatted down and touched the stone hearth. Charred newspapers littered the fireplace. She joined him and the sight of the recent fire raised gooseflesh on her arms.

He gave her a questioning look. "You've been here lately, Shel?"

Troubled, she shook her head. "Not for a month. And I never lit a fire. Silas made it clear it was too hazardous, with the dry season and the drought plaguing these parts. Last thing anyone needs in these parts is a forest fire out of control."

Nick walked around the chimney, studying the layout of the cabin. He peered out the windows. Usually this time of year the glass was grimy with dust, but not now.

The windows were clear and sparkling, as if someone had cleaned them.

"Silas send anyone out here to spruce up the place in the last month?" he asked.

She shook her head. "The cabin was the last thing on your father's mind."

"The spring's still running?"

She nodded. The cabin had been built with a plume running from the spring near the creek up to a long trough, providing fresh water if the well ever ran dry.

"Plenty of water makes this a good place to camp out. Or hide out." Nick frowned as he looked around. "Place is really clean. Too clean for a once-a-year cleaning."

She went to the fireplace and sifted through the ashes. Shelby pulled a piece of unburned paper from the hearth.

"Look, Nick. Someone's used this recently. This is a newspaper from last month."

She showed him the headline. His frown deepened.

"With all the fences in disrepair, anyone could get onto this property. Not just family. But who would want to camp out here?" she mused.

Nick prodded the ashes with the fireplace poker. "Someone who wants a place to hide out while they vandalize the ranch. Cabin's got perfect access to the back road, makes for an easy escape if needed. Plenty of canned goods and water."

When he checked the cupboards, Shelby's heart dropped to her stomach. The larder had been fully stocked this summer. She'd seen to it, for Silas insisted. Only a few cans of beef stew sat on the shelf.

A chill raced down her spine. Shelby clutched the straps of her pack, and felt her palms turn clammy. Whoever had been vandalizing the ranch knew this land, knew the back roads and the easy access. And they had been here recently. Maybe even as recent as yesterday, when they were at the cemetery burying Silas.

"What if they're still around? And armed?" she whipped her gaze around the small room, suddenly realizing how clean everything was, not even dust on the floorboards to show footprints.

Nick lifted the hem of his hoodie to display the pistol snug on his belt. "I guarantee I'm a better shot than he is."

"Or she. It could be a woman," she murmured, thinking of Natalie and how much the woman had talked about the ranch and how it would make a perfect location for her father's theme park.

She swiped a trembling hand through her hair. "We have a month, Nick. How can we find out who's doing this and come up with the money to pay off the mortgage?"

"Hey," he said softly. "We'll catch whoever's doing this. Don't give up that easily, Shel."

His thumb rubbed a sensitive spot on her lower lip. Nick stared at her mouth, his gaze darkening. Blood surged in her veins and her heart quickened. The last time she'd stood in this cabin with Nick, she'd been crying. He came searching for her, found her and enfolded her into his strong embrace. And once her sniffles had ended, his embrace turned different. He stared at her mouth the same way he'd done ten years ago.

"I'm not giving up," she said fiercely. "I never give up."

"Neither do I," he murmured, bending his head close to hers.

He kissed her.

She was too swept up in the moment to protest, too enraptured by the warmth of his firm mouth moving authoritatively over hers, feeling the subtle pressure of his lips, his scent wrapping around her like a warm blanket.

This is a bad idea, her mind chanted. *Go for it*, her body urged.

Shelby clutched his arms, holding on to him as his tongue gently thrust past her closed lips. A myriad of sensations pummeled her. Nick, kissing her like he'd done all those years ago, except his kiss was more assured. He was experienced, a man who knew how to kiss women and coax them into his bed.

Her eyes opened and she pushed at his chest. "Stop it."

Stepping back, he licked his mouth, as if still savoring her taste. His heavy-lidded gaze met hers, and she saw it sharpen with awareness.

"Trying to relive old times? Not going to work, Anderson. I'm not that same girl anymore."

A muscle ticked in his hard jaw. "I know. I lost control. Shel. You do that to me. This place…"

He turned around, jamming a hand through his thick hair. "Too many damn memories."

She was one of them. But she wasn't going to let him treat her like she had last time. Best to put distance between them.

Shelby went outside to grab a breath of fresh air, her nerves more rattled by his kiss than she would ever admit. It wasn't merely a kiss, but something deeper.

Connection.

Chemistry.

Nick Anderson was the only man who'd ever charged her body like that. Sex with other men hadn't even come close to the desire she felt with one kiss from Nick.

One kiss that would remain just that—one.

She walked around the cabin to the outcropping of

rocks by the wood plume that once funneled water from the stream and spring. Henry had built a root cellar near the spring to store vegetables. Far as she knew, it still existed. It also served as a good tornado shelter if you were caught in the open.

Or a good place to gather her composure, lost when Nick's mouth had captured hers. Shelby climbed over a boulder and went toward the spring. A hundred feet from the stream bed was a door set in the ground. A rusty ring protruded from the boards. Fishing out her cell phone and using the flashlight app, she then pulled the door open and descended into darkness.

The air was much cooler down here in the stone-lined cellar, and smelled faintly musty. Shelby ran her flashlight over the walls. Nothing here.

Except there was something, over in that corner. She walked over to it, and the closer she got, the more her heart raced.

Silas insisted on keeping nothing down here. Certainly never anything flammable.

The sight of the red gas can made her blood run cold. She touched the plastic, smelled the faint fumes. Next to the can was a lighter.

Footsteps sounded on the stairs. She looked up to see Nick peering down at her, his cell phone also used as a flashlight. Nick joined her and swore softly. "This isn't for a barbecue. Or to light a fire in the cabin."

"No." She rubbed her arms, suddenly very chilled. "You don't pour gasoline on an interior fire."

"But you do use it to torch something very big."

Someone had been here very recently. And they planned to do more than vandalize the ranch.

They planned to burn it.

* * *

If he ever needed evidence that someone threatened his family and his ranch, it was here, stored in the root cellar. Nick wasted no time calling the sheriff again. The cabin had decent cell phone coverage, thanks to a tower nearby.

He kept an eye on Shelby as they waited for the deputy to arrive on the back hollow road. He didn't like how pale she looked, the spark gone from those green eyes. He'd put the spark there with the kiss. Damn it, he hadn't meant to do that, but she looked so pretty standing with the shaft of sunlight glinting on her hair, her mouth so soft and warm...

Nick continued his search of the area. He found a footprint near the remains of the old mill, marked the spot with a cairn. If the cabin had been vacant all summer, he'd bet this was their culprit.

Shelby sat on the picnic bench by the stream, staring at the gurgling water. She'd abandoned her search for Henry's treasure after what they'd found. For a moment he stood, gazing at her. Forget the gold, here was a real treasure. Smart and strong, and all those curves, and her sweet mouth...

Nick turned away from the temptation of her body. Part of him wished he'd never come home, forget the funeral and burial, for what good was it to regret not saying goodbye to Silas? Not when so much distance had stretched between them, an ocean of anger and bitterness because Nick hadn't followed in his father's footsteps and remained on the ranch to manage the family business.

He'd carved his own way in life, made a career in the teams. Now he roamed.

Nomad Nick, his friends called him. Never the same place four weeks in a row.

The rumble of a car in the back woods alerted him. He went to the path cutting through the woods as the Nature County sheriff's deputy walked through the woods. Nick's stomach tightened.

"Nick Anderson," the man said, his drawl pronounced. "Hotshot hero finally came home. I'm surprised you're sticking around after your father's funeral."

"Jonah Doyle," he growled. "Now I have a real problem. You're it."

"Sheriff Doyle to you, Anderson." The man's gaze narrowed. "Where's Shelby?"

They walked up to the stream, where Shelby still sat at the picnic table. She scrambled to her feet.

"Hey, Jonah."

"Shelby, darling."

A flash of jealousy shot through Nick. Jonah was a homegrown boy who'd stuck around, unlike Nick. Made sense Shelby would be on friendly terms with him. She'd probably waited on him a few times at the restaurant. The logic still didn't calm the tightness in his guts. He had watched Shelby grow from a gangly, cute teenager into a woman with long legs and the kind of curves a man liked to trace with the palms of his hands.

He'd never had trouble finding a woman to warm his bed. Any woman. But now he found himself wanting more with Shelby.

Needing more.

Not a quick bout of sex, love 'em and leave 'em, all parties satisfied. A flash of pleasure, and then pack your duffel and ride away, never looking back.

More.

Something more satisfying and lasting than a one-night stand. Hell, not just sex to take the edge off, but long, slow loving, exploring a sinfully delicious mouth, trailing kisses all over her body… Waking up to know she'd be lying next to him, her eyes all sleepy, her hair tousled and her arms eager for him as he rolled over to greet the morning in his own special way.

But he wasn't sticking around. Not him.

Jonah was the kind of guy with his feet planted firmly in Barlow.

Like Shelby.

Nick suddenly felt like an outsider. Damn, on his own land, too.

"This way," Nick said curtly.

He showed Jonah the gas can and the lighter, but the sheriff shrugged. "Silas might have stored it here and forgot to tell anyone."

Shelby bristled. "I doubt it. He was very careful when it came to anything flammable by the cabin."

Jonah's expression remained guarded. "Sometimes old people get careless. And forgetful."

Nick didn't like the cavalier attitude of his former high school rival.

"There's a footprint."

Outside, Jonah examined the print Nick had marked and shook his head. "Could be anyone. With those fences all torn down, maybe a hunter looking for squirrel or rabbit. Doesn't mean much."

Small wonder he'd balked at calling the sheriff about the horse-apple prank.

"You're as useless as watered-down whiskey, Jonah," Nick snapped. "Would a hunter store gasoline in the root cellar or cut up tack in the stables?"

"Temper." Jonah didn't smile. "We know all about the vandalism. Silas had us look into it after the break-in at the house. We even patrolled a few times, but we can't station a man here 24/7."

"So you aren't going to dust for prints?" Shelby asked. "Because no one on this ranch stashed that can in the cellar. And I certainly didn't slash the tires on my truck."

Jonah removed his hat and ran a finger along the brim. "There's been talk in town about Dan wanting to force Silas's hand into selling."

The sudden intake of Shelby's breath warned him this was news to her as well.

"Talk from whom? Town gossips?" Nick got in Jonah's face. "Beaufort trying to stir up trouble?"

Jonah backed off, holding up his hands. "I'm only telling you what everyone else knows. Dan was at Martha Horner's real estate office last week, asking how much it would cost for a real estate appraisal on the ranch. All the ranch. He wasn't being quiet about it, either."

Shelby bit her luscious lower lip. "Dan never said anything to me. I keep the books, manage the bills and cut the checks. If he was shelling out money for an appraisal, he would have told me."

Jonah shrugged. "All I know is he told Martha when Silas went, they'd probably sell. Seems Felicity has a hankering to live in Knoxville, closer to her folks."

Minutes later, Jonah was headed back to his patrol car. Shelby looked around the grounds, her expression distraught.

"Right before Silas died, I asked Dan if we should think about selling a portion of the south pasture. I even mentioned it might be good to get a new appraisal to use as a bargaining chip with Beaufort, to know what the land is worth. He said there was no need. Why would he lie to me?"

Nick decided it was time to have a little chat with his cousin.

That afternoon, Nick waited for Dan in the study.

Nick had gone into Nashville and purchased battery-operated cameras, installing them outside the cabin. The cameras were the same kind of tracker cameras used on hunting trails.

Maybe now whoever used the cabin for storage would think twice about setting foot there. He also installed new steel locks on the root cellar and the front and back doors of the cabin. And using his savings, he bought a top-of-the-line security system with night-vision cameras for the outside of the garage.

He hated this room. With its dark paneling and oppressive, heavy furniture, it looked more like a funeral parlor than an office.

Amber fluid rested in the glass sitting on the desk before him. Nick raised the whiskey and saluted the portrait before him.

"Here's to you, Dad. You left me in a hell of a mess."

The liquid burned his throat as he sipped.

"But damn, you knew how to pick your liquor," he muttered.

The drink felt good, sharpened his senses. Nick glanced at the clock on the mantel as the door opened.

Dan came inside, frowning. "You're drinking already?"

"You're late." He set down the whiskey, ice cubes clinking against the glass.

Anger darkened Dan's face. "It's Sunday—the day I

spend with my family. What's so damn important you couldn't wait?"

Folding his hands on the desk, he leaned forward.

"When were you going to tell me about the appraisal, Dan? The one you asked Martha about as my father was lying on a hospital bed? Same time you were going to tell me how sick he was?"

Nick kept his voice quiet, focusing on his cousin's face. A bead of sweat formed on Dan's temple, slid down his lean cheek.

"Whoever told you that is a liar."

"Jonah Doyle may be an ass, but he's no liar."

Nick took a file folder Shelby had given him and pushed it across the desk.

"Explain why you've been spending money on video games and entertainment for your kids when this ranch has barely enough funds to purchase grain for the full-board horses."

Dan's expression became mutinous. For a moment, Nick had a wild flashback to his teenage years, when he'd sat in that very seat and Silas lectured him on fighting, drinking or any one of his numerous sins. Silas, his constant air of disapproval each time he looked at Nick. He'd tried hard to please him. He really did, but nothing was ever good enough.

The Belle Creek was more important to Silas than his only son. Nick found himself competing with horses and tractors and clients for his father's attention. Small wonder he'd taken the trouble, because at least when he'd gotten caught, Silas was forced to pay attention to him. Only instead of the affection Nick desperately craved, he'd been met with cold, hard disapproval.

Shelby, with her soft voice and sassy manner, had

made those times bearable. He'd leave Silas's study, stomp out in a temper, determined that he'd prove the old man was right, he was nothing but an out-of-control loser. Only instead of running away or breaking the law, he went straight to Shelby's trailer.

They'd talk and she always made him feel special. Different. Worth something, instead of the no-account failure his father said he was turning into.

Dan folded his hands across his chest, wrinkling the blue silk shirt. "I work hard around here, Nick. I stayed, stuck it out, unlike you, the hotshot hero who couldn't even bother to call home for Christmas!"

He went very still, struggling to control his temper. "I was deployed in places where they don't have access to phones, Dan. And that's none of your business. What was between Silas and me is private. Stop dodging the question. Why were you seeking an appraisal of the ranch without Silas's knowledge?"

His cousin's shoulders sagged. He rubbed his nose and his gaze darted away.

"Maybe Silas wanted it. Shelby doesn't know everything."

"Don't give me that crap. Except for the mortgage, which Silas took care of, Shelby knows every dollar, nickel and penny that comes in and goes out of this ranch. Including the two thousand you spent on a diamond for your wife." He flung the file folder at his cousin. Papers scattered.

Dan didn't pick them up. "It was our tenth wedding anniversary."

"And you couldn't get her something less expensive? Two thousand dollars, when the back pasture fence is broken, and we're behind on mortgage payments? Two thousand dollars goes a long way in showing the bank you promise to make good."

"Felicity had her jewelry stolen. I wanted to give her something to make up for it. You're a fine one to judge. You don't know how tough it was to hold this place together when the old man kept the house cold because he insisted heating oil was too expensive. Working your ass off for a measly allowance."

Nick sagged in the chair, suddenly weary. "No, I don't. But that's no excuse, Dan. Level with me. Would you sell if Silas left the ranch to you?"

Dan rubbed his hands on his trousers. "I don't know. Okay, I admit, I asked Martha about a real estate appraisal. I figured it would help convince Silas to sell part of the land. We have only a few horses rough boarding and the income isn't enough."

Nick looked around the study, thinking fast. "Fall's here, and winter's coming. More costs. But trail rides are popular this time of year. We could advertise, put the word out."

Dan's mouth narrowed and he sat straighter. "Why do you care? You'll sell the place and be on the road again before the ink is dry."

He couldn't blame his cousin. Hadn't he been contemplating the same thing? Nick stood. "Go back to your wife and kids. We'll talk later. From now on, you're on a strict allowance, per the legal agreement you're signing tomorrow. No more spending money on diamonds, video games or pedicures. If we're going to make this work, we have to cut back."

Dan glared at him. "Guess I don't have a choice if I want to stay. Welcome home, Nick. You walked back into a real mess."

Jake walked into the study as his brother pushed past him.

"What's got his goat?" Jake took the seat vacated by his brother.

"Money. What else?" Nick tapped the desktop. "How many clients do you have lined up for lessons this week?"

Jake sighed. "I had five, but three canceled. They made some excuse about kids having karate practice or soccer. I think the word got out and parents don't want them coming here because we can't guarantee their safety." Nick had hoped to build up the riding lessons for a quick cash infusion. Jake had a rep as a good trainer, patient and gentle with kids, especially the younger set.

They talked for a few minutes about the week's schedule. When Jake left, Nick leaned back in the chair. He'd come home to a real mess. And he didn't see how they could get out of it without selling.

Which would put Shelby out on the streets, without a home.

Chapter 8

Shelby wished she didn't have to work tonight. Sunday nights were usually quiet and tips were meager. Exhaustion crept into her bones. The uncertainty looming over them, along with the nastiness of last night's incident and the unsettling idea of someone storing gasoline in the root cellar, shook her more than she cared to admit.

Not to mention Nick's kiss in the cabin. That was the real reason for her jitters.

It was only a kiss. Meant nothing, not like it did back then. *Nick's kissed a lot of women, and you're not an inexperienced virgin.*

But she had to admit, the man knew how to move his mouth. He was pure sex, all those yummy muscles she longed to explore with her fingertips, run her tongue across that solid flesh as he lay back on the bed...

Do. Not. Go. There.

Sex with Nick was a very bad idea. She couldn't allow herself to drift into that fantasy, no matter how much she craved his touch. No matter how much the old feelings flared each time she saw him. She'd loved him ten years ago, with all the passion in her young heart. Now?

Her responsibilities to this ranch and her nephew came first.

Holding it together for Timmy's sake, she knew she couldn't let herself fall apart. Let herself become unglued. She was the strong one. Always had been.

"You're Southern, girlfriend. We Southern gals never let anyone see our spines bend," Ann often told her.

But damn, girl, did she really have to wear that stupid cowgirl outfit and the tight hose? Bad enough the skirt was too short.

She showered and shaved her legs, and after drying off, realized she missed a spot.

Sitting on the lip of the bathtub in her slip and plain cotton panties, she propped one foot up on the closed toilet lid and began lathering. Shelby scraped the razor over her calf, muttering an oath. *I'm not a* Playboy *bunny. For the lousy tips I get at the restaurant, you'd think that I was a real…*

"Sexy," a husky voice murmured.

Startled, she nearly cut herself, the razor sliding over her skin. Shelby clutched the instrument as she looked up.

Nick stood in the doorway. Her mouth watered and she forgot all about the razor and the stubble on her right leg.

Tan, wrinkled cargo pants rode low on his narrow hips. The navy-blue T-shirt stretched over his massive chest and hugged his big biceps. He looked scruffy, with a day's stubble covering his jaw and cheeks. The scar on his left cheek made him look rugged, like a pirate ready to ravish a maiden.

And oh, boy, was she ready to be ravished. Heat curled

in her belly, low and hot. How long had it been since she had sex? Seemed like forever.

Nick exuded a primitive sexuality that dovetailed into his warrior stance as he gazed down at her. Alert, ready, but the passion darkening his gaze indicated he was honed and ready for a different kind of battle.

In the bedroom.

Shelby was all too aware she had on granny panties and a satin slip with one strap spilling over her shoulder. Her hair was a tangled mess and she had been caught shaving her legs, a very private moment a guy shouldn't see.

Yeah, real sexy. I look more like a frazzled mom than a woman ready to wrap myself around Nick and stay there until I've had at least five orgasms.

"Six," she muttered. A guy like Nick who kissed as sinfully as the devil himself had to deliver at least six.

"Six what?" Nick leaned against the doorjamb.

Flustered, she waved the razor like a sword. "Do you mind?"

"Not at all. I can share. Need to brush my teeth."

His gaze darkened as he studied her leg, still lathered with soap. She couldn't help but lick her lips as she stared at his bulging muscles and those big hands and imagined the very wicked things he could do to her in bed, instead of her spending long hours on her feet waiting on overweight businessmen who wanted their steak rare instead of well-done.

Nick crossed the threshold. "Need some help?"

Before she could sputter an answer, he parked his very fine ass on the tub lip next to her. Then he took the razor from her hand. Nick glanced at her, his mouth quirking in a sexy smile.

"I promise, I'll be gentle."

And, oh, boy, he was sliding the razor over her bare, soapy leg. So gentle and slow, his brow furrowed in concentration as if he was painting a masterpiece instead of shaving her leg. Shelby put a hand on his shoulder to steady herself, feeling her heart race. The skin beneath his shirt was firm and so deliciously warm.

She imagined having all those muscles and that big body nestled close to her, sliding over her naked body as he stared down at her...

A throbbing pulsed between her legs as he leaned closer, slowly scraping the razor over the underside of her sensitive calf. He smelled delicious, like spices and woods and pure sex. His fragrance wrapped around her head, tendrils of it teasing her like a lick between her legs. A hank of his dark gold hair spilled down as he leaned forward, giving extra special attention to the sensitive spot behind her knee. As he gently slid the razor over it, Nick licked his mouth.

Shelby moaned.

Immediately he glanced up, concern clouding his gaze. "Did I hurt you?"

"No." *Not if you don't count the way my body hurts right now because all I want is for you to throw out that razor and let me straddle you, pull up your shirt and I'd lick you from stem to stern, my tongue traveling over those ripples on your abdomen...*

He finished and disappointment surged.

But then he dampened a washcloth and slowly stroked it over her leg, removing the excess soap. Nick paused at the edge of her panties.

His sleepy, sexy gaze met hers. "I'm getting you all wet."

She moistened her mouth. "Yeah. I know."

Nick traced a line along her panties. "And you have to go to work. I'll make you late."

"S'okay. I can be late." She leaned forward, shivering as his finger slid up her hip and began circling. Predatory. She was his helpless captive and couldn't move if the house was on fire or someone stood outside with a check for a million dollars and a plane ticket to Paris.

"I'd better go. Before I do something more than shave your legs." Intent glinted in his eyes and he gave that devilish little smile that had slain all the girls in high school, making them all sigh and whimper and dream.

"Like what?" she whispered. "Indulge me."

Nick's hand curled around her hip. He leaned forward, taking up all the space, all the air in the tiny bathroom. Steam misted the air, and she struggled to remember to breathe. He pulled back the elastic of her panties and dipped a finger inside, stroking her skin over her hipbone in a light teasing gesture.

And then regret etched his expression. He withdrew his hand and bent down, pressing a singularly sweet kiss upon her kneecap. "Not now. When I make love to you, Shel, it's going to be long and slow. Take my time with you."

"I have time. I have twenty minutes." The words fled her lips before she could snatch them back. What the hell was she thinking? She had a job. Responsibilities.

Sex with Nick Anderson wasn't on her to-do list. No matter how much her body cried out for his expert touch.

He smiled darkly. "Twenty minutes will barely get me started. Some things are meant to be savored, not rushed, darling."

Not fair, her aching body cried out. Leaving her like

this, unfulfilled and wanting. He stood, stretching out his body, and she saw the bulge at his groin. So he wasn't unaffected. That made her feel a little better.

Until he turned and displayed his oh-so-fine, tight butt. Nice and round and taut. Bet she could bounce a quarter off that sexy ass of his.

Nick ran a hand through his hair, making the ends tousled and sexy. She longed to do the same, caress that thick mass of hair, run her fingers down his chest, toy with his nipples and go lower...

She stood, banging her knee on the too-close toilet. Shelby bit back a juicy curse.

Nick looked concerned. "You okay, Shel?"

Nothing a night in the sack with you couldn't cure. "Fine," she muttered, rubbing her knee. "Mind? I have to get dressed."

"Need a ride to the restaurant? I can take you on my bike. Unless you've never ridden before."

"I know how to ride."

He gave her a long, lingering caress with his eyes. "I bet you do, sweetheart."

Shelby glared at him. "Nick!"

"That offer of the ride still stands."

Oh, that wicked smile of his, the way the light danced in his dark brown eyes, lit with sensual promise. "No. Er, thanks. Ann is picking me up." She hurried out into her bedroom, well aware of the scattered clothing on the bed, the rumpled pillows. And hell, the bed itself, looking so soft and warm and inviting...

Nick sauntered over to the door. She couldn't help but stare. He had the arrogant, confident swagger of a military man, erect bearing, shoulders thrown back, as if he knew his way around a room.

Especially a bedroom.

He had back then, all those years ago when they were teenagers. What would have happened ten years ago if he'd done more than kiss her? How would their lives have turned out?

Could she have stopped him from leaving the Belle Creek?

From breaking her heart?

The last thought reminded her of what Nick Anderson had done—turned and walked away. She wanted to have sex. She needed to be loved. Cherished. Held tight and given assurances that she came first. A man who would give her stability and would always be there when she needed him.

Not with Nick Anderson. Shelby knew she'd never come first in his life. She grabbed her panty hose from the bed.

"'Bye, Nick. Out," she ordered.

"I can help you dress." He winked at her.

"You can help by closing the door behind you. And entertaining Timmy while I'm gone. He gets dinner around six. Hot dogs are fine for tonight. Or there's leftover tuna casserole." Shelby sat on the bed and began to pull on the hose. "I'll be home after midnight."

He frowned. "I don't like you coming home that late alone. I'll pick you up."

"I'm fine."

"I'll pick you up," he repeated, that stubborn line forming a dent between his thick, dark brows.

Exasperated, she twisted around to look at him. "The restaurant doesn't close until eleven, and I have to cash out."

"I'll be there waiting for you at eleven." He folded his arms across his chest.

She knew him. He'd stand there, waiting for her to acquiesce until she caved in. Shelby sighed. Truth was, she hated that walk up the long, dark drive. Ann always dropped her off at the entrance to the ranch because she didn't want to wake up "the king and queen," as she called Dan and Felicity.

"All right. Eleven."

He nodded, turned and walked out.

Shelby dressed in record time, tugging the hated white fringed skirt on and making sure her cowgirl boots were spit polished so she could avoid another lecture by her manager. Voices sounded in the living room; Nick's was low and gravelly, and there was a higher-pitched one. Then a horsey laugh. Ann.

Giving a final pat to her cowgirl hat, she hurried out of the bedroom.

Her friend sat in the armchair by the door, ogling Nick, who sat on the sofa. Jealousy nipped her. Her best friend had big teeth, and was tall enough to play basketball, but she had a winsome way about her, with her teased blond hair, big blue eyes and friendly way of flirting and making men feel right at home, as if they were something special. Ann never wanted for a man.

Judging from the way Ann leaned close to Nick, she was working that special magic. Shelby cleared her throat. "You ready?"

Her friend gave a guilty start as Shelby walked into the room. "About time, Shelby! We're gonna be late."

Nick whistled. "You look cute, Shel." His gaze dropped to her feet. "Nice boots. They do great things for your legs. Especially your right leg."

The leg he'd personally shaved for her. His hot, hungry gaze met hers and for a wild moment she considered tossing aside the cowgirl hat, telling Ann she was sick tonight and then grabbing Nick's hand to march him straight back to her bedroom. He kept gazing at her, intent burning in his eyes.

And then she remembered the tuna casserole that was three days old, all they could afford to eat, and the payment due on her Chevy, which needed new tires, and Timmy's birthday. Sex with Nick Anderson was a luxury she couldn't afford because he'd cost her more than a lost night's pay. The price might even be her heart. There was too much between them for casual sex. What would she do when he walked out the door again, never looking back?

Shelby settled her hat more firmly upon her head. "Let's go."

She closed the door behind her, leaving Nick staring after her.

At the restaurant that night, business was steady, but not as busy as Saturday nights or Fridays. Her manager kept on her case, nagging her not to only wait on customers, but also clean tables, even though the busboy looked bored and kept sneaking off to text his pimple-faced girlfriend. She found the reason why when Natalie marched out from the kitchen.

Blond hair flouncing, her mascaraed eyelashes batting furiously, Chuck Beaufort's daughter wore a cream-colored silk dress more suitable for dining with crystal goblets and heavy silverware than a greasy, steak-grilling eatery. She pursed her thin, glossy lips and headed straight for Shelby.

"You were supposed to work last night," she accused Shelby.

"Ann took my shift."

"Well, you didn't clear it with me." Natalie folded her arms and tapped a spiked high heel.

"You know Silas Anderson died. I went to his funeral," Shelby told her, refusing to back down. "Silas was like a father to me."

Natalie looked sly. "Like a father. Of course, because your own father was a drunk, and a mean one who could barely hold down a job. It's a miracle you managed to graduate from high school with those genes you carry. Not like my father, who buys me anything I want. He gave me this restaurant. What did your father give you, Shelby, other than that dingy, rusted-out trailer that you called home?"

Struggling against the impulse to knock the girl flat on her face, Shelby drew herself up. "Too bad he didn't teach you good manners. Or maybe that particular talent doesn't exist in your gene pool."

She turned around, her stomach churning, and ignored Natalie's outraged sputter. Few in town dared to talk back to Miss Natalie Beaufort of the Beauforts of Nature County.

Not like Shelby, who had no family name.

My father was a drunk.

My mother was a drunk.

But I'm not my parents. Damn it, will that always taint me, like I'm carrying some sign around my neck saying Trailer Trash?

She'd struggled to hold down two jobs, attend college at night and pay her bills. Only through Silas's kindness in giving her free room and board had she managed.

Shelby would have done anything for Nick's father to repay his generosity.

Working at this crappy restaurant had been one small way to help with the ranch's bills. She'd have scrubbed floors in Natalie's house if it meant repaying Silas for what he'd done.

Because Nick's father hadn't merely given her a home. He handed back her self-worth and self-respect.

Both were traits that could be lost each time Nick swaggered near, his smooth gait hinting he could give a woman a great time in bed, his sexy mouth pursed in a cocky grin and that bad-boy attitude.

Was it in her DNA to be attracted to bad boys? Nick was a hometown hero, but a bad guy at heart. His rugged edges and rough side had only become more sharply honed with his military experience.

So focused were her thoughts on Nick that she nearly collided with Ann, who was coming out of the kitchen with a chef's salad.

"Watch it, Shelby!" Ann laughed. "You woolgathering again?"

She shook her head. "Had a little encounter of the Nastyville kind with our queen bee of the kitchen."

"What she say to you?" her friend demanded. "Want me to twist her panties in a knot?"

Shelby smiled. "She's just being Natalie. Can't help her nature. Like a rattler can't help its nature."

"I'd trust a snake before that one." Ann lowered her voice. "She said she was at your place earlier today, checking out how well her horse is doing. Claimed she smelled something fishy at the ranch. Wanted to make sure you weren't charging her for full board and giving her precious mare rough board. If I were you, I'd slip some horse apples into the back of her trunk, give her a real reason to smell something bad."

Her friend winked, then headed into the dining room to deliver her salad. Shelby stared after her, lost in thought. Natalie hadn't been at the ranch today. Not to show her face, anyway.

Was Chuck Beaufort's daughter the one behind the prank played last night and the gas can left in the root cellar?

Chapter 9

It had been a head-pounding night, the restaurant crowded with men watching the Tennessee game on the big screens. Tips were lousy and her feet ached. She was the last to leave because she'd stayed a little later to help the cook clean up, and was ready to crash into her bed.

And Nick expected her to ride back to the Belle Creek on...that?

Shelby stared at the Harley with unease. She'd never ridden a motorcycle before and right now, she was so dog-tired she feared she would fall off. In her haste to dress, she'd forgotten about Nick's bike. The short, fringed skirt would prove a real challenge.

"What's wrong? Never ride before?"

Black helmet in hand, dressed in a dark leather jacket, blue jeans and boots, Nick looked dangerous. Bad-boy extreme, his hair brushed against the collar of his jacket and his smile was sexy. A hint of wildness lurked in that smile, as if he planned to do more than ride them back home.

Shelby gave him a long, cool look as she adjusted the purse on her shoulder. "Not something like this."

"She's just like riding a horse." Nick gave the seat a pat. "Less temperamental."

"Except it eats less and doesn't pee on your shoes when you're in firing range."

He threw back his head. His deep, rich laughter caused a funny flutter in her stomach.

A rill of fear rippled through her. If she rode with him and took this risk, it meant leaving her world behind and trusting herself to this dark stranger who knew nothing of it.

"Shel?" Nick held out his hand. "I promise, I'll take good care of you and I won't let you go."

She studied the shiny metal, the numerous gadgets. "Tell me about your bike."

Approval radiated from him. He pointed out the midsection. "Twin B engine, makes the ride smooth and even. No vibrations." He flicked his fingers at the front. "Windshield, headlights. I used to have a smaller bike, without a windshield, but got tired of eating bugs on the highway when I had to travel across the country."

Nick bent over, jeans stretching smoothly over his taut bottom, and patted the box on the bike's side. "Saddlebags, with chrome studs, where I store my gear. Good for all the long-distance trips I make."

Shelby hitched in a breath. "I like the view," she murmured, staring at his very fine butt.

He squatted and flipped down a rubber-coated piece of metal. "These are for whoever rides with me. Footpads so you can rest your feet. Nicer than pegs."

Opening a saddlebag, he gestured for her purse. As he stored it in the saddlebag, she rested a hand on the leather seat, a little stab of emotion arrowing through her as she thought of women behind him, their hands clinging to him. "Have you ridden with many women?"

He gave her a burning look. "Yes, in the past," he replied evenly. "But none compared to you, Shel."

A warm tingling filled her. She sensed a deeper meaning behind his words, but didn't question it. Nick held out his hand. "C'mon, Shel. It's late and you must be dead tired."

Taking a step toward him was a step out in trust. She took a deep breath. What did she have to lose? She'd never taken risks before. It was about time to see what the rest of the world had to offer.

Shelby took his hand, felt excitement as a smile of pleasure touched his mouth. He flipped down the footpads and helped her onto the bike, but the skirt was way too short. Nick hesitated.

"Don't happen to have jeans or pants handy?" he asked.

Shelby frowned. "I'll manage."

Managing seemed to be her skill set lately. Never failing to adapt, make it work. For a wild moment, she wondered when a time would come when she didn't have to manage, and things would work for her instead of her working for them.

The front door of the restaurant banged open and Natalie stormed outside. Shelby's stomach tightened. Now what?

"Shelby, where are you going?"

"Home."

"You can't leave yet." Natalie put her hands on her hips. "Everyone else clocked out and you were supposed to scrub the ladies' room floor. And the men's."

Temper rising like molten lava, Shelby narrowed her

eyes as she walked closer to the restaurant owner. "Since when? That was always the assistant manager's job."

A smug smile touched Natalie's face. "Since tonight. I've rearranged everything. The last server to leave is responsible for cleaning the bathrooms."

It would always be like this. Natalie making the rules, changing them to suit her, and humiliating Shelby. Working eight hours for a few dollars in tips because Natalie made certain to give her the tables she knew were bad tippers. Natalie, who had tormented her in high school and continued to make her life miserable.

Would she ever be free of this woman's oppression?

"Shel, you want a ride home or what?"

Nick stood by the bike, waiting. His expression shuttered, but was unjudging. Fact was, Nick was the only one who never judged her. Never once thought of her as lower class because of her origins and her parents. Even Silas, who had given her many wonderful opportunities, had done so because he felt pity for her.

Nick didn't.

"I need this job," she muttered, as Natalie waited by the door.

Did she walk away and risk losing her sole source of income? Who would pay the bills?

He left the bike and came to her side.

"There are other jobs." Nick picked up her hand. "Jobs that were meant for your talent and brains, Shel. You're smart, educated and you're great with numbers. You deserve more than this."

It was the calmness in his touch, the absolute gentleness and his faith in her abilities that broke her. Shelby snapped like a tightly stretched rubber band. Nick was correct. She did deserve more.

"Go clean the bathroom yourself, you spoiled brat," she told Natalie. "It would be good for you to get on your knees for a change."

Natalie gasped. "You, you're fired! I want your uniform back by tomorrow morning. I'll mail your paycheck."

A knot of fury uncoiled inside her. The woman had it all planned. She had meant for Shelby to make one last mistake so she could wield her power. No more.

Shelby unzipped her skirt, shimmied it past her hips and then threw it at Natalie. "Here. You love it so much, you have it now. Hell, you can wear it. And you can't fire me, because I quit."

Off went the cowboy hat, sailing in the air at Natalie. Clad only in her worn fleece jacket, white collared shirt, white boots and panties, she glared at Natalie.

The woman stared at her, her mouth opening and closing like a fish.

Nick laughed and returned to the bike. He opened a saddlebag, removed a pair of gray sweatpants. "Here. Put these on. They're big, but will keep your legs covered. Mite cold out."

Then he gave a long, appreciative look at her lower half. "Black lace. My favorite."

Whistling, he closed the saddlebag. Shelby tugged on the pants, feeling warmth hit her legs.

Nick flicked a hand at the goggle-eyed Natalie. "'Bye, Natalie."

The woman stormed inside, taking Shelby's skirt and hat. Maybe it was a bad idea to quit when she needed the money, but right now she wouldn't think about that. For once, she'd live in the moment.

Shivering, Shelby shook her head. "Oh, wow, I don't

envy her. Have you ever seen the men's room after a
football game?"

Laughing again, he handed her the helmet. Nick
touched her cheek again.

"You're a hell of a woman, Shelby Stillwater. I'm
proud of you."

The brief kiss he dropped on her cheek warmed her
skin from the inside out.

Shivering from his touch, she put on the helmet he
gave her, the hard shell feeling as if she'd stuck her head
into a small cave. He chuckled and adjusted it so it didn't
swim over her smaller head, then flipped down the face
shield.

Proud of her? She'd quit her job and called the most
powerful woman in town a spoiled brat.

Nick settled in front of her, his broad back a solid
wall of muscle covered in black leather. "Put your arms
around me and just hold on. You can lean against the
backrest if you like."

Shelby's heart raced. Slowly she slid her arms around
his lean waist and leaned into him. The smell of leather
and his delicious, spicy scent flooded her senses. Pleasure filled her, as she snuggled closer, opening her thighs
to couch his. He tensed, muttered something and turned
the key. The bike roared to life as she settled her feet on
the footpads.

Nick turned. He cupped her chin with one gloved
hand.

"It's going to be okay. Trust me."

Trust him. Did she have a choice? Not just for the ride
home, either. Nick turned and she slid her arms around
his lean waist, her muscles tensing. Shelby squeezed her
eyes shut as they rode out of the parking lot. When they

reached the main road, she opened her eyes. The wide leather seat beneath her was comfortable, as promised. Wind gushed past her in a rush. Fresh air and the dank smell of the light rain that had splattered over the pavement filled her nostrils. The feeling was exhilarating and liberating.

Tomorrow, she'd think about the consequences of what she'd done. For tonight, she wanted to live for the moment, close her eyes and feel.

Shelby listened to the gush of wind racing past, smelled the delicious scent of Nick, his cologne and leather. She tried to relax and imagined they were without boundaries or restrictions.

His broad back felt like a sold, sheltering wall. Slowly, she released her fears as if they were dandelions floating in the wind. A new awareness replaced the fear. *I'm free. It feels like flying*, she marveled.

As he stopped at a red light, she shouted into his ear, "It feels like flying!"

Nick turned. "That's why I love bikes. Nothing else will do. I relish my freedom, to be able to go anywhere I wish. Want to go faster?"

"Yes!"

"Hold tight."

As the light changed, she gripped him harder, leaning against him. Wind whipped past them. Riding like this, nothing but open space before them, she understood why Nick chose this way to travel. The man was a maverick who enjoyed the open road.

As he pulled into the long drive of the Belle Creek, her heart sank. Nick loved his freedom. More than anything else. The Harley was a good reminder of that. He wouldn't stay here. Soon enough, he'd be roaring off toward the open road once more.

Nick drove to the front of the garage, put down the kickstand and shut off the engine. She removed the helmet, handed it to him. Then she slid off the bike, his sweatpants slithering down her ankles. Shelby tugged them up, holding them with one hand. The earlier bravado and the thrill of the ride had fled, leaving her cold and empty inside.

Nick put both helmets on the handles, retrieved her purse and followed her up the steps as she unlocked the door.

As he locked it behind them, she fisted a hand in the waistband of the sweatpants. "Thanks for the ride home. I guess you don't have to worry about picking me up tomorrow night, or the next because I'm now unemployed."

"There are other jobs."

"Right. By tomorrow, every single job I could get will be filled. Chuck Beaufort has all the power, Nick. You know what kind of influence he has. This is a small town and there aren't many choices."

"Shel, I'm not the enemy." His jaw tightened. "But damn it, I couldn't stand to see Natalie treat you like that any longer. What I said was true. You're smart, talented and you can get another job. Hell, I don't even know why you kept hanging around this ranch for so long. You could go anywhere."

Shelby compressed her lips. "Some of us don't have the luxury. We have responsibilities. Good night, Nick."

She trudged off to her bedroom, misery filling her. She could go anywhere.

Belle Creek was her home, the only real home she ever

knew. And when Nick flung his hands into the air and decided to give up and sell, she wouldn't have a choice.

She'd have to pack up and leave.

But he was right. Perhaps now was the right time to embrace change.

Chapter 10

Five days after Shelby had quit her job, she fell into a routine at the Belle Creek. Now that she wasn't as tired from working nights, she had time to paint. She set up her easel in the barn and, each morning, headed there to work.

Today the morning light spilled onto the wood floor, a haze glistening in the distance. Sitting on a bale of hay, she worked for two hours, each brush stroke soothing. Finally, satisfied with the results, she stopped. Dan had asked her to inventory every single piece of equipment in the old barn. Tomorrow, she promised herself she'd look for a new job.

Much as she knew it was best to put distance between them—shoot, an entire state of distance would be safest—Shelby didn't resist when Nick insisted on helping her.

Though the morning had dawned clear and cold, it warmed rapidly. Sunlight streamed into the old barn as dust motes danced in the beams. Inventory was boring, but essential work each year. Nick brought in a portable radio and tuned it to a popular country station.

Usually she worked alone, enjoying the solitude. Today she was too aware of the big man next to her, black Stetson on his head, the red-and-black-checked flannel shirt stretched tight across his deep chest, the smoky timbre of his voice as he called back to her the items to check off.

Even the subtle tang of his aftershave proved a distraction, lacing through the oil and gasoline smells of the tractors, and the hay stored by the animal stalls.

Clipboard in hand, he wrote down and checked off items as they combed through the barn. The iPad was more efficient, he'd argued, but this old-fashioned method of paper and pencil made her feel more in control.

She needed to feel in control of something.

They were interrupted by Mario, who came with the truck to get more hay for the stables. As she went through smaller items stored at the barn's back, Nick helped Mario stack a few bales into the pickup's bed. After Mario left, Nick swigged back a bottle of water, his strong throat muscles working. Sitting on a bale of hay, Shelby sipped from her bottle, fascinated by a bead of sweat trickling down his temple.

He set down the bottle and began moving to the beat of a lively song on the radio. "C'mon, Shel, let's dance."

Laughing, she watched him cut a smooth move across the weathered floorboards. Nick held out his hand, a spark in his eyes. "Show me what you've got, darling."

As she crossed the floor to join him, the song ended. The radio played Rascal Flatts's "Bless the Broken Road."

Slow dance. It didn't deter Nick. He reached out, pulled her into his arms and began a slow dance. Shelby didn't resist. It felt good, curled against his chest, his arms secure around her. The haunting melody surrounded them, spliced with the distant whinny of horses in the pasture, and the wind rustling through the treetops outside.

Nick was like the singer. He'd traveled a broken road for years, and had finally come home. Shelby sighed and moved with him, their bodies swaying. He was all hard muscle and sinew, and yet he held her gently, as if he cherished having her in his arms.

I could stay like this forever. Maybe this is the end of Nick's broken road, and I'm the one for him.

Reality nudged the edges of her daydream. Nick might be a drifter, but he wasn't home for good. He could continue to roam, and every minute she denied this fact, the more she stood to have her heart broken all over again.

As the song ended, she gently untangled herself from him. Nick looked down at her, an inscrutable expression on his face, those dark eyes filled with secrets.

"We should get back to work," she murmured, heading back for her clipboard.

Nick pushed a hand through his hair. "Let's take a break. How about a bite in town?"

Shelby gave him a wry look. "The Bucking Bronc?"

His little smile sent flutters of pleasure shooting through her. "I was thinking lunch at Flo's café. Grilled cheese and tomato, and hot tomato-basil soup."

Oh, so tempting. Shelby thought of her tight budget.

"You go. I want to finish this section of the barn by the time Felicity picks up Timmy from school."

Nick set down the clipboard and went to her. "My treat, Shel. C'mon. It's just lunch." He gave her a woebegone look. "Please? I need you to protect me. You won't let all those lusty waitresses jump me, will you?"

Couldn't help it, with that charming grin of his. "Oh, yeah, Shirley and Maude are real scary, Nick. They're more likely to jump all over Glenna when she gets a new stock of fabric in her shop. They're in love with quilting, not your amazing bod."

"You think so?" He came close enough for her to see the dark stubble dusting his lean cheeks and chin. Hadn't shaved this morning. He looked real sexy, too. "You think I have a hot bod?"

Shelby rolled her eyes. "I think you have a very large ego."

"Everything about me is big." Nick winked and his grin was so engaging, she had to laugh.

"Let's go, Shel. Take a break."

She took five minutes to splash water on her face and change from her grubby T-shirt into a knit cranberry sweater. Outside, Nick stood by the Harley. He handed her the helmet. She gave the bike a dubious look.

"That again? What about the truck?"

"The bike doesn't waste as much gas. And I like having you so close behind me." Nick winked.

They mounted the bike and roared off. Shelby felt the warmth of his body as she curled against him, her legs pressed against the hardness of his muscled thighs. Heaven was a motorcycle, even in the cold wind cutting through the thinness of her worn jean jacket.

Heaven was Nick Anderson, taking her for a ride.

She closed her eyes, adrift in fantasy. She could pretend they were cruising on a highway in France, headed away from the city for a day. Maybe find a winery and drink Bordeaux and eat yellow cheese, sharp and pungent. Spread out a blanket overlooking the grape vines, the sun warming them as they kissed beneath the sky…

Nick slowed down. She opened her eyes to see him turn right, toward the new shopping center built only two years ago by Chuck Beaufort Enterprises. Oh, right. Flo had moved her diner when the rent on Main got too pricey.

Nick pulled into the shopping center parking lot and cut the engine. She watched him toe the kickstand in place and remove his helmet. He pocketed the keys. He swung one muscled leg over the bike and held out a hand.

A sexy biker with a wicked smile and a tempting body. Shelby suppressed a sigh. It was lunch. Nothing more. Shelby removed her helmet, fluffed out her hair. Helmet head. If this was a date, and he was planning an afternoon delight, he was in for disappointment. She had too much work.

They walked the length of the shopping center toward the busy diner. And then they came to an office that read in bold letters Martha Horner Reality.

Nick ground to an abrupt halt as he scanned the photos in the window. His face grew angry.

"What's wrong?"

Silently, he pointed to the array of photos in the window. Shelby leaned close, her weary gaze scanning the real estate offerings. His index finger trailed across the glass to a flyer posted in the window. As she read the words, suddenly her hunger fled.

The flyer was advertising for investors in a ground-floor opportunity called Countryville, a venture that could create hundreds of jobs in the county. Prime views of the Smoky Mountains. Interested parties could call Martha's office.

But it was the photo on the paper that raised her blood pressure. Only one piece of land had that spectacular view of the mountains.

The north pasture of the Belle Creek.

Her furious gaze dropped to the elegant logo at the paper's bottom. Chuck Beaufort Enterprises.

"He's really going to do it. He doesn't even have the land!"

"He's confident enough he can grab it for a steal." Nick jingled the keys in his hand. "Did some checking in town. Seems Beaufort has been bragging about Countryville for a month now, how it will bring jobs to the town. Hotel as big as Opryland, with its own theater, swimming pool and…stables."

"But what if you don't sell?"

"Beaufort must think all he has to do is wait. Wait for the bank to foreclose on the ranch and then offer them a cash deal. With our acreage, he'd have the last parcel needed to build his park."

Shelby couldn't stand liars. But swindlers were worse.

"You know what this means, Shel. Whoever is doing all those things on the ranch to ruin our business is getting desperate, probably hoping to sell to Beaufort before the bank forecloses. Make a profit before it's too late."

His troubled gaze met hers in the yellow glare of the parking lights. She didn't need him to spell it out.

They had been looking at outsiders with a vested interest in forcing a sale of the Belle Creek to Chuck Beaufort. Natalie was the prime suspect. But no longer. Not with this news.

Whoever was doing all these things on the ranch wasn't an outsider after all. But someone with a prime interest in forcing Nick to sell before it was too late. And she could think of only one person that desperate, who had a wife with champagne taste and a beer budget.

His cousin Dan.

* * *

After lunch the next day, Shelby made Timmy a birthday cake, with real cinnamon icing. She looked over the brightly wrapped gifts purchased in town. Not much. Not what he really wanted—the new Nintendo. Heather had sent money for a birthday party, but it wasn't enough. Her sister's wire transfers had dwindled each month, and it made no sense. Timmy's parents loved their son, and wanted the best for him. Why were they being stingy with the monthly cash they sent Shelby for his care?

Shelby wanted to throw him a big party, but finances prohibited it. They did have roast beef for dinner, his favorite, and ice cream and cake, and Dan and Felicity promised to decorate the house with balloons and streamers to make Timmy feel special.

Wiping her hands on a dish towel, she looked out the kitchen window with its splendid view of the barn and stables. The ranch was bustling today. Not only had Natalie taken Fancy for a ride, but their other boarders had also decided to ride on the southern trail. Jake and his girlfriend, Lynn, accompanied them.

She should drag out her old laptop, review her résumé and start looking around for a new job. They needed the cash. No, she needed the cash.

But the afternoon was so pretty, and she was caught up on the bookkeeping, and it had been too long since she'd ridden. What good was it to live on a ranch and never take advantage of the trails? Might help to check out the fork on the old north trail, see if it needed work, and scope out the land for hunting. Deer season was popular in this area. They could open it for hunters or fall rides if Dan didn't sell that parcel, for the trail wended through the acres Silas had left him.

Every penny counted these days.

Minutes later, wearing a backpack stuffed with a water bottle, snacks and binoculars, she headed for the stables. Shelby wore her oldest jeans, a comfortable sweatshirt and her Western boots. She fetched Pantser from the pasture and saddled her. In the barn, the sharp machete they used for cutting back brush was missing. Instead, she grabbed big garden clippers and stuffed those into her pack. She decided to grab a rifle as well, just in case. Then she headed back to the main house. With all the incidents around here, she wouldn't take unnecessary chances.

Dan, working on the old tractor outside the barn, looked up as she rode by. He stood and wiped his hands on a stained cloth. "Where you headed?"

"Thought I'd take her on the north trail near the abandoned cornfield." Shelby scanned the distant field and frowned. "It only needs a little more clearing before we can bring in guests to ride on it. Want to come?"

His gaze darted away. Dan shook his head. "Got to get this tractor running so I can stack that hay from the field."

"Where's Nick?"

His cousin shrugged. "Out, I guess. He didn't say."

She knew he'd headed out early in the morning, had heard the front door open and close as she showered. And she was an early riser.

The roan snorted with impatience as Shelby leaned forward. "Where's everyone?"

"John, Mario and Hank are working on the south trail for tomorrow's group. Since this month is Halloween, I thought we could put out some scarecrows, pumpkins, spruce the trail up to make it more interesting."

"Sounds like a good plan."

She nudged Pantser onward.

Dan had good ideas, he just wasn't good at managing the money. Silas had been the one who kept things running smoothly. Grief pinched her. She missed him so much, his business sense and his keen sense of frugality.

Felicity didn't understand budgets or restraint. She supposed the woman had her good points. She was a good mother, and adored her sons. And Felicity hadn't always been so tense. Only in the last year, when finances started to dwindle, had she become more high-strung. Shelby had diplomatically suggested to Dan that he control his wife. Dan didn't listen.

But someone had to lay down the law to the woman. Maybe it was time to stop being nice and start playing dirty. Dark days meant dark action. Nick would agree. He wouldn't put up with Felicity's antics or complaints. He hadn't put up with Natalie, either.

Her stomach gave a pleasant jolt at the thought of Nick giving her a thorough once-over in her panties. Even in the dim light she'd seen the appreciative gleam in his dark eyes, the hunger. If she had been more welcoming, he'd have wound up in her bed.

Bad idea. Forget that Timmy slept only a few feet away and the walls were cardboard thin. Giving Nick Anderson access to her bed, and her body, was more dangerous than a lit match near that gas can they'd found. She'd combust all right. Go up in flames in his arms. No doubt he was a skilled lover. But after, he'd leave her cold and empty and aching.

Because it couldn't last. Nick couldn't last. He was a fleeting pleasure, as temporary as the pretty spring wildflowers that bloomed in the fields.

The sun glared overhead in the sky, a few storm clouds scudding across the bright blue. Her thoughts drifted to Nick, and the vulnerable, painfully emotional teen she'd been when he kissed her.

From the moment she and her family moved onto the ranch, Shelby had been too aware of the gorgeous, rebellious Nick with his tousled dark gold hair and cool brown gaze. Tall and gangly, and quiet, he stirred inside her feelings she'd never had. Her childhood had been spent trying to glue her family back together like a shattered china cup. After each drunken episode, her parents would fight, threaten to break up and Shelby would play referee.

Nick was the first person she'd ever met who looked at her as if he could see past the thin veneer of her brittle armor, into the real person that she guarded so fiercely from getting hurt. They would ride horses along this very trail, Nick egging her to race him, and her silly little girlish heart would beat faster.

They'd search for Henry's treasure on the property and swim in the water hole on long, lazy summer days.

And at night, they'd sit on wicker chairs on the wide wood porch of his family's home and talk about music, horses and their dreams. Nick loved country music and wanted to be a singer. Or a Navy SEAL—strong, invincible and tough. Shelby wanted to study art in Paris. It didn't matter that Nick was three years older. He was a good friend, and she had a crush on him.

But their friendship only mattered on the farm and gradually it faded. When she entered high school, it turned into a sweet memory to tuck away in her scrapbook. Her time with Nick was memorialized in an autumn leaf of brilliant crimson he'd found for her, the napkin he used to scribble song lyrics, a photograph of them sitting on sleds on the property's snowy hillside. In school, Nick was the tough, athletic track star who had a flock of adoring fans following him like ducklings waddling after their mother. He was older, too cool to associate with her, and she understood.

She could worship him from afar. Dream about a life with him, pretend there was hope.

When he'd kissed her in Henry's old cabin ten years ago, all her hopes and dreams collided like a meteor crashing to earth. And like that meteor, the shining moments turned into dust when he left and never said goodbye.

Shelby entered the woods flanking the cornfield, where the sun dappled the red and gold leaves littering the forest floor. A tangle of thorny blackberry bushes grew thick and wild, partly blocking the trail. The canes were thick and drought had left these dead.

Shelby dismounted, retrieved the clippers and began cutting. It was arduous work, for the canes were thick. Shame these bushes were dead, for she'd enjoyed picking the berries in the warmer weather and Felicity made excellent jam.

So much land. It would make a wonderful dude ranch. She'd even proposed it to Silas two years ago, suggesting they turn the main house into a bed-and-breakfast, even have a real homestead with chickens the guests could feed, and the big kitchen could easily be turned into a classroom, where Felicity could teach them how to can blackberries and cook real Southern dishes.

Silas had scowled and turned down the idea, saying he didn't want strangers on his family's land.

Well, tough luck. Look at us now, strangers getting ready to foreclose on the house and ranch.

She worked steadily on the thorny bushes as Pantser stood patiently by, swishing her tail.

How could Nick give all this up? This corner of Tennessee was sheer heaven. She loved it here, loved the clear open skies and the sounds of horses neighing across the valley in the early morning when they were turned out. On cold, crisp nights in winter, the stars seemed to burst out from the sky, so vibrant and sparkling and close it almost felt like you could touch them...

"Shel."

Shrieking, she jumped as a hand touched her shoulder. Shelby put a hand to her racing heart and carefully lowered the clippers. "Sweet Jesus, don't do that! Didn't you ever learn not to scare a woman with a weapon in her hand?"

Nick jammed his hands into his front pockets. His dark gold hair was as tangled and messy as the thick blackberry bushes. The blue-and-black-plaid flannel shirt hung loose on him, tucked neatly into his jeans. He wore his customary black leather jacket and a black Stetson, and a backpack was riding on his broad shoulders.

Cowboy biker, she thought absently, and then she scowled. "What are you doing out here, how did you get out here and what the hell do you mean, creeping up on me?"

Nick considered. "Lot of questions. Which do you want answered first?"

Shelby peered past him, didn't see a horse. "How did you get here?"

"Walked." He gestured to the woods. "Wanted to check out this trail. It's long, nice and flat for beginning riders. Thought it would make a good trail for riding again if we cleared it."

He cleared his throat as she gave him a pointed look and raised the clippers. Nick grinned.

"Nice knife. But you'll never get this cleared with that."

Removing the backpack, he fished out a long machete. He held it up and his grin broadened. "This is a knife, sweetheart."

Nick took a pair of thick yellow gloves from his back pocket and donned them. "We can clear all this faster if I hack and you pile."

They began a steady rhythm, Nick chopping the dead canes and Shelby clipping the thorny stems into smaller sections and piling them on the side of the trail.

Shelby shook her head as she cut a thick cane. "I should have known you took the machete."

"I don't mess around when it comes to hard work."

"You mean you work hard or you hardly work?"

The joke didn't coax a smile to his face. "According to Dan, I'm guilty of the latter."

Shelby sighed. "Give him a chance, Nick. You only got back and he's been running things here and helping Silas since the day you left. If not for him, the ranch would have gone belly up long ago."

He straightened and looked at her. "I give everyone a chance, Shel. Too bad no one around here is giving me a chance and they want to kick me out."

Bitterness tinged his voice. Troubled, she put a hand on his arm. "I think Dan is shell-shocked that Silas left the ranch to you. No one wants you gone, Nick." She squeezed his arm, feeling the thick muscle and sturdy bone. "I certainly don't."

When he gave her a long, thoughtful look, she blushed and removed her hand.

"Someone wants me out." He stabbed the machete into the ground, reached into his jeans pocket and pulled out a crumpled piece of paper.

Written in block letters was an ominous message:

You're worthless and useless. Leave now because no one wants you here.

She stared at the note. "Who would do such a thing? I don't recognize the handwriting." It wasn't a clear threat, but a taunt.

He took the note and stuffed it back in his pocket. "I found it in my pack this morning. Left the pack outside to air out. Whoever put that note in there either lives or works here."

Shelby's stomach tightened with anxiety. "It's a childish thing to do."

"It's the third one I found, Shel. Don't tell anyone else. I'm fighting an uphill battle as it is, trying to figure out how to find enough money to pay the bank."

Suddenly she was glad she'd brought the rifle. She'd been thinking of wild animals, not human threats. But the biggest threat they all faced walked on two legs, not four. They returned to work, Shelby lost in thought.

"Do you think whoever wrote the note is the one doing all the vandalism?" she asked.

"Not sure." His gaze hardened and he suddenly looked dangerous. "But I plan to find out. Don't go out alone anymore, Shel. I don't like you being alone and unarmed."

Shelby shrugged. "The worst I have to worry about on this trail is wild hogs. We used to get a few of them around here and Silas would shoot them, and we'd have a big pig roast. He'd invite all the local business leaders.

It was good for business relations. In the last four years, he got more and more cranky and antisocial. No more pig roasts."

"You do know the best way to bait wild hogs?" He hacked a thick vine and tossed it aside.

"Bacon?"

Nick's low laugh sent a shiver of pleasure down her spine. Not going there.

"Cupcakes. With vanilla icing."

Shelby wrinkled her forehead. "Are you serious?"

"I'm always serious about my hunting." He finished cutting back the bushes and eyed the results piled in the middle of the trail. "We could burn those, but not in this weather. I won't risk it."

Absently, she gathered the last handful of canes to push them to the side of the trail. A thorn pierced the thick fabric of her gloves.

"Ow!" Shelby tugged off the glove. A small droplet of blood oozed from her right forefinger.

"Want me to kiss it and make it better?"

Before she could speak, Nick took her hand, studied her injured finger. Then he raised it to his mouth and kissed it, his gaze never leaving hers. Her heart rate kicked up, and she remained motionless. Nick was a flirt, experienced in seducing women. But she was no longer that vulnerable teenager, desperate for his attention, who thought the sun rose and set on Nick Anderson.

Shelby tugged her hand free. "I'll live." The less contact she had with Nick, the better.

The sun shone high and bright in the sky when she'd set out, but it was getting later. "I want to go a little farther and then I need to get back. I want to finish preparations for Timmy's party."

As she untied Pantser's reins from a nearby bush, Nick's eyes twinkled. "Care to give me a ride?"

Riding with him on the motorcycle had already stirred up old feelings best buried. Shelby shook her head. "I don't want to strain Pantser. The exercise will do you good."

Nick's expression became guarded. "When are you ever going to forgive me, Shelby?"

Her heart kicked up a beat. "For what?"

"For whatever I did to you before I left here."

Her pride had been wounded enough. She shrugged. "It's in the past. I'm only looking to the future now, and trying to save this place from bulldozers."

His fingers gently encircled her wrist. "So am I. Let's walk, Shel."

The mere touch of his hand sent shivers coursing through her. Shelby didn't want to walk with him. She needed to focus on the practical. But the day was lovely and the man beside her tempting. Grabbing the reins, she led Pantser along the trail as Nick accompanied her. The path looked clear and wide, unlike her own personal path, which had grown very uncertain.

She began asking him questions about what he'd done since leaving the navy, learning that he had wandered across the country. Nick answered briefly, turning the tables on her. She began telling him about life on the ranch, and how challenging it was to care for a young boy.

A few minutes into their walk, Shelby asked the question burning in her mind since the day he'd left Belle Creek and hadn't returned. Until now.

"Why did you leave, Nick?" She gripped the reins tight, the leather making her palms sweat. "Did you run away from us? Me?"

"It was time."

"Why did you stick around so long? Why didn't you leave when you turned eighteen and you could legally join the navy?"

Why did you break my heart after we kissed and tell me I was too young?

He stopped, turned, his body tense. "That's a private matter."

"You ask me to share information about my life and you don't do the same."

Nick's jaw tensed. He stared at the trail ahead. Finally he looked at her, his gaze steady. "I stayed because of you, Shel. I wanted to make sure you would be okay. Remember that incident at the park when those boys teased you, and threatened you? You came home that day, crying, your knee all skinned, and you told me about it?"

A dull flush heated her face. She had been only thirteen, and three older boys from Nick's high school had called her trailer trash and worse. One, Martin Randall, had pushed her and laughed. The looks on their faces had scared her. "Hard to forget."

"I went after them." A tic started in his jaw. "I beat the crap out of them and told them to never, ever touch you again and warned them to spread the message. Hands off Shelby or Nick Anderson would make them pay."

Shelby's mouth opened wide. "You did that for me?"

At his nod, warmth filled her chest. All the times she'd thought he'd ignored her in high school when he looked out for her. The name calling had eased off after that, thanks to him. And no boy had ever threatened her again.

"I put Martin Randall into the hospital with a broken jaw. Silas beat my ass for that and he was going to make me apologize. I refused, and he kicked me out." He jammed his hands into the pockets of his jeans. "Return-ing home was really tough, but I felt I had to do it. For you, Shel. Someone had to watch after you and Heather, make sure no one took advantage of you. Yeah, Silas gave you a home, but he was so damn clueless when it came to many things. Someone had to watch out for you."

That was why Nick had run off when he was sixteen. And then he returned, and stuck it out until shortly after their kiss three years later. Shelby began to understand the complexities that drove Nick. "You never said any-thing. Dan said you left because Silas grounded you from going to that concert."

A small, bitter laugh. "Right. As if grounding me would do any good. I was tired of Silas treating me bad, but no way in hell would I ever apologize to that bastard Martin. It would give him power over me, and then he'd feel free to go after you."

All the while Nick had ignored her in school he had been her quiet protector. After the incident, he'd taught her self-defense moves, training he'd increased when he returned home. Shelby touched his arm. "Thank you, Nick. Thanks for being there for me."

He gave her a sideways glance. "I never talked about it because I didn't want you thinking you couldn't defend yourself and you'd always need me around."

She had needed him, and showed him that day in the cabin with her eager kiss. Her smile dropped as they kept walking. Soon after that kiss, Nick left for good.

"I did need you. As more than a protector, Nick. I was crazy about you and that day you kissed me, you broke my heart."

There. It was out, in the open, and no longer swirling in her head. She no longer cared if the words gave him power over her, for speaking them had empowered her. Shelby knew she could move forward now.

He gave a heavy sigh. "You were too young and innocent, Shel, and if I had stuck around any longer, it would have ended badly. For both of us. I'm sorry I hurt you, but sometimes the hardest decisions are the right ones, and walking away from you, when I wanted to do more than kiss you, was the right one to make." His jaw tensed. "I don't want to talk about it anymore."

Wind kicked up the dirt and leaves on the path. Shelby noticed a large round patch on the trail and kicked the decaying leaves. The ground before her suddenly gave way and she stumbled. Nick quickly caught her arm, pulling her back. His dark gaze widened with concern. "You okay?"

Shaken, she pointed to the ground. "There's a hole under the leaves."

They squatted down and uncovered the hidden hole about two feet deep. Mouth flattened, Nick stared at it.

"This isn't natural. Someone shoveled out the dirt, replaced it with brush and leaves to make it look flat. If you had been riding…"

I would have ridden into it, and Pantser would have fallen, maybe breaking her leg. Or a guest riding could have done the same, and been badly hurt.

Shelby shuddered.

They cautiously made their way farther down the trail, leaving the horse tied to a tree. A few yards away, they discovered two more holes. Now it was clear, it was deliberate.

Sitting back, he dusted off his hands. "That's it. Trail's officially closed. We'll take the riders on the south trail only, and I'm going to personally inspect it before each ride. And install more trail cameras as a deterrent against whoever the hell is doing this."

He helped her stand, strong fingers gripping her arm. Nick looked as steady as ever, while knots tensed her stomach. As they started back to the house, Nick stayed close to her, his gaze sharp as he kept watching the fields.

Nick removed his hat, swiped an arm across his forehead. "From now on, don't ride out alone. I put Mario, John and Hank and a couple of their buddies to work fixing those fences. Making them electric and cordoning off the south pasture. Only way someone can get to those trails is through the barn and stables."

"That costs a lot."

"Leave the expense to me. I have a little money. I'm more concerned about you now. You okay, Shel?" Nick cupped her cheek, searched her eyes. His touch sent little electrical currents sizzling through her.

"I am now."

"Less people know about this, the better. Felicity will get hysterical and worry about the kids taking pony rides, and Jake will tell Lynn, and Lynn will tell others."

She understood. If word got out, they'd lose even more business.

As they walked back to the stables, Nick kept alert, his gaze constantly roving. She appreciated his protectiveness. A far more troubling thought kept nagging her.

The saboteur was getting clever, planting traps to hurt people. What would happen next, and could they stop it before someone got seriously hurt?

Chapter 11

Timmy's birthday party became the celebration everyone sorely needed. As Timmy played video games with
Mason and Miles in the basement recreational room,
Shelby sat at the nearby table with Dan, Felicity, Jake and
Nick. Jake's girlfriend, Lynn, wasn't there. Jake hadn't
said much, only that they decided to start seeing other
people. He said this with his usual self-deprecating shrug,
as if it hadn't mattered. Nick understood.

Jake was the cousin he liked the most. In a way, he
and Jake had a lot in common. They were experts at hiding their emotions.

Nick watched Shelby keeping a motherly eye on
Timmy. Certainly the attraction between them still
held—in fact, it was even more powerful. But Shelby
kept him at a distance. He understood. Nick could sell
the ranch, pack his bag and leave, whistling as he rode
off, never looking back. Like before.

He had to convince her that he would do all in his
power to save the ranch. Nick sensed Shelby was the glue
holding Belle Creek together.

"We need to find a new source of income." Dan sipped his beer. "I've been thinking if we decorated the barn with hay bales and pumpkins, and scarecrows, charged admission and had people come through to search for old Henry's treasure, we could make a decent amount to stave off the bank. We planted pumpkins in the field by Henry's cabin, should be ready for picking about now. Maybe even do a pumpkin patch. Families love 'em."

Nick leaned back in his chair, thrusting his thumbs through the belt hoops of his jeans. He always did that when thinking. Old habit from childhood. Mentally he calculated how much he'd have to spend to make his cousin's idea work.

"Let's do it. I'll fund expenses from my personal account. Wagon rides, too. Pumpkin patches are real popular. And you could set up a small store, selling that delicious jam of yours, Felicity."

Felicity actually blushed with pleasure, and for the first time, Nick saw what had attracted Dan. She was quite pretty when she smiled. Almost human. "I'd have to have help with the canning."

"I'll help," Shelby volunteered. "And we can have a craft fair. The ladies who have a quilting club in town have plenty of crafts they'd love to sell."

Nick leaned forward, warming up to the idea. If Belle Creek were to survive, everyone had to pitch in and feel they were a part of the process. Teamwork made the SEALs effective, and the same could work here. "We could set up booths. Charge them a fee for the table, a reasonable one. Dan, does the Freelander farm still have goats and donkeys?"

At his cousin's nod, he continued, "See about them

renting out their livestock for a small petting zoo for the children."

"Pony rides," Felicity suggested, her glance going to the boys playing on the sofa. "The children would love them. Mason and Miles will loan their ponies. Macaroni is excellent with small children."

This had to work. Surely, it would. All they needed was a healthy infusion of cash.

Nick traced a bead of condensation along his beer bottle, remembering the people his father had cultivated to visit the farm each fall for wagon rides. "I'll get the license in town, get the word out. If we start now, we can be ready the weekend before Halloween. I still have some clout in town. Maybe even rustle up some local talent for a concert at night."

"Takes time to get a license." Dan looked worried.

"Not for me. I'll get it done."

He would, too. For the first time, Nick felt hopeful. The plan had to work.

He gave Shelby a meaningful glance. "I'm closing off the north trail for now. It's too remote and clogged with brush. I don't want anyone near that trail. Jake, take the riders this week on the hillside trail. It's got terrific views of the mountains. I'll get started on the permits and licenses tomorrow. Maybe reminding folks of what this farm meant to the community, all the good times they had here in the past, will draw in more trail riders as well."

Jake frowned. "Might take a while to harvest all those pumpkins. Sure we'll make enough money for the bank loan?"

Shelby nodded. "If Nick fronts the expenses, we can make enough to make a huge difference and maybe buy more time with the bank. We can charge fifteen dollars a head, eight for children under ten, and run it Friday, Saturday and Sunday. We'll need to hire extra help, including parking attendants. Could get pricey with the expenses."

"Let me worry about that. The challenge will be pulling off all this in a short time frame," Nick told her.

The real challenge was the person vandalizing the farm. Shelby bit her mouth, and he swallowed more beer, fascinated by her lush lower lip.

"We need extra security as well. Crowd control."

"Leave that to me." Nick rolled his empty beer bottle in his palms. "It's all settled then."

When Dan and Felicity went to check on the children's game, and Jake fetched another beer, Shelby pulled Nick upstairs to Silas's study with the excuse they needed to talk.

Nick shut the door and leaned against it as she stood before the empty, cold fireplace. "Nick, what about keeping all those visitors safe with the vandalism going on around here? Do you have the funds to hire security guards?"

He'd already considered that. "I can hire one or two rent-a-cops. That should suffice. Whoever is doing this might be scared off. They work in the shadows, and opening the farm to crowds means more eyes. Especially if they're searching for Henry's treasure."

"Is that a risk we can afford to take?"

"We have to, Sweet Pea. Otherwise, I don't see how we can drum up enough cash to keep the bank from breathing down our backs." Nick folded his arms across his chest. "I have enough in retirement savings and my mutual funds to pay for some of the money owed, but not enough. We need this kind of big event to regroup."

"Does this mean you're in this to stay?"

Nick hesitated. He'd promised until the end of the month, but what if they couldn't come up with the cash? So tempting to merely sell and leave. But not with everyone being affected like this.

This was his farm, his land, his family.

For the time being, he'd remain. "I promised you, I'd give it my best, Shel." He gestured to the door. "Let's get downstairs before Dan and Jake think I'm up here having my wicked way with you." *Which I would enjoy, very much.*

They returned downstairs. The video game was winding down. Felicity glanced at the clock. "It's way past their bedtime. Dan, Jake, Nick, will you clean up while I get them upstairs?"

"That's right, you have the easy job," Jake quipped good-naturedly.

Dan laughed. "You've never tried getting your nephews to bed after a sugar rush, Jake. Cleaning up is a cakewalk."

Almost on cue, Miles and Mason began protesting as their mother herded them out of the room. Jake and Dan began clearing the table of paper plates, jesting about the times they'd fought to stay up late. Nick helped her pull down the balloons and streamers, as Timmy curled up on the sofa.

Nick glanced at the little boy, his heart tugging as he saw Timmy's eyes close. "Why don't we let Dan and Jake take care of this? Look at that little guy. He can't stay awake. Let's get him to bed."

He picked up Timmy, who gave a mighty yawn. "C'mon, sport. Been a big night."

Timmy shook his head. "If I go to bed, it won't be my birthday anymore."

"If you don't go to bed, Aunt Shelby can't read you a good-night story," Nick told him.

"And your mama and daddy sent a very special gift for you, only to be opened once you were in bed." Shelby smiled at her nephew. "Don't you want to open it?"

Timmy suddenly seemed more alert. "Yes!"

They said good-night to Dan and Jake and headed upstairs. Once inside her apartment, Nick helped Timmy get ready for bed as Shelby got the special gift Heather had asked her to purchase. When Timmy was settled under the covers, she sat on the bed's edge and handed him the present.

Tearing off the red-and-blue wrapping paper, Timmy stared at the gift. "A book?"

"Not just any book." She took the copy of *Charlotte's Web.* "I used to read this to your mama when she was your age. It's a story of lasting friendship."

Sorrow shadowed her eyes for a moment. Nick's chest tightened. He remembered Shelby telling him about those nights, reading to Heather as their parents fought. Nighttime stories had given both sisters a sense of escape, far from the cruel realities.

Nick sat in the corner chair by the window, moving a few trucks and Legos first, as Shelby began to read. Her voice was low and soothing and soon Timmy's eyes closed. She set down the book, tucked in the covers around him and kissed his forehead.

"Good night, six-year-old boy," she whispered.

Nick followed her out, closing the door. He couldn't see how Heather and Pete could leave the little boy here.

If he had a family, he'd fight tooth and nail to stay together.

"Want some tea? I made sugar cookies for the party, and stashed some in here."

Nick nodded. Anything to stave off sleep, and the memories that fought to the surface each night.

Anything to spend more waking moments with the fascinating, sexy Shelby. He sat at the counter as she bustled around the tiny kitchen, setting the kettle on the stove.

"You're a wonderful mama to your nephew, Shel. He's a fine little boy, thanks to you."

Shelby brought two cups to the counter, along with the sugar cookies. They sipped their tea. Shelby ran her tongue along the cookie, her gaze distant. "I used to visit your house when I was little. Remember Mabel's sugar cookies?"

He nodded. Mabel had been a wonderful cook, and a good person. "I remember asking if I could help, but Silas said baking was a woman's job. He'd send me out to muck the stables."

"I'm sorry he was cruel to you, Nick." Shelby touched his hand. "You deserved better. I was so caught up in how nice he was to me, I failed to understand, or accept, that Silas could be a right bastard to you."

Granules of sugar dusted her wet mouth. Nick stared, enraptured as if caught up in a dream. That mouth of hers, hell, it had tempted him ten years ago when he was nineteen. Back then it took all his restraint to stop kissing her and walk away.

Walk out of her life for good, because he knew if he stayed, he'd ruin her future. All his life, Silas shouted that he was no good, a loser who wasted his time. Nick assured himself he ran away to join the navy to escape from the hell of home. Now, looking at Shelby as she slowly ran a tongue over her lower lip, he knew the real truth.

He ran away from her. From the sixteen-year-old who had captured him with her sweet nature and sinful mouth, and the woman he knew she'd become.

Shelby, who didn't care he was the ranch owner's only son. Shelby, who took him by the hand into the bathroom to clumsily dab ointment on his split lip after he'd fought with the local bully. He knew Silas would beat his ass for fighting, and at fifteen, he was damn sick of the old man always lecturing him as much as he tired of the belt whooping his sore ass.

He'd nearly run away, but Shel stopped him.

So she'd applied cosmetics to his face, and made him look like a zombie. Then she'd done the same for herself and announced to everyone that she and Nick were cast in roles for the school play.

No one suspected a thing. Her pantomime of a zombie had made Silas laugh, deflected his father's suspicions. By the time Silas found out about the fight, his anger abated.

Shelby, always there for him. Shelby, who ran into the woods to hide her sobs when her vicious father hit her in a drunken fit. He'd held her close that day. She was only eleven and the bruise marking her pale white cheek enraged him. Made him want to do a little punching of his own. But he'd hugged her tight, handed her a dirty handkerchief and whispered, "Never let them see you cry. 'Cause it makes them even more powerful."

Now Shelby looked so woebegone, so forlorn, he wanted to gather her into his arms and swear she'd never hurt again. Promise her anything. He hated seeing her like this, as if someone kicked her hard and she lacked the strength to get up.

"Do you ever find yourself regretting the past?" she asked. "Wonder what would happen if you had a do-over for the last ten years?"

"All the time." He moved closer. "How the hell I ever left you is beyond me."

She gave a tremulous smile. "And now you're back."

"And here with you."

Nick reached out and stroked her wet, sugar-dusted lip and then he did what he swore he'd never again do.

He lowered his mouth to hers and kissed her. He kept the contact light, enjoying the subtle flavor of her mouth, the softness of her plumb lips, the startled sigh as she leaned into him.

Curling one hand around her head, he brought her closer and deepened the kiss. Nick thrust his tongue deep into the warm, moist cavern of her mouth, tasting tea, sugar and the unique damn-it-to-hell delight that was uniquely Shelby. Blood raced through his veins as his pulse kicked up, and his body thrummed like an electrical wire. He wanted this—no, needed this. Connection. Feeling. He'd been so damn numb for so long he thought he'd lost everything, hiding behind a sarcastic laugh and a sneer for the world.

Wonderful, fabulous, gritty Shelby had brought him roaring back to life. Beneath his jeans, he was hard. He kissed her, letting her know a man's desire, not a boy's, the kind of kiss you give a woman before you lay her down and love her long into the night.

His hands left her nape and explored lower, unfastening the top buttons of her blouse. Nick slid a hand under her blouse and cupped her breast. She fit perfectly into his palm. Gently he kneaded her hardened nipple, teasing lightly as he flicked his fingers over the cresting bud.

Moaning, Shelby grabbed his shoulders, holding on as if she was drowning. He was sinking as well, awash in pure pleasure. Nothing mattered but this moment, and Shelby. Need flooded him, such desperate need he'd die if he couldn't have her.

Nick broke the kiss and stared down at her, at the sleepy confused passion glazing her eyes, at her mouth swollen from his possession. Then awareness dawned. Red flushed her cheeks and she pulled her blouse shut, as if realizing what they'd been doing.

You. Bed. Now. He struggled to think in complete sentences instead of grunting like a caveman. Impossible, when his body was surging with the need for sex, him so hard it hurt. No one would suffice but Shelby, her tangle of wild curls, her big eyes staring up at him as he moved deep inside her.

"What are you doing, Nick?" she whispered.

"What I wanted to do ten years ago, and stopped." Nick cupped her chin and gazed into her eyes.

A hardness entered her gaze. "I'm no starry-eyed teenager anymore."

"No, you're a woman now. We will be lovers, Shelby." He touched her cheek, marveling at her satin skin, flushed with anger and passion. "I want you in my bed, and what I want, I always get."

Shelby shuddered as he leaned close and nuzzled her neck, dropping tiny kisses on it. "When did you become so single-minded, Nick?" she whispered.

"When I joined the teams." He nipped her tender skin and then soothed the sting with a long lick. "We never give up. Never quit."

He ran his hand down her back, stroking her to accustom her to his touch. It had been too many years since he'd touched her this way, but time rolled backward as if they were teenagers again, stealing away a few precious moments for themselves.

Then she jerked away, putting out her hands like a traffic cop.

"What you need is a hard dose of reality, Nick Anderson. I'm not the loving-and-leaving type. You should have learned that ten years ago." Shelby pointed to the sofa. "I'm headed to bed. I have a long day tomorrow. Good night."

Blinking, he stared after her as she stormed away. And then he chuckled ruefully.

Shelby thought he'd back down that easily? She didn't know anything about SEALs.

Never give up. Never quit. Especially when it came to something he wanted.

Nick could be quite ruthless when it came to that.

Chapter 12

The next morning, Nick coaxed Shelby into joining him for a ride instead of painting in the barn. He needed the fresh air and exercise. He hadn't forgotten the kiss of the previous night, and judging from the wariness in her eyes, neither had she.

But she was cordial enough, and soon they had saddled the horses and were riding.

They were riding on the main trail that afforded a splendid view of the mist-shrouded Smoky Mountains. The air was tinged with a hint of approaching winter, and it brought spots of rosy color to Shelby's cheeks. She looked so damn pretty today, her long hair held back in a tortoiseshell clip, a favorite jean jacket keeping away the morning chill. And those long, delicious legs that haunted his fantasies.

Nick inhaled a lungful of fresh, clean air. After the last place he'd bunked, waking up to the stench of the garbage Dumpster just outside his window, this good country air cleared his head. Tempted him to stay a while longer. But if he couldn't come up with enough money for the back payments Silas owed, he wouldn't have a choice. The bank would foreclose.

The knowledge curdled his blood. He turned to look at Shelby, who looked so pretty in the misty light, her hair swinging gently in a ponytail.

That the Belle Creek still operated, the horses were healthy and the buildings well maintained, was due to her.

Nick leaned forward, the leather saddle creaking. "Do you know how amazing you are?"

Shelby turned her head. "Amazing at what?"

"Everything you do, Shel. Holding it together."

She looked troubled. "I'm not doing such a great job lately. Some days it feels like it's all falling apart. Being a mom is exhausting, especially when he's sick. I worry about him, but I think today he should be all right. He's only running a slight fever. I brought him over to stay with Felicity, he doesn't seem that sick, but I want to make sure he's not coming down with something."

"He's sick? You sure about that?" Nick remembered all the times he'd faked a temperature with the thermometer placed on a hot light bulb. "He seemed very alert this morning at breakfast. He really loves the new video game Dan and Felicity got for his birthday."

Shelby stopped her horse. Pantser tossed her head and snorted, as if in agreement with Nick.

"You saw him at breakfast? He was sick in bed."

"Not when I was up at five. Seemed mighty interested in his cereal."

Shelby narrowed her eyes. "That kid…"

She turned the horse around, heading back. Grinning, Nick did the same. He hoped Shel wouldn't be too hard on Timmy.

They rode at a canter on the trail, cutting through the

pasture, when Nick spotted a thick black curl of smoke rising through the trees. His pulse raced.

"Fire," he yelled at Shelby, kicking his mount into a gallop.

Nick leaned forward in the saddle, letting his horse have his head, holding tight with his knees while he dug out his cell phone from his jeans. He dialed 911 and barked out instructions.

That suspicious black line made his heart drop to his stomach. With the drought, if the fire spread, the entire ranch could burn. He raced over the trail, dirt flying up beneath his mount's pounding hooves.

Now he could see the smoke rising from the barn. The barn that Timmy liked to hide in to play his video games.

Shelby galloped ahead of him and slid off her horse. Jake was running from the stables with Hank and Mario. They uncurled the hose at the pump.

Mario turned on the pump, but only a thin trickle of water came from the hose.

"Son of a... What the hell," Jake yelled. "Water pressure is too low!"

That pump had worked fine three days ago. Knowing the ranch was a tinderbox, Nick had checked it himself. More vandalism.

Shelby raced to the front of the barn, and picked up a small black baseball cap.

His blood ran cold.

"It's Timmy's," she shouted. "Timmy!"

Jake dropped the hose. He shoved a hand through his hair and ran to the door, but drew back as billowing black smoke poured outside. "What the hell is that kid doing inside the barn?"

Nick leaped off the horse. Orange tongues of flames licked the sides of the barn now.

"Timmy!" Shelby screamed.

His heart dropped to his stomach as he heard a small voice cry out. "Aunt Shelby, help me!"

Nick caught her, forcing her back. "Stay here."

Tearing off his T-shirt, he wet it with the thin stream of water from the hose. Nick held the shirt over his face and raced through the open door. Tremendous heat and black smoke slammed into him. Flames licked the left side of the wood barn, leaping up to the loft to ignite the hay stored there. Timmy loved sitting by the stalls by the hay to play his video games. Acrid smoke choked him as he crawled low, searching for Shelby's nephew.

Nick spotted something by the green tractor near the hay bales. Lungs burning, he ran over, breathing through the wet T-shirt. Timmy was on the floor. Coughing violently, Timmy pointed to his foot, pinned between the wall and the tractor's back wheel. "I'm stuck."

With deliberate coolness, Nick talked in a low, soothing murmur to Timmy as he pushed back the tractor and untangled his foot. Throwing the wet shirt over Timmy's head, he scooped the boy into his arms. Racing for the exit, he coughed, the thick black smoke blinding him. Tears gushed from his eyes. He could barely see. Focusing on the light streaming through the black smoke, he stumbled forward.

Gotta make it, gotta make it…

His bum leg suddenly gave out and he fell to his knees, nearly dropping Timmy. Behind him, the hay loft exploded into flames. Cinders flew into the air and he knew if they remained here a minute longer, they would both die.

Not on my watch.

Timmy sobbed and coughed. The terrified child in his arms fed him strength. He could do this. With every last ounce of effort, Nick struggled to his feet and forced himself to the exit.

As he emerged, Jake grabbed Timmy and ran away from the barn, yelling for Hank to help Nick. But it was Shelby who slid an arm around him, guiding him away from danger. Nick collapsed on the ground, desperate for fresh air. His leg ached like a bastard.

Mario and Hank crowded near him, congratulating him on his bravery as Shelby called for the arriving paramedics.

"You're a real hero, Nick. You saved his life," Hank told him.

An EMT slapped an oxygen mask on him.

"I'm checking on Timmy." Shelby leaned forward and kissed his sooty cheek. "Thank you, Nick."

Struggling to breathe, he gulped down fresh lungfuls of oxygen. Nick waved a hand to protest. The two EMTs ignored it, and made him stretch out. Grateful for the rest, he lay back, wincing as muscles in his bad leg jumped.

That injury nearly caused him to collapse and drop the little boy. Was it ever going to get better? Hell, he'd quit the teams because he feared letting down the other guys, and failing them in a crisis.

Now, because of his past injury, he'd almost let Shelby's nephew die. As the paramedics shut the vehicle door, Nick didn't feel like a hero.

Shelby couldn't stop shaking inside.

The barn and everything inside were ruined. But Timmy was alive. Safe. So was Nick. Firefighters had the blaze under control, spraying a steady stream of water.

Leaving Jake and the stable hands to deal with the fire's aftermath, she had driven to the hospital.

The emergency department's waiting room had only one other occupant, an elderly woman reading a magazine. Shelby sank into a battered chair. Shaking badly, she buried her head into her hands.

Thanks to Nick, Timmy would live. But Felicity and Dan weren't anywhere on the ranch. Jake said he hadn't seen Dan since early that morning.

Who would set the barn on fire? Was it another move to drive Nick into selling?

Suddenly she remembered her easel and paints. She'd left them there, planning to paint each morning. Instead, today she'd gone riding with Nick. If she'd been in the barn, would the arsonist have knocked her cold, leaving her to die?

Shelby felt as if someone had kicked her in the stomach. Drenched in sweat, soot coating her face, she felt as if her legs would give out. She called the only person whom she could trust in an emergency. Ann answered on the first ring.

"Honey, are you okay?" her best friend asked in her thick accent. "I heard about it through the grapevine. Oh, Shelby, is Timmy going to be all right?"

Shelby blew out a breath. "I'm here at the hospital, waiting to see him. The doctor said he'll probably be here at least for a day to make sure he's all right. Nick saved his life. He's here, too—they admitted him for smoke inhalation. Ann, who would do such a thing? Try to kill a little boy?"

"It's a horrible, horrible thing, Shelby. Maybe whoever set the fire didn't know Timmy was in there. Maybe they're getting desperate. Can't Nick just sell and cut his losses and leave?"

"And I'll be homeless."

"You'll always have a place with me, honey. You can find another job in town without that bitch Natalie jerking your chain. Your sister will be back in less than a year, anyway. Belle Creek is too dangerous, Shelby! Is Jonah any closer to catching whoever is doing this?"

Shelby gripped her cell phone tight. "I don't know. I think after today he's going to have to put more men on the case because now it's attempted murder. It's one thing to cut up horse tack or damage property, another to set fire to a building and nearly kill a child."

There was silence for a minute on the other end. Then Ann said softly, "Honey, do you need me to come down there? Is there anything I can do? Want me to stay at the ranch with you until Nick gets out?"

"No. I'll be okay. I'll let you know if I need anything. Thanks, Ann."

As her friend murmured goodbye, Shelby thumbed off the phone. What would she have done if Timmy died in the barn? She'd never have forgiven herself.

Her trembling hands scrubbed the legs of her jeans. Heather trusted her with her only son, trusted her to keep him safe. Safe wasn't the ranch. Not now. The pranks and vandalism had escalated beyond mischief. What next? Would someone take a shot at Timmy as he walked to the main road to catch the school bus?

Thank the good Lord for Nick. Nick, whom she'd dismissed as a bad boy intent only on his own pleasure.

The man was a true warrior, a real hero. Seeing him dash into that burning barn, risking his own life, made her realize the qualities that shone through him that he downplayed with his grin and teasing manner.

Not all men had the mettle to put their own safety second, and the welfare of others first. She began to understand Nick preferred to hide behind a mask of a charismatic grin and indifference.

All the men she'd dated paled in comparison. They were nice, mild guys, even-tempered and even amicable, like Jonah. They had dated a few times but never really clicked. Nothing could compare to Nick and his raw sexuality, his personality.

Silas had been good to her, kind and generous. But sometimes it was easier to treat a stranger's child better than your own. Perhaps. All Shelby knew was that Nick was here now, and he'd promised to stick around to see it through with the ranch. Nick, shouldering the burden, taking on responsibilities his father had placed on him. The others were only concerned with the ranch and what the finances meant to them, like Shelby. Making sure they had a home and a business.

Not Nick. He could easily cut his losses, sell the place and walk away. Her heart warmed. Maybe he wasn't as much of a careless nomad as she thought.

Maybe it was time someone told him exactly what he was, and how much he meant to the ranch. And to her.

Nick hated hospitals. He'd protested, wheedled and even struggled as the paramedics strapped him onto a gurney and loaded him into the ambulance. Now, lying in a hospital bed, hooked up to oxygen, he tried to relax. But his skin felt stretched tight and his head spun, not just from the smoke, either.

Someone set the barn on fire. They could have killed Timmy.

Old memories surfaced. Dragging Vinny out of the Humvee, struggling to breathe past the pain as bullets sang out. Then the blackness of nothing…and waking up to a hospital bed, much like this one.

Helpless, weak.

Nick had vowed to never be weak.

No choice then, like now.

What was the point of his life, anyway? No longer a SEAL, fighting to keep his country safe. Hell, he couldn't even keep this ranch and its occupants safe.

He knew the gas can meant someone planned to torch the place. Yeah, the security cameras he'd placed there and the extra precautions he'd taken were good, but not enough. Never enough.

Never good enough.

Guilt pricked him. Why couldn't he have done more?

Loser, a tiny voice whispered inside.

The ghost of his father's voice echoed inside his mind. *You'll end up dead in a ditch somewhere in Nashville if you keep going like this.*

No, Dad, I'll end up in a hospital bed, hooked up to these damn machines. But Timmy was safe, and alive, and that was worth it.

Same as it had been worth it to save Vinny's life.

Being a SEAL had meant everything. But when he'd awakened in that other hospital bed and realized he could never run as fast, maneuver as quickly and be the athlete he'd once been, Nick made the decision to quit. It had been the toughest decision. But he had to be the best, and with his reflexes slower and his body injured, he didn't want to risk his teammates' lives. SEALs functioned like a well-oiled machine. When one guy went down, he dragged the others with him.

He still had his buddies, like Cooper and Jarrett. Hell, his former teammates were more family than Dan or Jake. But they were settled now. Happy.

They had something he longed for, but didn't know how to obtain. All Nick knew was the wandering lifestyle he'd led since leaving the navy meant he was never alone long with those doubts pummeling him. The demons inside him kept whispering in Silas's voice that he was headed to ruin.

At least he had a private room, where no one could see him like this, sprawled in a hospital bed, too exhausted to move. He wondered if the nurse could hang a sign on his door—No Visitors. As far as he was concerned, the longer the door remained shut, the better.

A soft tap at his door. Aw, hell. He hoped it wasn't Dan, Felicity and their kids again. Felicity had been weeping, her eyes red and her makeup smeared. Dan had looked stricken and the kids had been shell-shocked. After inquiring if Nick needed anything, Dan told him he was taking the family out of town for a few days. The barn fire had scared the living daylights out of them.

And then Dan had lowered the hammer.

"I'm going to sell the acres Silas left me. I'm sorry, Nick. It's gotten too dangerous. There's a farm in Knoxville that's looking for a manager. I'm headed out today to interview with them, and Felicity is going to look at houses we can rent until we get ready to buy one."

Nick wished him luck. He couldn't disagree. If he had a family, he'd bolt as well. But he'd promised Shelby to give it his best to save the farm.

"Come in," he called out.

Shelby walked inside, Shelby with soot streaking her pretty face, her cranberry sweater and jeans smelling like smoke. Something tight in Nick's chest eased. The worry clouding her big eyes centered on him as she took in the IV pole, the stupid mask covering his face.

A bit of heaven. No one had worried about him in a very long time.

What would it be like to come home every night to her, feel her arms wrap around him tight as if she never wanted to let go?

But he wasn't the sticking-around type, as she had reminded him. Wanderer.

What the hell am I searching for, anyway?

Right now, a way out of this damn hospital and back to the ranch, so he could get back to work. Get back to finding the bastard who thought it okay to torch a barn and nearly kill a small child. Nick's fury rose. He clenched his fists in impotent rage.

And then coughed again.

Shelby's hand smoothed his brow. "Easy, tough guy. You're not going anywhere. Just relax."

Her hand felt great against his warm brow, smooth and cool. Caring. Too good. He could easily get used to this, used to Shelby.

"Timmy?" he rasped. "How is he?"

But then tears filled her eyes and she blinked hard, as if trying to push them back. "You saved him. He inhaled smoke and he'll probably be in here another day, but he's alive. You're a hero, Nicolas Anderson."

Deeply uncomfortable with the label, he shook his head. Heroes were noble men who sacrificed everything. He wasn't one of them. Because as soon as the ranch was financially in the clear, he was gone.

Heroes were ordinary men who stuck it out. Not guys like him, always running away to the next destination.

She remained on his bed, stroking his hair. Damn, she was a sight for any man, sooty or not. His heart tugged as he thought of how worried and panicked she was, nearly losing her nephew.

Nick reached up, clasped her hand. Couldn't speak without coughing, but he squeezed her hand in reassurance. And then he thumbed away a single tear trickling down her cheek.

Shelby smiled softly, reached for the tissue box at her bedside and wiped her eyes. "I'm fine. And you're going to be fine, too. The barn—" she gave a little laugh "—that's not so fine. Everything's a loss, but it can be replaced."

He sagged against the pillow. Damn. He'd hoped the firefighters had managed to save part of the structure. The tractor he planned to use to tow the wagon for the hayride, the corn husks for the maze, the tools he needed for repairs. All gone.

He slammed a fist against the mattress. Shelby placed her palm over his hand. "No, Nick. It's just stuff. It can be replaced, eventually. You and Timmy can't. When I saw you run into the barn, Nick, I was praying you'd come back. I thought I had lost you for good."

"Yeah. Well, I'm made of flame retardant." He grinned, but she did not smile back. Instead, she squeezed his hand.

"How long are they keeping me?"

"Until later today. Maybe overnight." She picked up his hand, kissed it. "If you're a good boy and rest, and do what the doctor says."

Worry riddled him. Stuck in here meant leaving the ranch vulnerable. Shelby vulnerable. If anything happened to her... His hand itched for his gun. When he found the bastard who did this, nearly killing her beloved nephew, he'd make him pay.

But he hadn't been a SEAL all those years without learning discipline and patience. And priorities. His main priority was ensuring his family, and Shelby, were all safe at the ranch.

"Maybe you should move out. Until we catch this ass who's doing this. You, Dan and his family, and Jake. At least you for now. Keep you safe."

Shelby blinked hard. "Nick, the ranch is my home as much as it is yours. I don't run. We made a deal, remember? We're in this together."

He coughed and she adjusted the cannula over his cheeks. His throat still burned, but he had to convince her. Because he didn't know if the arsonist who'd done this would resort to even more desperate measures.

"That was before..." He dragged in a deep breath. "This got deadly, Shel. What about Tim? The apartment's too isolated."

A stubborn line indented her forehead. "Then I'll move into the main house until you get out of here. Felicity will have to bite me."

He laughed, which turned into a fit of coughing. Shelby poured him a glass of water. Damn that woman, all spark and sass, stubborn as him. Nothing put her down.

A quiet knock on the door and Jonah walked inside. Nick set down the glass and narrowed his eyes.

"What the hell are you doing here? Come to tell me there may have been a fire?"

Jonah's gaze flicked from him to Shelby. "I'm here to give you an update on the investigation."

Shelby bristled. "You mean there actually is an investigation now? A little late, Jonah."

The man shuffled his feet, and withdrew a small notepad from his jacket pocket, along with a pen. "There is now. Tell me what you saw. Anything."

For the next several minutes, Shelby and Nick filled in Jonah on all the incidents.

"What about the barn?" Nick asked, struggling to sit up. Damn, he hated looking weak, especially in front of Jonah. He never forgot how Jonah beat him out for the football team in high school.

"It was definitely arson. Fire chief found an empty gas can in the ruins."

He and Shelby exchanged glances. She scowled at Jonah. "I told you that gas can wasn't in the root cellar by accident."

Nick put a calming hand on her arm. "How did it start?"

"Could have been anything. A match, an electrical spark. Chief will give me a full report when they finish digging through the ruins." Jonah shook his head. "I'm assigning a special team on this case, Nick."

"Nice of you to finally believe me," he said angrily. "Maybe if you had listened to me earlier, Timmy wouldn't be in the hospital and I'd still have a barn. Or maybe you wanted the place to burn down—"

"Nick, please," Shelby interrupted.

Jonah sighed. "I believe you now. Truth is, I thought all these things were high school pranks. Kids, fooling around. And maybe..."

Nick waited.

The man's gaze met his. "I pushed this to the back burner because it was you, Nick. I never did forgive you for pulling that stunt when we were kids and boosting my dad's car, driving it into the pond. My old man worked real hard for that car. We weren't rich, like your family. Didn't matter that Silas bought him a new one. I resented you because you got away with everything, while the rest of us had to work hard for what little we had."

Guilt flashed through Nick. "Would it make you feel better to know that Silas beat me for that, and made me work extra hours mucking out the stalls?"

Jonah grinned. "Only if you fell face-first into the manure pile."

He stuck out a hand. Nick shook it.

"Truce."

Jonah would never be his friend, but he needed the sheriff's help now. "You can make up for not believing me about the gas can and the other things."

"How?"

"Keep an eye on the place until they spring me." His gaze shot over to Shelby. "And Shelby. She's alone and vulnerable. I don't like leaving the ranch unguarded."

"I'm not vulnerable," Shelby snapped. Then she bit her lush lower lip. "But you're right about the ranch. It is too wide open for more incidents. Whoever did this isn't satisfied anymore with leaving notes or ruining tack or digging holes on the trails."

Mentally he went through his personal finances. Paying extra security would drain his savings even more after he'd paid the bills for the pumpkin patch, but it was necessary.

Jonah shook his head. "Two of the guys agreed to a security detail at the ranch. No charge. Can't spare them more than a couple of days, though."

"I can pay." Nick struggled with his pride.

"Not necessary. Silas did a lot for this town. It's time to pay him back."

Soon, he would be home. Hell, he'd be home today if he could. But at least with Jonah's men patrolling, the house and grounds would have extra eyes looking for trouble.

The sheriff looked at him, nodded. "Got to get back. Take care, Nick."

When Jonah left, Shelby remained, sitting on his bed and smoothing back his hair. He closed his eyes, suddenly weary. Her concern spread through his chest, warming him. Felt good to have someone care about him. Hell, he could get used to this.

No, you can't. Because you'll eventually leave and go searching again...

For what?

For the first time since he left the navy, Nick wasn't sure. What the hell was he looking for, anyway? Another dead-end job, cash for a paycheck? Another quick bout of sex, satisfying his body's demands but leaving him as empty as before?

He'd been so busy wandering, hopping from city to city, that it kept all his demons at bay. They swirled around in his head now, taunting him much like the old man's voice.

Shelby deserved a sticking-around kind of guy, someone to marry her, give her lots of babies and make her happy. Give her a home where she could feel safe and secure. Put those roses back on her cheeks, the spark in her eye and coax free that gurgling laugh.

Not him.

Nick let her stroke his brow. Touch him. He'd give

himself this small luxury of Shelby, allow himself to dream that she could be his for life.

For now.

Because he suspected soon enough, he'd be walking out of her life again. This time, for good.

Chapter 13

Despite his doctor's protests, Nick left the hospital early the following morning. He didn't like leaving the farm unguarded, and Shelby unprotected.

Once home, he made a few phone calls. If they were getting the Anderson pumpkin patch underway, he needed help. Two of Silas's friends who owned farms agreed to loan him tools, their tractors and other items needed. Not only that, but they also volunteered to help set everything up. They would stop by later in the week with the necessary items.

Next, he went into Silas's study and opened his own personal laptop to check the network monitor he'd installed on the ranch's Wi-Fi router. The firmware program he'd designed himself protected the network, allowing him to improve security against malicious attacks.

It also allowed him to inspect all the IP addresses visited by anyone using the ranch's Wi-Fi. In light of the barn fire and the increased threat of violence, he pushed on. He had to find the person behind these acts, and if it meant cyber spying, he would do it.

Later, he would ask forgiveness. Forgiveness, in light of the fact that Timmy had nearly lost his life, was much better than permission.

He also shut down the ranch's social-media accounts and opened new ones with stronger password protection, giving access only to himself.

Nick suspected the same person who burned down the barn and created the other problems was connected to the social-media hacking. His thoughts immediately went to Chuck Beaufort. The developer had much to lose if he couldn't acquire this land. That theme park needed the acreage and the water rights and main-road access. And Chuck's daughter had access to the stables and the trails since she boarded Fancy here.

Beaufort was the person who stood to gain the most if Nick decided to sell.

He looked over the results of the latest scan. Nothing extraordinary, except Shelby had visited several banking sites in the past week, and a site listing jobs in France. Sighing, he leaned back. Shelby should leave Belle Creek. She had a lot of talent, and the ranch stifled her artistic ability because she seldom had a chance to paint.

For now, he had a much larger concern. He packed a few things in a backpack.

Dan and his family were in town shopping. Jake had gone to Nashville to check on ordering a new tractor, and Shelby was at the hospital, visiting Timmy. Kid was due to come home later today.

His blood boiled as he thought of the boy dying in the barn fire. The sabotage had escalated beyond malicious pranks. Even with Jonah and his deputies promising to investigate, the arsonist could strike again.

To prevent any more injuries, he'd laid down strict rules. No one on the farm was to go off alone. Even the staff were working in pairs as a safety measure.

Nick made himself the exception to the rule. Mostly, he worried about Shelby. She was gutsy and accustomed to roaming the property alone. He remembered her when they were growing up together. She was a cute little thing, tousled long curls, always messy, always tagging along after him. Even back then when he was young, he recognized a kindred loneliness in her. Maybe that was the reason that he became attracted to her back then, when they were small enough to play as innocent children. But when he grew older and she grew older, a spark of attraction burst into a flame.

He had few regrets in life. Nick believed in living on the edge and making the most of your life. It was one of the reasons why he became a Navy SEAL. But he did have one regret, when he'd been too young and arrogant to fully comprehend the consequences of what he'd done to Shelby. He didn't regret kissing her, no, that was an action he was damn glad he'd taken. He regretted the haunted, painful look on her face when he told her he couldn't stay.

Pushing aside thoughts of Shelby, he turned his attention to the fire. There was no reason for the water pressure to be that low. Someone must have cut the pipes leading to the water hole. Years ago, his father had laid down several yards of piping from the pond, both for irrigation and for the pump at the barn.

An hour later, his backpack and tool bag sitting in the cargo basket, Nick set out on an ATV to trace the water line. The piping system on the farm worked much like a sprinkler system in a homeowner's yard. While working as a handyman during his travels, he'd repaired a few of those.

The above-ground white pipes were easy to spot, and maintain. The narrow road leading to the water hole was soft dirt; a well-used horse trail. Views of the mountains were prettier here, and the riders could admire the sun glinting off the water in midday. He passed a soft sand corral used for training horses. Ringed by sprawling trees, the pond was naturally fed by underground springs. But they'd always called it a pond.

Decades ago, Silas had set it up to pump water from the springs to the outlying barn and pastures. The water pump system should have worked to extinguish the barn fire. The pipe to the barn ran in a narrow ditch bordering the trail.

At the culvert in the road, the pipe led to a T joint, with another set of pipes leading to the fields for irrigation. There was a shut-off value at the T joint. Nick climbed off the ATV, carrying his tool bag.

It wasn't needed, for the shut-off value came off easily in his hands. Inside the pipes was a rag. He swore. No wonder the water pressure had been insufficient. Someone deliberately clogged the water flow and set fire to the barn.

Nick removed the rag and glued the shut-off value in place. He returned to the ATV and followed the trail to the water hole.

Memories assaulted him as his gaze landed on the one-hundred-foot-tall sycamore tree near the bank. How many times had he climbed that tree on the wood rungs he'd nailed to the trunk? He and Silas had built a platform on a long, sturdy limb, the beginnings of a tree house. That project had been abandoned when his mom fell ill, and eventually died. The platform had turned into a refuge after that. He'd been only eleven, grief-stricken and numb, for he'd not just lost his mother, but Silas had died to him that day and stopped being the father who treated him well.

Despite his best attempts to remain hidden, Shelby always found him. She would sit with him on the half-finished tree house as he released all his pent-up feelings about losing Mom. Even gave him that stuffed bear with the chewed-off ear she lugged around.

Shelby, who had been more of a friend than even Dan, who'd acted like a big brother.

Nick stripped off his clothing and dove into the springs from the platform he and Silas had built in happier times, when they'd worked together as father and son. Before his mom died, and Silas's world died with it. The cold water hit him like thousands of stabbing needles. Nick grimaced, but he'd felt worse during his time as a SEAL. The water was clear, sandy at the bottom. He swam underwater, following the pipes to ensure none were cracked or sliced.

Satisfied all was well, he began swimming in long, sure strokes across the pond. He needed this exercise, needed to feel he was in control of a body that no longer functioned like a well-oiled machine. Hospitals tended to do that to him.

How many times had he and Shel jumped into this water during the summer, splashing each other and laughing? It was his love of water that led him to becoming a SEAL. He could swim across this pond ten times without hesitation.

Determination arrowed through him with each stroke. He could do this. Ever since leaving the navy, he felt adrift. Flotsam on the current of life. Once his life had purpose. Being a SEAL was everything to him, hell, it was embedded in his identity. Silas never knew how driven Nick had been to prove the old man wrong, that he wasn't going to end up dead in a ditch somewhere, homeless and alone.

Except after he left the teams, he had to start all over. And nothing he could see about his life served the same purpose. Except for now. If he never did another thing in this life, he had to save this farm. Or at least, make sure he found whoever threatened his family. And Shelby.

Nick swam underwater to the shallow end and stood.

Only to see Shelby on the bank, staring at him.

If she had any doubts about Nick being fully recovered from the smoke inhalation, they vanished in a heartbeat. Naked, he stood thigh-deep in the water, sleek and wet. Each curve of his biceps, the thickness in his wide shoulders and the rippling muscles in his abdomen caught her wide-eyed attention. He looked as gorgeous as a Greek god. Water dripped down his hair, beaded on his impressive chest, droplets tracking through the hair marching in a fine line down to his...

Oh, my.

Heat suffused her as she jerked her gaze upward to his scowling face. Nick marched out of the water. Now she could see other scars dinging his long, powerful legs, especially the nasty one high on his right leg.

His expression looked dangerous, and she backed off as he approached.

"What the hell are you doing out here alone?"

So he wasn't mad at her for catching him skinny-dipping. Shelby shook her head. "I could ask the same of you. At least I'm wearing clothing. Who goes swimming naked in October in that water? Are you nuts?"

"I'm a SEAL." He stalked past her, grabbed the white towel from the shore near his backpack. "Or at least I was. Cold water is nothing to me."

"I see."

He glanced down at his right thigh and his jaw tensed. "Yeah, you've seen all right. Like my road map of wounds?"

"Wasn't looking at those. I was talking about your lack of shrinkage."

But despite her gentle, teasing tone, Nick's scowl deepened. Then he knotted a towel around his lean waist, and shoved a hand through his wet hair. "I used to swim ten laps around this pond without losing breath. Now I can barely do three."

"You just got out of the hospital!"

"That's no excuse. I said the same thing to myself when I was discharged from the hospital. And here I am, more than two years later, and I'm still not back in the same shape. I'm way out of shape."

Shelby wanted to shake sense into him. Nick wasn't out of shape. He wasn't Dan, with a small beer belly, or Jake, who never walked any distance on the farm because he was plain lazy. Nick's body was a testament to how athletic he was.

"Nick, you're too hard on yourself. Stop it. You risked your life to save your teammate, just as you risked your life to save Timmy. That takes a lot of courage. You're still strong. Give yourself time to heal," she said softly.

He snorted. "Right. How much longer will it take for

me to get back into top shape so I can re-up, and regain
what I lost when I quit being a SEAL?"

This wasn't the confident Nick Anderson she'd known,
the man who never quit. But someone had to tell it like
it was, because he needed honesty.

"Maybe never. You told me being a SEAL isn't all
about strength, but mental perseverance. You have to
heal from the inside before you can address the physical issues, Nick."

He turned away from her, regarding the pond as if it
taunted him. "Wait while I get dressed, and I'll take you
back on the ATV."

Clearly, the scars he bore cut much deeper than into
his skin. She had to do something to tease him back into
good humor. Between almost losing Timmy, and Nick,
and the destroyed barn, she felt ready to snap. As did he.
So she did something for the good of them both, guaranteed to make him quit wallowing in self-pity.

She stole his clothing and jumped on the ATV, tearing off toward her apartment.

"Shelby!"

His roar rose above the grinding whir of the vehicle. Grinning, she kept going, knowing he was chasing
her. But not in that towel. Nope, she knew for certain
he was...

Shelby turned her head. Yup. Stark naked, running
after her, the towel gripped in one fist. Her grin widened
as she pressed the gas pedal. *Let's speed it up, Nick. See
what you've got.*

His outraged yells continued to follow her down the
road. Finally as the burned-out barn came into view, she
slowed down. That should suffice.

Nick raced over to the ATV, winded, but not as much

as one would expect, and grabbed his backpack and clothing off the rear cargo basket. He knotted the towel around
his waist again. As he opened his mouth, probably to turn
the air blue with curses, she turned and grinned.

"And you said you were out of shape."

Nick's expression eased, smoothing out from a severe
scowl. Ah, he got it.

"You are a minx," he murmured. "You should be
spanked."

"Don't get my hopes up."

Dark eyebrows shot upward. "Don't tempt me. I'll
save fun and games for later. Right now I should spank
you for riding on this machine without a helmet. You
know the rules."

She felt abashed. "Sorry. I was in a rush, forgot it. I
went looking for you and couldn't find you. I was afraid
you overdid it."

"Because I'm still weak." He said it with a forced
smile.

She blew out a breath. "Because you might not be
fully recovered, Nick. So stop acting as if you should
be a superhero around here, and then getting upset with
yourself because you can't do it all. It's not doing anyone
good, least of all you."

His expression turned serious. Thoughtful. Drawing
closer, Nick reached up and tucked a lock of hair behind
her ear. "You're the only one who dares to tell it like it
is, Sweet Pea. Thanks. I needed that push."

So close. Close enough for her to inhale the spicy scent
of his aftershave, and see that small area on his chin,
where he'd nicked himself shaving. See the intriguing
flecks of gold in his dark brown eyes.

Close enough to taste the richness of his mouth, the

sensual curve of his full lower lip. No thin lips for Nick, no—even his mouth was a work of art. She looked at the jagged scar on his cheek, and reached up to gently trace it with a fingertip.

"You were always beautiful before, Nick. Even more so now with your scars, because I know the price you paid for them. I'm so thankful you came home to us. I really have missed you, Nick."

His gaze shuttered as he drew back, away from her touch. Once more, he distanced himself. Embarrassed that she'd revealed too much, Shelby hopped off the ATV and turned her back on him. "I'll let you dress, and then you can drive. I think I've done enough for today and I need to get back because they're discharging Timmy. I only came home to grab his favorite shirt before heading back to the hospital. I thought he'd feel better wearing it."

Clothing rustled, and the sound of a zipper dragged upward filled the silence between them. She turned finally and he sat in the driver's seat. She climbed onto the seat behind him, thankful he'd taken the larger, monstrous ATV and not the smaller one used for navigating the trails.

When they reached the garage and she'd climbed off, heading for her truck, Nick blocked her. "Shelby, I missed you, too." His gaze searched her face. "More than you know. You're the only one here I trust."

Trust. As in friendship. All the teenage insecurities she'd felt rushed back like a tidal wave. Nick muttering that he had to leave and they were friends, nothing more. Making her feel as if she'd been a fool for kissing him.

"Right. Shelby the reliable, good ole Shelby, who is always there when you need her." She laughed a little to cover her anger. "A good friend, indeed."

"No. Not like before, Sweet Pea. Not friendship. This isn't like before. It's much more." He gently traced a line across her mouth, his touch trailing fire in its wake. Making her want him all over again.

Trembling, she closed her eyes, feeling his finger graze over her chin, down to her neck. Her nipples pushed against her bra, eager and straining. Oh, wow, with one touch he set her on fire, making all her past boyfriends seem fumbling and awkward. She enjoyed sex, and while they'd been accommodating in her needs, they hadn't equaled Nick.

Nothing could ever equal him.

Then she felt him touch her. He unbuttoned her blouse. Immobilized with sheer need, ignoring the cool air brushing against her bare skin, she opened her eyes.

He pulled open her blouse, lifted up the cup of her bra and looked down. Her sluggish brain kicked into gear. Shelby yanked the ends of her blouse together. "Nick! What are you doing?"

"Taking a peek. Fair play. You did see me naked."

That jaw-dropping grin had probably coaxed more women into undressing than she could count over the years. His seductive, deep voice, and the twinkle in his eyes… Impossible to be angry at him. Not with that boyish charm. But she'd be five shades of fool to let this go further, because he'd already broken her heart once. Shelby didn't intend to go for a second round.

Buttoning up her blouse, she ignored the heat rising from her throat to her cheeks. "Why don't you get ready and come with me to the hospital to pick up Timmy?"

His playful grin dropped. "If you need me, I'll come with you, but I'll call Jonah first to see if he can send one or two of his deputies. I'm not sure when Jake's returning from Nashville and I hate leaving the farm unguarded."

Words better than an icy dive into the pond. Shelby nodded. She didn't like him being alone here, either, not with an arsonist prowling around. Letting him know this would ding his self-confidence.

It wasn't that she worried he couldn't handle trouble. She couldn't handle anything else happening to Nick. Or Timmy. With a start Shelby realized they were the two most important people in her life. Her sister was thousands of miles across the sea, and had become secondary.

"Call him. I know he'll be happy to send a couple of guys over to watch the place. And it would be nice for Timmy to see you again. He really likes and admires you."

And so do I. But that's something I can't let you know.

She kept those thoughts secret and guarded as they made the preparations to return to the hospital for Timmy.

Because if she had it her way, Nick Anderson would never again know how very much he occupied her thoughts, and finally had started to occupy her heart as well.

returning from the pond, *Shelby* retreated upstairs to her bedroom for much-needed privacy. The close encounter with Nick had sent her hormones soaring. She needed distance.

Shelby finally sat down to check her email. Lately all she received were notices from vendors who contacted her when their emails to the farm went unnoticed. Wincing, she scanned through a stack of emails, mostly vendors, some spam. A few were from locals interested in booking trail or wagon rides. Those she forwarded to Jake, who handled renting out the horses.

Another email, sandwiched between the spam and angry vendor emails, caught her eye. Heather. Finally! She hadn't heard from her sister in more than three weeks, despite all the emails she'd sent. Shelby opened it, eager to read an update.

Hi, Shelby! Pete and I are heading back tomorrow. He broke the contract. Long story, but there's great news! Can't wait to see you and Timmy. We're flying into Nash-

as if Hea... ...ing, ...olved
around her e... ...een the
case? Shelby doing ... make up
for neglectful, uncaring ... ...ng her life-
style to fit Heather's so Heat... ...band practice in high school. Shelby giving ... money when
Heather needed a new car. Shelby orga...izing Heather's
expensive wedding, Shelby making sure Heather had everything she needed.

Shelby caring for Timmy for months so Heather's husband could earn money overseas. The pattern stared her starkly in the face.

Nick was right. She did put everyone else's needs before her own. Especially when it came to her baby sister.

Shelby rinsed out her cup in the sink. She packed Timmy's favorite shirt and then grabbed her keys to drive to the hospital. She wasn't packing a damn thing of Timmy's. No, this time Heather wasn't coming first. Her son was.

The next evening, Heather and Pete still hadn't arrived by eight thirty. Shelby had given up calling and waited downstairs on the patio. There was a distinct chill in the air, but she'd donned Nick's jacket. Warm, lined with sheepskin, it smelled of him, spicy and masculine.

As promised, Jonah had sent two men out to the farm to patrol and make their presence known. Privately, he'd told Shelby and Nick he suspected an inside job.

Shelby had thought so as well. Natalie had the most to gain by driving them to sell sooner rather than later.

After finding out Heather was coming here, Nick had discreetly mentioned sleeping in the main house. Typical of the new Nick. Thoughtful, not wanting to intrude. Grateful for his understanding, she saw him in a new light. Ever since returning home, he'd been responsible. Practical. Gone was the daring rebel who didn't care about others. Maybe Nick had changed.

Heather certainly had not. Living in Iraq hadn't made her more responsible. Shelby tried texting again, but Heather didn't answer.

Where were they?

Finally, as the clock slowly dragged closer to nine o'clock, a car entered the driveway and pulled up before her garage apartment. Heather and Pete climbed out of the back. Relief flooded her. They were okay, just late.

Shelby ran and hugged her sister as Pete and the driver began unloading the luggage. Shelby stepped back to study Heather. Her sister was two years younger, and hadn't changed, except her ash-brown hair was longer. Her merry blue eyes sparkled, and she looked slightly plumper, but fashionable in a faux-fur-lined hooded coat with shiny brass buttons, silk-and-wool pants and stilettos that Shelby knew were quite expensive. Amused, she realized she still wore her faded jeans used for riding, worn Western boots and a jacket that had a slight tear in the sleeve.

She'd been too concerned about Heather to bother changing.

"You look cute." She pointed to the jacket. "New clothing?"

"Michael Kors." Heather beamed. "It was a great sale."

Good thing Pete made plenty of money. Heather had compensated for being poor as a child by wearing designer clothing and insisting on the best for her family. While Shelby wasn't as obsessed with fine clothing and expensive living, she couldn't blame her. Life in the cramped trailer on the farm had meant pinching pennies and wearing hand-me-downs, always afraid in school that other girls would notice. Or worse, the time Natalie Beaufort laughed because Shelby wore a pretty flowered dress Natalie had donated to Goodwill.

After hearing of the incident, Heather had told her to throw the dress out. Shelby didn't. She valued good clothing too much. Instead, she spent the afternoon with scissors, shortening the sleeves and adding lace so the original design had changed enough to make it "hers."

At least Heather looked well, though slightly tired.

Shelby pointed to her watch. "You're late. You said you'd be here at dinnertime."

Heather shrugged. "I know, but Customs was a bear. And then we had a problem getting an Uber. The airport was really busy!"

"You couldn't have called as soon as you made it through Customs? Let me know? Timmy was looking forward to seeing both of you."

Guilt flashed across Heather's face. "I'm sorry. How is he? I miss him so much, I can't wait to see him! Can we all have dinner together? I'm starved."

"Timmy and I already ate, but I can heat up leftovers for you and Pete if you've haven't eaten yet."

"Oh, good. We were in a rush and didn't have time to stop."

The driver pulled away and Pete came over and hugged her. Tall and slender, with a shock of brown hair and a cowlick, he was a quiet man who deeply cared for Heather and Timmy. Shelby liked her brother-in-law. He worked hard, and kept Heather stable and happy.

"So good to see you, Shelby. Can I take our luggage upstairs?" Pete asked.

It could clutter her small living room, but they'd manage. "Sure. Just store it by the sofa. I'm afraid I don't have much room, but we'll make do."

He nodded. "Thanks for looking after Timmy for us, Shelby. You're a lifesaver. I'll never forget how much we owe you for this. Mind if I look in on him? I can't wait to see him."

She smiled. Her brother-in-law was as thoughtful and pragmatic as Heather was forgetful. "Go ahead. He's asleep in the bedroom on the right, down the hall."

As Pete took the two big suitcases upstairs, she turned

back to her sister. "You hit the jackpot with him, Heather. And your son. He's an amazing little boy. Loves it here. Heather, why didn't you answer my texts?"

Heather frowned and pulled a cell phone out of her pants pocket, and then groaned. "Oh, darn, Shelby. My phone died and I don't have a charger. It's packed. I never got your texts. I'm sorry, honey. I really am. It's been so crazy since we arrived, and I got sick at the airport."

Irritation dissolved into sisterly worry. "The long flight must have been a bear. Are you all right?"

"Fine, only queasy at times."

The glow on Heather's face... It clicked. "You're pregnant!"

Beaming, Heather nodded. "Four months. You're going to be an aunt again, Shelby. And Timmy will have a little brother or sister by this time next year. It's why we've returned to the States. The contractor hiring Pete let us go, with the condition he finishes the work remotely. All they need are the plans now that the groundwork's been laid."

Laughing, Shelby hugged her again, glad for her sister. Heather deserved this happiness, a family of her own and enough money to feel secure. She'd dreamed about it all the time while growing up.

And what about you? a small voice whispered inside her. *When will it be your turn?*

Soon. Now that Heather and Pete are home, it's my turn to relax and let someone else take charge.

"So what are you going to do now? Did you find a place yet in Nashville?"

Heather's eager expression changed. "Pete found a terrific job, with a good salary, in Seattle with a tech firm. They want him to start next month and meet the team he'll be working with as soon as possible, so we're headed out there."

Shelby's heart sank to her stomach. "Seattle! That's across the country. I don't know if I can move that quickly."

"I'm sorry, Shelby. There won't be room." Heather twisted the wedding ring on her finger. "We rented a very small apartment, and with the baby coming, it'll be really crammed. And I need to bond with Timmy again before the baby comes, so I want lots of alone time with him. And my mother-in-law is coming when the baby arrives to stay with us for at least two months. You understand…"

Her sister's words turned into babbling nonsense. Stricken, Shelby stared at her sister. When she finally surfaced for air, she said quietly, "You promised we'd all live together. You begged me to live with you, and you promised free rent until I could find a job. No matter where you ended up, Heather."

"I know, but things changed, you have to understand, Shelby. Why, you can find a job in Seattle after we're settled there? I'm sure you could get a good job and a place of your own…and by then the baby will have arrived."

Tuning her out, Shelby stared at the seemingly endless rolling fields. Once more, she'd set aside her own needs for someone else, and once more, they had disappointed her.

"Nick was right," she murmured. "It's never going to change."

Heather's gaze sharpened. "Nick? That tomcat? He's back here?"

"Yes. He now owns the farm. Silas left it to him. Didn't you read my emails?"

Another flash of guilt in her sister's eyes. Eyes so much like their mother's. "I meant to, but we were busy packing everything and organizing to move back here. Everything happened so quickly."

"Ah. Is that why you stopped sending money for Timmy's care?"

This time, Heather wouldn't meet her gaze. She worked the wedding ring so much it spun around her finger like a merry-go-round.

"We needed every last penny for the move and buying a new car. Pete's former roommate in Nashville found him a great deal on a barely used car to get us across the country, but the guy wanted cash only. And I figured with you living here rent-free, and Silas was always so good to us and treated us like his daughters...well, you could manage. I mean, Nick now owns the farm and they've always been rich."

More excuses. Heather never asked once how Shelby had been faring. How her life had been, or how she felt about seeing Nick again. Nor had she asked about the farm or what was happening there.

It wouldn't matter. She was upset with Heather, but her sister didn't need to know how bad things were here. It was for the best that they take Timmy and get him away, to a place where arsonists didn't burn barns and nearly kill little boys.

"When we get settled in Seattle, I'll pay back every last dime. I swear it, I mean..."

Suddenly drained, she smiled. Heather was her only sister, and all the family she had left. "It's okay. Come upstairs, and I'll fix you something to eat."

"I'm sorry, Shelby, about the last-minute arrangements. We can find a motel in town."

"Don't be silly. You're pregnant and Timmy's here. I have fresh sheets on my bed, and it's a queen. I can sleep on the sofa."

Shelby pasted a too-wide smile on her face as they trudged upstairs. She would let Heather and Pete have her bed. Because she'd always been the big sister who set aside her own needs to care for others.

Old habits died hard.

Heather and Pete were taking Timmy and leaving today.

Over breakfast the following morning she'd tried to process the news, but Shelby felt as if someone had smacked her with a two-by-four across the face. Now, as she watched Heather throw Timmy's clothing into his suitcase, she tried to keep her equilibrium. Her world was tilting on its axis.

Timmy was outside with his father, saying goodbye to Macaroni pony. Nick was with them. He'd shown up at the apartment after breakfast to greet Heather and Pete. Questions had lingered in his eyes, but he hadn't asked anything, only agreed to escort them to the stables when Shelby asked.

She sat on Timmy's bed, clutching his one-eyed teddy bear. "I thought you were staying at least a week!" A week would give her time to say her last goodbyes to Timmy, whom she would miss dreadfully. A week would stave off the terrible loneliness swimming in her chest with the knowledge that her only sister was leaving and going far away.

And she didn't know when she'd ever see her again. How could she afford a plane ticket when she had no job, and barely two hundred dollars in her checking account?

"We have to get to Nashville by noon because the guy selling the car wants to sell it on his lunch break. He's got another buyer if we fail to show up." Heather tossed Timmy's Spider-Man underwear and white T-shirts into the case.

As she went to shut the lid, Shelby scooped up the plastic bulldozer—Timmy's favorite. "You have to take this. He'll be asking for it."

Heather dumped the toy into the suitcase. Her sister glanced at the trucks, cars and blocks littering the floor of the postage-sized bedroom.

"We don't have room for all those, so can you pack and ship them to us in Seattle?"

"Sure," Shelby said dully.

Clinging to the teddy bear as if it was *her* stuffed animal that kept away the nightmares, Shelby followed her sister down the stairs. Heather insisted on carrying Timmy's case.

In front of the garage a car sat, its engine running. Heather handed the suitcase to the driver. "Here's the last one."

Nick, Pete and Timmy walked up the driveway. Timmy ran to the car and turned to his father with a frown. "Daddy, you and Mama going away again?"

Pete squatted down, looking at his son. "Yes, Timmy, but you're going with us. We're never going to leave you again."

Tears spilling down her cheeks, Heather hugged Shelby tight. "It's best if we leave right away," she said, sniffling. "I love you, Shelby. Thank you for everything."

Openly crying now, Heather climbed into the back

seat, leaving her husband with Timmy to say goodbye to Shelby.

Heather never had been able to tolerate a scene when their parents fought, and didn't like drama any more now.

Nick squatted down and hugged Timmy. "Goodbye, sport. Don't forget what I told you."

Nick shook hands with Pete. "Good luck." With a meaningful look at Shelby, he jerked a thumb at the house. "I have a conference call with the mayor if you need me. Dan and Felicity and the kids are away and Jake's still in Nashville, seeing about a new tractor."

Her heart beat faster as Nick walked away. Now came the hardest thing of all. How could she say goodbye to this little boy who had captured her heart a year ago, who had been her entire world for thirteen months? She had rearranged her schedule, her priorities, her life around him.

He was the first one she saw in the morning and the last one at night, for she always checked on him before going to bed.

I'm going to miss you so much. Shelby bit her lower lip, struggling to control her emotions.

Bending down, she hugged Timmy. "Goodbye, sport. I'll take good care of Macaroni pony for you."

A small frown puckered Timmy's face. "You're not going with us, Aunt Shelby?"

"I can't. But I'll come visit." *Someday. Somehow. I don't care where you are, I'll come visit, when I can.*

She started to walk away, but Timmy pulled free of his father. "No! No! Please, Aunt Shelby. Don't leave me, don't leave me!"

Pete grabbed his son's hand. "We have to go, Timmy," he said firmly.

Struggling to be free, Timmy wailed, kicked and screamed.

She rushed to him, kissed his forehead. "It's okay, sport. You belong with your mama and daddy. They're going to take you to a wonderful new place, and you'll have lots of new adventures. They love you so very much and they're going to take good care of you."

Tears clung to his long lashes. "But I won't have you and Macaroni pony. And Nick won't be there to keep me safe or play Legos with me."

Throat closing with emotion, she brushed back his hair. Stubborn cowlick, just like his daddy. "You have your daddy now, honey. He missed you so very much and he'll keep you safe. And Mama will read you night-night stories and tuck you in, and be there when you get home from school each day. They're your family. Please, you have to go with them now. It's going to be okay."

She handed him the teddy. He smiled through his tears.

"Here's Teddy. Hug him tight and wish him good-night and I'll hear it. Teddy is a good messenger."

Timmy hugged the bear tight. "I'll tell him. But will you call me and tell me a night-night story over the phone?" he asked, his lower lip jutting out.

Shelby blinked hard to keep the tears at bay. She looked at Heather, who was openly crying. "Your mama will read you a night-night story, but I promise I'll call."

She kissed his forehead again. "Now be a big boy, just like I asked, and go with Mama and Daddy."

"Come on, Timmy," Pete said gently. He picked his son into his arms, and mouthed *thank you* to Shelby.

He buckled Timmy into the booster seat, and then sat in front beside the driver.

As the car drove away in a cloud of dust, Shelby waved hard until she thought her arm would break. *What the heck*, she thought dully. *It can't hurt any worse than my heart right now.*

Chapter 15

Nick worried about Shelby.

All the next day she avoided him, insisting she had the books to balance and bills to pay. He left her alone until dinnertime. He knew what it was like to say goodbye and struggle to keep your emotions in check.

At dinner, she'd vanished. He ate leftovers Felicity had in the fridge, and then went to find her. There was only one place Shelby would go. He went outside into the clear, starry night, buttoning his jacket. Damn cold out. A wicked cold front was sweeping across the valley. He had to find Shelby before she froze.

The ATV was inside the four-car garage below Shelby's apartment. Giving silent thanks Dan had left the two ATVs there, and not in the barn that had burned down, he strode into the garage, found the keys in the ignition of one vehicle and started it up.

As he headed out along the north trail leading to Henry's cabin, thoughts spiraled in his head. Awfully smart of Dan to garage the very pricey ATVs. But why the garage? In the past, the machines, along with the tractor, were housed in the barn. They used them to get to the pumpkin garden, and the fields where they grew hay.

Dan also had mentioned taking his boys on the machines for joyrides.

Was Dan the arsonist who burned down the barn? Maybe his cousin was tired of the responsibility, and resented Nick for inheriting everything after all the years Dan had worked his ass off for Silas.

But if Nick sold the ranch, what would Dan get?

Dan had a very good reason for forcing Nick to sell, and leave. He wished he could trust his cousin.

Jake, on the other hand, seemed ready to cut his losses and move on. He'd mentioned something about moving to Kentucky, getting a job as an assistant trainer at a reputable stable known for producing Derby winners.

Seemed like everyone was ready to move on. Except Shelby. She was planted here as surely as the magnolia tree by the garage. Sturdy and resilient.

Ruminating over what she must be feeling, he navigated past the thick trees, the headlights of the vehicle picking out the dirt trail head of him. Cold air whipped his cheeks as he drove, careful not to speed. This trail had been groomed, but with the barn incident, anything could lurk here.

When the cabin finally came into sight, he saw a glow in the windows. Someone was there, and had lit a fire. Nick parked the vehicle at the slope of the hill, climbed off and walked on the woodchip path to the front door. Maybe she didn't want company, but tonight, he wouldn't give her a choice.

Lightly tapping on the front door, he waited a minute and then opened it.

On a blue wool blanket, Shelby sat before the brick

hearth of the fireplace, where a small fire crackled. She looked so forlorn and woebegone, he wanted to gather her into his arms and promise her no one would ever hurt her again. But he couldn't.

Nick softly closed the door, his boot heels clicking against the hardwood floor as he approached. Damn, it was cold. He put more logs on the fire, built up the flames and then tugged off his boots and socks and set them before the now roaring fire. Only then did he join her on the blanket.

By the glow of the flames, he could clearly see the tear tracks on her cheeks. Gently, he wiped one away with the pad of his thumb.

Shelby sniffled. Nick said nothing, but held out his arms, and she went into his embrace. He stroked her hair, wishing he could provide more comfort, wishing her sister hadn't arrived when she did and hurt Shelby. She was one tough woman, and it twisted him up inside to see her this broken.

He knew what it was like to have family reject you, no matter how hard you worked at getting their approval. Nick sighed. Silas and Heather were worlds apart in personality and temperament, but for one thing. They never appreciated those closest to them, the ones who would give up everything to make them happy. They were too blind when it came to everything except their own lives.

Heather still had time to change. For Shelby's sake, he hoped the hell she would, before it was too late, like it had been with Silas and him.

Giving another heartbreaking sniffle, she buried her head against his shoulder, wetting the checked flannel fabric of his shirt. "What are you doing here, Nick?"

"Watching after you. All your life you've taken care

of everyone else. Your folks, sister, Silas, my family, Timmy, even me. I reckon it's time someone looked after you for a change."

She gave another heartbreaking sniffle. "He's gone, Nick. My Timmy. He was mine for a whole year, and now I don't know when I'll see him again. Everything's changed. I was supposed to go with them. Heather, Pete and Timmy are all I have left."

Nick kissed the top of her head. "No, they're not. You've got me, Sweet Pea. I'm not blood, but I'm here for you."

He couldn't help it. Nick drew back and stared into those wet emerald eyes, teardrops clinging to her dark lashes. Gently, he kissed away a salty droplet trickling down her cheek. Over and over he delivered tiny kisses to her face, letting her know he did care.

Shelby slid her arms around his neck, and caressed his nape. Man, the things she did to him…he should stop now, before this went too far. Ten years ago, he'd convinced himself he'd be heading into hell in a handbasket if he followed through on his passion for Shelby.

Drawing away, he gazed into her eyes and realized he didn't want to stop.

"Nick, I'm not sixteen anymore." She traced a line over his mouth. "I want you. Do you want me?"

Taking her hand, he slid it down to the hardness in his jeans. Her gaze grew languorous with desire.

"There's no bed big enough for what I want to do to you," he murmured. "And what I want to do to you now is barely legal."

Yeah, he might go to hell, but the ride with Shelby this time would be worth the price.

* * *

Nick Anderson had always held her heart. Never had she forgotten about how he made her feel—cherished and safe and desirable.

Even though he'd crushed her young, childish love for him, she secretly harbored a dream he'd return one day. Now he was here, in her arms. Not wishing to think about the consequences, her body aching with sheer need, Shelby cupped his face, her thumb tracing over the wicked scar on his cheek. She stared into his eyes, seeing past pain and hurt, and desire. Healing this man of all he'd endured here at the ranch and abroad as a SEAL wouldn't be easy, but for tonight, they would share their bodies and forget about all else.

Nick removed his shirt and flung it aside as she tugged the sweater over her head.

Fingers trembling, she helped him yank down his jeans and boxer briefs. He was large and hard. Ready for her. Nick unfastened her bra clasp, and helped her out of the garment. His gaze darkened as he studied her breasts, her nipples pearling. Gently he palmed them, teasing the tips with his thumbs as a shudder raced through her.

"I've dreamed about this for ten long years. You haunted my thoughts, Shelby. I've always wanted you." He took her hand, placed it over his heart. "I kept your memory here, so I could never forget you. When I was lying in the hospital bed, banged up and hurting so bad I wanted to die, I thought of you and it gave me the will to fight for another day."

Shelby traced the scar on his cheek. "Nick, I kept you in my heart as well. I'm so glad you never gave up, and came home to us."

He kept playing with her breasts as she closed her

eyes, bracing her hands on his shoulders. Each stroke sent a lick of fire between her legs.

He skimmed a warm palm along her hip, making all her nerves jump and sizzle. "I like women who are clocks."

Shelby regarded with amusement. "Say what?"

"Hourglass figures." His smile was wicked and filled with sexy promise.

"With my butt, I'm more like Big Ben."

Nick rolled her over onto her stomach, and cupped her bare bottom. "Hoo-yah, baby, don't diss your sweet ass. Lots more to squeeze, and love."

Then he gently rolled her over, so she was stretched out on her back. Nick kissed her mouth, her chin, raining tiny kisses down her body. He settled between her thighs and pushed them open wide. Then he put his mouth on her.

Shelby drifted into a haze of pleasure, the sensations building higher and higher with his tender loving, until they reached a crescendo. She screamed as the orgasm slammed into her. He stayed with her, kissing her all over and then sat back on his haunches. Nick removed the condom from his wallet, tore off the foil wrapping and sheathed himself. He stretched on top of her, his gaze heated as he stared down at her in the firelight.

"You are so damn sexy, Sweet Pea. So beautiful," he murmured.

Nick pushed inside her with a groan, all hardness and heat, his chest sliding over her sensitive breasts, his muscled thighs wedged between her outstretched legs.

It had been a long while since she'd had sex and at first he hurt a little. Shelby winced, but wriggled closer with a moan.

It felt so good, each long stroke filling her, his satisfied groans filling the empty spaces inside her heart. They moved together, golden firelight playing over their bodies, the wind moaning outside in unison with their groans and sighs.

He bent over her, his fingers reaching between them to tease her wet, feminine flesh and stoke the heat higher.

Shelby gasped as the heavenly sensations increased, and then she shattered in a powerful climax that wrung a sob from her throat. Nick dug his fingers into her arching hips, threw back his head and groaned, coming deep inside her. He said her name over and over. He stayed still for a moment, shuddering with pleasure, his muscled body heavy upon hers as she stroked the back of his head.

Then with a sigh, he pulled away and rolled them to the side. Hearts pounding, they lay wrapped around each other. Nick stroked her hair as she nestled against his shoulder. A cold draft billowed across the floor, cooling the sweat on their bodies. Silence draped between them for a few moments, broken only by the wind rustling the leaves outside.

"I'd love to stay here all night with you, Sweet Pea, but without much firewood, we're gonna freeze to death and there's no bathroom."

She snuggled against him. "You're a guy. You don't need one. All you need are the trees."

Chuckling, he smoothed back her tangled hair from her face. "I was thinking of you, darling. And getting some real heat, other than the kind we can make here on the floor. I want to make love to you in a soft bed, the kind you deserve."

"I don't mind the floor."

His chuckle turned deep. Nick grinned. "Maybe, but

I only brought one condom, darling. And I'm going to need plenty more tonight."

Arousal curled, hot and tight, in her belly. And then she remembered the earlier events, the tears on Timmy's face, and the abandoned toys she'd promised to pack and ship to him in Washington.

"I don't know if I can return to my place, Nick." Panic tinged her voice. "Too many memories of Timmy. It's why I came out here tonight to be alone."

He kissed her, a brief kiss filled with promise. "You can. I'll be with you, Sweet Pea. Trust me."

It was getting mighty cold in the cabin, and much as she thought spending the night with Nick here would be romantic, her practical side knew it wasn't a good idea. Shelby hunted around for her clothing and dressed in a hurry. By the time they made it out to the ATV with the help of Nick's flashlight, her teeth were chattering.

He made her climb on before him, and snuggled close to her as he started up the engine. They drove slowly back to the main driveway, a mixture of sadness and excitement arrowing through her. Sadness because of losing Timmy. Excitement because she was spending the night with Nick Anderson, the gorgeous man of her dreams.

It won't last, a tiny voice whispered inside her. *He's going to leave.*

But tonight she wouldn't think of the future. Tonight was for the distant stars glittering overhead through the trees like fistfuls of shiny diamonds. Tonight was for feeling Nick's muscled body close against hers, and the desire pulsing through her veins.

Tonight was for dreams.

When he pulled in front of the garage and they were climbing the steps to her apartment, she felt a flutter of unease in her stomach. Tension knotted her body. Making love with him in the cabin had been spontaneous, at least to her, even if he planned it. This was taking a big step forward. Nick admitted he hated spending the night with a woman because he was a solitary sleeper.

Would he hold her close for a few minutes after they made love, and then tiptoe off to his sofa bed? Pretend making love to her had been a memory and nothing more?

"We're not spending the night here," he told her as she unlocked the door. "But there's something inside you need to see."

"So we're staying together?" She gave a little laugh.

"I'm not leaving you alone in that bed tonight, Sweet Pea." Nick picked up her hand and kissed her knuckles. "I plan to hold you all night long. But first, I have a surprise for you."

Surprises had always been bad. Shelby didn't like them. Surprises were her parents leaving her alone, barely fifteen, to care for her little sister. Only by Silas acting as legal guardian had they skated by the authorities. Surprises were things like her sister announcing she was moving across the globe, and leaving Timmy under Shelby's care. All for the money, not really caring what Shelby's plans were.

And then there were the really nasty surprises, like the type the saboteur left.

"I'd rather know now, unless you won the Powerball and you plan to split it with me."

A short laugh. "Darling, you deserve the whole jackpot. But I didn't win the lottery. You'll have to come with me to see what it is. I promise, you'll like it."

Nick was her lover now. It felt good, but odd to think of him that way.

Because she didn't want him as a fleeting memory of a sweet night of making love. She wanted more. Even if she couldn't have more.

The living room was clean, the sofa put back instead of being pulled out as she'd left it this morning. Shelby gave him a questioning look, but Nick smiled. "We've been busy. Check out Timmy's room. Go on."

Her heart sank as she thought of seeing the empty bed, the toys scattered on the floor, the unbearable quietness. Shelby walked to the room across the hallway and opened the door.

She gasped.

Gone were the colorful Batman curtains she'd hung at the double windows. White blinds replaced the curtains. No more twin bed bureau, or any of the posters he'd used to decorate his room. Instead, the room had been stripped down to a plain wood desk with a gooseneck lamp, an office chair, gray cabinets, a bookcase filled with books. An art easel sat in one corner, along with a small stand filled with paints.

She touched the paints with a wondering hand. All new, and brushes as well. Shelby glanced up at Nick, who was leaning against the doorjamb.

"I felt bad you lost all your art supplies in the fire. And I reckoned you'd feel more comfortable sleeping here if this room functioned as a studio to foster your talent. I didn't get rid of Timmy's stuff—it's all in the closet if you want it."

How long had it taken him to do this? Nick understood her secret dream of becoming an artist. Nick knew her preference for watercolors, not acrylics or oils.

Fresh tears filled her eyes, only these were different tears. She turned to him. "Thank you. This is the best gift anyone's ever given me, Nick."

His mouth worked, and he looked intense. "You need to pursue your dreams, Sweet Pea. It's about time you treated yourself to a grand adventure of your own. From the time I met you, you talked about being an artist. Now it's your turn to create."

He gave her rear a gentle pat. "Go pack an overnight bag and I'll wait for you downstairs."

Shelby tossed clothing and essentials into a small suitcase, her heart beating hard. She wouldn't think about the quiet command behind his smoky voice. Not tonight. Tonight was for creating magic, and pretending that she and Nick could share more than sex and passion.

They walked along the dirt road to the main house, the wind cutting through her like a knife. It was quiet. Too quiet. Unease filled her. She didn't like being so alone here on the ranch, with everyone gone. But there was Nick, and there hadn't been any incidents since the fire. Maybe things had calmed down a little.

Maybe the person trying to drive them out had decided to let the bank do its work and start foreclosure.

Nick insisted on carrying her suitcase. The nearly full moon provided sufficient light as they walked across the dirt road to the main house. At the front porch, she hesitated. Never had she spent the night here. It felt as if she was breaking a rule.

He opened the door and swept her a low bow. "After you."

"I don't know, Nick… I don't live here."

His gaze was serious. "I do. I own the Belle Creek,

Sweet Pea, and you can bunk anywhere you want. To-night, you're sleeping in style. No hard floor for you."

She gave him a slight smile. "A real bed with sheets?"

Nick winked. "I even washed them, just for you."

He took her hand and tugged her up the stairs. "Where are you going?" she asked. "Not that awful pink monstrosity."

"Hey, that pink monstrosity was once my room. Don't mock my style."

"Ruffles and all," she teased.

At the landing, he swung her up into his arms and she laughed. Jake's room was across the hallway.

"Jake wouldn't mind if we used his room for the night. He's never there," she pointed out as Nick strode into his former bedroom. "He was always with his girlfriend. We all thought Lynn was the one. She works as a nail technician while she's going to college and she has pink hair."

"He broke up with her one week ago." Nick marched across the threshold of the pink bedroom and gently deposited her on the bed. "He told me Lynn got too clingy. I don't want to talk about my cousin's sex life tonight, Sweet Pea. Tonight is for us alone."

He kissed her again, sending all her senses scrambling all over again. As they stripped again, she could only think of the moment, wishing it would last forever.

An hour after they'd made love, Shelby couldn't sleep. Sitting up in the bed, she watched Nick. Arm flung over his head, he lay on his back, looking as innocent as a child.

All the lines smoothed out from his face as he slept, the scar on his cheek softer in the warm glow of the bedside lamp. He looked defenseless.

Knowing how powerful his body was, and how he moved, she knew it wasn't true. Nick Anderson was as defenseless as a tiger. She blushed, remembering how he'd moved inside of her. Her body tingled and ached from the hard loving.

Her feelings for him grew deeper every day. But what would happen if he decided to sell the ranch and leave?

She'd been crushed ten years ago when he abandoned her.

This time, she knew he'd break her heart for good.

Chapter 16

One week after making love with Shelby, Nick felt even more restless than when he'd first arrived at Belle Creek.

Sex with Shelby had filled Nick with a troubled longing. The sex was fantastic, but equally so was holding her close to him, feeling her warm, soft body in the dark night. Listening to her breathe, his world felt centered for the first time since he'd left the navy. He could easily drift into contentment with this woman, envisioning a life complete with marriage, kids and life on the ranch.

Yet deep inside, he felt a restless urge to leave. Shelby was apple pie, stability and all the comforts of a home he wasn't certain he wanted. Or deserved. The emotions she stirred threatened to quell the restlessness he'd felt. And that bothered him, because he wasn't certain how he'd adjust permanently to life as a rancher. Or a husband. Or a father.

After they'd made love that night, he hadn't time to dwell on his growing feelings or his very male hunger, because both Jake and Dan returned home. Everyone stayed busy preparing for the pumpkin patch at the ranch.

Shelby had moved into the house, sleeping in the pink guest room at Nick's request. With everything that had to be done, he felt better having everyone under one roof at night. Even Jake obeyed Nick's edict, grumbling good-naturedly about sleeping in his own bedroom. The new security system Nick had installed at the house meant one less thing to worry about. To make doubly sure everyone was protected, he moved his belongings into the basement rec room.

There were no more stolen kisses with Shelby, or nights spent making long, leisurely love in borrowed beds. Nick woke before dawn and worked nonstop until way into the night. Meals were quick bites grabbed haphazardly, or takeout Felicity ordered. By the time he fell into bed, exhausted, Shelby was upstairs asleep.

Today was opening day. Shortly after dawn, Nick rode out over the trail where the hay wagon would pull happy families later. He wanted to ensure all was perfect. The proper permits had been secured, electrical lines laid down for extra lighting, portable toilets installed—everything was set. Nick also purchased a small liability policy as a condition of securing the permits for the festival.

Satisfied the trail was good, he galloped back, and then dismounted. Nick led Tiny Dancer back to his stall to wipe him down and currycomb the horse. As he reached the stall, he saw something taped to the door. He unfolded the white square of paper. His temper rose, and he crushed the paper in one trembling fist.

Damn it. He'd thought these childish notes were over.

**You think you're a big hero but you're a loser.
Go away before you get hurt.**

He stuffed the paper into his jeans pocket and started working on drying off Tiny Dancer. The note was supposed to mock him. Well, whoever wrote it didn't know him well. It took more than mere words to get under his skin. Still, he was glad that he'd hired extra security guards for the start of the pumpkin patch. Jonah Doyle even promised to spare a deputy to stop by and patrol at random.

Nick finished currying Tiny Dancer, put oats into his feed bag and gave him a pat. Feed was expensive, and the ranch was running on a shoestring budget. After this weekend, they should have enough cash.

"Enjoy your treat, big guy," he told the horse. "Next week you'll have plenty more."

He returned to the house to grab coffee before the workers started arriving to set up the booths and vending trucks.

Shelby was in the expansive kitchen, sitting at the breakfast bar, reading a newspaper and drinking coffee. Clad in a blue-and-pink flannel shirt and matching sleep pants, she looked sexy as hell. She glanced up when she saw him and her expression softened upon seeing him.

"Hello, stranger. Want some java juice?"

In a few strides, he was at her side. "No, what I want is you, Sweet Pea." Nick framed her face with his hands and dropped a kiss on her soft, warm mouth.

Her fingers laced around his wrists. "Me, too, Nick." A delicate flush tinted her cheeks. "I've missed you."

Not as much as I'm going to miss you when I finally leave. The thought startled and unsettled him. Was he truly entertaining the idea of walking away? Leaving Shelby and the ranch?

And go where?

But he couldn't deny the tug of restlessness that increased each day he spent at Belle Creek. Too many years roaming with the navy, and then on his own, had made it difficult for him to settle.

Nick looked at Shelby, the softness on her face, the sparkle in her eyes and the flush on her cheeks. How could he leave her, after discovering how much he'd started to care?

Nick didn't want to think about it today.

They were all ready to go.

Shortly after four o'clock, the crowds started to arrive. Minivans filled with children, big pickup trucks rumbling down the road to park in the pasture.

Felicity proved surprisingly clever at organizing the event. Nick had hired men to bulldoze the ruins of the burned barn, but debris still remained. They'd built a wood fence to hide it and Felicity and Shelby painted colorful pumpkins on the planks.

At the ranch's entrance, Felicity placed hay bales with pumpkins and corn stalks. Right inside the entrance, where clerks sold tickets from booths Nick had rented, she and Shelby had set up rocking chairs, hay bales, corn stalks and dolls with farming overalls before a sign that read Anderson's Pumpkin Patch. A photographer snapped family photos at the exhibit, selling the digital prints to those who wanted a memento of their special day's outing.

Nick checked the tractor to make certain it was properly hitched to the wagon. He straightened his Stetson and looked back at the children and their parents clustered together on the bales of hay lining the wagon that served as seats.

He stood by the wagon, and tilted back his hat. "Hi, everyone. I'm your driver, Cowboy Nick. I'm taking you on a ride through some of the prettiest country God ever created in these parts. As the sun starts to set behind those mountains, it'll get a little spooky, so hang tight. Be sure to keep a look out for the scarecrows. They have a habit of jumping out of the cornfield."

"I'm not scared of scarecrows," one tyke yelled out, and everyone laughed.

Nick leaned his arms on the wagon's side. "You're a brave soul. You scared of ghosts?"

The boy shook his head.

"Good, because we're headed to the old cabin, where it's said Henry buried his treasure. You may catch a glimpse of his ghost. Everyone ready?"

"Yes!" a chorus yelled back.

"Okay, everyone say, 'Giddy up, Cowboy Nick!'

Giggles and laughs. "Giddy up, Cowboy Nick!"

Grinning, he started the tractor and with a jerk, the wagon pulled forward. Humming a country tune, he waved at the children picking out pumpkins in the fields. Shelby was in charge of the little ones near the bounce house, and Jake was overseeing the corn maze. Mario, Hank and John ran the petting zoo and the pony rides, while Felicity was in the large tent he'd rented, supervising the craft fair and farmer's market. Big stalks of corn, apples and fresh cider were sold as well.

Local vendors had set up food and drink stands, where one could purchase a refreshing soft drink or bottled water. The delicious smells of fried dough, cotton candy and steak sandwiches dripping in cheese and onions wafted on the breeze.

Corn stalks, bales of straw, pumpkins and gourds decorated the trail as they chugged along the trail. Jake had even erected a few skeletons set up as scarecrows, rigging them to wave their arms as the wagon passed. Even the weather cooperated, with temperatures in the sixties and no rain in sight.

The crowds had been bigger than anticipated, but Nick had hired extra hands for security and for crowd control, just in case. He'd nearly drained his savings account, too. But if it meant saving the ranch, and finally seeing the debt cleared so they could finally operate in the black, it was worth it.

"Are we really going to see old Henry's ghost?" one of the kids in back shouted at him.

"I bet you will. He hangs around the cabin to guard his treasure," Nick yelled back over the roar of the tractor's motor.

"That treasure is a myth, Nick Anderson," shouted Harvey Glen, the town mayor. He laughed as he slung an arm around his wife as their two young children laughed and bounced up and down on the hay bales.

"That's what you think, Harvey." Nick grinned and slowed the tractor as they came to the first of Jake's skeleton scarecrows. As the tractor rolled close, the motion sensor on the skeleton triggered and the skeleton waved its arms. Children gave delighted shrieks.

The waning sunshine felt good on his face as he headed across the pasture to the cabin. It was a good day, and everyone was enjoying themselves. No more threats, for the security guards patrolling ensured that.

We're going to make it. For the first time, he truly believed he could do what his father had asked.

Nick glanced backward at the parents and their children enjoying themselves. Maybe this wasn't his calling, but it was a welcome change, and it felt good to make people smile.

The hum of an ATV roared in the distance. He turned his head, saw someone following him, motioning to stop. Nick frowned and slowed the tractor and then stopped. Dread filled him as the rider climbed off. Jonah Doyle in full green uniform. Not smiling, either.

"Jonah." Nick jumped down from the driver's seat. "Odd time to pay a social visit. Unless you wanted to hitch a ride on the wagon?"

The sheriff compressed his thin lips. "I'm sorry, Nick. I have to shut you down."

Protests rang out from the children, and the parents exchanged confused looks.

"Why?" Nick gave him an even look, even though he already suspected the reason.

"I don't have a choice, Nick. Your permit got canceled due to lack of insurance."

"What lack of insurance?" he demanded. "I bought a liability policy four days ago!"

Doyle shoved a paper at him. The words seemed to dance on the paper before him. His insurance policy had been canceled. No explanation, just words promising a refund in the mail.

"You're telling me all these people are going to have to leave, right now? The insurance covers us for today's events." Thinking fast, he locked gazes with a startled Mayor Glen. "I would argue in court that I didn't get a twenty-four-hour notification."

Mayor Glen cleared his throat. "Jonah, surely you can grant an extension, at least for tonight. Give people a chance to enjoy themselves."

"Not up to me, Harvey. Without a permit, the town

council will be on my case. Unless you can assure me otherwise." Jonah exchanged knowing looks with Nick.

Nick fully understood. If the mayor agreed to keep quiet, they could keep running the pumpkin patch at least through tonight.

"What do you say, Harvey?" Nick broadcast his most charming smile. "You don't want to disappoint all these good folks who came here for fun tonight."

"No, I don't. I'll handle this with the council. As long as you promise you won't open again tomorrow, Nick." Harvey puffed up his chest. "I'm taking a huge gamble here."

Nick breathed a small sigh of relief. "I promise."

"Tonight only. It's all I can do." Jonah looked at the wagon, his jaw tight. "Enjoy your ride."

His smile more forced, he continued running the tractor along the trail, trying to keep up the friendly guise of Cowboy Nick. All the while inside him, Navy SEAL Nick wanted to find Chuck Beaufort and beat the living crap out of him.

When he returned the hay wagon to the entrance, and handed over responsibility for driving the tractor to Mario, Nick headed into the house to make phone calls. A short time later, he emerged. No luck. No insurance company would issue an emergency rider to the ranch's liability policy.

Beaufort must have found out about the insurance policy Nick purchased from one of his companies.

He headed into the tent. Beneath it, Felicity and Shelby sat at a picnic table, eating roasted ears of corn. His heart sank as he looked at Shelby. So pretty and animated, she fit right in. She looked so happy; he hated delivering the news.

"Look what I found," he drawled, walking up to them. "Two of the prettiest ladies in Nature County."

"Oh, pish." Shelby waved her hand with the corn. "You old charmer."

"How's business?" he asked.

"Excellent. Tomorrow will be even better." Flushed, Felicity set down her corn. "I got so many compliments on my peach jam. I sold all fifty jars."

Nick lowered his voice. "I'm afraid you won't, Felicity. Tonight was our last night. Our insurance policy was canceled."

Felicity's prim jaw dropped, while Shelby's eyes filled with tears. "No, Nick. We can't!"

He squeezed her hand. "I'm afraid we have no choice."

When the last visitor had left, and the vendors were packing up, unhappy at losing business over the weekend, but agreeing to a partial refund of their fees, Nick held a meeting under the tent. Tomorrow it would be packed up and returned to the rental company.

The only person absent was Jake, who'd agreed to watch over Mason and Miles as they stabled the ponies and fed and watered them for the night. Felicity, Dan and Shelby sat on chairs at the rented tables. Shelby had tallied the night's intake and while they had made a decent amount of money, some of it had to be refunded to pay back the vendors.

He was too upset and restless to sit. Almost all his savings was gone. And for what?

Loser, a little voice inside him whispered.

He told the voice to shut up and turned to face the others. "Jonah and Harvey did us a huge favor by allowing us to remain open tonight. Otherwise, we would have had to shut down entirely and anger a lot of people who paid good money for a fun evening."

"Who shut us down?" Dan demanded.

"It was Beaufort. Lyon Freedman may run the insurance company, but it's owned by Beaufort, and as soon as he found out, I assure you, he canceled the insurance policy. I couldn't get a rider on the ranch's policy to cover us and keep the permit."

Dan muttered under his breath. "I wish we could get back at that bastard."

"Language, honey," Felicity told him. She twisted her hands. "Is there anything we can do to buy more time?"

Nick had already considered the options. "It's time to pay him back at his game. Dan, when is that town council meeting on the zoning change? The one Beaufort needs to build Countryville?"

Dan pulled out his cell phone. "Monday at five. The council usually meets at seven, after dinner. Odd they called this special meeting so early."

"Maybe so hard-working folks wouldn't come to it." Anger filled him. "Dan, start making phone calls to everyone you know to let them know about the meeting. Beaufort can't get off that easily."

"I can do one better." Dan's eyes narrowed. "Mayor Glen's an old fishing buddy. I'll call him and ask him to push back the meeting until seven. Suggest that if he doesn't those with an interest in bringing new business into town won't have a chance to hear all the reasons why the land should be rezoned."

A hard smile tugged up the corners of Nick's full mouth. "Do it. Shelby darling, cancel all your plans for Monday. We have a date."

Shelby looked at Nick. "Are we storming the castle?"

"You got it, Sweet Pea. You and I are going to that meeting. And come hell or high water, or both, we're going to stall Beaufort in getting his precious theme park."

Chapter 17

Nick had a plan, and it involved her.

On Monday, after breakfast, they headed into town.
For the next few hours, they shopped at the local stores,
and chatted with people Nick hadn't seen since his father's funeral. Each time Shelby spotted someone she
knew who'd done any kind of business with Silas, she
and Nick stopped to talk.

They went to lunch at Flo's café, where Nick turned
heads. He was handsome in his long hair, and even the
scar on his cheek gave him a mysterious flair. As they
sat at a corner booth, Nick facing the door and his back
was to the wall, Shelby heard other patrons whispering.

"They're all speculating about you," she murmured,
glancing at the menu Flo had personally brought over
to them.

"Hope it's good."

"With you, it's always good." Her gaze went to his
scarred cheek. Nick was solid here in town.

And even though she'd spent the past eighteen years
living here, and all her adult life working hard at the

ranch, she still felt slightly insecure around some town leaders because of her parents. Nick might be branded a nomad and a prodigal son, but they welcomed him back with open arms.

Not speculative looks, as some did with her, as if waiting to see if she'd order a beer and pass out drunk on the floor as her daddy sometimes did. Or shoplift clothing, as her mother once did at Sally's Fashion Barn. Silas had to pay her bail on that one, and her mother promised to never do it again.

Silas had been a godsend to Shelby and her sister, Heather. But even he could not erase all the suspicion people like Natalie harbored simply because her parents hadn't been respectable.

At a booth across from them, two town council members sat, eating lunch. They kept giving her suspicious looks, as if expecting her to steal the salt and pepper shakers. She overheard one say loudly, "Thank the good Lord her parents are gone, at least. Worthless drunks."

A blush lit her cheeks. "I'm never going to be good enough for some of the town officials," she muttered, glaring at the glass of ice water Flo had set before her.

His hand reached over, covered hers. "You are good enough, Sweet Pea. Don't mind their opinions."

Nick picked up her hand and brushed a soft kiss across the knuckles. His mouth warmed her, and her nerves tingled from the contact. Shelby smiled, but his words failed to reassure. Her family's reputation had been forged in alcohol and public fights.

His family's reputation was forged in reputable business relationships and long-standing roots in town.

Shelby looked at Nick. In his plain blue T-shirt, leather jacket, faded denim jeans and biker boots, he looked tough. A stranger, who might breeze into the café and get hostile looks from locals who were protective of their own. But this was Nick, and clothing mattered little compared to his family name.

On the other hand, her outfit was stylish, yet not lavish. The beige knit sweater fell past her hips, combined with tight jeans, knee-high brown leather boots and a soft cashmere scarf around her neck. Shelby knew she looked good, and her clothing was as fashionable as Natalie Beaufort's wardrobe.

I might as well be wearing sackcloth. Because some in town, like Mayor Glen, will always eye me with suspicion, as if I'd steal the salt and pepper shakers off the table.

"Well, hello, stranger. Haven't seen both of you in a while."

The familiar drawl cheered her. Shelby looked up as Ann stood at their table in a waitress uniform, a big smile on her face.

"What are you doing here?" Shelby jumped up to hug her friend, who laughed.

"After you quit, there was no point in staying at that greasy spoon." Ann snapped her gum and tapped her pencil on the pad as Shelby sat down again. "Natalie was mighty angry, but there was nothing she could do."

Touched by her friend's loyalty, Shelby felt a lump in her throat. "Thanks, hon. Maybe I could get a job here as well."

"You? You're too smart, Shelby. You could easily work in Nashville as an accountant. Or find a job in a little art boutique. Why stay here in this dump?" Ann swept the café with a visible sneer. "There's nothing here for people our age. That goes for you, too, Nick Anderson. You're too young to get stuck in a backward town like Barlow."

"I'm an old soul," Nick joked.

"Barlow isn't backward," Shelby protested.

A cynical look came over her friend. "Oh? The same town that labels you only because you had loser parents, Shel? No, it's not backward. It's stagnant. Why you stay here is beyond me. You have a college degree, a chance to make something of your life."

She sighed. "Maybe you're right."

"You know I am. You can get a career outside the farm and Barlow. Me?" Ann shrugged. "All I can do is get jobs waiting tables."

"Don't say that." Her tone came out sharper than intended. "You're very smart, Ann. And with a little luck and searching, you can find a better job."

A distant look came over her friend. "Yeah. Maybe someday I will."

Shelby and Nick gave their orders. As Ann lowered her hand, Shelby grabbed her friend's right wrist.

"Whoa, where did you get the sparkler?" The princess-cut diamond had to be a full carat. Surrounded by baguettes on either side, the white gold ring looked mighty expensive. "Did you get engaged and fail to tell me, girl-friend?"

Ann tugged her hand away, a flush covering her cheeks. "Wrong hand, silly. It's a little gift from my new boyfriend."

She felt guilty at neglecting their friendship. "I didn't know you were dating someone special."

"They're all special. This is just my flavor of the week." Ann laughed and winked at Nick. "Want to be next?"

Nick returned the wink and slid his hand over to cover Shelby's palm. "Sorry, darling, I'm taken."

Ann gave a big smile. "Well, good for you both. You'd

better treat Shelby right, Nick Anderson. Or I'll have my new boyfriend beat you up."

"I'm scared," Nick quipped.

"You should be, big guy. He weighs all of a hundred and twenty-five pounds, and most of that is in his glasses." Ann laughed and they joined in.

Ann waved her pad. "Be right up."

He gave the departing Ann a thoughtful look. "Her boyfriend must either be in love or have plenty of disposable cash. That ring is at least six thousand dollars."

Shelby was glad of it. "She deserves a decent man who will treat her right."

Nick gave her an intent look. "So do you, Sweet Pea."

Are you the one? The question was on the tip of her tongue. But here was not the place to ask, not with Flo's crowded with eavesdroppers.

I'll ask him. Soon as this business with the town council is over.

She had to, because she needed to know where she stood with Nick Anderson, no matter what his plans for the ranch were.

At 4:00 p.m. sharp, Shelby met Nick outside by his truck to drive into town for the council meeting. Her jaw dropped upon seeing him stride out of the house, keys jingling in one hand. Gone were the wild, tangled dark blond locks spilling down to his collar. His hair was clipped neatly, and he'd shaved the day beard. Most surprising was the black blazer, crisp white shirt and pressed black trousers he wore, along with polished shoes.

She'd been there when he received the haircut, but combined with the new clothing, he was a completely different man. Handsome before, now he was knock-down gorgeous and stylish.

Shelby's mouth quirked up in amusement as Nick swept her a low bow.

"You shine up very nicely, Nick Anderson."

He ran a hand over his shorter hair. "Reckoned I should dress for the occasion. The biker look only goes so far with local officials."

For this meeting, she'd chosen a turquoise blue embroidered shirt with ruffles, spanking new jeans and her western boots. Instead of pulling back her hair into its usual ponytail, she let it fall loose around her shoulders.

In a briefcase, she carried her speech and notes about Belle Creek's history. Beaufort might try to muscle the council into the zoning change, but she was prepared to dazzle them with reminders of the ranch's long-standing history with the town.

"You look amazing," Nick murmured, as he opened the door for her. "Good enough to eat. Maybe I'll save you for dessert later, after this circus sideshow we're headed to."

Blushing, she climbed into the truck, fisting her hands in her lap to hide their shaking. Public speaking wasn't her strong suit, but if it meant thwarting Beaufort, she'd preach to a stadium filled with people. Shelby had spent several hours last night practicing her speech before a mirror.

They arrived early, as planned, and found two seats in the auditorium close to the stage, where the long table had been set up for the town council.

As people drifted into the room, Nick reached over and held Shelby's hand. Felt good, and his touch grounded her, especially when Chuck Beaufort arrived. He glanced at Shelby, nodded at Nick and took the seat in the front row.

The meeting began, and Mayor Glen read out the proposed zoning change. Then he opened the floor for comments. Tension knotted her stomach. On the stage were the town's most prominent citizens, and she knew they didn't have a high opinion of her. How could she hold her own against them? Make them listen to what she said?

Chuck Beaufort was first to the microphone. In his Italian silk suit and red power tie, Beaufort looked relaxed. Confident, as if he'd already convinced the council to vote for the zoning change. He began his speech, and every single word felt like a hammer on her head.

"Benefits will be many for this town. The future is here and the opportunity is now. The zoning change my company requests will bring jobs to many. It will bring in revenue and growth."

When he finished, Shelby bristled. Nick put a calming hand on her arm, but she shook it off. She marched to the microphone and cleared her throat. "I have something to say."

Forget the planned speech. She decided to speak from the heart, and hopefully, it would hammer home her point to those listening. Though he had finished speaking, Beaufort stood nearby, as if to counter anyone who dared to speak out.

"Benefits will be many to Mr. Beaufort. He's the one who will profit the most. Is there a guaranteed promise of jobs for people in the town, or is he going to bring in his own people from Nashville?"

The developer looked away, a flash of guilt in his eyes. Oh, yeah, she knew he was. Promise jobs to locals on the premise of building the park and then give the jobs to the workers from miles away.

"Developing this land and bringing in a theme park will bring tourists, yes, but lots of traffic and problems," she continued. "Our infrastructure can't support it. It means the burden of more taxes on us for roads, water and sewage, law enforcement and fire protection. Barlow will lose everything we stand for, everything that brings this community charm. I swear it, Barlow will turn from a strongly knit small town into a tourist trap."

She kept hammering at them, but the town council looked at her with the same blank stares as the cows on the Cherrywood Farm next door.

When she finished, Shelby's shoulders sagged. No use. They were sold on Beaufort's proposal, and once the zoning change was approved and the development approved, there was nothing to stand in his way.

Nothing but Nick Anderson and a contract of sale for the three hundred acres Beaufort needed.

The timer dinged, and her five minutes were up. Shelby stepped back, her shoulders straight.

Until Beaufort took the microphone again. "Very eloquent speech, Miss Shelby. Very noble of you to defend the ranch, even though you have no ownership in it."

That sucker punch nearly knocked the breath out of her. Ignoring the frantic waves of the mayor, she gave it right back to Beaufort.

"I don't have the deed to the farm, but I have ownership of it. Everyone does, because the farm has been here for five generations. We all own a piece of its history, as much as we share Flo's café and picnics by the river and the 4-H club. It's what makes this town a real community, not merely a place to live. And if you're too greedy to understand that, then you don't understand what keeps most people in Barlow."

Silence for a moment. Beaufort looked stunned, as if no one ever dared to speak back to him. Then from the back of the room she heard a familiar raspy voice.

"You tell 'em, Shelby!"

Glancing back, she saw Vern Dickerson stand, straight and tall, giving a fist pump to the air. He wore his veterans ball cap. Then he applauded.

The applause began to spread, and it thundered through the room. Filled with pride, she smiled and resumed her seat.

She'd stated her piece, and it felt wonderful. Judging by the approval of the crowd, they thought it was wonderful, too.

The grim faces of the town council disagreed.

Nick gave a gentle squeeze of her hand. "Thanks, Shel," he murmured.

Harvey Glen and the other council members weren't looking at her. They looked at Beaufort. The developer stood nearby, his grin making him resemble a fat Cheshire cat. Elation faded. What was the use? They were on the developer's side. Thought his park meant an infusion of cash, and jobs.

It wasn't her farm. She was only an employee. Maybe it was time to move on. Get a real home of her own, instead of spending all her time trying to save one that seemed impossible to rescue.

Her spine might have looked plenty straight, but she felt ready to crumble. Nick took one look at her.

"If that's all the public has to say, then I move that—" the mayor began.

"Hold on a moment, Harvey," Nick called out.

Climbing over Shelby, Nick approached the microphone. He gave a pointed look to Beaufort, who finally sat down. Then he didn't address the council, but turned to face the packed auditorium.

"Most of you know who I am. Nick Anderson." A slow, charming grin. "I'm the one y'all prayed for in church when I was growing up because my dad said I would be the death of him, and y'all loved Silas."

A few chuckles. Nick continued, his Deep South drawl much more pronounced.

"Y'all call me a hometown hero. I'm no hero. I was doing my job as a SEAL, just like all the other guys who fought. Some paid with their lives. Now I'm back home and I'm asking you to be heroes and vote against this zoning change.

"My family's farm is in trouble. No secret in town. The farm has been a part of this community for five generations. But I'm not addressing my problems. I'm addressing the problems that will happen if you vote on this zoning change and bring in big-city business to this community. All the traffic that will clog up Main Street, the tourists who will bring in more business, yeah, but we'll need more motels and restaurants. Big chain ones. No tourists are gonna come to Main Street to eat at Flo's. All that will be gone. Just a concrete jungle with flashy lights. All that pretty hometown charm gone forever.

"This town's always had charm, warmth and a good dose of neighborly kindness." Nick swept his hard gaze over all the town council. "What's going to happen to the Barlow I grew up in? The town that held a concert each year to raise money for the youth center? The town that came to my family's farm and took sleigh rides at Christmas?"

Murmurs sounded among the audience. Nick turned back to the town council.

"And yeah, Barlow sure could use an infusion of cash-spending tourists. I've been thinking, with the big country-music convention that comes to town each year, no reason why we couldn't throw a concert at the farm of our own. Showcase local talent, and pull in big names from Nashville who'd be happy to help."

He pointed at Mayor Glen, who looked interested. "Harvey, you have connections to agents of some of Nashville's stars. If you could coax some big names into playing on the farm, well, I'd be happy to set up the land for the concert. Might even stretch it to two days, make it a country-western Bonnaroo. Smaller, of course."

He flashed that to-die-for grin again. "Flo, darling, I reckon the tourists would love that homemade cherry pie you make. You could set up a stand, we'd have food concessions, the works. And people would need places to stay, so there would be a need for more motels. I reckon once they came and saw our small-town charm, they'd want to return for shopping on Main for quilting supplies or picnics by the river, even a petting zoo." He pointed to Howard Freelander. "Howard, I bet if you set one up, people would love to bring their kids and buy some of your wife's apple butter."

Now the murmurs rose to excited voices. The council looked impressed—most of all, Mayor Glen, who owned a musical instrument shop in town that sold vintage guitars. Shelby silently cheered on Nick. All the things she'd said had fallen on stone-deaf ears with the town council. They ignored her. But Nick wasn't having that. They would not ignore him. Not now. Not ever.

He was an Anderson. A hero.

Mayor Glen pounded the gavel. "Order."

"If you want, I'd be happy to work up a proposal for you to look over." Nick hooked his thumbs into the belt loops of his trousers. "Sound good? I'd need two weeks to work on it."

He glanced at the other four members of the council. "I move that the council postpone the business of the zoning change until three weeks from today."

"Hey, wait a minute," Beaufort argued, but Mayor Glen pounded the gavel again.

The council voted 4-1 to postpone the zoning change. Nick stood up and gave Beaufort a mock salute as the man scowled at him.

Then he took Shelby's arm, escorting her out of the room as people called out to him, waved and smiled at him. And they waved at her as well. For the first time, Shelby felt like a real part of this community.

When they had climbed into the truck and were headed back to the farm, Shelby thanked him. Nick smiled, a real smile this time.

"I'll need your help with writing the proposal, gathering the information. Dan's, too. He was great at organizing the pumpkin patch. I'm sure he can work out the details on the land, how many facilities we'll need, the works. Maybe get the town to pay for the sheriff's office for security details."

"That was very good. The council listens to you."

Nick gave a self-deprecating shrug. "They know Beaufort's development sounds good for the town, but it'll change everything. I reinforced what you said, Shel."

"Does this mean you're staying? Or was that all a speech to delay things?"

Nick sighed. "I promised you I'd stay until we got the money or the bank foreclosed, Shel. I aim to stick to that."

"And after? If they vote on the proposal, or they don't, what are you doing then?"

One hand on the steering wheel tightened to white-knuckle intensity. "Let's take it one step at a time. Can't we celebrate the victory of Beaufort not getting his way?"

One day at a time. Oh, she was so good at living that way. And tired of it, never having a future, always being the responsible one to make sure all flowed smoothly. Suddenly it wasn't good enough. "We need to figure out a plan for next month if the council doesn't approve your plan, Nick. Did you see Bob Miller's face? He voted against the postponement. He's firmly in Beaufort's pocket. He'll find a way to get the others to turn down whatever you come up with."

Nick turned his head, frowning. "When did you turn into such a pessimist, Shelby? What happened to the girl who was determined to make the best of it?"

Anger bubbled up inside her. It finally exploded like a firecracker.

"She grew up, Nick. Someone had to, while you were off, not caring what happened here, not sticking around. Someone had to deal with the repairs, the bills, your father getting sick and someone trying to run us off the property and sell to Beaufort. You never wrote. Never kept in touch."

He pulled off to the side of the road and shut off the engine. Nick twisted his body around to face her.

"If I hadn't left, Silas and I would have come to blows. My old man was right. I was headed on a highway to hell and ruin, and that's why I left, Shelby. The navy straightened my ass out. Don't lecture me about responsibility.

I sent money home when I could. When Jake wrote and told me things were tight, I sent more."

Stunned, she stared at him. "Jake never said a word about it."

He pushed a hand through his hair. "I told him I didn't want Silas knowing where the money came from. I knew how proud the old man was, and how he'd never turn to me for help. I did write. I did keep in touch."

Tension made his jaw taut. "I wrote Dad a letter after boot camp. Told him about how I needed the navy to straighten out, kick my butt into shape. Told him my plans for being a SEAL and how I wasn't going to give up until I made the teams. And then I made the teams and called home to tell him. He promised to show up at the ceremony. He didn't. Said he had to deal with a horse show."

Shelby swallowed hard. "I'm sorry, Nick. He did. It was a crazy time, none of us could spare a moment. He wanted to fly out there, but we needed that revenue."

"I can understand that. But I became invisible to him after I became a SEAL. I wrote, because Silas hated email. I asked him to tell you, Jake and Dan and his family about what I was doing. He never wrote back. I wrote him again, and he never wrote back. Finally, after ten letters, I gave up. What was the point? Jake was the only one who wrote one or two letters. No one else did. Not one letter, email or phone call. I'd get deployed down range, not knowing if I was going to come home in a body bag, and the worst part of it? I had no family who cared if I lived or died."

Her heart tumbled to her stomach as he fisted his hands, his breathing ragged. "I'd walk off that plane and all the other guys had girlfriends, wives, fathers, mothers, families and friends to greet them, wave flags, give hugs. Me? I had no one. So I figured all of you wanted it that way, and I never looked back."

At a loss for words, she remained silent a moment. All the years she'd resented Nick for leaving a family she thought was gold, thinking he was too good to stay in touch with his father because he was a hotshot SEAL. All the time he'd been pining for connection from home. Wanting his dad to keep in touch. And Silas had never done so.

"We never got those letters." She struggled to speak as emotion closed her throat. "Silas never told us. Not me, anyway. And Jake never said anything. I know you had problems with your dad, but he was a good man. He was strict and tough, but I know he loved you, Nick. He told me how worried he was about you in the navy. Each time we heard another SEAL got killed in action, he'd pray it wasn't you. He was very proud of you, Nick."

Shadows lingered in his dark, haunted gaze. "Then why didn't he ever tell me, Shelby? When I got wounded and ended up in Walter Reed, I thought about calling home. I needed him. But then I remembered all those times he told me I'd never amount to anything, and here I was, broken and bloody, failing him all over again. No one was there for me."

Shelby couldn't help it. She scooted over to his side, and her arms enveloped him. Nick resisted at first. "I'm here for you now, Nick."

His wide shoulders finally lost their tension as he relaxed in her tight embrace. He rested his cheek against her hair. "I'm so broken still, Shelby. I can't believe he's gone, and I never had a chance to say goodbye. No one told me he was that sick."

Tears stung her eyes. "He didn't want anyone worrying. It wasn't until it was too late, and he wound up in the hospital, that we realized how sick he was. Silas never said a word about the letters. I'm so sorry, Nick. We didn't even know you'd been wounded until your lieutenant called. And after you got discharged from the hospital, we couldn't find you. Silas told me he figured you wanted to be alone."

He kept stroking her hair, as if the motion anchored him. "I went through a bad period after I left the hospital, Shel. Even slept on the streets for a while, trying to regain my sense of purpose. If it weren't for my former teammates, I'd probably be dead by now. My good friend Cooper set me up with a job near Bethesda, and Jarrett got me a set of wheels. He lectured me like a big brother, got my head straightened out."

Silently she thanked those friends, and felt a stabbing regret that his own family had let him down. Just as her parents had failed her, Nick's family hadn't supported him, either. There were many layers to this man, and she'd unpeeled one of them.

Gently, he untangled himself from her tight grip. "Hey, darling, don't cry. It's okay now."

Shelby sniffled. "All those wasted years. If I knew you'd written to Silas, tried to stay in touch, I'd have demanded he answer you."

Nick smiled a little. "I know. You were always there for me, Shel. Thanks."

"So does this mean you're going to stay?"

Chuckling, he wiped away a tear with the pad of his thumb. "We'll see, Sweet Pea."

They had a big job ahead of them.

Chapter 18

Leaden light filtered through the frilly pink curtains at the bedroom window as Nick awoke the next morning. The sky was gray with the approaching dawn. He stared at the ceiling, amused at the stars glued there. Peace filled him. Last night, making love with Shelby had been incredible. He could spend a lifetime with her, and never get enough.

Curled against him, Shelby slept, her long hair tousled, a faint red mark on her neck where he'd loved her last night. Nick stroked the mark of his possession, reminding himself to be gentler in the future. She had delicate skin.

Her eyes fluttered open and she gave him a sleepy smile. "Good morning, hot buns."

Chuckling, he stroked her hair. "Hot buns?"

"You do have a very cute butt. What are you doing awake?"

Nick grinned, liking the new nickname. "Admiring you," he said softly.

Shelby reached out, touched his cheek. "I could do the same to you. Except it's too early."

"It's almost six," he pointed out.

"Well, you promised we could sleep in."

"This is sleeping in, sleepyhead," he teased, tugging at a strand of her silky hair. "Even if the stars are still out."

At her puzzled frown he pointed upward. Shelby sighed. "Those stars make me sad."

"Then let's pull them down and toss them into the sky, where they belong." He didn't usually get this whimsical. "I don't want to see you sad."

"It won't matter. Felicity put them there, and no one had the heart to tell her to take them down." Shelby glanced upward. "They were for the baby."

His stomach gave an unpleasant lurch. "What baby?"

"A little over a year ago, she was pregnant with a daughter. But Felicity miscarried at five months. This bedroom was going to be hers." Shelby rested her head on Nick's shoulder. "It's why she's become so rigid in the past year, between the loss and the ranch losing money. Felicity tries to control whatever she can, because it seems like everything is slipping out of her grasp."

Now he understood his cousin's wife better. Nick was glad she seemed to be making a turnaround. But today he didn't want to talk about his family. Today was for celebrating a small victory, and for Shelby.

Rolling over, he gave her a deep kiss.

Shelby looked up at him tenderly as he pulled away. "Why, Nick Anderson, you must be a morning person."

"Yes, I am."

And then he pulled her into his arms once more to show her exactly how much he was.

* * *

Nick showered quickly and dressed in a flannel shirt and gray sweatpants.

Shelby had fallen asleep, a slight smile on her face, when he emerged from the bathroom. Nick grabbed his cell phone and left the bedroom, closing the door behind him.

Whistling, he went downstairs to make coffee. When it was finished he fetched a big mug with a horse on it and poured a cup. Standing at the French doors overlooking the pasture, he admired the sunlight dappling the oak and magnolia trees near the house.

His cell phone rang. Nick picked it up from the kitchen counter. Jarrett was an early riser, like him. But this wasn't Jarrett's number.

"Kurt," he said, answering the phone. "What's up that you're calling before seven on a Tuesday morning?"

A long, heavy sigh. "I'm sorry, Nick. Bad news. The bank has called in your loan."

The phone nearly fell from his fingers. Nick gripped it so tight, his fingers hurt. "What the hell? When? How?"

He listened to the details, his stomach tightening. When he hung up, Nick nearly threw his cell across the room. Instead he sat at the table, and buried his head into his hands. Should have known that son of a bitch wouldn't want to stall.

Beaufort. Beaufort hadn't liked being thwarted at the council meeting. He still pulled the strings, and now he'd pulled the ranch's loan.

They had twenty-four hours to pay back the entire loan, not just the sixty thousand dollars for the back payments and the balloon that had been due.

There was no way on earth Nick could pay back a loan of that magnitude in one day. Bracing his hands on the kitchen table, he stared out at the pasture that had been in his family for five generations.

He was going to have to sell.

Nick was selling the ranch, leaving her homeless.

Shelby struggled to breathe as he told her the news over breakfast. They were alone in the house, as Dan and his family had gone back to Knoxville to look for a new house. Jake was spending the night in town with friends.

She could only stare helplessly at him, unable to summon even a fake smile as she'd done when her sister left.

His chocolate-brown gaze remained steady, the small tic in his cheek the only evidence of emotion. "The bank called in the note last night, Shel. I'm going to make all the arrangements. By tomorrow afternoon, Belle Creek won't be mine. I'm meeting Kurt Mohler at his office downtown later today to sign the papers."

A tremendous roar sang in her ears. She wanted to shake her head, get rid of the sound buzzing there. It sounded like the crash of all her hopes and dreams.

"Nick, you can stall for more time… Silas would be heartbroken."

He tensed and shoved a hand through his hair. "I already informed Dan and Jake. Dan and his family made plans to move to Knoxville. Jake has a bead on a job training champion jumpers in upstate New York. As for Hank, Mario and John, I'm going to give them severance, of course."

She bit her lip. "So I'm out of a job. And the apartment, too, it seems."

"Soon as I have the cash from the sale, I'm putting thirty thousand dollars into your personal account for all you've done for the ranch, Shelby. It's enough to fund a

fresh start, or go to Paris and study art." He shoved a hand
through his thick, short hair. "I'm afraid you'll have to
vacate the garage apartment. I'm certain Beaufort will
want everything emptied so he can demolish it. I can
help you with that."

Her voice held only a slight quaver. "And where are
you going?"

Nick flicked his hand into the air. "I don't know yet.
Maybe head south to Florida for the winter."

Tightness compressed her chest, so tight and hot she
could barely breathe. Shelby looked out the French doors,
struggling to comprehend his words. Her helpless gaze
took in the oaks and sycamores turning brilliant colors,
the horses peacefully cropping grass in the pasture. All
this would soon vanish. She tried to memorize it, as one
would memorize each brushstroke of a favorite painting.
She couldn't move, couldn't make herself leave him, leave
the table and return home to make arrangements to find
another place to live.

Home? She had no more home. After eighteen years
of security and stability, she felt adrift. A festering panic
seized her—she knew this was the end of something quite
precious and important and perhaps she'd never get it
back. Not the home she'd known for nearly two decades.

Nick.

Shelby wanted to hold on to the moment, to capture it
like artists put ships into bottles. She wanted to turn back
the clock to the moments before her world crashed down.
Nick was leaving, moving on, and what they had shared,
the laughter, sharing and love, was about to vanish.

It hadn't been more than mere sex, or friendship. It
had just...been.

He wants to get rid of you. Time to move on, and pick

up the pieces and get out. Don't be a fool and stand here, letting him see how much he's hurt you. C'mon, Shelby, have a little pride and dignity.

But it hurt far too much, an excruciating pain that settled in like an old friend stretching its legs, the same hurt that haunted her ten years ago. This time, it was worse. Shelby gripped her coffee cup so tight her hands hurt. Gathering her lost composure, she forced herself to speak slowly and quietly, forcing down the bubble of hysteria that wanted to shriek and holler.

"Thank you for the kind offer, Nick, but I'll find a place on my own. Pay me what the ranch owes me for the work I've done for Belle Creek. No more."

"Fine. Seeing as you haven't taken a salary six months, it's more than thirty thousand dollars."

"I can't believe you're doing this. Nick, there has to be a way to fight it," she blurted.

He closed his eyes and rubbed the bridge of his nose. "I've done all I can."

"So you'll pack up and leave. Run away like you did ten years ago." Misery engulfed her and she released her hands on the coffee cup. She hurt enough, without having this pain. Shelby rubbed her aching fingers.

Mouth compressed, Nick stared at the doors. "I'm not running. But I know when it's time to give up."

"Like you gave up being a SEAL? Gave up on Silas and trying to understand him? And now you're giving up on Belle Creek." Her voice dropped. "On us, Nick. I could have helped you make this work. I was willing to try. You're stronger than you think, Nick. Don't give up. You have it in here—" she pressed a hand to her heart "—to give it a fighting chance."

A tic began in his cheek. "I gave it a fighting chance,

Shelby, but I know when something is futile. Unless you have two hundred and fifty thousand dollars to spare, Belle Creek will be sold. As for my father, that's my private business."

"This is your home." She pushed away the coffee cup. Liquid sloshed over the side, spilling onto the table. "My home, too."

The cheek tic became more pronounced. "Why stay here, anyway? Barlow isn't special. Take the money, start new someplace else. Go to Seattle with Heather, travel, but don't stay here. There's nothing here for you."

She gave him a long look, filled with sadness, anger and hurt. "Yes, you're right. I thought there was, Nick. There was you. But not anymore."

Leaving him sitting at the table, she went upstairs to gather her things. She had much packing to do, and not much time.

Her heart ached with each step she took up the stairs.

Chapter 19

He had something special with Shelby, and now it was lost.

Nick felt like the lowest kind of worm as he rode on his Harley to the graveyard. Maybe his dad was right. He was a failure. He'd given up on the ranch. Given up on a future with Shelby, the only woman he ever truly loved.

Startled at the thought, he pulled into the cemetery. Love? Yeah, he had done it all right. Fallen in love with the girl next door, the one woman he would yank out his eyeteeth to prevent anyone from hurting.

No, you did a good enough job of that yourself.

Near a group of trees and a serene pond, Nick parked his bike on the access road and switched off the motor. Bypassing the graves with their bronze vases of red, blue and pink silk flowers, he headed for the mortuary, where the ashes were interred. On the marble facade were bronze markers. One read simply Anderson. Silas and Marlene.

He rested his hand against the cool marble, his throat closing.

"Hey, Dad." He swallowed hard, looked around. No one here. So quiet. Peaceful. A fountain bubbled in the midst of the pond flanking the building. Oak, maple and hickory trees had begun to shed their colors.

Seasons changing. Life going on.

So many regrets.

A bronze vase of red and blue silk flowers sat atop the marker reading Silas Anderson. Someone had thoughtfully placed the flowers there to remember Silas.

Shelby, maybe. Or Jake or Dan. He was glad they'd done it. Made the place seem less cold and bleak.

He struggled to contain his feelings. Needing control, he began to read the nearby markers.

Anderson, Judith.

Nick blinked back tears and stared at the stone. He'd never come here, never had a reason, for Silas wasn't sentimental and after losing Nick's mom, he said visiting the dead was a waste of time. *Best way to honor your mother is hard work, doing what she wanted for you*, Silas had snapped when Nick had timidly asked about visiting her grave.

He never noticed the name. Too much of a coincidence. Anderson, Judith. A small round photo was set into the marble. A round face, laughing eyes and dark hair.

Pretty, animated. A relative?

Nick studied the other markers. His uncle Charles. Aunt Ida next to him. Dan and Jake's mother, Gert, and their father, James.

Who was Judith Anderson?

Only twenty-four years old when she died twenty-nine years ago. Silas never mentioned a cousin or any other relatives. Yet here she was, buried in the family crypt.

Someone had left a faded teddy bear, its brown fur turned nearly white, beneath the marker.

A note was scribbled next to it. He picked it up, unfurled it.

Miss you, sweetheart. My love will always be with you.
Johnny

Who was Johnny?

Nick didn't like mysteries. Liked them less with his family. Silas wasn't around anymore to ask. Maybe he should have come home sooner. Maybe he could have talked the old man into going to the hospital quicker, giving him a fighting chance. Moisture stung his eyes. He didn't wipe away the tears, but let them flow this time.

"I'm sorry, Dad," he whispered, looking up at his father's bronze marker. "I'm sorry I disappointed you. Sorry I didn't come home sooner so I could say goodbye."

He removed his SEAL pin from his jeans pocket, and placed it next to the red and blue silk flower arrangement.

"This is for you, Dad. I hope wherever you are, you're proud of me. I did it for me, but I did it for you, too."

Nick walked to a nearby bench and sat, burying his head into his hands, releasing the grief over all the lost years. Maybe that was their problem. Too much alike, clashing against each other. He thrived on challenges, like Silas had. Sought them out, needing adventure and action—he hadn't been content to stay in Tennessee, his feet firmly planted on the ground like his cousins had.

Yet now, he realized there was more to life than roaming. He'd been restless, impatient to grab adventure by both hands. The rebellious teenager was gone now, replaced by a man sobered by too many brushes with death.

Maybe life was about a different kind of adventure, the type you had when a woman waited for you at home, and you never knew what the next turn in the road with her would bring.

He felt the pull of the road already, but it wasn't as insistent as before. Because of Shelby. Not just the ranch. Shelby, with her willingness to fight, to rise above everything life doled out to her and make it count. Shelby, who sacrificed everything to take care of her sister, and her nephew.

While he'd run away to seek thrills, she'd been staying here in Barlow, her feet firmly planted on the ground. As steady as the flowing seasons.

Shelby deserved a second chance, just as Belle Creek did.

Filled with dread, Nick dug out Silas's letter from his pocket and finally read the rest of the letter.

When you were young, I was hard on you because I feared you were headed to a bad end. If I was too tough and didn't show enough affection, I am sorry. You are too much like your father, stubborn and proud, but I love you. I only want the best for you. You're a grown man now, and you've done well. Find a good woman, Nicolas. Find her and hold her close, and never let her go. She'll be the one to stick it out with you through the hard times and celebrate the good.

I had faith in you all those years ago, son, and I have faith in you now. Don't let our feud be the reason Belle Creek is destroyed. Years of living

history are etched in that soil. We Andersons owe it to the town, to good people like Shelby, who love the ranch, to save it. No matter what you decide, I'll always be proud of you.
Your loving father, Silas

Nick smoothed out the paper with a trembling hand. His old man was proud of him. No matter what. Words he'd always longed to hear stood out in stark relief on the white paper.

Selling Belle Creek to Beaufort was selling himself out, and depriving the town of a landmark. He could do this. Hell, Shelby had faith in him. Shelby believed in him. Hometown hero.

No, only a man determined to do what was right, and save a living piece of history.

Swallowing hard, he dug out his phone and scrolled through the contacts. Maybe there was a way to save Belle Creek after all. He did have friends. Before he'd been too damn proud to tell them, same as he'd been too proud to ask for help after he'd been sprung from Walter Reed.

Jarrett Adler answered on the first ring. "Nomad. Coop told me your family home was in trouble. You okay?"

Nick leaned his arm against the tree. "Jarrett, I have a favor to ask…"

Two hours later, Nick waited in the office of a local attorney Jarrett recommended. The wire transfer of the cash and the legal documents would take another hour. Plenty of time before the midnight deadline imposed by the bank.

Take that Beaufort, he silently thought.

Former Navy SEAL Jarrett Adler had married into a very wealthy family. And Lacey, Jarrett's devoted wife, readily agreed to paying the two hundred and fifty thousand dollars Belle Creek owed to the bank, and giving Nick a new mortgage with a more reasonable interest rate.

He'd already texted Shelby with the terrific news, and left a message on Jake's phone. Now he dialed Dan's phone number. His cousin sounded cheerful, but Nick cut him off with the news. "I'm not selling to Beaufort."

Silence on the line. Then Dan spoke in a weary voice. "Make up your damn mind, Nick. You suddenly find all that money under a tree?"

Nick looked at the sleek table and the bookcases lined with law manuals. "Something like that. I found a way to pay off the mortgage without selling outright. Called an old buddy."

"Why?" Dan blurted.

"Shelby said something that made me change my mind. And Silas did as well. I'm doing this for her." He paused. "For the entire town. Belle Creek is living history."

"Shelby." A snort. "She's interfered too much. Silas always listened to her, not his own damn kin. Shelby should learn to shut up."

Anger curled low in his belly. "Shelby has done a hell of a lot for Belle Creek. Stop insulting her. I'll have provisions for you and Felicity—"

"Provisions won't put a down payment on the house we're buying in Knoxville. You're being a selfish bastard, Nick. If it weren't for Jake, we'd never have money to even rent."

"When you get home, we're going to talk, Dan."

"I'm nearly there. Left this morning to return back

to Belle Creek to retrieve some things. And when I see Shelby, I'll give her something to think about."

"Dan, wait…"

The line clicked off. Nick studied his phone with a frown. His cousin was clearly upset that Nick had decided against selling for a profit. There went the cash Dan counted on to buy the Knoxville house.

Was Dan the person behind all the vandalism at the ranch, and the arson?

Jake had given them rental money. Of course, Jake was a bachelor, who eschewed spending money and liked to sleep in the stables.

Then again.

Nick clicked on his phone and accessed his notes about the list of websites he'd jotted down that Jake had visited in the past two weeks. Nothing unusual, except Jake had been accessing his bank account a lot. Same as Dan had. And he had the log-ins and passwords for both accounts, thanks to his cyber hacking skills.

He went to the website of the bank Jake used, and entered his cousin's log-in and password. Then he scrolled through the deposits and withdrawals to see how much money Jake had given Dan.

Son of a bitch.

Nick told the receptionist to have the attorney handle the wire transfer to the bank to pay the mortgage. Sick with worry for Shelby, Nick raced out of the office. Shelby was alone at Belle Creek. And if what he suspected was true, trouble was headed straight for her.

Chapter 20

Homeless again.

Shelby knew she could move in with Ann temporarily, but she hated imposing, especially since her friend was dating someone new. At least now she didn't have to worry about Timmy. Instead, she'd phoned a few places and found a boardinghouse in town. It would suffice until she figured out her next step.

Seattle? Too far, and Heather and Pete needed time alone with Timmy. Shelby thought of her watercolors, and her love of art. Nick was right. It was time for a fresh start. By selling the ranch, he forced her into doing the one thing she'd dreaded, and longed for, her entire life. Change.

Shelby finished packing her suitcase. Later, she'd ask Nick to sell the furniture. She wanted to start fresh, without any burdens. Her heart ached as she swept her gaze around the apartment. Of everything on Belle Creek, she'd miss Nick the most.

She headed to the house to say her private goodbyes to each room. Dan and his family were returning tomorrow to pack their belongings. Jake was probably with his new girlfriend. He'd texted her earlier, telling her that he would be gone most of the day.

No doubt Beaufort would bulldoze the house as soon as the ink was dry on the contract to sell.

When she finished downstairs, she went through each bedroom. In Jake's room, she paused at the French doors opening to the balcony, and then opened the doors to air out the room. Jake always kept this room so clean and neat. Seldom had he slept here.

For the first time, she wondered why Nick's cousin never stamped his personality onto this room. He was family, and Silas always treated him well. Her fingers trailed over the spotless bureau. Jake had won trophies in equestrian jumping competitions, including a Rolex awarded to him when he rode Readalot in the Winter Equestrian Festival in Wellington, Florida. Jake had been so proud of that Rolex.

Had he sold it?

She opened the top drawer and rummaged through the items. Socks, jockey shorts. A smile touched her face at the old joke Jake used to always recite. *Can't be a good rider without your jockey shorts.*

No Rolex. But a piece of paper caught her eye, stuffed way into the back. Shelby pulled it free.

A check for ten thousand dollars made out to Jake, from Chuck Beaufort. Hand trembling, she stared at the numbers.

Jake was working with Beaufort. Not Dan, as Nick suspected.

She had to alert Nick, fast. Maybe he could stop the sale, use this as leverage to get a judge to stall for time. As she fished her cell out of her jeans pocket, she saw a text from Nick. Shelby started to read it when footsteps sounded outside the bedroom door.

"You know what they say about snoops," a deep voice drawled. "Curiosity killed the cat."

She started to turn, and something hit her head hard. Then the darkness rushed up and she felt no more.

Her head pounded, and her jaw ached. Shelby woke up to find herself on the cabin floor. Arms and legs trussed, she could not move. The stench of gasoline filled her nostrils.

Blinking hard, she forced herself to focus. *Don't panic. Panic won't solve anything.*

Her vision finally cleared. She scanned the room. On the table close to her was a metal laptop and a case bulging with papers.

Jake stood by the back wall, splashing liquid onto the wood beams. There was a woman with him. The woman turned.

"Ann?" Shelby struggled to sit up. "Ann, help me!"

"Right." Her best friend laughed. "Help you? You brought all this on yourself, you stupid bitch. Nick should have sold. He would have sold to Beaufort if not for your little pep talk. Now, we have no choice. Once you're dead, and the cabin's gone, Nick will be so filled with guilt he'll change his mind. He won't want to keep Belle Creek. He'll sell to Chuck, climb on that bike of his and take off, never looking back."

Her best friend had been her enemy all this time. Feeling utterly betrayed, Shelby looked at Jake, who ducked his head. He tossed aside the empty container as Ann removed a lighter from her pocket.

Shelby looked at Jake, desperate to reason with him.

"Jake, this is murder. You're not like this. Please, don't ruin your life. They will find out. Nick will find out."

Jake laughed. "Nick? He won't. And I'll be long gone. Nick, the hero! My whole damn life with Silas, all I ever heard about was how wonderful Nick was, how smart and clever."

He seized her hair and she cried out. "You know why Silas never found out where Nick was stationed, or deployed? Because I burned all those damn letters. I was sick and tired of hearing about my damn cousin."

Understanding came to her. Jake had hidden away all his anger and jealousy. All the time Silas was being hard on Nick, he was also praising his son to Jake.

"You set the barn on fire! You almost killed Timmy!"

A shadow touched his face. "I didn't know the kid was in there. I swear it."

Encouraged, she pressed on. "You're not a murderer, Jake. You're better than that."

He shook his head and went to the table to join Ann. "No, Shelby, you're wrong. I'll do anything to get away from this damn prison. It's too late."

She was going to burn alive. Shelby thought fast. Greed had brought them to this point. Perhaps greed would work to buy her time.

"Before you light that, you should know the secret of Henry's treasure will die with me."

Both Jake and Ann turned.

"I know where the treasure is."

"Where?" Jake fisted his hands. "Uncle Silas never told us."

"He never searched as thoroughly as I did. I lived in this cabin for a week when he was renovating the garage apartment."

A small lie, but Jake wouldn't know, for at that time he'd been on the equestrian jumping circuit.

"Tell us where it is." Ann held out the gun. "Or you die now."

"Untie me and I'll tell you." She forced down her fear and stared Ann straight in the eye. "Won't do you any good if I'm dead."

Jake loosened her bonds as Ann trained the pistol on her. Shelby marched to the fireplace, her head pounding, her heart racing. She had one shot at this…

Pretending to stumble, she started to fall, then she kicked Jake hard. Jake grabbed her as he staggered backward, and as he did, she twisted hard. He released her with a cuss as they started to fall.

"Shelby!"

That dear, familiar voice filled her with hope and fear.

"She's got a gun," Shelby screamed out in warning.

Nick charged into the room, cocking his pistol. Ann fired back, but she was no match for Nick's skills. She dropped the gun and raced for the back of the cabin.

Shelby was on the move, swinging wildly at Jake. *Don't miss, don't miss…*

Contact! She hit him hard with the steel casing of the laptop, and he staggered back. Nick tackled him and slugged him hard on the chin.

Recovering from the earlier blow, Jake tackled Nick. Nick elbowed the back of Jake's head and the man did not move. Then she heard a window breaking. Ann laughed as she crawled through the broken window, and then she tossed in the burning candle. The back of the cabin went up in flames with a loud whoosh of air. Black smoke filled the air and filled her lungs.

"Let her go," Nick shouted. "Shel, get out of here."

"Jake."

"I'll get him."

He dragged Jake out of the burning cabin as Shelby ran to the water pump, using the hose to spray the cabin. Soon, sirens rang out in the air. Nick secured Jake's wrists with his leather belt and then helped her spray down the walls.

"I thought you were dead," Nick said hoarsely. "Dan told me he was headed back here to talk to you. I never imagined Jake was the threat."

"How did you know I was here?" She handed him the hose and hugged him hard, her heart racing still.

"Cyber spying. I read an email from Ann to Jake, telling him of the plan to 'dispose' of you in the cabin. Once you were gone, I'd sell out of guilt. Damn, Shel, I almost lost you."

She regarded him with a stern look. "And how did you cyber spy, Nick Anderson? Did you install some kind of software that spied on me as well?"

The sheepish look on his face told the answer. "On everyone who used the ranch's Wi-Fi. Sorry. I only examined the network communications that looked suspicious. It was originally to protect the ranch from outside hackers, not for capturing sensitive data on the network. But after Dan told me he had money from Jake to rent a house in Knoxville, I hacked into Jake's bank account and saw several healthy deposits from Chuck Beaufort."

"You're forgiven."

Minutes later, the police arrived with the fire department. Jonah Doyle rushed over, looking at Jake on the ground as the firefighters took to spraying down the flames.

"Guess you found the culprit, Anderson." The sheriff gestured to one of the deputies. "Bob, take them back to the house."

In his patrol car, Jonah's deputy took them back to the house. As they pulled up into the drive, Felicity and Dan stood near their truck.

An unconscious Ann was sprawled out on the driveway.

"What happened?" Nick demanded.

"We saw the fire and Felicity went inside to see if anyone was home. Ann came driving up in the ATV. She was dirty and sooty and had a knife. She told me if I didn't give her our truck, she'd kill me." Pride was evident in Dan's voice as he looked at his wife. "Felicity came out of the house and beaned her."

"What did you use as a weapon?" Shelby asked.

Her expression one of astonishment, Felicity looked at the unconscious Ann. "My mother's canned peaches. I asked Mom for more to sell. I thought every dime would help."

"Killer fruit," Nick quipped as the deputy hauled the moaning Ann to her feet and hustled her into the patrol car. "First you with the laptop, Shel, and now Felicity with fruit. No one messes with our women."

"My wife, the champion fighter of canning." Dan slid an arm around Felicity and hugged her tight.

Telling Dan about his brother was going to be tough. Nick drew his cousin aside. Shelby gestured to Felicity to join her on the porch to give the two men privacy.

"I never did like Ann." Felicity frowned, and looked at Shelby. "Did you know she called you a trashy hick last year when she came to the ranch to check on her horse? I overheard her saying it to Natalie."

Shelby blinked. "No. Why didn't you tell me?"

The woman sighed. "I was still recovering from losing the baby. My head was messed up. At one point, I hated the world, and I really didn't like how you seemed to be first in Silas's affections. I'm sorry, Shelby. You were so nice to me, and I wanted to be friends, but I felt too insecure. You're so smart and motivated…and all I know how to do is can fruit."

The woman's confession stunned her. All the time Shelby had thought her snobbish as she tried to make friends with her, but Felicity felt too shy to reach out.

"You're underrating yourself," she told her. "You're an amazing wife and mother. And you were wonderful with Timmy. Thank you for that."

Nick and Dan returned to the porch. Dan slid an arm around his wife's waist. He looked pale, but stoic.

Nick joined Shelby on the porch steps. "I don't want you to move until the EMTs get here to check out you."

Shelby smiled, resting against Nick. "I'm fine."

He cupped her chin. "Let's have the EMTs determine that. I'm still insisting you go to the hospital to get checked out."

"Really, I'm going to be okay."

It was going to be okay.

Better than okay.

Chapter 21

Ten days after the fire, it was time to make a fresh start.

Jonah Doyle and his deputies had hauled Ann and Jake off in patrol cars. Jonah then paid a visit to Chuck Beaufort, taking a pair of handcuffs.

After his arrest, Beaufort arranged for a plea deal with the district attorney's office. He'd confessed to hiring Jake to sabotage the ranch and leave threatening notes for Nick in exchange for a percentage in the theme park Beaufort planned to build. Ann, who had loved to eavesdrop on Natalie at the restaurant, had overheard the developer talking to Jake one late night. She'd blackmailed both to get her own cut, promising to run Shelby out of town. It was Ann who left the roaches and the rat in Shelby's locker at work.

Desperate to keep his secret, Jake became lovers with Ann, stealing Felicity's jewelry so they could have quick cash to buy a new truck no one could trace. They planned to leave Barlow and live in Kentucky.

Dan and Felicity had agreed to remain at the ranch, with Dan in charge of restoring Belle Creek to its former glory as a showpiece for equestrian jumpers to train. The money would come from the sale of the cabin and its surrounding fifty acres to a local preservation foundation, which planned to restore the cabin and open it to tourists. The sale of the land allowed Nick to partly repay Jarrett, who asked only for the ranch to be part of the underground railroad he was building for battered women to stay in safe houses. The garage apartment would make excellent temporary guest quarters for those women on their way to a new life and new identity through Project SOS.

Nick hadn't asked her to move out of the garage apartment. Neither did he say she could stay. Instead, he'd been closemouthed about any future plans for her.

Today, Nick insisted on taking her out to the burned cabin. Riding on the ATV, they passed Dan supervising a group of construction workers rebuilding the barn. He waved to them.

When they reached the cabin, it saddened her to see the ruins. But at least the fire hadn't spread to the entire structure, thanks to the diligent efforts of the Barlow fire department and Nick's zealous insistence on maintaining the pump at the cabin.

Nick parked the ATV and helped Shelby climb off.

Hands in his jeans pockets, Nick studied the charred ruins. "A piece of history is gone. But it will be rebuilt."

"The kind of building Chuck Beaufort wouldn't like to see. Thanks to you, and your friend Jarrett, Belle Creek is saved." She leaned against him as he kissed the top of her head.

Picking their way through the ruins, they walked through the cabin. The fire had claimed the back portion of the cabin, but the front had been spared by the fire department.

Shelby looked at the fireplace, remembering how she and Nick had made love here. She touched the masonry, trailing her finger along it, and downward.

"Seems odd old Henry's treasure was never found," he murmured into her ear.

Crouching down, her fingers combed over the soot-stained bricks. "Nick, did your dad ever check this fireplace? Is it the original?"

"Yeah, he said he did. The bricks should be all original. Dad was meticulous about maintaining the history of the cabin."

"Then what about this marking?" She pointed to a pair of bricks on the fireplace's right side, near the hearth. Both bore small heart symbols.

He frowned. "Could be Henry carved the hearts. Or something else."

Taking out his knife, he dug into the mortar and then removed two bricks, revealing a hollow space.

Shelby peered at the findings as he removed a small packet of papers. Nick began scanning them as Shelby looked inside the hollow, wondering if Henry's treasure was there as well. Finally he looked up, his eyes filled with wonder. To her surprise, tears swam in his dark eyes.

"What's wrong? Are the letters clues to where Henry buried the gold?"

"They're letters. Love letters from John James to Judith Anderson."

Shelby sat on the floor as he handed her the papers. "Who are they?"

"My real mother and father."

He read to her parts of the letters. Judith Anderson

was Silas and Marlene Anderson's only daughter. Against her father's wishes, she started seeing John James, an aspiring country singer, who once was in trouble with the law for petty larceny. Worried the flighty singer would never give his daughter a stable home, Silas forbid Judith from seeing John.

"They used to meet here in secret." Nick set down the letters and looked around the cabin. "I was probably conceived here."

Judith died giving birth to Nick in a private hospital far from Barlow. Silas arranged to put his name and Marlene's on Nick's birth certificate and they raised the baby as their own, not wanting the child to grow up with the stain of illegitimacy.

"That's why Silas was so hard on me," Nick mused. "He was afraid I would turn into my real father, without a stable source of employment, and turn to petty crime."

Picking up the letters, she read the eloquent prose. John James might never have been the stable husband Silas wanted for his youngest daughter, but Nick's father loved Judith. Absorbed in the words and the adoration in them, Shelby finished reading the last letter, her heart turning over.

"It's so sad. He really adored her and kept sneaking in here after she died." Sniffing, she touched the papers. "This is his last letter to her, shortly after she died. Silas offered him money to leave and never look back. He had no choice. He was flat broke, and brokenhearted."

Nick scanned his phone. "I Googled his name while you were reading. John James is still alive. He became a singer in a band and he lives in Nashville and works at a recording studio."

"Your real father."

"I'm going to contact him. I have a father who's still alive, and needs to see his son." Nick put away his phone. "These letters are the treasure, Shel. But I think there's still more inside that hollow in the fireplace. Why don't you look?"

She reached into the hollow and withdrew a diamond ring. "Nick, how did this get here?"

"Sleight of hand." He took it from her and slid it on her left ring finger.

"Shelby Stillwater, will you do me the extreme honor of becoming my wife?"

Tears filled her eyes. For a moment, she was afraid to breathe.

His steady gaze searched hers. "Sweet Pea? I promise to never roam again, if you're at my side for life."

"Yes. Yes. Yes!" She flung her arms around him.

His kiss was tender, sweet, with an undercurrent of the passion they'd shared before this very fireplace. He smoothed back a stray lock of hair.

"I reckon we could have an early summer wedding, here on the ranch if you want. By then the ranch should be operating in the black, as long as Dan has free rein to implement his ideas and hire trainers for young equestrian jumpers. And a honeymoon in Paris."

"Paris?"

"There's a summer session of watercolor painting I found. Six weeks long." He kissed her again. "A very long honeymoon to fulfill your dream of studying art in France."

"What about your dream?" she whispered, staring into his eyes.

He picked up her hand with the engagement ring on it. "My dream is right here with you, Shelby. There's no place I'd rather be. All those times I wandered around the country, I felt lost because I didn't have you. Not anymore. You're my GPS, my guiding star. I don't ever want to lose you again."

As he kissed her again, she sighed against him. Maybe they would never find Henry's treasure. It didn't matter.

The real treasure wasn't gold, or an historic cabin and the promise of riches.

It was right here, with Nick Anderson. The troubled, angry boy who held her heart. He'd left home to become a Navy SEAL and fight for his country and then got lost along the way.

Lost no more. He was home to stay.

* * * * *

Look for the next thrilling installment in
Bonnie Vanak's SOS AGENCY *series, coming soon!*

Don't forget the previous titles in the series:

SHIELDED BY THE COWBOY SEAL
NAVY SEAL SEDUCTION

Available now from Harlequin.com!

Get 2 Free Books,

HARLEQUIN

ROMANTIC suspense

Plus 2 Free Gifts—

just for trying the

Reader Service!

"You don't think I can do it?" Her chin jutted out and her
lips were pouty. Not that he was thinking about kissing
her at this particular time.

"I know you can do whatever you want to, Halle. You
pulled me out of a raging river, for God's sake. That's not
the question."

"The river was still by the time I got to you. Tell me,
Alastair, what do you think is the issue? What's your
point?"

"The concern I have is how you're going to make
enough money to not only keep Bluewood running, but to
invest in its future. How will you ensure a legacy you can
leave to our child? That's a full-time job in and of itself."

Tears glistened in her eyes as she bit her trembling
bottom lip. Not that he was looking at it for any particular
reason. "I'll do whatever I have to. It's how my daddy

raised me. Fords aren't quitters. Although Dad always found time for me, always let me know that I was first, the priority over the ranch. He was bringing in a lot more money when I was younger, though. I don't know if the ranch will ever get back to those days." She wiped tears off her cheeks.

"Are you sure you want to take on another full-time job on top of the ranch? With a new baby?"

"That's the question, isn't it?"

"That's part of what brought me here, Halle."

She grabbed a napkin from the acrylic holder on the table and wiped her eyes, then blew her nose. He made a note to order the finest linen handkerchiefs for her, with the Scottish thistle embroidered on them. Her hands were long, her fingers graceful. Would their child have her hands?

Her long, shuddering breath emphasized her ramrod-straight posture. He was certain she was made of steel. She rested her sharp whiskey eyes on him.

"Go on."

"Marry me, Halle. For the sake of our child, marry me."

Find out Halle's answer in
THE BILLIONAIRE'S COLTON THREAT
by Geri Krotow, available November 2017
wherever Harlequin® Romantic Suspense books
and ebooks are sold.

www.Harlequin.com

THE WORLD IS BETTER
WITH
Romance

Harlequin has everything from contemporary, passionate and heartwarming to suspenseful and inspirational stories.

Whatever your mood,
we have a romance just for you!

Connect with us to find your next great read,
special offers and more.

 /HarlequinBooks

 @HarlequinBooks

www.HarlequinBlog.com

www.Harlequin.com/Newsletters

HARLEQUIN

A *Romance* FOR EVERY MOOD™

www.Harlequin.com